# The Road to Pearl Harbor

The
Coming of the War
Between the United States
and Japan

BY HERBERT FEIS

PRINCETON NEW JERSEY

PRINCETON UNIVERSITY PRESS

ISBN 0-691-01061-7 (paperback edn.)
ISBN 0-691-05632-3 (hardcover edn.)

First Princeton Paperback Printing, 1971
Seventh Hardcover Printing, 1971

Printed in the United States of America
by Princeton University Press, Princeton, New Jersey

THE first article of the first (1854) treaty between America and Japan read:

"There shall be a perfect, permanent, and universal peace, and a sincere and cordial amity, between the United States of America, on the one part, and the Empire of Japan on the other, and between their people, respectively, without exception of persons or places."

The night before the attack upon Pearl Harbor, on reading the last Japanese notice that meant war, the President said to Hopkins, ". . . we have a good record." Standing before the International Military Tribunal for the Far East on trial for their lives, the chief figures in the Japanese government said the same. I have tried in this book to see into the gradually opening archives of that final term before the war: and thus to tell how and why the war came about.

The reader may wish to know before he begins the main sources from which this narrative is derived. The most important among the many were:

*For the account given of the policies and actions of the American government*

1. The State Department archives.
2. Drafts of the history of military plans and arrangements preceding the outbreak of war, which is being written from American and British official records at the direction of the Joint Chiefs of Staff.
3. Selections from the papers of President Roosevelt deposited at Hyde Park.
4. The full private diaries of the former Secretary of War, Henry L. Stimson, the former Secretary of the Treasury, Henry Morgenthau, Jr., and the former Ambassador to Japan, Joseph C. Grew.
5. Conversations with officials of the American government who participated in the events narrated—particularly:

Eugene H. Dooman, former Counselor of the American Embassy in Tokyo

Joseph W. Ballantine, former member of the Far Eastern Division of the State Department

Sumner Welles, former Under Secretary of State

Dean Acheson, former Assistant Secretary of State

Stanley K. Hornbeck, former Adviser on Political Relations, Department of State

Maxwell M. Hamilton, former Chief of the Division of Far Eastern Affairs, State Department.

Some of these individuals in addition made available notes or memoranda on particular points.

*For the account given of the policies and actions of the Japanese government*

1. The records, particularly the exhibits, of the International Military Tribunal for the Far East.

2. The records of the International Military Tribunals which met at Nuremberg.

3. Selected documents from the captured German and Italian archives.

4. The diary of Marquis Koichi Kido, Lord Keeper of the Privy Seal during the most critical phases of this period; and the Saionji-Harada memoirs—a running account of the doings within the Japanese government, as kept by Harada, the secretary to Saionji, the last of the so-called Elder Statesmen of Japan, and reviewed by Saionji.

5. Special studies of the Japanese situation and policies prepared by or for the Military Intelligence Division of the Supreme Command, Allied Forces, Tokyo, from Japanese records and discussions with Japanese officials.

As regards both the American and Japanese records, the several investigations by the executive and legislative branches of the American government of the events preceding the Pearl Harbor attack are a voluminous and indispensable source of information. They provide not only a vast collection of documentary material, but also, in the form of oral and written testimony, the results of probing the memory of many witnesses of this journey into war.

Both in the research for and in the writing of every part of this narrative I have received much help. The State Department granted me full access to all pertinent records. This permission was made the more valuable by the patient and constant assistance of the members of that Department, in various sections, in locating in the voluminous and complex archives the many thousands of papers which contained the story. Of the many who thus aided me I would mention in particular Dr. G. Bernard Noble, Chief of the Division of Historical Policy Research, Mrs. Arlene Pratt, Mr. M. B. C. Chambers, and Mr. Frank Smiraglia. For help in conveniently securing the records of the trials of the German diplomats, I am obliged to Mr. Jack B. Tate and Miss Katherine B. Fite; and for facilitation of my use of selected captured German and Italian documents, to Professor Raymond J. Sontag and his staff.

To many officials, past and present, in the Department of the Army, I am indebted for similar help in locating and acquiring copies of captured Japanese records, both those presented to the International Military Tribunal for the Far East, and certain special studies of prewar Japanese policy prepared for the Supreme Commander of the Allied Forces; especially to General William H. Draper, Jr., former Under Secretary of War, who opened the way for me; to General Douglas MacArthur and his staff, particularly General Charles A. Willoughby, Assistant Chief of Staff, Military Intelligence, who supported my search for this source material; to Mr. Joseph B. Keenan, former Chief of Council for the Prosecution of Japanese War Criminals, and Colonel Edward H. Young, Chief of the War Crimes Division, who arranged for me to have continuous use of the same material later in this country; to Colonel Carter W. Clarke, who was good enough to assemble for me the whole of the file of intercepted Japanese messages, known as "Magic";

To Captain T. B. Kittredge, U.S.N., of the Historical Section, Joint Chiefs of Staff, I am greatly indebted for enabling me to consult drafts of various studies that are in preparation of our military planning and decisions before American entry into the war, and also for his patience in discussing these matters with me;

To former Secretary of War Henry L. Stimson, for allowing me to use pertinent parts of his unpublished diary, to Mr. McGeorge Bundy, and Mr. David H. Clift of the Yale University Library, for facilitating its use; to the former Secretary of the Treasury, Henry Morgenthau, Jr., for allowing me freely to read and draw upon that absorbing and voluminous record which he assembled (a combined register of the activities in which he was a participant and witness, and collection of documents); to our former Ambassador to Japan, Joseph C. Grew, for providing me with a full set of the many volumes of the diary that he kept while at Tokyo, and for talking over with me the experiences and views recorded in these pages. All had an eager interest in having the whole story known, told, and understood;

To Miss Grace Tully for her enjoyable talks about White House matters within the realm of her recollection, and for her help in obtaining
access to the collection of papers of former President Roosevelt at
Hyde Park; to Mr. Stanley Hyman of the Franklin D. Roosevelt
Memorial Foundation, for guiding me in the search for and among
these papers; to Dr. Wayne C. Grover, Archivist of the United States,
for arranging that I might consult these Archives; and to Dr. Herman
Kahn, Director, and Dr. Edgar B. Nixon and the other members of the
staff of the Franklin D. Roosevelt Library, for their cordial reception
and their aid;

To many of my former colleagues in the State Department for searching their memories in regard to the events recounted: among them
Eugene H. Dooman, who gave the manuscript a corrective reading at
an early stage and contributed facts and ideas, though his judgment
of many important points differed, I know, from that in the text;
Sumner Welles; Dean Acheson; Stanley K. Hornbeck; Maxwell M.
Hamilton; Joseph W. Ballantine, who also made available to me a copy
of the Nomura manuscript; Max W. Bishop and Ruth Bacon; Donald
Hiss; Joseph C. Green who allowed me to read the notes he kept as
Chief of the Division of Controls; to Samuel Boggs for advice on the
map problem.

To Justice Felix Frankfurter for taking many hours of a summer holi-
day to read the typescript and for blending critical advice with encouragement; to the Hon. Hu Shih, former Chinese Ambassador in Washington; to the Hon. Nelson T. Johnson, former American Ambassador to
China and Minister to Australia; and to the Hon. Eelco N. van Kleffens,
former Foreign Minister of the Netherlands Government in Exile, for
information on matters within their experience; to Mr. Robert E. Sherwood for further material on points of which he has written in his book,
*Roosevelt and Hopkins;* and to Mrs. Mary D. Keyserling of the Bureau
of Foreign and Domestic Commerce, for assembling important statistical
material on American oil shipments to Japan; and to Mr. Paul H. Nitze
of the State Department, for copies of the *Strategic Bombing Survey;* to
Mr. Laird Bell of Chicago for trying to locate the papers of former Secretary of the Navy Knox, even though the effort failed; to Miss Ruth
Savord, Librarian of the Council of Foreign Relations; to Professor
William L. Langer of Harvard University for lending notes on several
important points; and to Dr. E. A. Goldenweiser, of the Institute for Advanced Study, for help in translating German documents.

The help given me by many people in the government must not be taken as indicating any kind of official approval, sponsorship, or responsibility. This book is the work of a private scholar.

To the Institute for Advanced Study at Princeton, New Jersey, for appointing me to membership, and for essential and extensive assistance in the doing of the job: to Professor Walter W. Stewart, a fellow Member, who favored the undertaking and was constant in his stimulus; to Miss Jocelyn Farr for doing the wearisome tasks of typing, checking, and keeping the manuscript in order; and to my wife, Ruth Stanley-Brown Feis for sharing the long and hard strain of doing the job and preparing the Index.

H. F.

*Institute for Advanced Study*
*Princeton, New Jersey*
*February 1, 1950*

# CONTENTS

[ xi ]

CONTENTS

Map follows page 20

# PART ONE

# SEPARATION

# CHAPTER 1

## The Arc of Opposition

JAPAN, from its seat on the small island of Honshu, wanted to be arbiter of Asia and the Western Pacific. The wish throve in poverty and pride, finding company in thoughts which made it seem just. The Japanese people came to believe that the extension of their control over this vast region was both natural and destined; that the other people living there needed the guardianship of Japan as much as Japan needed them. The Japanese armies sailed across the China seas under a banner which proclaimed peace, justice, and partnership for all. The bayonets were merely to expel the devil who would not understand their "true intentions."

By 1937 the banner had been carried far. Large and populous areas of the mainland of Asia (Korea, Kwantung peninsula, Manchuria) were compelled to submit to the Japanese rule. But the wish for a greater realm did not come to rest.

Inner strains, felt in all parts of the toiling land, kept it alive. The home islands were getting more crowded; all usable land was being farmed; the extra young men and women from the rural districts were being forced to seek a living in the workshop or factory. An anxious attempt was under way to expand both old and new industries. But capital was short and progress depended on being able to get the needed raw materials from foreign lands. Still the country was intent on having an army and navy equal to those of far wealthier powers. The sum of its needs and ambitions, in short, was beyond its scanty means.

And in the mid-thirties these means came in hazard. Japan was finding it hard to sell its own goods abroad. The worldwide depression was reducing foreign demand. Worse still, many foreign lands were raising their import barriers, making them higher, more rigid, and more pointed against Japanese products. The country still had ample reserves of gold —almost half a billion dollars—to take care of even a sustained deficiency of income. But if and when these ran out, Japan would have to drop back to a poorer standard of life, and a lesser rating among the powers. The Army and excitedly patriotic youth preferred another solution; to extend the realm of Japan's Empire.

The situation abroad made it seem possible for Japan to do so; not only possible but urgent. Two movements were under way in China which not only upset Japanese activities in that country, but threatened its control over Manchukuo and Korea. Chinese nationalism was coming alive, and being rude and demanding. Japan was being nagged, as were the Western Powers, to give up all privileged positions in China and to dwell therein only by leave. Many thought that before long this would result in virtual expulsion of all Japanese interests from China. At the same time, Communism was spreading among the masses in the north. Serving this doctrine, and served by it, was the old enemy, Russia. The view formed, particularly in the Army, that it was essential that Japan make its will felt toughly and quickly in China.

Simultaneously, the situation in Europe seemed to favor a bold attempt to make Japan strong and self-sufficient. Germany and Italy were challenging Britain and France. This seemed to offer a chance to make them pay for the safety of their colonies in Asia; to cause them to share the gains derived from them, perhaps the control. The United States had so neglected its Navy and Army that it could not fight a war in the Western Pacific. Besides, the American people would not, it was judged, go to war to rescue China or protect European colonies.

Japan felt entitled to take from the western countries all it could. Had they not—particularly the United States—always begrudged Japan its progress? Were they not forcing her back to a meager life by harsh bans upon trade, access to resources, and immigration? Had they not refused to join in efforts to prevent China from being unruly and hostile? If it came to war, would not the real fault be theirs? Feelings of this kind, a disciplined resentment, made foreign protests seem only another proof of selfishness.

So conditions lured Japan onward, and so ran the justifying thoughts.


But how was the advance to be managed? By strategy or by force; or, in the sanctioned language of Japanese officialdom, "by diplomacy or defense"? [1] If the old tales are a true record, the Japanese take even more

---

[1] As expressed in the guiding program adopted by the Hirota Cabinet on August 11, 1936, in a formal statement, entitled, "Decisions of the Five Ministers Conference of International and National Policies": ". . . the fundamental national policy to be established by the Empire is to secure the position of the Empire on the East Asia Continent by dint of diplomatic policy and national defense, mutually dependent on each other, as well as to advance and develop the Empire toward the South Seas." Proceedings of the International Military Tribunal for the Far East sitting at Tokyo (subsequently referred to as *Far East Mil. Trib.*), Exh. No. 216.

pride in their strategies than in their arms. The first resort of those with ends to gain—whether good or bad—was ruse and cunning: the talented man, by these means, leading the stronger enemy into foolish defeat. Only when himself surprised and at bay did the warrior use arms.

In the situation which Japan wished to master there was great need for maneuver. For there were at least two countries both stronger than itself and free to oppose it—the United States and the Soviet Union. And there was one respect in which Japan was most vulnerable to the stratagems of others. It lacked the basic means for a long struggle. Through bent back and patient scheming it had drawn from the outside world crucial elements of its present strength. These might be denied at any time.

Hence the call upon the gifts of persuasion and deceit by which the admired figures of the past had so well served Japan. The problem was to achieve passage to a position where Japan need not fear the power of others either to deprive it of vital supplies or face it with overbearing force. It could be solved, the strategists reckoned, by disguising Japan's aims, by moving step by step, by choosing weak spots first, by using favorable turns of event, by keeping opponents divided.

This was the design that failed. Rather than yield to those whom it had tried to outwit, Japan threw herself against them.


Against the bent of Japanese policy, the American government strove day in, day out—during the dreary years of the mid-thirties. It condemned Japan's breaches of treaties and resort to arms. It protested the harm done to Americans. It abetted Chinese resistance and would not recognize the legitimacy of Manchukuo (taken over by Japan in 1931). It repelled pleas of need and avowals that Japan was seeking only to guard peace and order in the Far East. If such was its real purpose, the American answer always was, why did Japan ignore the treaty system created for that very end; and instead create war and disorder?

And all the while, the American government proclaimed the rules of good conduct in a peaceful and prosperous society of nations. Sometimes there were four, sometimes five, sometimes seven, sometimes more. They were a retaining wall against Japanese claims; a way of trying to protect China; and a guide to the route along which Japan might redeem itself.[2]

[2] Of all these principles the one which caused the most stubborn difference between the United States and Japan was the traditional demand for the open door in China—

These measures summed up to a rigid opposition. But this was an attitude rather than a program. Most Americans were, during this period, anxiously resolved not to take part again in the quarrels between foreign countries. They had little hope that we could settle them and much fear that we would be caught in them. Thus a line came into being which the men in office feared to cross. They could speak up in defense of traditional national interests. They could comment, plead and protest against the angry tide of outside events. But they could not take, or thought they could not, any action that might carry us towards or into war.

Under this imposed restraint the government nurtured patient hope. Before the Manchurian venture (1931) Japanese diplomacy had been calm, and seemingly in rhythm with western ideals. Some of the leaders who made it so had lost position. Some had died. Some had been killed because of their beliefs. But a chance remained that, if not deeply hurt or offended, Japan might, after others had brought distress, turn again to men of the same kind.

There were elements in Japan, influential elements, who were known to have great doubts about and dislike for what their country was doing. A few revered elder statesmen were spreading caution. There was open worry among those bankers, traders, and industrialists who foresaw the opposition Japan would meet. Senior naval officers were talking informed sense. They had seen much of the outside world and knew how large were the seas which the advocates of expansion wished to bring under Japanese rule.

The continued resistance of China was counted on. The Japanese armies were failing to bring that "incident" to an end, or even to bring the end into sight. Sometime, the American authorities hoped, the Japanese people would grow weary of the effort and cost; the Navy would grow impatient at the drain upon Japan's strength; resistance to Army domination would spread. Then a more temperate group could regain control of Japanese affairs. With them a just ending of the quarrels in the Pacific might be arranged. Threats or pressure, it was feared, would spoil the chance.

One other thought figured in the guidance of American policy. Decisive success in the use of compulsion might have some undesired results. If Japan were brought to sudden collapse it might no longer be an

called by the historian, Charles A. Beard, "the dangerous and shadowy shibboleth of the Open Door . . ." *President Roosevelt and the Coming of the War, 1941* (New Haven, 1948), p. 240.

effective opponent of Communism in Asia. Unless the retreat from Manchukuo were well managed, the Communists might win control of the land, not China. This gave cause for wishing a settlement by consent, rather than by coercion.

Such were, in brief, the shaping ideas behind American dealings with Japan until the course of the war in Europe made us feel that we also were in danger. Up to then (1940) we refrained from threats and coercion, either alone or in concert with other countries. All the traits of this period of isolation became most visible when Japan invaded China in July, 1937, and the injured signatories of the Nine-Power Treaty met in Brussels to decide what to do. A short account of this episode may serve as prelude—somewhat separated as it must be—to the later events of which this narrative will tell.

## CHAPTER 2

# The Last, Lost Good Chance: 1937

WHEN, in July 1937, the Japanese Army marched into China, we were trying to make foreign policy out of morality and neutrality alone. These neither prevented the advent of trouble nor provided effective ways of dealing with trouble.

As instance of our attitude at this time, take the exchange between the British government and ourselves, not long before Japan entered China. Neville Chamberlain, on succeeding Stanley Baldwin as Prime Minister, found himself heir to a stack of notes in which the American government set forth a creed for all the world. After brief study he sent comment quizzical. No matter how much, he said, the British might wish to observe this creed, it could not do so because of the German threat. It was in the grace of the United States, he added, to lessen this fear by amending the Neutrality Act to distinguish between the aggressor and victim. Britain, he said, because it was unaided, wished to avoid trouble in Europe and the Far East at one and the same time. Therefore, his cold communication asked, should not an effort be made to reach an accord with Japan?

There was starch in both pleats of our answer. The idea that the United States should openly and in advance take sides in the European situation was regarded as out of the question. In the Congressional contest over the neutrality law, just ended, quite the other opinion had prevailed. As for the idea of seeking an accord with Japan—that was against both our grain and our wishes. Our answer (of June 1, 1937) hid our refusal to do anything in a discourse upon the way in which we believed something might be done: "It is the traditional policy of this country not to enter into those types of agreement which constitute or which suggest alliance. We feel that the governments principally interested in the Far East should endeavor constantly to exercise a wholesome and restraining influence toward conserving and safeguarding the rights and interests of all concerned, and toward preventing friction and development of tensions. We believe that consultation between and among the powers most interested, followed by procedure on parallel lines and concurrently, tends *to promote the effectiveness of such efforts*."

Such prose was not chosen, as the reader may think, for this occasion. It was regulation, "general issue," for our diplomatic notes; a uniform of ponderous precision.

The war between Japan and China started on the night of July 7, 1937, at the Marco Polo Bridge, ten miles west of Peiping. At first it seemed as if it might be only a local conflict between military units. But soon it became clear that the Japanese Army had other plans.[1] The Prime Minister, Prince Konoye, despite his avowals of regret, did not prevent the Army from marching on. Again and again in this narrative we shall meet him, so behaving. Before long the Japanese troops were in Peiping and Tientsin, in control of the railways going south, and advancing on Shanghai.

The assault upon China was a threat to the position of every one of the Western Powers in the Pacific. It smashed what was left of the Nine-Power Treaty on which hopes for peace in the Pacific had been based.[2] The disturber, Japan, was weak compared to the injured countries. It was, as well, dependent upon them for the means of keeping its armies in the field. They could have obliged Japan and China to settle their dispute peaceably. To have done so, the compelling powers would have had to endure some strain, cost, and danger. Japan would almost certainly have defied them at first. It might even—though this is most doubtful—have entered into war with them all. But the resistance would soon have crumpled. While it lasted, however, the United States would have had to occupy the front line, and many of the rear lines as well.

Not too trying a test, it might be thought, of what could be done by parallel and concurrent action. But it turned out (as will be seen) that the only concurrent action taken was to do nothing. The only parallel

[1] As well stated by Joseph W. Ballantine in "Mukden to Pearl Harbor," *Foreign Affairs,* July 1949: "Although the Army had thus chosen the time and place of the attack, it was a natural consequence of fixed national policy calling for establishment of a solid footing on the continent."

[2] The first paragraph of Article I of the Nine-Power Treaty of Washington, signed by Japan on February 6, 1922, read: "The Contracting Powers, other than China, agree: (1) to respect the sovereignty, the independence, and the territorial and administrative integrity of China." The nine powers were the United States, Japan, the British Empire, France, the Netherlands, China, Portugal, Italy, and Belgium.

action was an attempt by each to place the blame for doing nothing on the others.

Minds were ransacked in a search for effective ways of causing Japan to desist, while staying uninvolved. Unhappily none was found. The American government issued (July 16, 1937) a formal statement of the principles which it implored all countries in the Far East to observe. These were the same as those which Hull had been propounding ever since he took office. To him they were, as he wrote later, "solid, living, all-essential rules. If the world followed them, the world could live at peace forever. If the world ignored them, war would be eternal." [3] We were to repeat them like a litany to the very hour of war.

The Japanese government had one answer for the outside world, another for its own people. That which was addressed to the United States made a show of agreeing with Hull's principles, while disputing his grasp of the facts. That made at home disposed of the matter pertly: "The sole measure for the Japanese Empire to adopt," Prince Konoye said to the Japanese Diet, "is to administer a thoroughgoing blow to the Chinese Army so that it may lose completely its will to fight."

The Chinese government asked us to mediate. We refused on the ground that if we tried, the Japanese government would be angered and aided in its bid for support at home. A little later, we said the same to a British proposal that the United States join with it and France to effect a truce and to act as mediators. Hull explained at a press conference on August 17 that he found himself between two extreme views:

"One is the view of extreme internationalism, which rests upon the idea of political commitments. We keep entirely away from that in our thoughts and views and policies, just as we seek, on the other hand, to keep entirely away from the extreme nationalists who would tell all Americans that they must stay here at home . . ."

Using discretion, the President chose not to apply the Neutrality Act to the war in China. He thereby risked the criticism of those both in and out of Congress who had placed the act upon the statute books. But his unspoken reason was accepted by most—that to apply the act would hurt China and help Japan. Besides, if the American government declared Japan and China to be at war—a step from which both those governments were holding back—it might be regretted. Names count; a war might be harder to end than an incident. The rules of war might bring us into a dispute with Japan over our right to trade with China. Japan, it was true,

---

[3] *The Memoirs of Cordell Hull* (New York, 1948), I, 536.

was left in a position to obtain arms in the United States, but it did not need them.

What it wanted was oil, scrap iron, and other raw materials. The United States was providing these sinews of war. Whether or not to continue to do so, became the moot point. There were several groups of convinced advocates of restrictions. During the first half of 1937 Japan had bought in the United States 1.3 million metric tons of scrap iron and steel—far more than ever before. It, as correctly guessed, was adding to the reserves upon which it could fall back in case of embargo or war. The subject had been examined before the advance into China by a committee of which Assistant Secretary of State Francis B. Sayre was chairman. In May 1937 this group had reported back that "examination of all aspects of the matter leads the committee to the conclusion that immediate restrictive action would not be required or justified." This study was, with the President's knowledge, passed on to members of Congress who wanted to subject this trade to regulation.[4]

The State Department stood by this conclusion during the first weeks of trouble in China. There was refuge in the lack of legal authority to control exports. But as Japan pushed on and killed the helpless civilian masses within the Chinese cities it grew less happy with this answer. The press began to dramatize the fact that means for this cruel warfare were being secured in the United States. Thus an illustrated article in the *Washington Post* of August 29, 1937, stood under the following headlines: "AMERICAN SCRAP IRON PLAYS GRIM ROLE IN FAR EASTERN WAR. JAPANESE RAIN DEATH WITH ONE-TIME JUNK. GUNS, BOMBS AND BATTLESHIPS, ALL MADE FROM OLD METAL, SHIPPED ACROSS PACIFIC IN GROWING AMOUNTS."

This was an appeal to conscience rather than a political argument. It found a leading advocate in former Secretary of State, Henry L. Stimson. By letter printed in the *New York Times* he made a vigorous and cogent statement of the reasons for suspending our trade with Japan in war materials. The course being followed, his argument contended, "threatened to bring upon us in the future the very dangers of war which we now are seeking to avoid."[5] This letter appeared one day after the President in Chicago (on October 5) spoke of a "quarantine" of aggressors. In the middle of a speech which otherwise just rotated around old axioms, he spoke some startling sentences:

[4] The Schwellenbach Resolution (S.2025), introduced March 30, 1937, and various similar legislative proposals.
[5] *New York Times*, October 7, 1937.

"It seems to be unfortunately true," he said, "that the epidemic of world lawlessness is spreading.

"When an epidemic of physical disease starts to spread, the community approves and joins in a quarantine of the patients in order to protect the health of the community against the spread of the disease. . . .

"War is a contagion, whether it be declared or undeclared. . . ."

What was this, if not a proposal that the United States join in a concerted plan of opposition to Germany and Japan? So it was read to be even after Roosevelt's puzzling comment at his press conference the next day. Upon being asked whether this speech was a "repudiation" of the Neutrality Act, he answered: "Not for a minute. It may be an expansion." [6]

His thought may have been that the purpose of the Neutrality Act was to stay at peace, and the purpose of a "quarantine" would be to compel others to observe peaceful ways.

But, whatever the name, most Americans were against the idea. They did not think that the epidemic could reach them. They preferred to try to isolate themselves, rather than join in an uncertain effort to wipe out the disease. The proposal was too sudden, too off the cuff, too different from the President's former comments on the foreign situation. A few vigorous groups hurried to its support. But the rest of the country and Congress were opposed. A sack of silence was wrapped around the remark. It was put in quarantine for three unhappy years.

The impulse of other governments to do anything about the war in China had been weak and fearful before. Now each felt the more warranted in thinking first and last of how to safeguard itself, no matter what the general outcome. The Prime Minister of Britain seemed to get caustic satisfaction from this proof that we were not ready to act. In a private letter he wrote: "I read Roosevelt's speech with mixed feelings . . . seeing that patients suffering from epidemic diseases do not usually go about fully armed . . . [there is] something lacking in his analogy. . . . When I asked [the] U.S.A. to make a joint *démarche* at the very beginning of the dispute, they refused." And in another letter, he added: "It is always best and safest to count on nothing from the Americans but words." [7]

[6] Press Conference, October 6, 1937, *The Public Papers and Addresses of Franklin D. Roosevelt* (New York, 1941), 1937 Volume, p. 423.

[7] Keith Feiling, *The Life of Neville Chamberlain* (London, 1947) p. 325.

Japan and Germany, of course, measured the episode. Roosevelt had put out his hand to pluck the nettle short. When they saw him draw it back, and even deny the gesture, they ceased to fear what might be done at the meeting at Brussels, soon to begin.

[2]

That conference was a funeral rather than a birth. It was called in tribute to a mood that was past and to pledges that were breaking. The participants (members of the League of Nations and parties to the Nine-Power Treaty) were without a common program and failed to form one.

The Assembly of the League of Nations had declared that Japan was a breaker of treaties and a war maker. The American government had spoken up bluntly in support of this judgment. Thus all that joint censure—moral pressure—could do had been done. What more or else could the offended nations do? Mediate? Their own opinion forbade any terms which would allow Japan to emerge as victor over China. Find other ways to satisfy Japan's discontents and fears? They were not willing to offer what Japan aspired to have. Compel Japan to desist by concerted pressure, supported by force, if need be? None was ready to take the risk, unless the United States would stand before and behind them in all dangers. All this, the talks before the conference made clear. Still it met—if only to put a wreath on the grave of the scheme of a peaceful order in the Pacific.

The State Department, in advance of the meeting, surveyed the Far Eastern scene with more disposition to allow that there might be some admissible basis for Japanese action than ever before or after. There was a wish and sense of need for something more than a policy of repression. The conference, it was laid down in several well-drawn studies, ought to cause Japan to desist from its current course. But it ought also to seek to give Japan a sense of economic and political security. This was to be done by assuring it, first, of raw materials and markets, and, second, by devising ways that would prevent the Soviet Union and China from misusing the chance they would get. Admirable prescription, but neither at Brussels nor later was a way found to fill it and presently it was forgotten.

The President—one week after the quarantine speech—saw fit to quiet suspicions that we were about to enter into a pact which might lead to war. In a radio address on October 12, he said: "The purpose of this conference will be to seek by agreement a solution of the present situation in China. In efforts to find that solution, it is our purpose to cooperate with the other signatories to this [Nine-Power] Treaty, including China and Japan."

This was matched by words which Chamberlain addressed to the House of Commons on October 21: "I suggest that it is altogether a mistake to go into this conference talking about economic sanctions, economic pressure and force. We are here to make peace, not here to extend the conflict."

Shortly before the conference convened the American and British governments again swapped views. Foreign Secretary Eden sent a note (October 19) to Hull, stating that neither watchful waiting nor moral condemnation would have any effect. The extension of active aid to China and the disruption of Japanese economic life might be effective, the British analysis continued, but these measures would be hard and dangerous. They could not be effective at once. Japan might blockade China or even attack countries applying pressure. Therefore, his note concluded, before entering on this course countries would want mutual assurances that they would come to each other's defense. This would not only give them needed protection, but be a sign of joint strength that might cause Japan to yield.

Hull did not dispute this analysis. But he again made clear that the American government did not think the conference should discuss sanctions. Its purpose should be, he answered, to find a solution by agreement, not by force. And again, he rejected the imputation, coming from London and Paris, that the lead was ours.

The advice given Norman Davis, our delegate, was in accord with these ideas. His aim, the President told him before departure, should be to mobilize the moral force of the nations who wished peace, and while doing so to "observe closely the trend of public opinion in the United States to take full account of it." Davis, though dissatisfied with his part, took care not to forget this advice.

The conference was depressed from start (November 3) to end (November 24). The governments drew no closer together. The American delegation refrained from definite initiatives of any kind. The British were just as careful not to propose anything that could get them into trouble. From first to last, their representatives at Brussels affirmed that Britain was ready to discuss the possible use of collective sanctions; and that it would go as far as and as fast as the United States was ready to go.[8] But it would join in punitive action only if a broad mutual defense pact was made. As Sir Ronald Lindsay, British Ambassador in Washington put the matter to the Under-Secretary of State, Welles, on the 13th, ". . . the British Government was tied by the leg in Europe and was not in a position to undertake any possible hostilities in the Pacific unless it were possible to be assured in advance that it would receive military and naval support from the other signatories of the Nine-Power Treaty."

The French government was against doing anything. It would consider positive action against Japan, it said, only if there was "complete solidarity," along with a joint guarantee of the defense of Indo-China.[9] The Dutch government, owing to the exposed position of the East Indies, said as little as possible. The Scandinavian countries (Norway, Sweden and Denmark) said that the whole point of view of their peoples was that they did not want to be involved in anybody else's quarrels, no matter who was right and who was wrong. Their idea was that the sooner the conference adjourned the better. The government of the Soviet Union said it would join in any action that Britain and the United States were prepared to take. But its purposes were suspect.

The Japanese saw to it that the officials assembled in Brussels did not gain faith in one another. Kurusu, then Ambassador to Belgium, passed around a telegram from the Japanese Ambassador at Washington which stated that the American government was not behind its delegation, and that leaders in Congress were harshly critical of the fact that they were there at all.[10]

Within ten days it was, as Davis reported to Washington (November 14), clear that the governments present at Brussels would keep their hands folded unless the United States proposed some positive measure, with all that might mean. The American government remained unwilling. But it did not want the conference to adjourn with dramatic swiftness. A continuation of talk, it was thought, even though it did not lead to any decision, would have a useful moral effect.

But by November 24 even the talk was played out. The conference, doomed before it met, disbanded. There was a lesson to be learned from the rout. The only way in which the war in China could have been well ended was by firm collective action, action that would have offered

[8] Statement of Foreign Secretary Eden to Norman Davis, November 2, 1937.
[9] Reports of the American Ambassador to France, William C. Bullitt, of talks with the French Premier Blum, and French Foreign Minister Delbos, October 22–23, 1937 and reports of Norman Davis from Brussels, November 6–7, 1937.
[10] Report, Davis to the President and Hull, November 21, 1937.

Japan an inducement for peace and met refusal with compulsion. But this lesson was not learned, or even stated boldly, until three years later —too late to prevent tragedy.

The failure of the Brussels Conference could not be made up. The last good chance to work out a stable settlement between China and Japan was lost in 1937.

## CHAPTER 3

# 1937-39: Japan Goes Deeper into the Stubble

THE war in China dragged on. The Japanese Army went deeper and farther into the stubble. By the middle of 1939 they had gained control of the five northeastern provinces (as far south and west as Kansu) and down into Central China through Hankow. They had won the main port cities along the Chinese coasts, and the islands off them.

But still Japan could not bring the struggle to an end, either by stratagem or force. Terror did not wipe out resistance in the front and the rear and at the sides. Nor yet soft words, secret pay for desertions, chosen agents, or assassination. Puppet governments were created in North and Central China, as in Manchukuo before. But the Chinese people refused to heed them. Some became known as Opium governments, since their chief revenue was derived from stimulated traffic in that drug. Outside sympathy was steadfast.

Even the soldiers were finding the stay long and the end hard to foresee. Eighteen months had passed since General Matsui, Commander of the Expeditionary Force at Shanghai, sent his New Year greetings:

"Riding north and south for scores of years,
    I have worked for the renovation of Asia but alas!
    In a war camp I greet my sixty-first year
    Even so, death shall not overtake my youthful hope." [1]

A careful watch was kept upon the amounts of weapons and materials sent to the armies in China. Yet they were a drain upon men and means. Civilians in Japan were allowed less and less of scarce products but this did not compensate. Whatever was used up in China of steel, machines, and vehicles was so much less for new factories and arsenals at home.

---

[1] Written at Nanking, New Year's Day, 1938. General Matsui was commander of the army that sacked Nanking. Death overtook him in Sugamo Prison; he was sentenced to death by the International Military Tribunal for the Far East, and hanged. His poetical mood was not always wistful, as may be seen from his military orders. For example, the passage in his statement of October 8, 1937, issued to clarify the intentions of the Japanese Army in the Shanghai area: "The devil-subduing sharp bayonets are just on the point of being unsheathed so as to develop their divine influence." *Far East Mil. Trib.*, Exh. No. 3411.

Whatever of oil and weapons, was so much less for the forces that might battle Russian armies in the north, or conduct an advance to the south.

In each foray, cause was given for American complaint. As the Japanese foot soldiers slogged their way over the Chinese countryside, they lost prudence and pity. As Japanese planes bombed crowded Chinese cities, American schools and churches were destroyed, American businesses were hurt, American lives were lost. Wherever the Japanese armies went they chased or squeezed out all foreign activities.

America became angered. The economic and political causes of the struggle dropped out of mind; its brutality and disregard of American interests took their place. Though still diluted by dislike of war, the resolution formed that Japan must not be allowed in the end to win in China.


The picture of Japan before American eyes grew more sinister. We had grown used to its image as breaker of the peace in Asia; almost at home with it. Now it began to appear on the screen as a member of a vicious gang, a plotter, along with Nazi Germany, of trouble all around us. For Japan seemed about to join the Axis.

In January 1939, Prince Konoye, who had been Prime Minister since the beginning of the war in China, gave way to Baron Hiranuma. Konoye had seemed to want to cling to friendship with the United States, no matter how he might abuse it. Hiranuma was thought to be hostile to us and eager to work with Germany and Italy. He had long been one of the main figures in the leading reactionary societies of Japan—the Kokuhonsha. This had stood for Fascism within Japan, the rule of the soldier class, the belief that Japan could survive and prosper only by its strength in arms.

The first measures of his government seemed to confirm these impressions of the meaning of the change. Japan took over places that could be convenient bases for attack on western possessions in the Southwest Pacific. On February 10, 1939, it occupied the island of Hainan, off the coast of Indo-China between Hong Kong and Singapore. In March it claimed sovereignty over the great expanse of sea in which the Spratly Islands were scattered, some 700 miles southwest of Manila; these coral islands contained useful anchorages for light naval forces and aircraft. Neither of these extensions could be accounted for by the war in China. Both were signs of naval reckoning. They were taken as indications that Japan was thinking forward to a struggle in the Southwest Pacific.

These advances were, it was surmised, related to plans to draw closer to the Axis. On February 8 Grew sent along a rather full report on the talks between Japan and Germany, then in progress. Hull was worried. But his response was still the acme of caution lest he step into the net of foreign diplomacy.[2] The Ambassador was authorized to caution the Japanese government against the association. But he was told that he should seem to be speaking for himself, and to avoid any phrases that would connect our position too closely with that of Britain. In the guise of personal opinion, Grew conveyed Hull's message to the Foreign Minister, Arita. He left the interview with the sense that the Japanese government would reflect longer before taking any decisive step.

It was deeply divided, of that there was no secret, over the question of what kind of accord to make. One part, led by the Army, wanted an all-out partnership; the other wished only a pact against the Soviet Union. The American government longed to prevent the combination. But all it did—all it felt able to do—was to cast a silhouette; to stalk, stick in hand, along the horizon. Best not, Hull judged, to use the half-measures allowed him, such as public warnings and an extension of the "moral embargo."[3] Dependence on the United States and the British Empire for vital raw materials was known to be one, if not the chief, of the reasons why the more careful elements in Japan were able to resist the rest; why Hitler was being told that Japan could not afford to alienate the democracies.[4] But Grew warned that if we tried to sway the decision by denying these materials, or by threat of doing so, it would go against us. The advice, which fitted the commanding American wish to stay out of trouble, was heeded.

For a time this policy of *existing* as a great power, without *acting* like one, seemed to work well. The Japanese government was reported to be firm in its refusal to help Germany beat down Britain and France.

[2] Grew's report of February 8 and Hull's response of February 10 are printed in *Papers Relating to the Foreign Relations of the United States: Japan, 1931–1941* (Washington, 1943), II, 161–63.

[3] In June 1938, the American government had asked the makers and exporters of aircraft, aircraft parts, engines and armaments, of aerial bomb and torpedoes, not to send these products where they would be used to bomb civilian populations. The appeal worked. No more were sent to Japan. This action became known as a "moral embargo"; perhaps because it rested on moral appeal and not on law, perhaps because it was regarded as a moral reproof.

[4] The Japanese government was, in fact—as its since opened records show—telling the Germans that this was the chief reason why Japan "was not yet in a position to come forward as an opposer of the Democracies." See the telegram from Ribbentrop to Ott, the German Ambassador in Tokyo, April 26, 1939, in which the German Foreign Minister summarized the history of the negotiations which had been taking place in Berlin. *Far East Mil. Trib.*, Exh. No. 502.

Foreign Minister Arita confirmed this in a talk with Grew on May 18, just before the Ambassador left for the United States. He assured Grew that any agreement that might be signed would not contain any political or military obligations except those required to combat Communist activities. However, he added, if Britain and France should enter into an alliance with the Soviet Union, Japan might be obliged to change its position. Though the State Department thought this assurance honestly meant, it was not wholly relied on. The Japanese records, since opened, show how hard the Foreign Minister (and his colleagues of the same mind) fought to make it valid.[5]

In May—as Hitler's voice was rising to its highest pitch—the Prime Minister, Hiranuma, asked the United States to join Japan in an attempt to keep the peace in Europe. But the tenor of his proposal showed that his ideas of how peace was to be kept were in line with Axis wishes, not with American. They visualized concessions by the "have" to the self-styled "have-not" nations. This was confirmed in a secret talk he had with Eugene Dooman, who was in charge of our Embassy in Tokyo during Grew's stay in the United States.[6]

Japan, the Prime Minister said, was ready to sound out Germany and Italy in regard to a conference to find a solution for the world's troubles, if the President would sound out Britain and France. As regards the terms of settlement, little was said. But again, Hiranuma's interspersed comment seemed to mean that he thought that the proper terms would be a payment by Britain and France to Germany and Japan. No doubt such was his idea. But this—we now know from Japanese witnesses—was only one phase of his thought. The Prime Minister really feared to be dragged into a war between Germany and the West while the war with China remained unfinished and the Soviet Union remained free. And he was frantically trying to prevent his cabinet from being split asunder.

By whatever line of purpose this peace bid was inspired, Hull was suspicious. His reply, sent by *mail,* was in effect advice that before trying to solve the world situation Japan might well first clear up the disorder of its creation in the Far East.[7] Japanese forces in China were at this time using brutal tactics to humiliate and expel the British settlement at

---

[5] See Chapter 4, where the story of events within the Japanese government is told.

[6] The proposal was made to Grew who cabled it on May 18 before leaving for the United States. The talk with Dooman was on the 23rd. Grew's cable and Dooman's memo of the conversation are printed in U.S. Congress, *Joint Committee on the Investigation of the Pearl Harbor Attack, Hearings* . . . (Washington, 1946). Part 20, pp. 4133-39.

[7] The text, dated July 8, is printed, *ibid.*, 4171-74.

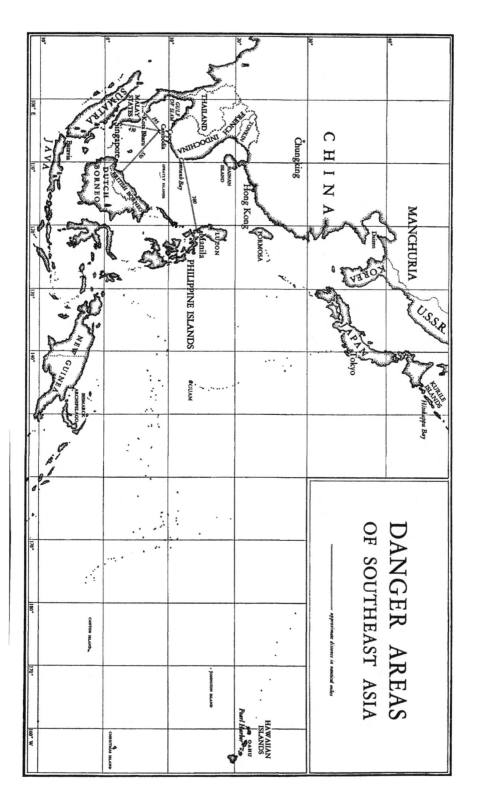

DANGER AREAS
OF SOUTHEAST ASIA

—— approximate distance in nautical miles

Tientsin. They were bombing Chungking, and some of the missiles struck close to the residence of American diplomatic representatives and the American gunboat, *Tutuila,* stationed in the Yangtze. Hull did not like this peace talk, punctuated by blows in the ribs. Neither did the American people.

But the government remained wary of any measures that might involve the United States in war, either in the Pacific or in Europe. Thus when on May 20, the British Ambassador consulted Welles about possible joint reprisals against Japan, he had been told that the American government wished to continue on its own way, without entangling ties. It might, Welles had added, acted by itself as the situation developed.

One reason for this reserve was not far to seek. The President was about to urge Congress to amend the Neutrality Act so that arms produced in the United States might again be sold to nations at war. The country was to be persuaded that the change was on the safe side; that it would improve the chance that the United States could remain at peace. The advocates of the amendment pleaded that if Hitler knew that Britain and France could equip their forces in the United States he might take longer thought. Or, if he did not and provoked war, that Britain and France could better defend themselves and thus serve our defense. While the issue was being debated, Roosevelt did not dare risk any dispute with Japan or association with Britain which might alarm the country.

For all the caution, his plea to Congress did not prevail. As before, the request for amendment was met by the argument that the sale of arms abroad would be preface to American entry into war. On July 11 (six weeks before the outbreak of war in Europe) the Senate Committee on Foreign Relations voted by twelve to eleven to defer decision until the next session of Congress in January 1940. Hull properly entitled his account of this event, "Neutrality Disaster." Like a slap in the face, it knocked out of mind any idea of a concerted program to deal with Japan.

[2]

But still, the American people favored both these things. Hull found himself called upon to span this crevasse between wish and will. He resorted to a measure which would reduce Japan's future value as an ally of the Axis—yet one of which Japan could hardly make a fighting issue. On July 26 the American government served notice to terminate the Treaty of Commerce and Navigation between the United States and

Japan. After six months we would be free to control or end our exports to and imports from Japan.

This was an act of separation—before which Hull had long paused. Several months previously, in April (we are still writing of the darkly clouded prewar period of 1939), he had all but made up his mind to do less. It was planned merely to denounce only some sections of the treaty and to replace even these with a short-term commercial accord. Then a show of feeling in Congress against Japan caused Hull to risk the more serious measure.

Key Pittman, Chairman of the Foreign Relations Committee of the Senate, had introduced a resolution authorizing the President to end trade with Japan.[8] Hull had thereupon concluded it was best to postpone even the partial denunciation of the treaty. He was afraid that this step, which was meant only as forewarning, would get caught in the debate over the Pittman resolution and the revision of the Neutrality Act. Then he might get carried farther and faster than he wanted to go, or lose such freedom of action as he had. During June and July the confusion of counsel had grown worse as still other proposals were advanced in Congress to end or control trade with Japan.[9] One of these, presented by Senator Vandenberg on July 18, resolved that the United States give notice to Japan of intentions to terminate the treaty.[10] Seeking a way through the tangle by touch and trace, Hull decided to go along with that—though it came from the other side of the Senate.

He had asked Pittman to postpone his own bill to the next session of Congress. If, he informed Pittman at the same time, Congress should pass the one which Vandenberg sponsored, the Executive would give it careful attention. On July 26 the Senate Committee on Foreign Relations had discussed this idea. A majority of both the Democrats and Republicans were in favor, but there were dissenters. It seemed likely that the debate in the Senate would be long, and that harsh words against Japan would be spoken. The President and Hull made up their minds to go ahead on their own. That day the termination notice was given to the Japanese Ambassador.

[8] This was S.J.Res.123. It would have authorized the President to embargo the export and import of goods or to restrict monetary exchange and credits, if he found that any party to the Nine-Power Treaty was endangering the lives of American citizens or depriving them of their legal rights and privileges in violation of that treaty.

[9] Particularly, S.J.Res.143, introduced by Senator Schwellenbach, providing for the control of exports used in violation of the sovereignty, independence, territorial, or administrative integrity of any nation.

[10] This was S.Res.166. Its purpose was explained, "So that the Government of the United States may be free to deal with Japan in the formulation of a new treaty and the protection of the United States' interests as new necessities may require."

For this act the American government had more than usual reason. American trade was being completely controlled to suit Japanese plans, and American business within China was being ousted at all points reached by the Japanese Army. Japan had forfeited both legal and equitable rights to economic protection under this or any other treaty.

Such was the course of affairs which induced the decision to cancel the whole treaty. Perhaps it might turn out well; perhaps badly. The United States was committed to nothing final. The battered Chinese government would be encouraged. Contrary to fears of the experts, Japan might be sobered. If not, and Japan joined the Axis or moved south, then it would be best anyway, to stop suckling the Japanese armies.

The misgivings as to how Japan would react, it can now be perceived, were excessive and premature. The treaty notice was a surprise and shock. The Japanese government made excited efforts to find out what would happen after the treaty expired. Of his response, Hull wrote later:

"I was careful to give them no enlightenment. I felt that our best tactic was to keep them guessing, which might bring them to a sense of the position in which their flagrant disregard of our rights and interests in China was placing them." [11]

The opponents within the Japanese government of a complete alliance with the Axis had for the time being prevailed. The adverse views of the Navy, in particular, had told. But the advocates of the liaison were still trying to have their way, and using every means, straight and crooked, of getting it. The treaty notice seems, as far as the Japanese records in hand show, to have merely made the dispute hotter, without changing the balance.

About this time, Hull's postal reply to the Prime Minister in regard to a joint effort to prevent a war in Europe arrived in Tokyo. Its substance was already known by the Japanese government. But Dooman deferred delivery of the formal answer. For, as drafted, he thought it could be read as meaning that the United States would not make up with Japan until the war in China was ended, and ended as we wished. Hull would not make clear whether this was or wasn't his thought. Some small changes of language were made. And more time was allowed to pass, so that the answer would not be connected closely with the notice about the treaty. Finally on August 8—three weeks before the start of the war in Europe—it was handed in.[12]

[11] Hull, *op. cit.,* I. 638.
[12] The series of messages exchanged between Dooman and the State Department over these questions is printed in *Pearl Harbor Attack,* Part 20, pp. 4191 *et seq.*

The State Department did not want to give the Japanese fire-eaters new brands to flourish. It did not want to give the others proof that the United States could not be appeased. But it wanted to make clear that our opposition was firm, and untouched by fear that Japan would combine with Germany. Let the Japanese government, it was thought, when deciding its course, brood on our power rather than count upon our good nature. In this mood Hull, during July and August, read Dooman's informative accounts of the resumed dispute within the cabinet over the terms of alliance with Germany. These told of the Foreign Minister's resolute refusal to promise to join in war against Britain (and the United States), of the Navy's firm support of this refusal, of reports that the Minister of War would resign in order to force a change in the cabinet, and of rumors of assassination.

For all that this reported crisis in Tokyo could mean, it got only left-over attention. For, at that moment, it seemed only marginal to the greater crisis in the West. Our greater interest, our stronger feelings, our prime diplomatic efforts were directed there. The American government did not want to fix its position towards Japan until it had a clearer view of what the situation in Europe was to be.

Hitler did not keep either Washington or Tokyo guessing much longer. On August 22 the news came that Germany and the Soviet Union, with dramatic swiftness, had made up their quarrel. They had agreed to stay at peace with one another, and to provide each other with a great quantity of supplies.[13] The most curtained mind could see that this meant that war would come in Europe very soon. But in the Far East—it was almost as clear—there would be a respite. The program to which Japan was devoting itself would be most certainly upset. The schemers for empire had led Japan into a morass. Japan, hurt and isolated, would, it could be seen, need time to adjust itself.

But the tale of what occurred next will be more truly grasped if, before going on, we look into the Japanese records, since open to the student. These enable us to know much more now than the American government could know then about what happened between Japan and Germany in those months of 1939 of which I have been writing.

[13] The two main articles of the Treaty of Nonaggression between Germany and the Soviet Union, of August 23, 1939, read: Article I. "Both High Contracting Parties obligate themselves to desist from any act of violence, any aggressive action, and any attack on each other, either individually or jointly with other powers." Article IV. "Neither of the two High Contracting Parties shall participate in any grouping of powers whatsoever that is directly or indirectly aimed at the other party."

## CHAPTER 4

# The Dismay of the Japanese Strategists: August 1939

HIRANUMA, gaunt in speech as in look, upon hearing of the German-Russian pact remarked that this turn of events was "intricate and baffling." Well he might think so. For Japan was in a very different spot from the one in which it had planned to be. To see why, we must look back into the record.

The original impetus towards an alliance with Germany had come from a wish to have allies in the struggle against Communist and Russian activities and influence in East Asia.[1] But the sponsors were not unaware that a loose association with that country might serve other purposes as well. It could shrivel up the impulse of the League of Nations to impose restraints upon Japan. It might also cause the Chinese government to become more responsive to Japanese wishes.

These were the magnetizing thoughts that had drawn Japan into the Anti-Comintern pact with Germany, initialed on October 23, 1936, and signed on November 25 of the same year. The published parts could be read as making the pact what the parties said it was—merely an agreement between them to aid each other in resisting the foreign activities of communism. Both denied that it had any undisclosed feature. But the denials were false. In a secret attached agreement, it was provided (Article I) that if either country were threatened or attacked by the Soviet Union without provocation, the other would not give relief to the Soviet Union; and that the two countries would consult about the measures to use to preserve their common interest. Further (Article II), that neither would conclude a political accord with the Soviet Union which did not conform to the spirit of this pact—except with the consent of the other.[2]

---

[1] The justification of the then Prime Minister (Hirota) and Foreign Minister (Arita) are included in the Report of the Investigation Committee of the Privy Council, November 20, 1936. *Far East Mil. Trib.*, Exh. No. 484.

[2] The whole accord comprised: (1) The pact for concerted defense against the Comintern; (2) a supplementary protocol; (3) the secret attached agreement; (4) four annexes

A great effort had been made by the Japanese government to convince the world that this pact had no purpose nor effect, except to fend off communism. Thus the Japanese Foreign Office announced on November 25:

"It should be pointed out that in connection with, or behind, this agreement there exists no special agreement whatsoever, and that the Japanese Government have no intention to form, or join in, any special international bloc, for any other purpose and finally that the present agreement is not directed against the Soviet Union or any other specific country." [3]

Some hours earlier the Foreign Minister, Arita, had left another thought in the mind of the Privy Council: "The substance of the secret agreement has considerable possibilities of development depending on the intention of the two countries, and if there should arise any danger of an outbreak of war between Japan and Soviet Russia there is still room to push the discussion beyond the provisions of this agreement." [4]

To the American and British governments profuse assurances had been given that this Anti-Comintern pact was in no way a danger to them. The Japanese government may have been self-deceiving. It is likely that at the time the Japanese government did not realize in how many ways or how deeply any link with Germany (and Italy) would affect its relations with Britain and the United States. [5]

The tie-up with Germany had proved useful almost at once. Hitler refused to participate in the Brussels Conference in 1937; and he kept the Western Powers so alarmed about what he would do while they tried to discipline Japan, that they did not dare do anything. For this and other favors Japan had been content with the benefits of the association. But not Germany. During the next two years it had become displeased with the extension of the war in China. For that war was using up means that Japan might need, if called upon, to deal with Russia. Thus Germany had tried to bring peace between Chiang Kai-shek and the Japanese government. When this effort came to nothing, the German government was angry at the failure, believing one cause to be Japan's refusal to state

---

to the secret pact, these being letters exchanged between Ribbentrop and the Japanese Ambassador in Berlin, Viscount Mushakoji, agreeing on interpretations of the pact and the secret attached agreement. Only the first two were published. A good translation of them is printed in *Foreign Relations: Japan*, II, 153–54; and, of the unpublished parts, in *Far East Mil. Trib.*, Exh. No. 480.

[3] This statement was a long explanation of the need for defense against international communism. It is printed in *Foreign Relations: Japan*, II, 155–56.

[4] Minutes of the Meeting of the Privy Council, November 25, 1936. *Far East Mil. Trib.*, Exh. No. 485.

[5] Italy joined this Anti-Comintern pact on November 6, 1936, but did not become a party to the secret protocol.

its terms clearly.[6] It was also displeased because Japan would not promise a privileged position for German economic and trade interests in North China and Manchuria. The Japanese Army refused to limit its own claims.[7]

But when the chance came to have Japan as a full ally, Germany had been ready to pass by these grievances. In the summer of 1938 (during the first Konoye Cabinet) the idea of converting the Anti-Comintern pact into a political and military alliance had turned into a serious project. General Oshima, the Military Attaché in Berlin, was used for the job—in preference to the diplomatic staff. He informed Ribbentrop that "the time had come in the opinion of the Japanese Army to conclude a general defensive alliance between Germany, Italy, and Japan—which would provide for reciprocal assistance if any of the three powers were attacked by another without provocation." [8] The German and Italian officials were receptive. Oshima drew up a text with Ciano and Ribbentrop and submitted it to Tokyo.

On August 29, 1938, the five most important ministers of the Konoye Cabinet had approved the idea of entering into some further accord with Germany and Italy. But they had rejected the text transmitted by Oshima. Their thought was that the new pact should be an extension of the Anti-Comintern pact: that the Soviet was to be the chief object; that care should be taken to avoid alarming the United States and Great Britain; and that any political or military obligations should be suspensive, that is, effective only when and as the partners might later agree. These limiting features had not suited either the Japanese or German enthusiasts. A fight began within the Japanese government that continued to the very day that Germany made a deal with the Soviet Union. The basic difference, clearly seen and freely discussed, pivoted around the question whether the coming war would be against Russia or the West. Germany wanted a pact that would apply against either or both.

In October 1938, the Konoye Cabinet had made Oshima Ambassador to Germany. The appointment was at the behest of the Army General Staff and the Minister of War, General Itagaki. Another and even more excited worker for a total pact with the Axis, Shiratori, not long after

---

[6] As stated in the cable of the German Ambassador in China, Dirksen, to von Neurath, Foreign Minister, January 17, 1938. *ibid.*, Exh. No. 486 G.

[7] *ibid.*, Exh. Nos. 591, 593, and 594.

[8] As related by Ribbentrop to Ott in a telegram on April 26, 1939, *ibid.*, Exh. No. 502. Details about the origins and early phases of this negotiation are to be found in the interrogations of Oshima, *ibid.*, Exh. No. 497, and in the deposition of General Ugaki, Minister for Foreign Affairs, May–September 1938, *ibid.*, Exh. No. 3580.

had been made Ambassador to Italy. Both Oshima and Shiratori obeyed the orders of the Army High Command in Tokyo, rather than those of the Foreign Office.

Oshima had been certain of himself and the strength of the forces behind him. He submitted revised texts of a full alliance and called upon the Japanese cabinet to approve them or make way for another cabinet that would. The Konoye Cabinet dealt with his first try, in October, merely by inaction. But the succeeding cabinet, headed by Hiranuma, found it could not dispose of his second attempt that way. Support for a close and complete association with Germany had become too strong, especially within the Army. So strong and assertive that Oshima became sure Japan would sign the submitted draft. So sure that Ciano and Ribbentrop became sure, and began to arrange the exact time and place of signature.[9] It was at this point that Grew learned what was going on; and the American government—as related—began to convey warnings, garbed as Grew's private thoughts.

The opponents of a full alliance had held fast. More than seventy times during the spring and summer of 1939 the Hiranuma Cabinet found itself wrangling over the toil-worn texts. The points at issue were three: whether the pact would apply only in the event of war with the Soviet Union—or also in the event of war with others; whether or not in case any of the parties found themselves at war the others should be unconditionally obliged to join; and whether the pact was to contain a promise of "effective military support" or something less. The three points were related to each other.

The Prime Minister, Hiranuma, had been ready to go a long way to meet German wishes, but not so far as the Army wanted. Resort was had to every method of wearing out the resistance of the peaceful and prudent members of the government. Among the means used by the friends of the Axis to have their way had been: false reports to the Emperor, suppression of information, forged drafts, leaks to the press, arranged displays of hostility towards Britain, and threats of revolt and murder.

In opposition, the Foreign Minister, Arita, had stood firm against any obligation that might bring Japan to war against the United States or Britain. Conservative financial and business circles were no less op-

---

[9] It was to be on January 28 or 30, 1939, at Berlin. Memorandum of von Mackensen, German Ambassador in Italy, January 3, 1939. *Far East Mil. Trib.*, Exh. No. 3584.

posed. The court circle, including the Emperor, was gloomily against the pact. The Army and nationalist groups tried to frighten the officials in that circle by stirring up popular feeling against them. They spared the sacred person of the Emperor, while managing to revive memories of the time when his forebears were kept in seclusion.[10] But, it was the Navy which really had prevented the consummation of a full alliance. The Navy Minister, Yonai, and the Vice-Minister, Yamamoto, had been as stubborn as the spokesmen for the Army.

Again in February, Oshima in Berlin and Shiratori in Rome had tried to turn the trick by disobedience and deception. They attempted to create a situation from which the Japanese government could not retreat. They objected to orders brought to them by a special commission, headed by Prince Ito, a Foreign Office representative. They asked Tokyo to recall them, as a way of forcing a crisis. They told the German and Italian governments that they would resign, cause the cabinet to fall, and bring about a military government.[11]

"Just what is to be done?" the Emperor had asked the Prime Minister about the first of April, "in the event that Shiratori and Oshima do not conform to the directives of our Government concerning the strengthening of the Anti-Comintern Pact?"[12] A week later the question still sought an answer. For the two ambassadors had continued to repeat that Japan would participate in a war against Britain and France. The Emperor reproached the Minister of War, Itagaki, for his sanction of such conduct. But the imperial rebuke was phrased with care lest the Minister of War resign and create a crisis.

Germany had then lost patience and demanded a decision. The response was like one of those sets of boxes of which the Japanese are fond: within each there is a smaller one. The Japanese government offered to sign a pact of general scope on condition that it be allowed to issue a public statement at the time of signing. This would explain that the pact was intended to deal only with the Soviet Union and that other countries need not fear they were meant. Ribbentrop answered that

[10] Many details of this attempt to subdue the court are given in Parts 19 and 20 of the "Saionji-Harada Memoirs," and in "Kido's Diary" (Diary of Marquis Koichi Kido, who later became Lord Keeper of the Privy Seal, and the most influential of the officials around the Emperor). English texts of both these works were prepared for the Supreme Commander, Allied Forces, and extracts from both were presented as exhibits before the International Military Tribunal for the Far East.

[11] *The Ciano Diaries, 1939–1943*, edited by Hugh Gibson (Garden City, N.Y., 1946), entries for March 6 and 8, 1939, and the depositions of Nagai (Miziko), *Far East Mil. Trib.*, Exh. No. 3587.

[12] According to the account given by Matsudaira, Chief Secretary of the Privy Council, to Harada.

"this interpretation, which is in direct contradiction to the text of the agreement is quite out of the question for us." [13]

Baffled, but still avid for the benefits of association with Germany, the government had not given up. On May 4 Hiranuma addressed a personal appeal to Hitler through the German and Italian Ambassadors in Tokyo. The essence of this message was: "As far as the strengthening of our relations is concerned, I can affirm that Japan is firmly and steadfastly resolved to stand at the side of Germany and Italy even if one of these two powers were attacked by one or several powers without the participation of the Soviet Union and to afford them political and economic and, to the extent within her power, military help. . . . [But] Japan is, in view of the situation in which it finds itself, neither presently nor in the near future able to extend to them in a practical manner any effective military aid. However, it goes without saying that Japan would clearly grant this support if it should become possible through a change in the circumstances." [14]

In other words, the Japanese government had offered to enter an alliance of general scope, provided it could retain freedom to decide what its action would be in a crisis. It would enter the circle, if the circle were made of rope not of iron, so that it could twist and turn. Ribbentrop at once asked the passed-by Ambassador, Oshima, for his rendition of the meaning of this message. Would Japan, Ribbentrop asked, consider itself at war in the event that Germany was at war, even though it did not give military aid? Oshima said "Yes."

This answer had provoked another crisis within the Japanese government. The Foreign Minister, Arita, thought it arbitrary and inexcusable. The Prime Minister and the Minister of War defended the reply and refused to have it withdrawn. Arita thereupon said he wanted to resign. But the Navy persuaded him to stay. It was at this juncture that the Prime Minister had tried to get out of his trouble by proposing to Washington, as already told, that Japan and the United States join together to avert war in Europe.

The Emperor had remained cool to the alliance. When so informed, the Chief of Staff of the Army was awed but not subdued. Some of the advisers around the Emperor grew anxious that if he continued to play a part in this quarrel revolt would follow. Thus Kido, then Home Secretary, remarked to the last of the Elder Statesmen, Prince Saionji, that

---

[13] Telegram, Ribbentrop to Ott, April 26, 1939, *ibid.*, Exh. No. 502.
[14] Telegram from Ott to Ribbentrop, May 4, 1939, *ibid.*, Exh. No. 503. For interpretation, see supplementary telegram of May 6, Exh. No. 504.

"in the later years of Emperor Komei's reign, the Shogunate completely changed the officials about the Emperor. Perhaps something along that line will occur. In order to lead the Army, but still to make it appear as if we were being led by them, we must also make it seem as if we understood the Army a little more."

The court might become scared, but not the Navy. Still it sacrificed more of its freedom of decision to the Army's wish for an alliance. A compromise had been reached to the effect that Japan should promise to enter the war certainly and at once if the Soviet Union were one of the enemies; but that if it were not, Japan should have the right to choose its time of entry. This formula was put up to the German government in a tentative way on June 5.[15]

Two days later, June 7, the Polish Ambassador in Tokyo told Arita that his government had indisputable evidence that the contact between Germany and the Soviet Union had become active. Arita had dismissed the idea. But on second thought he made inquiries of his diplomatic missions abroad. When, on June 20, a secretary of the Japanese Embassy quizzed the Germany Foreign Office, he was told that all rumors of talk about political matters were "fake," that the talks with the Soviet Union concerned only economic affairs.[16] That was the last that the Japanese government was to hear of the matter until the pact was ready for signature and seal.

Ott, the German Ambassador in Tokyo, who knew nothing of the talks with Russia, had meanwhile continued to try to find out what the latest Japanese offer was worth. He found the task puzzling. The Prime Minister and the Army construed it in a very positive sense. The Foreign Minister and political circles made much of its reservations. But one thing must have been clear to Hitler: that only if the Soviet Union were among the enemies could Japan be counted on as an ally. This was exactly opposite to the program upon which he had now begun to base his plans.[17]

The Japanese advocates of the alliance had not been deterred by the receipt of notice on July 26 that the American government wanted to terminate its treaty with Japan. As late as August 11, according to Ott's reports to Ribbentrop, the Minister of War said that the Army had resumed its fight for the alliance; that in the last resort, he, Itagaki, would

[15] Telegram, Ott to Ribbentrop, June 5, 1939.
[16] Memorandum, German Foreign Office (Woermann), *ibid.*, Exh. No. 2723.
[17] Or, as related in a letter from Hitler to Mussolini (about August 30), "Japan was ready for an alliance against Russia in which Germany—and in my view Italy—could only be interested in present circumstances as a secondary consideration."

risk his resignation; that this action would bring down the cabinet; that the issue would be forced within a few days; and that he would send further word directly through Oshima and Shiratori, thus avoiding the Foreign Minister.[18] But this last mistaken effort had failed. The Minister of War, despite his threats, had not been able to have his way. Ott thought that his resignation and a cabinet crisis had become unavoidable. This report arrived in Berlin at almost the same time as a message from Moscow confirming Molotov's wish for an agreement with Germany.[19] Of this the Japanese government had still guessed nothing.

The Army leaders had urged Hiranuma to go to Berlin and Rome, to persuade Hitler and Mussolini to take what Japan offered. These desired partners were to be convinced that it was not lack of desire, but the clamp of circumstance, which made Japan shy about giving all that was asked. When Prince Saionji had heard of this he had remarked: "Somehow it does not make sense. It is like a dream." It was no dream, but it was a pursuit of a pact that had become a phantom. Its life had derived from a common fear and enmity—the Soviet Union. Now Germany was about to adopt the enemy as a friend, and to urge Japan to do likewise.

[2]

Germany and the Soviet Union had not come together over night. The first messages had passed in early June—like glances exchanged by members of two unfriendly gangs who happened to meet on a dark street.[20] They both began to wonder whether they might not work with, not against, one another.

[18] Telegram, Ott to Ribbentrop, August 18, 1939, *ibid.,* Exh. No. 2198. This report is borne out by the account of events in "Kido's Diary," particularly the entry for August 7.
[19] Telegram, Schulenburg to German Foreign Office, August 19, 1939. *Nazi-Soviet Relations, 1939-1941; Documents from the Archives of the German Foreign Office* ([Washington] 1948), pp. 64-65. Published by the Department of State; edited by Raymond James Sontag and James Stuart Beddie.
[20] As early as May 20, 1939, Stuart Grummon, the Chargé d'Affaires of the American Embassy in Moscow, sent Washington an intimation of what was about to take place. He cabled that Schulenburg, the German Ambassador in Moscow had just seen Ribbentrop; that the Foreign Minister, obviously reflecting Hitler's views, had said that since the activities of the Comintern were no longer important, there was no longer an ideological bar between Russia and Germany. Further that the Ambassador had been asked to convey to the Soviet Government discreetly that Germany entertained no animosity toward it, and to try to find out what the present Soviet attitude is toward relation between the two countries. Great care, Ribbentrop had said, was necessary in order not to alarm Japan.
A German Foreign Office memorandum, May 29, 1939, noted that Molotov had told the German Ambassador in Moscow that the resumption of commercial negotiations was subject to clarification of the political relations between Germany and the Soviet Union, and pondered what that meant. *ibid.,* p. 10.

The German government knew, of course, that if it made up its quarrel with Russia Japan would feel deserted. It was obvious, as Schulenburg, the German Ambassador in Moscow, wrote to Weizsaecker, the State Secretary in the Foreign Office, on June 5, ". . . that Japan would not like to see even the smallest agreement between us and the Soviet Union." [21] But this does not seem to have caused Hitler to pause a moment before the better chance. No concern was felt over the plight in which Japan would find itself. Hitler and Ribbentrop seemed to have been fairly sure, in fact, that Japan would soon get over the hurt, and follow in Germany's trail.

Russia made it very clear that it would expect Germany to cease siding with Japan and induce her to show friendliness. Or, as Molotov put the matter on August 14 to the German Ambassador, it would be essential that Germany cease to support Japanese "aggression." [22] On the next day, the 15th, and again on the 18th, a basis for a deal having been confirmed, Molotov reverted to the subject of Japan. When he recalled how Germany had been trying to draw Japan into a pact against Russia, no denial was made. The German government was now in complete accord with the idea of "German pressure on Japan." It was understood that Germany was to influence Japan to improve its relations with the Soviet Union and to settle the border quarrels. [23]

No matter, any longer, how the anguished argument within the Japanese government turned out. The prime purpose of a possible alliance with Germany was being changed without notice. Up to then it had been to gain an ally against Russia. Thereafter it was to become a question whether Japan would also accept Russia as a friend and join Germany in the attempt to despoil the western Powers.

In such a turnabout, it may be remarked, there lay almost complete certainty of ultimate war between Japan and the United States. For if Japan and Russia came together, the Japanese longing to expand could only turn south. There it would menace vital sources of supply and communication routes, and surround the Philippines.

By August 21 it was judged safe to let Japan know what was afoot. Among the qualities of the Nazi regime that Oshima had found most admirable was its habit of quick and ruthless decision. Now he had full chance to appreciate it. The news was telephoned to him by Ribbentrop

[21] Letter from Schulenburg to Weizsaecker, June 5, 1939, *ibid.*, p. 18.

[22] Letter from Schulenburg to Weizsaecker, August 14, 1939, *ibid.*, p. 46.

[23] Memorandum by Schulenburg, August 16, 1939, *ibid.*, pp. 53–54; Hitler's message to Stalin, August 16, 1939, *ibid.*, p. 58; and Ribbentrop's talk with Stalin and Molotov, night of August 23–24, 1939, *ibid.*, pp. 72–73.

that evening. Ribbentrop was at the Berghof about to leave for Moscow, and could not find time to see the flurried Japanese friend before his flight. So Oshima paid a midnight call upon Weizsaecker. "The Japanese Ambassador," that German official informed Ribbentrop, "as usual showed himself well disposed. At the same time, I discerned in him a certain uneasiness, which increased in the course of the conversation." [24]

Weizsaecker was soothing. He assured Oshima that Germany wanted to maintain its friendly relationship with Japan, and esteemed personalities like Oshima who had acted most vigorously to that end. Its arrangement with Russia would, he went on, beginning to indicate the new strategy, put Germany in a position to bring about a period of quiet in relations between Japan and Russia. Since it was clear as day, he blandly continued, that for Japan as for Germany, England was the prime enemy, the agreement which was being reached with Moscow would serve the interest of both nations.

But for the Japanese government the experience was like opening a mail box and having a pack of hornets dash out. It was angry at the lack of notice, dazed, and incoherent. The strategists were left without a ready answer; they had been fooled before the eyes of their enemies. The Prime Minister informed the Emperor (through the Lord Keeper of the Privy Seal) . . . "that the affairs of State cannot be carried on with the situation as it is today. With the conclusion of the Russo-German Non-Aggression Pact, Japan's foreign policy is in a state of having been practically betrayed. This is a failure in foreign policy which resulted from the unreasonableness of the Army. In order to serve in accordance with Japan's singular loyalty to the Emperor, I (the Premier), shall, on the one hand demand the Army's reconsideration and set an example; and on the other, since I cannot justify myself to the Emperor, I shall apologize and resign." [25]

---

[24] Memorandum by Weizsaecker, *ibid.,* p. 70. Weizsaecker is the prototype of the trained, career foreign official whom dictators found it useful to retain in order to conduct selected business and maintain contact with the professional diplomatic world. Their presence was helpful in leading other countries to believe that the foreign policy of the dictatorship might at any time conform to traditional standards; be less ruthless and dramatic. The officials stayed in office partly out of love of it, partly with the thought that they might influence their rules or their country for the better. The transcript of the trials of Weizsaecker and some of his colleagues in the German Foreign Office (which is cited later) is of substantial interest to the student of this feature of the conduct of foreign affairs, of the relationship between permanent staff and political chiefs in a dictatorship.

[25] "Saionji-Harada Memoirs."

The press, for once, admitted it may have been foolish. Despite some reserved doubt about an unrestricted alliance, it had chattered much about the Tripartite Pact, in the making. Even the Army was resentful. The pact with Germany would make it easier and safer for the Soviets to maintain a large army on the Manchurian front, and for the Communists to penetrate, if not invade, Manchukuo and Mongolia.

On August 25, the Foreign Minister informed Ott that the Japanese government was about to enter a solemn formal protest against the pact with the Soviet Union. For in its opinion, this pact was a serious infraction of the secret attachment to the Anti-Comintern Pact.[26] Therefore, the Japanese government could not continue with the talks about an alliance with Germany and Italy. But this statement was softened by a wish to cling on to future chances; Germany might win and still be in a position greatly to help Japan. Thus Arita added that, while the Japanese government felt itself compelled to take this position, it was willing to continue its friendship with Germany and was looking for a suitable way.

We may anticipate a bit to trace the note of protest of which Arita spoke. It did not reach its mark for several weeks. Oshima showed the paper to Weizsaecker, who, after reading it, said that it would receive "an ill-tempered answer, which would not be serviceable to the friendly relations between Japan and Germany. . . ." Thereupon Oshima took it back.[27] Leaving Tokyo in the dark, he kept the protest until he felt it could be presented without effects damaging to his wishes. The time came round; on September 18 he delivered it. By then the campaign in Poland was won. He could count on a better humor in Berlin. So "slightly bashful, he finally turned it over with words that suggested Germany could forget it now." [28]

Within Japan a hasty search began for some combination which would be able to maintain domestic order and adjust Japan's foreign policy. The critics did not have the daring to oust the Army from a share in it. Even those who had worried much about the alliance with Germany

[26] It was, of course, a blatant violation of Article II of the secret attachment which specified that "The High Contracting States will not during the validity of this agreement and without mutual assent conclude any political treaties with the Union of Soviet Socialist Republics which do not conform to the spirit of this Agreement."

[27] The text of the protest is given in *Far East Mil. Trib.*, Exh. No. 782. Weizsaecker's memorandum of this talk (August 26th) with Oshima is printed in (United States) *Department of State Bulletin*, June 16, 1946.

[28] Memorandum by Weizsaecker, *Far East Mil. Trib.*, Exh. No. 734.

thought it essential that the new Prime Minister be acceptable to the Army. They were afraid of internal disorder. The Army leaders submitted to the opinion that for the time being Japan must move with care. But they did their best to secure a selection that would not reject association with the Axis later on, if the battle went well for Germany.

The choice, after many nervous conferences around the Throne, fell upon General Abe. The Army thought it could count upon his understanding. The other groups thought that he would exert control over the Army and govern its will. The Emperor sealed the choice by observing that "The Army would co-operate with Abe since he understood matters concerning it, and thus let him try out." [29]

Who was the proper person for War Minister? The Emperor expressed the wish that the person to be selected for that position should be suitable for he "ought to co-operate with the Prime Minister and purge the Army thoroughly, or diplomatic intercourse and internal administration will be impossible." General Hata was given the job. He had been Chief Aide-de-Camp to the Emperor and remained close to him. But, to anticipate again, the Army had no intention of permitting him to run its affairs; and presently it forced him to submit and resign.

Admiral Nomura, a sober, solid naval officer, of friendly inclination towards the United States and Britain, was chosen as Foreign Minister. For a short time it was thought that there would be a purge in the Foreign Office too, a riddance of the clique attached to Shiratori, which had bedevilled previous Ministers of Foreign Affairs. Shiratori, himself, was recalled from Rome at his own request, the better to push his ideas at home. Oshima was allowed to remain in Berlin until later, when, for the same purpose, he too returned to Tokyo. Many other changes were made in the Foreign Office; but they were neither thorough nor lasting.

The members of the new cabinet having been selected, on August 28 Hiranuma stepped out. "The German-Soviet Pact," he announced in going, "has produced a new, strange, and baffling situation in Europe, in view of which Japan must be prepared to abandon old policies and to form new ones. . . . This causes the Emperor to worry again; . . . as a Japanese subject, it would be nothing less than becoming familiar with the Emperor, and slighting the favor shown to me—were I to remain in my present position." [30]

General Abe took office on August 30 (Tokyo time). The next day

[29] The account of this change of government is drawn largely from the "Saionji-Harada Memoirs," and "Kido's Diary."
[30] *Far East Mil. Trib.*, Exh. No. 2728.

Germany invaded Poland. On September 3 Great Britain and France declared war on Germany. The new government avoided any statement of neutrality. It resorted to an involved and three-ply explanation of its ideas. "Confronted by the recent outbreak of a European war," the statement published in Japan began, "the Government of Japan plans to avoid becoming involved in that war . . ." But tucked into the notes sent the nations at war, informing them of its intentions, was advice that they withdraw their ships and troops from areas in China controlled by Japanese forces.[31] And in the longer public statement issued by the new cabinet on September 13 on its policies there was much to show that Japan was not really chastened. The utmost effort was to be made "to realize self-supply and self-sufficiency in regard to national defense." This was in part to be achieved by an economic program that would unify Japan, Manchukuo, and China.

In sum, Japan had been thrown out of its stride by the pact between Germany and the Soviet Union. But it was going to keep on trying to beat China into submission, and cling to the aim of attaining a new order in East Asia.

[31] This is printed in *Foreign Relations, Japan*, II, 9.

## CHAPTER 5

# Separation but Still not Enmity:
# the Winter of 1939-40

JAPAN continued to seek a new order in East Asia, but by itself and with shrunken notions. On August 26 the Japanese Ambassador in Washington, Horinouchi, paid a call of contrition upon Hull. This was three days after the signature of the German-Soviet Pact and two days before the Hiranuma Cabinet gave up office. He said that his government had decided to abandon all negotiations with Germany and Italy, and that he expected that Japan would have to adopt a different line of foreign policy.

The Ambassador found that this turn was regarded in Washington as an accident, not a change of heart. Itself engaged in deception, Japan had met deception. This being so, Hull saw no reason not to repeat, as he did, American causes of complaint. The American attitude, he went on, was guided by known principles; it would not be bent to fit the curves of Japanese policy. Tersely he concluded, "The future of American-Japanese relations lies largely in the hands of Japan. American policy is a policy of friendliness and fair dealing toward all nations. It will not change."

The Japanese statement of September 3 that it would stay out of the war in Europe was read with mild satisfaction. The President and State Department could feel roughly pleased with the way in which their recent handling of Japan had worked out. At least Britain and France would not have at once to divide their forces to protect their colonies and sea routes in the Far East. The United States would not have to decide at once whether to let Japan run loose or risk war. A break with Japan had been avoided; the way to a peaceful settlement in the Far East left open. But, by cancelling our treaty, we had called attention to our disapproval. Time remained to test further the results of a firm but unaggressive policy of opposition. The temper of the American people and the state of our armed forces made it expedient, if not compulsory, to go on that way.

This type of policy, it may be remarked, best suited the nature and skill of the Secretary of State. He was given to sifting a difference into its smallest particles; to enduring a strained situation long. And all the while, and every hour, subtly he tugged at the cords of trouble so that it might unravel as he wanted. These were the qualities that shaped our diplomacy during the period ahead. The American government hugged its convictions hard, waited, and began to put itself in a better position to deal with whatever might come. Any and all actions, the effects of which could not be measured in advance, were avoided. This period lasted till the coming June, when decision was forced upon us.

As before, the chief argument within the American government concerned the question of whether or not to continue to provide Japan with the sinews of war. The issue, as a tactical one, came to the fore in September. The American government was trying to bolster British and French resistance to the "friendly advice" that they pull out of China. Dooman, our Chargé d'Affaires, thought a hint from us was in order. He asked consent to tell the Foreign Minister, merely as his own opinion, that if Japan took any steps to force Britain and France out of China the American public would become less inclined to continue to supply raw materials and machinery. Hull said no. But on September 7 Hull himself asked the Japanese Ambassador a question:

"How does your Government expect us to prevent the Congress and the country, if we should attempt to do so, from taking up the question of our monetary and financial and trade relations with your country and dealing with it in a way that you can well imagine in the light of all the circumstances?" [1]

The art with which this inquiry was carved is worth notice. Not even the most edgy official could assert that the Secretary of State had made a threat. He had merely given the Japanese government a reminder of circumstance and asked it to use its imagination. The men who were to try in the coming months to mislead the American government would have been well advised to reflect upon the talent which phrased this question.

For its part the American government would not consider any idea that the troops and ships which we had in China be withdrawn. It continued to call Japan to book for all the damage which American interests in China were suffering as a result of the warfare in that country. Thus, Hull made it very clear to the Ambassador that we "expected the Japanese Government to present concrete evidence of the manner in which

---

[1] Hull's memorandum of this conversation is printed in *Foreign Relations, Japan*, II, 12-14.

the legitimate grounds for complaint on the part of this Government were to be removed and that this Government did not feel called upon to take the initiative in making any suggestions of this character." [2]

But with advent of the war a new reason emerged for checking some exports. The American government was itself beginning to accumulate reserves of many raw materials of which this country was short, and which would be needed in the event of war. Some of them, it may be noted, came mainly from the Southwest Pacific—rubber, tin, quinine, Manila fiber. Foreign countries were buying these in the United States, taking supplies away faster than the American government could gather them.

A group scattered throughout the government were convinced that it was vital to stop this drain, whether Japan minded or not. Unless the United States had adequate stocks of these critical and strategic materials, they stressed, it would find itself disabled, both in diplomacy and in war. But Hull was given other advice. Those of his staff who were concerned with commerce did not believe such action urgent or essential.

He was spared the pain of decision. The President made it for him. He passed down word that the government should first try to control the trade in these materials in some other way. For the time being, he did not want to ask Congress for authority to do so. His caution came from fear lest any proposal which could be read as meaning that he foresaw war might cause Congress again to refuse to revise the Neutrality Act.

On September 26 the President asked all the private interests concerned to cease the export of eleven named raw materials. The appeal was effective. Export of these materials practically ended. Japan made no protest. It was maintaining similar controls.

The Presidential caution was rewarded when on November 3 Congress agreed to the desired revision of the Neutrality Act. The section which forbade the export of arms, munitions, and implements of war was repealed. But this action gave no clear clue as to whether Congress had grown more disposed to permit the Executive to take sides in the wars that were going on in Europe and Asia. The process of amendment did not reach the preamble of the Joint Resolution. It still read, "to preserve the neutrality and the peace of the United States and to secure the safety of its citizens and their interests."

Some had favored revision because they thought it was time that the United States should play a part in the world situation. Others did so

[2] *ibid.*, II, 39.

because they thought that repeal of the ban on the export of weapons would make it easier to continue to remain aloof. Thus the House of Representatives stood up to cheer Representative Wadsworth, whose speech closed with the citation of Theodore Roosevelt's advice to "speak softly but carry a big stick." Then it did the same for Representative Rayburn, who said that the new law forbade "the things . . . that got this country into the war twenty-two years ago." Hull kept mum—up to the ceremony of signing. Then all he said was: "I desire to repeat with emphasis what I have consistently said heretofore, to the effect that our first and most sacred task is to keep our country secure and at peace, and that it is my firm belief that we shall succeed in this endeavor." [3]

Between "will" and "won't," the President and Hull thought, the time for decision had not come. Let matters between us and Japan take their course, opinion form as it took the further measure of them. They would not foretell what ought or must be done when January 26, 1940, came round, and the treaty with Japan expired. Grew, home on leave from Japan, found this attitude disturbing. Beneath the waiting he seemed to detect a wish to strike against Japan and a vague belief that this could be done with impunity. Of his efforts to dispel this notion he wrote in his diary, upon his return to Tokyo (October 1939): "In both my talks with the President I brought out clearly my view that if we once start sanctions against Japan we must see them through to the end, and the end may conceivably be war. I also said that if we cut off Japanese supplies of oil and that if Japan then finds that she cannot obtain sufficient oil from other commercial sources to ensure her national security, she will in all probability send her fleet down to take the Dutch East Indies. The President replied significantly, 'Then we could easily intercept her fleet.' "

Grew was moved by portents, not by evidence. There was no plan in the autumn of 1939 to use sanctions against Japan. There was a state of mind, becoming more confirmed, which forbade compromise with Japan. Sooner or later, states of mind express themselves in action. After the treaty was cancelled, anything might happen. Grew wanted the American government to divert the indicated course of events by again seeking a settlement with Japan; and, as a way of showing its wish to remain friends, to propose some temporary substitute for the treaty. Another entry in his diary at this time summarizes his affirmations:

[3] *New York Times*, November 5, 1939.

"I believe that we should now offer the Japanese a *modus vivendi,* in effect if not in name, that we shall commence negotiations for a new treaty, withholding ratification until favorable developments appear to justify. . . .

"In my view the use of force, except in defense of a nation's sovereignty, can only constitute admission of a lack of good will and of resourceful, imaginative statesmanship. To those who hold that it is not enough for these qualities to exist on one side—my answer is that they do exist in latent form in Japan and the function of diplomacy is to bring them into vigor. Shidehara diplomacy has existed. It can exist again." [4]

The President and Secretary of State shared the hope expressed in the final sentence of this entry. But where were the reasons for the belief that this change could be effected by a mere show of patience and good will, as Grew seemed to think? While they had the treaty, Japanese governments had not valued it enough to listen to us. Why would they begin to do so now—if the treaty were restored? Both the President and Hull wanted prior proofs of a change in aims and methods. Grew's idea was rejected. He was told, instead, to speak out upon his return to Japan in a way that would bring home to both the government and people of that country that trouble was ahead unless they changed their policies.

The text of the speech in which this was to be said received much study within the State Department. It was to be resonant but not threatening. Grew reconciled himself with the thought that if American policy was not to conform to his ideas, it was best, anyhow, that Japan be plainly told what it was to be. In that way, at least, the risk of war through ignorant misjudgment might be lessened.[5]

Grew delivered his notice that the American government would not back down, and that, therefore, if trouble was to be avoided the Japanese Army must. During the weeks that followed, it seemed to the American government to be having some measure of effect. There were signs—which proved to be passing—that the Japanese government might deal less harshly with American interests and activities in China; the Japanese government promised to reopen the Yangtze River to foreign traffic. But these small acts of care were offset by the efforts to create a puppet Chinese government in Nanking and thereby to disavow Chiang Kai-shek's group as the legal government of China. Washington called the new regime by its true name and refused to recognize it. The warning spoken by Grew, it appeared, would be defied.

[4] Unpublished diary of Joseph Clark Grew, October entry, 1939.
[5] Joseph Clark Grew, *Ten Years in Japan* (New York, 1944), p. 295.

But Hull still paused. Opinion was divided and uncertain. On November 6 Senator Pittman predicted the Congress would authorize the use of economic pressure on Japan. Senator Vandenberg contradicted him at once, warning that such threats were the first step towards war itself.

Anything of that sort that was done would have to be done alone. Compelled to fight their own battle in Europe, neither Britain nor France wanted trouble in the Far East. If it should become necessary to protect their own position in that region, they were ready to compromise with Japan. As explained by Lord Lothian, the British Ambassador (on November 21 and subsequently), his government favored some accord between China and Japan "on a basis which would be fair and equitable to both sides, but with the realization on the part of both China and Japan that each side would have to make concessions." The French government leaned the same way.

But the American bent stiffly the other way. Thus Welles, then Acting Secretary, told Lothian that the American government could not and would not do anything to bring pressure on China to make a peace which was not just or which assigned a preferential place to Japan in China. Hull lectured Lothian in the same sense, on December 15. The American government, he asserted, had done its utmost to bring about a fair settlement in the Far East; but in his view Japan was bent on turning the whole of China into a vast Manchukuo; the American government could not consider such a policy and would not depart from the position and principles which it had been defending since first Japan began its conquest of Asia.

The British and French authorities bowed to our judgment, but with a reminder that if it were wrong the first blows would hit them and not us. They remained uneasy. So did Grew. He resumed his efforts to make sure that the American government did not enter into, fall into, the error of thinking that Japan would yield to pressure. Thus, in a long and considered dispatch sent on December 1, he wrote in part:

"On one issue [Japanese] opinion can be definitely said to be unanimous: the so-called New Order in East Asia has come to stay. That term is open to wide interpretation, but the minimum interpretation envisages permanent Japanese control of Manchuria, Inner Mongolia, and North China."

Sanctions, he was sure, would not cause Japan to give up its program in China, but would arouse it to fight—since it was a nation of hardy warriors, with an ingrained spirit to do or die.[6]

[6] Dispatch, December 1, 1939, Grew to the State Department.

This estimate agreed on the whole with that made within the State Department. But Grew's advice did not seem to jibe with it, but rather to issue from some do-or-die professional instinct of his own. How or why diplomacy could win the day, if Japan was so hard set upon the creation of a new order throughout Asia, remained unclear. Hull decided that the best course for the time being was merely to prolong the uncertainty. To refrain from the use of sanctions which might produce a crisis, but also to refuse to give Japan any guarantee as to what the United States might do in the future. On December 14 the President approved this course.

Grew, as expected, questioned the decision. So did the British and French. Hull's answer to Grew, on December 20, stated that while he also desired to give the Abe Cabinet every chance to increase its influence over the Army, he had the impression that at the bottom it was as keen as the Army to extend Japanese power over Asia. Though more prudent, perhaps, because better informed of the risks, it was hardly less ambitious. To Lothian (on December 15) he repeated that the United States could not consider any policy that would enable Japan to achieve a victorious peace.

By the turn of the new year, 1940, it was settled that we would neither renew nor replace the treaty. The United States kept itself free to end at any time the shipment of goods vital to Japan. When told of this decision, Nomura, the Foreign Minister, was bitter and depressed. For the first time, Grew noticed, he did not accompany him downstairs after their talk.

But no crisis was to be forced. Trade with Japan was to be allowed to go on in much the same way as when the treaty was in force.[7] Japan was left unhindered to win or lose the battle in China; to scheme for a southern empire or renounce the dream.

As the momentous new year, 1940, began, the American government would not compromise its ideas, and Japan would not compromise its purposes. Of the two, the government of Japan was the more frustrated. Unable to move either ahead or back, the Abe Cabinet, formed during

[7] Except for a further extension of the "moral embargo." This applied to the export of the means of war from the air. On December 2 the President extended it to include metals essential to airplane manufacture, including aluminum, magnesium, and molybdenum. On December 6 he also included all plans and plants or technical information of service in the production of aviation gasoline. The Japanese Ambassador protested these extensions on January 6, 1940. Hull answered on the 27 by giving him a long list of the instances in which Japan had bombed the civilian population of China. *Foreign Relations, Japan*, II, 204-209.

the period of shock over German desertion, was forced to give up. Of its experience in office more is now to be learned from the Japanese records. Let us see briefly what they tell before going on with the narration of events in Washington.

[2]

Grew had warned that unless the United States relaxed its opposition to the Japanese program the Abe Cabinet would fall. He was correct. It had been asked to do the impossible: to serve the New Order for Greater East Asia without exciting Britain and the United States.

For a while, as told, the Army was persuaded to be less careless in its treatment of American interests in China, and even to consent to the reopening of the Yangtze River to foreign trade. Nomura stamped on every new flicker of purpose to align Japan with Germany. For Ribbentrop sought to convince the new cabinet that the pact which Germany had made with Russia could be a boon. It was, he expounded, to make possible a quick German victory over Britain, and that victory would open the South Pacific to Japan. A great partnership was open to Japan. He would, if allowed, complete it by mediating between Japan and the Soviet Union. This remained the governing German conception until the talk between Hitler and Molotov in November 1940; to form so great a group of covetous nations that the United States would quail. Nomura was impassive.

But the seekers of the alliance, like Oshima, did not give up. They counted on the Army. Even in the shadow it remained able to prevent any settlement with China. Failing in this, they reckoned that the cabinet would fall. Presently the Army would gain control of Japanese policy again, and the alliance with the Axis could be formed. All this it would take some time to bring about, but they were sure it could be brought about.

The Abe Cabinet went on to the end with its attempts to get the American government to accept the leaves for the root. The demands made by the Army for the means of conducting the war in China grew. Rice and other essentials of living became scarcer and dearer. Political parties spent themselves even more in intrigue.

Had the American government agreed to enter into some temporary accord to take the place of the treaty—as Grew urged—the cabinet might have remained in office a while longer. But not much longer, and surely it would not have lived through the events of the summer ahead. Its resignation (in January 1940) was noted in Washington without qualms. Like the Axis observers, the American government judged it to be too weak to reverse Japan's course, even though granted time.

General Abe yielded to Admiral Yonai as Prime Minister. The choice was much influenced by the wish to keep relations with the United States and Britain from growing worse. Yonai had been Secretary of the Navy in the two previous cabinets. He had been the most stanch opponent of an alliance with Germany. Arita returned to the office of Foreign Minister. He had been in that office in 1936 when the Basic Principle of National Policy was written down—which specified that, while the New Order in East Asia was being realized, the United States and Britain must not be turned into enemies. A supple man, yet afraid of the Axis connection.

The choice of these men was taken by Hull to mean that the refusal to renew the treaty was having good effect. Grew became less despondent about the outcome of our obstinacy, noting in his diary: "a new and healthy attitude and point of view are gradually emerging which may be capable of achieving a great deal, if not rebuffed by us." [8] But the German watchers were not cast down. Ott merely remarked that two or three more transit governments might be needed in order to bring Japan back into the German orbit.[9]

This new cabinet was even more haunted by tales of assassination than the one whose place it took. The thought of violence—of the use of killing weapons—is a radioactive one. It was inside Japan.

[8] Entry, January, 1940.
[9] Telegram, Ott to Ribbentrop, December 31, 1939, *Far East Mil. Trib.*, Exh. No. 3503.

PART TWO

# HOSTILITY

## CHAPTER 6

# The First Waves of German Victory
# Reach the Southwest Pacific:
# April 1940

WITH the treaty out of the way, those who believed that Japan should and could be forced to change its course, became more active. Their views were most ably advanced by Henry L. Stimson, former Secretary of State. As always, his words commanded respect. For they were imbued with a sense of great things, not small; of courage and the duty of a country as strong as the United States.

His letter printed in the *New York Times* of January 11, 1940, still gives today—as it did then—the impression of a stern and sure fullback going through the center of the opposing line. It was a straight rush from a moral position to a strategic goal.

For three years, Mr. Stimson wrote, American resources—especially oil and scrap iron—had aided wrongdoing in the Far East. Since there was no adequate alternative source of supply for these materials the responsibility was almost wholly focused on us. The American people were, he thought, united in their adverse judgment of Japan's attack on China—but there was fear that if we did anything to prevent the wrong, that would lead into war with Japan. "Experienced observers," he contradicted, "have promptly recognized and publicly stated that such a fear was without credible foundation; that the very last thing which the Japanese Government desires is a war with the United States . . ." The Japanese—the train of his analysis went on—could not bring a regime of peace in China with security, law, justice, order, and stability; on the contrary, only more misery and fear, hostility, and violence. So, if the United States wished to bring the war in China to an end, the way to do so was by ceasing to provide the means for carrying it on. It was essential that the Japanese military organization should be discredited in the eyes of the patriotic Japanese people. For until they realized that their Army was embarked on a failing venture it was not likely that they would cease to support it. Then, and then only, would peace in the Pacific come into sight. Thus, the argument concluded, the United States should act in accord with its beliefs; and forcibly, not feebly.[1]

Both the reasoning and the sentiment expressed by Stimson had much appeal. For the first time, the public opinion polls—shallow gauges of informed thought—seemed to show that American opinion was in favor of ending this trade.[2]

But to the officials who had the decision to make, various main points seemed suffused with doubt. If the Japanese Army, for whatever reason, got into greater trouble in China, would it become discredited? Or would it, by placing all blame on us, be able to win more tenacious loyalty? And if, as a result of our action, Japan should really be faced with defeat in China, would it give in or would it make a desperate attempt to save itself by war? Mr. Stimson's opinions on these points seemed to them dubious, and his dismissal of the chance that Japan might dare to fight the United States too confident.

Congress still had before it several bills written with Japan in mind. Some, like the Pittman resolution, would have given the President merely authority to restrict export of specified products. Others, like the Schwellenbach resolution, would have made it mandatory for him to do so. Their existence on the calendar of Congress was itself deemed useful by Hull. But he did not know whether or not he wanted any of them to become a law. Day by day he fingered that question, like a pianist who was not sure what would come out of a struck chord. Moved by caution and patience rather than by faith, he decided that it was better to wait; to invite still the small chance that the course of the wars in China or Europe might cause Japan to draw back without being forced to do so.

Thus, without public appearance or plea he permitted, as did the President, a divided Senate Committee on Foreign Relations to discard the menacing measures. He did not court a display of Pittman's fitful hot temper by taking sides against him. But his unhappy anxiety seeped into the committee rooms of Congress and dampened the impulse to act. Bills to restrain trade with Japan, to restrict the export of iron and steel scrap remained unpassed.

---

[1] Five years later, as Secretary of War, Stimson was to write another letter: the one that brought this failure to an end in a more tragic way; the one which proposed to President Truman that atomic bombs be dropped upon Japan.

[2] Samuel Eliot Morison has remarked about this, "of course the voters were not told, and could not be told, that an almost certain consequence of the embargo that they wanted was war with Japan." *History of United States Naval Operations in World War II, The Rising Sun in the Pacific* (Boston, 1948), III, 39.

This uneasy pause lasted through the winter of 1939-40, the winter of the "phony war" in Europe. The Japanese armies went further into China, showing even less regard than before for American lives and property. As far as the State Department could judge, the Yonai Cabinet, while fostering a cool view of the situation, was effecting no real change in Japanese policies. While, within the Diet, it was being accused of kowtowing to the United States. Both the Prime Minister, Yonai, and the Foreign Minister, Arita, seemed to be counting upon the progress of the Japanese armies in China to bring the United States round. In the meanwhile Yonai was asking us to forbear from coercion—in the light of a common wish for peace. To the Diet he said (on March 23):

"The question of a general embargo is a serious one both for the country imposing the embargo and the country upon which it is imposed. If one false step is taken, danger lies ahead for both countries. I do not believe the United States would risk applying a general embargo upon Japan. However, we must be prepared for any eventuality. The Government is giving every consideration to this point."

The conduct of the cabinet was taken as showing a wish for peace without resolve or power to achieve it. All the more so, since the Japanese government after months of shifty intrigue finally set up the puppet government for China. This action Hull, on March 30, in full accord with the President, denounced, saying that ". . . the setting up of a new regime at Nanking has the appearance of a further step in a program of one country by armed force to impose its will upon a neighboring country and to block off a large area of the world from normal political and economic relationships with the rest of the world." [3] At the same time it was announced that the Export-Import Bank would grant another loan to Chiang Kai-shek. The British, with a gulp, followed the American lead.


Other irritants swiftly followed.

The German invasion of Denmark and Norway on April 9 had quick radiations in Tokyo. The Foreign Minister, Arita, a few days later (April 15) issued a statement in regard to the Dutch East Indies. Its expressed point was not subject to objection: "The Japanese Government," he declared, "cannot but be deeply concerned over any development accompanying an aggravation of the war in Europe that may affect the *status*

[3] *Department of State Bulletin,* March 30, 1940.

*quo* of the Netherlands East Indies." But in Washington the occasion and purpose were suspect. Was Japan only warning both sides in the war to leave the Indies alone? Or was it seeking a reason to send its own forces south? The opinion of General Pabst, the well-informed Dutch Minister in Tokyo, was calming. He thought that Arita was merely on guard lest the Dutch government invite the British to take charge of the Indies, in presentiment of a German invasion of the Netherlands. Grew also was inclined to believe this the only purpose.

Perhaps, Hull thought, but only perhaps. In some of the language used by Arita there seemed to be an insinuated claim of special interest. For instance, the comment that "With the South Seas regions, especially the Netherlands East Indies, Japan is economically bound by an intimate relationship of mutuality in ministering to one another's needs." [4] What did this statement mean? Much of the Japanese press began at once to expound it as a claim for Japanese supremacy in the South Seas.

Even before this episode, Japan had been making unusual requests of the Indies; had been pushing for advantages that would bring the Indies into the service of the Greater East Asia program. On January 12 it had given notice to the Dutch government of the termination of its Treaty of Judicial Settlement, Arbitration, and Conciliation with the Netherlands. By the terms of this treaty the parties were pledged to settle all disputes by peaceful means. Three weeks later (on February 22) it had given the Dutch government an outline of what Japan wanted of the Indies. The main features were: a lowering of trade restrictions; greater facilities for Japanese enterprise in the Indies; easier entry for Japanese merchants, employees, and workers; mutual control of the press.

The Dutch government had studied these proposals, torn between dislike of them and fear of refusing them. Its answer had been delayed; and on March 8 the Japanese government had renewed the requests in a note given to the Dutch Minister in Tokyo, General Pabst. At the time of Arita's statement these were still under study in Batavia, with a tag attached recording Pabst's opinions. This read: "If we give in on the so-called less important points, if we give the Japanese even a finger's breadth of their demands, they will quickly ask the whole of our country."

All this Hull knew. He decided to paste up his own thoughts alongside those of Arita. In accord with the President on April 17, he pointed out that any change in the status of the Netherlands Indies would directly affect the interest of many countries, not only Japan. Further, he implied

[4] *Foreign Relations: Japan,* II, 281.

that the only country that might intervene in the Indies was Germany. He recalled that in 1922 the United States, the British Empire, France, and Japan had each given formal notice of its firm resolve "to respect the rights of the Netherlands in relation to their insular possessions in the region of the Pacific Ocean." [5] The British government echoed Hull's remarks. The Dutch government went further; it gave fresh assurance that no matter what happened the economic relations between the Indies and Japan would be continued. Further it promised not to seek (or accept) outside help to protect the Indies.

The Japanese government professed to see no reason for the excitement. Arita's statement, its Ambassador in Washington said to Hull, was a simple act of prudence, innocent, akin to the protection extended over the Americas by the Monroe Doctrine. To which Hull dryly answered that the Japanese formulas did not seem to work out that way, as witness Manchuria and China. The Ambassador turned this blowy corner of debate by remarking that the United States was sending a consul to Iceland and inquiring about developments in Greenland.[6] Mistrust sharpens the wit. Could this be taken to mean that the Japanese government found the connection between our principles and our strategy as loose as the American government thought theirs?

The *logic* of the mutual suspicion was sound. Such difference as there was, the student can comment, lay in the inner thread of the desire. It came out in the test—when and as the desire got the chance to satisfy itself. The American government was sure that if American armed forces were, as a consequence of the war's events, placed in strange locations, they would be used as guardian, not conqueror. The Japanese did not share this belief in our own good intentions. And we had no faith in theirs. If only there were some looking glass which gave forth an image of intentions, so fixed and clear that it would look the same to all!

Talk is a poor substitute for such a mirror. This, various American officials (Grew, Dooman, and Sayre, High Commissioner for the Philippines) found out in their talks with Arita during the next few weeks. With Dooman the Foreign Minister could speak without an interpreter, and his report roused long thoughts in Washington. Arita (April 26) pleaded that the American government must take a sensible and practical view of the Japanese plan for a new order in the Far East. He was ironic about the prospect of the re-emergence then, or after the war, of a liberal world economy, on which Hull based his efforts at persuasion. Japan, he

[5] *Department of State Bulletin*, April 20, 1940.
[6] *Foreign Relations: Japan*, II, 283–84.

said, was subject to threats of boycotts, sanctions, and embargoes. There-fore, it had to acquire access to raw materials which would make it equal to the self-sufficient empires, and secure in the event of war. The eco-nomic ventures which Japan were conducting in China, the exclusive chances it was acquiring, were to serve that end. American business was being displaced, not out of commercial greed but only for permanent reasons of self-defense; it would be allowed to operate within the bounds so set.

Thus he drew aside the cloak of vagueness in which Japanese diplo-macy was habitually clothed. The American government was not at-tracted by the exposed anatomy of purpose. Japan might or might not be historically justified in wishing to become strong and an equal of the strong. But by what means and at whose expense? And, if it had its way, could it be trusted to use its strength justly? Who would know whether the mind within the body would be sound or unsound?

The purpose of Arita's exposition was to persuade the American gov-ernment that Japan was not unfriendly to the United States, or by nature or wish aggressive. The effect was the opposite. Would it not be well advised, the State Department began anew to debate, to cut the flow of war materials to Japan? Was it not prudent to do so? The risk that they might be used against us was increasing. The chance that we would need all or most of these materials for our own military effort was growing. Had this not become the only possible way, as Stimson had argued, to bring about a change of mind in Japan? A change in Japan's mind, for we would not change ours. But there remained the haunting contrary thought: that by taking the step we should make war certain and near.

Hull tossed and twisted among the throbs of opinion about him. He informed Congress that if it was deemed necessary to control the export of iron and steel scrap as a measure of national defense, no considerations of foreign policy stood in the way. But he ignored Treasury suggestions, which were becoming bolder and more frequent, that the scope of the moral embargo be enlarged. And he went on evading Senator Pittman's reminders that his, Hull's, support was needed to secure approval of his resolution. In other words, Hull continued during this interim to attend on events.

The next moves were more swift and upsetting than any reckoning. On May 10 Germany began the invasion of Holland, Belgium, and

France. They fell within a month. Japan would see in their collapse and Britain's plight a shining chance to come into what it deemed its own. How was it to be kept from making itself master of the bereft colonies to the south—Indo-China, the Dutch East Indies, Malaya?

# The Grave Dilemma Before the
# United States: May 1940

THE President and the Secretary of State sought first of all to remove any real reason for Japanese action against the Indies. Thus, at once, on May 10, Hull proposed to Lord Lothian that both their governments again assure Japan that they would not disturb the status of, or in, the East Indies. Before London responded, word came from Tokyo that Arita had summoned the German, Italian, French, and British Ambassadors to tell them that events in Europe had sharpened Japanese concern over these Dutch colonies. Afraid that this was the signal for Japanese action (planned, and perhaps even already begun), Hull hurried to repeat publicly what he had said before: that many countries, among them Japan, were pledged to respect the status of the Indies, and that any disturbance of it would prejudice the peace and security of the entire Pacific area.[1]

Roosevelt acted to make sure that a slip in time might not cause a slip in history. The Dutch government, he knew, had asked the British and French to assist in the protection of its West Indian islands (the two important oil centers of Curaçao and Aruba).[2] He was worried lest the Japanese use this as an excuse for moving into the East Indies. The Japanese memory, it was supposed, would recall that the British had once, at a far earlier time, taken over these eastern islands from the Dutch and held them five years. He, therefore, now asked the British government through Lothian to strengthen the American hand in Tokyo in three ways. First, by confirming at once and publicly that it would not intervene in the East Indies; second, by arranging that the Dutch government, also at once and publicly, confirm that it had no need nor intention of asking such help; third, by announcing that the British and French troops in the West Indies islands would be taken away at the earliest moment.

---

[1] Hull, *op. cit.*, I, 891, writes: "Since expressions of 'concern' had been an introductory phase in the ominous pattern of many Axis military movements, I issued a further statement on May 11."

[2] *New York Times*, May 12, 1940.

So close did the chance of Japanese action seem to the President, so important to make haste, that he urged Lothian to get an answer by the next day, which was Sunday. Lothian did, informing Hull that the British government would at once do what we asked. The British Embassy in Tokyo (on the 13th) passed on these assurances to Arita. He responded by saying again that Japan had no intention of entering the Indies. The chief concern of Japan, he averred, was to insure the continued inflow of raw materials from these islands. Sir Robert Craigie, the British Ambassador in Tokyo, expressed the opinion that the Dutch government would not interfere with this trade, nor would the British with the exports from Malaya.

Thus far and no further the American government was willing to go in order to avert a Japanese coup. It would make no gesture that might have to be supported by action. Thus the President did not respond to Churchill's request, in his personal message of May 15, that the United States send naval forces to Singapore. Nor would he even attempt to state what he would do, if anything, if Japan moved against the European possessions in the Pacific.[8] When (also on May 15) the Australian Minister, Casey, informed Welles that his government would find it most helpful if we would state, both privately and publicly, that it was "not prepared to entertain any attempt at intervention in the Dutch East Indies," Welles said we wouldn't.

Though the American government thus would not promise to save the Indies, it remained anxious about their fate. Apart from the other reasons, our own supplies of rubber, tin, and quinine were at stake. Of none of these had we yet sufficient reserves for a crisis.

On the 16th, when the Japanese Ambassador came to see him, Hull found himself being put on the defensive. He was quizzed about the situation in the Dutch West Indies. The British and French activities there, he explained, were only a small extension of patrol operations, carried on to prevent any attempt of hostile groups to get control of the islands. They would, he said he knew, be ended soon. The Ambassador was sceptical. He wanted details and, upon getting some, he wanted more—till Hull was aroused. What was the purpose, he asked the Ambassador, of this examination? Might it be that Japan was preparing a case in defense of an invasion of the East Indies? The Ambassador flatly

---

[8] As Admiral Stark wrote to Admiral Richardson, Commander in Chief of the Pacific Fleet at Hawaii, on May 27, "Suppose the Japs do go into the East Indies? What are we going to do about it? My answer to that is, I don't know and I think there is nobody on God's green earth who can tell you." *Pearl Harbor Attack*, Part 14, pp. 943-44.

denied that this was so, saying that his government was satisfied with the situation there.

Hull, in turn, was sceptical. He was, and remained, convinced that at this time Japan was seeking to develop a pretext on which it could enter the Indies.[4] The memorandum which was made of this conversation ended: "I still interpret the Ambassador's visit as one under instructions to develop a pretext to support Japan in connection with its plans and purposes toward the Netherlands East Indies."[5]

In the islands, the local military and civilian officials thought that Japanese warships might appear in their harbors any day. They hurried with plans to destroy the oil fields and refineries which, it was assumed, would be the first objective of Japanese attack. Then, and for many months after, they feared that the attack might be provoked by an American refusal to supply Japan with oil.

The Japanese records in hand permit us now to comment upon these opinions and fears. The Japanese denials of any intent or plan to seize the Indies by force at this time were honest. The Yonai Cabinet was genuinely afraid of being taken by surprise. It feared that either Germany or Britain—and more probably Germany—would arrange with the Dutch government (in or out of Holland) for a transfer of authority. It was also worried lest some incident occur which the Japanese Army would seize upon to justify some unordered action of its own. These anxieties lay behind the quizzing of Hull.

But, that being said, the Japanese government cannot be acquitted of a design to bring the economic and political life of the Indies within its orbit; to have and to hold if Holland went under. On May 16, the same day that the Japanese Ambassador in Washington cross-questioned Hull, the Japanese Consul General paid a call upon Hubertus J. Van Mook, the robust official in charge of the economic affairs of the Indies. In his words, the Consul General delivered "condolences, requests, and veiled threats almost in the same breath." Two days later (the 18th) Japan spelled out what it wanted. It asked a written promise that no measure would be taken to hamper the export to Japan of specified minimum quantities of thirteen raw materials; among them bauxite and oil in far larger amounts than Japan had ever obtained from the Indies.[6] More

---

[4] See Hull, *op. cit.*, I, 893.

[5] *Foreign Relations: Japan*, II, 288.

[6] Japan asked 250 thousand metric tons of bauxite, all that the Indies produced and almost all Japan needed; of oil, 1 million metric tons, almost double Japan's previous imports from the Indies. This was, however, only about one-seventh of the total production of the Indies and about one-fifth of what Japan needed.

ominous still, was simultaneous demand that the Indies enter into a new and extensive basic accord on the other items in their economic relations. And soon, as will be seen, the Yonai Cabinet was to ask still more; and even so the governing cliques of Japan were making ready to discharge it from office, because it was not asking enough.

The German government had not made known its ideas about the status of the Indies. When it did, on May 22, it proffered something different and more than had been asked by Japan. Ott, as ordered, told Arita that the German government "was not interested in the problem of the Netherland East Indies." [7] The Japanese government spread this word to the press. Publicists made much of it, as German consent to whatever Japan might choose to do in the whole of the Southwest Pacific. This was a true reading; the now open correspondence between Ribbentrop and Ott, his Ambassador in Tokyo, makes plain that Germany intended the answer to prompt Japan to take over the Indies. But it did not. May passed and June came and the spotlight moved on.

## [2]

As the German armies moved through France, the dilemma before the American government became truly grave. The United States, and the United States alone, was in a position to try to restrain Japan. But its only ready instrument was diplomacy. At that moment—when it was not known whether the British Empire might not be forced into a peace which would yield much to Japan—economic measures seemed of little value. To threaten war seemed reckless.

At the time of the fall of France, the whole regular American Army consisted of 230,000 enlisted men and 13,500 officers. Due to past error and neglect, the United States could not fight a war in the Pacific and at the same time come to Britain's aid. Beyond that, the President, the Army, and Navy were all compelled to reckon with the worst possibility: that despite anything the United States did, Britain would be defeated. Then all our force and attention would be needed to prevent the outposts of this hemisphere—in the Atlantic and Pacific—from falling into unfriendly hands. The Joint Army-Navy Planning Committee were deeply immersed in the study of what measures to take if Britain fell

---

The other important raw materials sought were manganese ore, nickel ore, wolfram ore, tin ore, scrap iron, rubber, chrome, and molybdenum.

[7] Telegrams, Ribbentrop to Ott, May 20, 1940, Ott to Ribbentrop, May 22, 1940. *Far East Mil. Trib.*, Exh. Nos. 517 and 518.

or yielded. Plainly it was no time to risk a war with Japan except as a last resort, even if the American people had been so inclined.

And they were not. Neither of the political parties was suggesting or advocating such a course. The election campaign was starting. Democrats and Republicans alike were bidding for votes by vows and affirmations that the United States must stay out of war. They continued to do so through the momentous summer months when the fate of the Pacific as well as that of Europe was at stake. The caustic and accusing student of Roosevelt's foreign policy during this period, Charles A. Beard, is better justified in his comment on this point than on some others: "Indeed, in respect of foreign policy, the striking feature of the political campaign of 1940 was the predominance of the antiwar sentiment among Democrats and Republicans . . . At no time during that contest did President Roosevelt or Mr. Willkie or any other responsible party leader venture to propose openly that the United States should become involved in foreign wars or should adopt measures calculated to result in war. On the contrary, as far as the two great parties were concerned, the only choice before the voters was between two candidates . . . engaged in outbidding each other in the solemnity and the precision of their pledges to maintain the neutrality and peace of the United States." [8]

What was there left then except diplomacy, to try to cause Japan to remain quiet? Diplomacy with a shadowy border on which silhouettes of future American armies and navies were dimly etched?

[8] Charles A. Beard, *op. cit.*, p. 7. The pertinent planks of the two platforms were as follows:

The Democratic platform avowed: "The American people are determined that war, raging in Europe, Asia and Africa, shall not come to America. We will not participate in foreign wars, and we will not send our Army, naval or air forces to fight in foreign lands outside of the Americas, except in case of attack. . . . The direction and aim of our foreign policy has been, and will continue to be, the security and defense of our own land and the maintenance of its peace."

The essence of the Republican statement on the same subject was: "The Republican party is firmly opposed to involving this nation in foreign war." The rest of the platform consisted of an attack on its party opponents for having spent so much money and having achieved so little improvement in our military establishment. It expressed readiness to support "all necessary and proper defense measures proposed by the Administration in its belated effort to make up for lost time: . . ." but also deplored "explosive utterances by the President directed at other governments which serve to imperil our peace," and went on to "condemn all Executive acts and proceedings which might lead to war without the authorization of the Congress of the United States."

Both parties were later to excuse themselves by their shrewd use of the term "foreign wars."

[3]

Hull began to search for ways and means to influence Japan. Or, as he was to express it later, he began with "a fine-tooth comb and a microscope [to] go back over our relations with Japan and see if it [was] humanly possible to find something additional with which to approach them and prevail upon them not to gallop off on a wild horse." [9] Time was the object—time for Japan, time for Britain, time for the United States.

But it was to be bought without payment in the coin wanted by Japan. Ambassador Grew, on May 30, was told to begin talk with the Japanese Foreign Minister and to do his utmost to persuade him: first, that German victory would not bring security or prosperity for Japan and, second, that partnership with the United States in expanding trade and promoting welfare by peaceful means would serve Japan better. His remarks, it was suggested, might include a reference, factual in tone and substance —to the ways in which the United States was proceeding with plans quickly and greatly to increase its military power. This was the lean essence of a tuberous message.

A denial of any intent to appease was appended. "It is of course essential that we at all points guard against creating an impression or giving ground for any inference that the United States has modified or will modify its position of opposition to policies and courses, whether of Japan or any nation, which involve endeavor to achieve various possible national objectives in international relations by use of force."

The composers of this instruction toured the whole circuit of the State Department, taking on clauses at each stop. The ponderous caution, just quoted, was added at the insistence of the senior adviser on Far Eastern Affairs, Stanley Hornbeck. He thought he detected signs of a tendency to concede to Japan, if only a little and only under the cover of fair formulas. This he had argued (in a memorandum of May 24) would be read as a sign of weakness, and as a "Go" signal akin to that recently given by Germany in regard to the East Indies.

Grew welcomed the chance to see what he could do. But first he tried to get something more with which to bid—some spark of promise. The hand he had been given by Washington, made up only of intangibles, looked weak. And weak, indeed, it was.

"Within Japan," he explained in two most well-informed cables sent

[9] Hull, *op. cit.*, I, 895.

on June 3 and 4, "ideas and principles were wildly tumbling about." There were, he reported, great differences of opinion as regards the nature of a settlement with China and the means of bringing it about. One influential group was advocating an agreement with the Soviet Union to divide China; and some of its members were urging as well the seizure of the Indies before the final German victory. Another group was basing its program upon close alliance with Germany against Britain—thus to become a partner in writing the terms that would dispose of European colonies in the Pacific. Both of these groups sought to turn out the government. But, Grew's analysis continued, there were still steadfast advocates of the view that Japan should seek to settle the war in China by cooperation with the democracies, and refrain from the use of force anywhere else. They were in dire need of support. Thus he asked to be authorized to indicate that as soon as there was concrete evidence that Japan was ceasing to impose its will on China the United States would grant it economic benefits.

Within the State Department another brief battle ensued. At the end Grew's orders remained unchanged. He was advised on June 4 that Hull thought it best that he eschew specific mention of "possibilities of helpful economic and financial co-operation."

The French armies were scattering towards the south; the British armies were being pushed to the beaches of Dunkerque; Holland was entirely under German occupation. The British government was again suggesting that it would be well to bring about a compromise between Japan and China.[10] The American government stood stock-still in the position it had taken when Japan entered Manchuria in 1931 and the heart of China in 1937. It counted on its (and China's) ultimate power to ward off Japan's expansion in the Pacific. Whether sooner or later, whether by diplomacy, or the offer of economic support, or the use of economic pressure, or in war, was for the future to decide.

Senior officers of the Army and Navy, making up the Joint Planning Committee, on June 26 reported on the European war situation. On the 27th they presented to General Marshall the tenth and final draft of their views on the "Basis for Immediate Decisions concerning the National Defense." These had been worked out in anxious tension keyed to

[10] On the urgent advice of Craigie, whose messages and talk are recorded in Grew's diary, entries for May 21, and 31, 1940.

the news, and their main features were already known to the President, and approved by his chief advisers.

The war estimate assumed that the British Empire would still be standing in the fall and winter of 1940, but thought it doubtful that Britain itself could continue to be an active combatant. It advised against immediate American participation in the war. Our policy in the Pacific should be, it was recommended, defensive only; but our main fleet was to be kept in that ocean pending further events. There it would stand to support a concept upon which we might fall back in the worst emergency. Foreign powers were to be notified that the United States regarded the British and French possessions east of the International Date Line within the sphere of application of the Monroe Doctrine; and hence their sovereignty could not be transferred to others, either by force or treaty.

Thus, had Britain fallen or been forced to capitulate, the United States might well have tried to check and limit Germany's and Japan's claims in the Southwest Pacific. But each time Churchill spoke, the emergency seemed farther off and less likely.

The talks between Grew and Arita, as it is not to be wondered, arrived nowhere. The Foreign Minister agreed "in spirit and principle" with our ideas for a better world. While doing so, he recalled some hard knocks which Japan had received because the world was not better. In the past, he said, his country had sought freedom of movement for its men and trade; but both had been shut out by foreign countries. What it had to sell was bought or rejected at the convenience of others; and what it had to buy was subject to the will of others. In short, he rehearsed again the Japanese case for wanting a share of what others had.

Thus, in language more roundabout than ours, he tried to turn Grew's intimations into offers. Would we stop aid to China? Would we not enter into a new short-term treaty? Would we not recognize the new conditions in East Asia? Might not Japan and the United States each agree to preserve its own sphere of influence in the Pacific Ocean? Grew answered that before any such definite measures could be discussed the United States and Japan would have to agree upon fundamental policies and principles. These he then restated at greater length than ever. Nowhere did they admit Japan to a privileged place, neither in China nor elsewhere in Asia.

This gambit was played through by Grew and the Foreign Minister in long and thorough sessions of talk, usually in the private houses of friends, during the next month.[11] Only a diplomat as conscientious as Grew could have moved so smoothly through the game. But even he felt impelled to enter in his diary at the end of June: "The vicious circle is complete, and how to break it is a Chinese puzzle which taxes imagination."

The entry stated the fact. Arita refused an American proposal made on the 24th that the United States and Japan should exchange notes affirming their wish to maintain the existing situation in the Pacific, except through peaceful change. Then five days later (June 29) he had recourse to the radio. Almost, by then, overcome by advocates of expansion, he made himself spokesman for the conception of Greater East Asia under Japanese control.

Japan, he declared, would leave no stone unturned to end all help for Chiang Kai-shek; for the sword that Japan had drawn in China "is intended to be nothing other than the life-giving sword that destroys evil and makes justice manifest." After thus blessing what the squalid Japanese armies were doing in China, he mounted and, as Hull had feared, galloped off on a wild horse. He roamed over all the lands and seas of Asia.

"The countries of East Asia and the regions of the South Seas are geographically, historically, racially and economically very closely related. . . . The uniting of all these regions in a single sphere on a basis of common existence, insuring thereby the stability of that sphere, is a natural conclusion. . . . This system presupposes the existence of a stabilizing force in each region with which, as the center the peoples within that region, will secure their co-existence and co-prosperity as well as the stability of their sphere." [12]

Japan was to be the stabilizing force. Arita tried to avoid the disquieting effect of these ideas abroad by stating that this extension of the Japanese sphere was to be achieved "by peaceful means." This last phrase was not missed by the Japanese Army, and they did not like it. Now we know that Arita spoke as he did in the hope of outwitting those who were trying to defeat him, and against their objection.[13] The Army was afraid that the Yonai Cabinet might still keep itself in office by such bold

[11] The main talks were held on June 10, 19, 24, 28, and the final one on July 11. Grew's memoranda of the talks are to be found in *Foreign Relations: Japan*, II, 67, *et seq.* He observed his instructions very closely, even as regards the language that he used.

[12] *New York Times*, June 30, 1940. The full official text of this speech is to be found in *Far East Mil. Trib.*, Exh. 529.

[13] A further account of the circumstances in which this speech was made is given in Chapter 10.

talk, without real vigor behind it. The speech was a dislocated gesture which failed. It did not save the cabinet and it aroused the United States.[14]

Even though the speech might be, and in the State Department was discounted, it marked a main turn in the situation. For even before these words were spoken, the Japanese government had begun to flash the "sword that destroys evil and makes justice manifest" at several places in Asia, outside of China. The gleam was clearly visible.

[14] "JAPAN," the *New York Times* of June 30 headlined its report of this speech, "DEMANDS VAST SPHERE IN EAST ASIA AND SOUTH SEAS."

CHAPTER 8

# Japan Starts on the Road South:
# June 1940

DURING the second half of June the Yonai Cabinet (1) served demands on the Pétain government to allow a Japanese military mission to operate in Indo-China, (2) asked the government of the East Indies to guarantee the continued supply of raw materials wanted by Japan, (3) threatened the British government with war unless it took its troops out of Shanghai, and closed the frontier between Hong Kong and China and the road from Burma into China. By these measures China would be cut off from all the outside world. American loans would no longer be of use. The air lift over the Hump with cargo was still in the future. Japan would place itself in a position where it could endure, if not ignore, American pressure.

The Japanese and French governments had long been bickering over the traffic between Indo-China and China. Shipments against which the greatest objection was taken had been stopped. Growing impatient, Japan had in April smashed the railway line from the air. Foreseeing the end, the Governor General of Indo-China, General Catroux, agreed to suspend the movement of all munitions and war materials to China. But the Japanese government was not satisfied with this promise. On the 18th of June—the day after France asked Germany for an armistice—the Four Ministers' Council decided to demand not only an end of this traffic, but also the right to keep military observers in Indo-China to make sure of it. It was resolved that if the French refused, force would be used.[1] These demands were presented swiftly, and on the 20th they were accepted.[2] This was the first pointed threat against the European colonial

---

[1] "Kido's Diary," entry for June 17, 1940.

[2] *The Private Diaries (March 1940 to January 1941) of Paul Baudouin* (London, 1948), p. 146. The daily notes kept by the then Secretary of State for Foreign Affairs in the French government at Vichy contain an extensive running account of what took place between Tokyo, Vichy, the French authorities in Indo-China, and the Japanese armies in China and Indo-China in this and later stages of the Japanese entry into Indo-China.

empires of the Pacific. The northern border of Indo-China connects China with Siam and Burma.

The State Department learned quickly of the Japanese intrusion. It was assumed to be only the start of a further movement south. And perhaps to have even grimmer import: a concert with Germany, and Japanese entry into the war against Britain. For, the query came to mind at once, would Japan begin to thrust itself into Indo-China without German consent and aid?

Enemy records make it possible now to know what actually happened in that regard. As guessed, the German government had been asked in the very first phase of the affair to extract a quick answer from Vichy. While it was still thinking over what to ask Japan in return for the favor, the Japanese government sent another message to Berlin, worded like a valentine. Kurusu, the Japanese Ambassador in Berlin (serving in place of Oshima), was ordered to congratulate the German government on its great victory. On so doing, he was to point out that Japan had a marked interest in Indo-China and ask that Germany make known its willingness that Japan have a free hand in that colony. Ribbentrop had already said as much about the Dutch East Indies. He might, Kurusu was also told, adduce certain reasons why Japan deserved this chance; first among them because of its services in forcing the United States to keep its fleet in the Pacific Ocean. He might also explain that by this advance Japan could end its dependence on the United States and the British Empire, and compensate Germany by providing raw materials from the sphere about to be acquired.

Kurusu spoke as told, and with vim. But he found that the German government, now installed in Paris and looking across the Channel, felt no need to give without getting. Ott, from Tokyo, was advising Berlin how the Japanese request could best be put to use. It would, he cabled, be well for Germany to grant Japan's wish, but it had better make sure that it did not turn around and use the blessing to bargain with the United States. Therefore he urged that if consent were given it should be in a way that would bind Japan tightly to Germany, and in a form that the Yonai Cabinet could not reject without danger of having to give way to one closer to Germany.[8] Ribbentrop took some time to think out how to follow Ott's advice.[4] While still so engaged, the French gave in. This first

[8] Telegram from Ott to Ribbentrop, June 19, 1940, printed in the *Department of State Bulletin*, June 16, 1946.
[4] Within the German Foreign Office the request was met with a measuring sneer. The notes prepared for Ribbentrop by one of his assistants, Wiehl, began, "The thanks of Japan for the friendly attitude of Germany in the China conflict come rather late." *ibid.*

occasion for any quick, positive German answer to Japan passed. Within a few weeks it was superseded by Japanese requests of wider range. Meanwhile Japan sent the first units of its military mission into the province of Tonkin.

The government of the Indies was harder to browbeat. But still, on June 6, as the German troops poured into France, it sent a conciliatory answer to Japanese requests that it had hitherto ignored. The promise asked—that no measures be taken to restrict exports to Japan of the specified raw materials—was given. The oil sought by Japan, although much more than the Indies had supplied before, would be provided if the contracts were closed in time. The oil-producing companies in the Indies were told to give the matter thought and not to reject buying offers about to be made. But as regards entry and place for Japanese enterprise and emigrants, the Indies government gave little or nothing. It answered that it was already being generous, and that its curbs were necessary to protect the native population or vital interests of the Kingdom. In summary, the Dutch offered to provide more essential materials, but refused to let the Japanese obtain a larger place in the economic life of the Indies, or control of a larger part of its resources.

On June 28 Arita, launched upon his Greater Asia campaign, probed into the meaning of certain parts of this Dutch reply of June 6. He asked whether it could be read to mean that the Dutch government undertook to export at least the specified quantities of the specified materials to Japan *under any circumstances.* "Should you," Arita ended his note, "have any objection to this interpretation, I shall be grateful if you will let me know." What circumstances did he have in mind? The American government guessed that Japan was seeking to obligate the Indies to supply oil even if the United States stopped doing so. Should this happen, the American measure would be nullified. Even worse, the United States and the Indies would be separated from each other.

The American government was being kept informed day by day of what went on. It would not phrase its thoughts as advice, since it was not willing to accept the responsibility of being wrong. But it spoke its opinion aloud in the hearing of Dutch diplomats—to the effect that Japan was not likely to use arms to enforce its demands. The governors of the Indies were by no means sure this opinion was correct. But anyhow, they were resolved not to do what they did not want to do, or at any rate, not much. They took refuge in delay and reticence.

[2]

While thus striving, during late June, for access into Indo-China and the Indies, Japan counted upon our absorption in the European catastrophe. The surrender to the German armies, the aged Pétain taking charge of beaten France, the dispersion of the French fleet, the weather on the Channel, the words of Churchill: these were the matters that flowed over the American mind and spirit.

Absorbed we were; and, as told, engaged in figuring out how to adjust our diplomacy and military plans to the worst that might occur. But not to the neglect of what was under way in the Far East. As the arsenals were searched for arms for Britain, Hull and Grew, as also told, strove to keep Japan quiet. Within their talk of the benefits of peace the alert listener might detect the beat of a distant drum. The Japanese government pretended not to hear or care; but the records show it did. The Japanese Navy remained wary about a long war with the United States— a war that would be begun with only limited reserves of oil.

But in London the sound of this drumbeat could not be heard. The British government was afraid that Japan would use the chance, in league with Germany, to conquer Malaya and the Indies. Alone, without American help, Britain could not defend them. With our help it could at least try.

On June 10 Lothian, on Churchill's orders, had asked Hull whether the United States would enter into joint conferences in regard to fleet movements in the Pacific and the Atlantic. Hull had replied that he doubted whether there would be any occasion for such conferences. Whatever this answer might mean, it could not have comforted the British. Three days later the Dutch government had asked whether we would be willing to have the Asiatic Squadron of the Pacific Fleet make contact with the Dutch naval forces in the Indies. Welles had answered that no practical way was seen to do so. Further, he had said, that such a step might arouse Japanese suspicion, and prejudice the position of the Indies.

Then on June 27 the British Ambassador (accompanied by the Australian Minister) asked Hull to decide whether Japan should be opposed or appeased. Japan was demanding that Britain withdraw its troops from Shanghai, close the Hong Kong frontier, and the Burma Road. The British government recognized—the memo went on—that if it did so the future security not only of the Empire, but of the United States as

well, would be imperilled. But, alone, it could not oppose Japan's demands to the point of fighting a war in the Pacific. Two courses seemed
open. Pressure might be increased upon Japan by imposing a full embargo or dispatching warships to Singapore. Or another effort might be
made to win Japan over by making a pleasing offer of terms for the solution of the Far Eastern situation. Britain would cooperate in whichever
one of these two policies the United States selected. The case for settling
with Japan was stated more flatly in an Australian note of June 29, which
observed that "if the United States and the British Empire compromise
now and negotiate together with Japan, the concessions that we can give
together are very likely to be considerably less than Japan will be able
to take by war."

Both the President and Hull appreciated Britain's desperate need to
find ways and means of guarding its supporting empires in the Far East.
But they did not want to adopt either of the methods proposed. Hull,
talking to Lothian on June 28, ruled out the embargo and the dispatch
of warships to Singapore. He also refused to join with Britain in paying
Japan to remain quiet. It was unlikely, he explained, that Japan would
listen to any kind of arrangement for the Far East that the American
government would care to sponsor. It was not for the United States, he
said, to offer benefits at the expense of other powers. However, there
would be no objection on our part if Britain and Australia should test
the chances of an accord by offering economic advantages. But the bargaining, he cautioned, must not be at the expense of China, nor of the
principles on which the United States stood. This meant, in substance,
that Britain, France, and Holland would have to give to Japan whatever
might be given.

Britain can be absolved for seeking any way to hold its position in the
Far East in this summer of 1940. The forces that could be recruited from
this region, the supplies, the naval bases, would all be vital in the struggle
with Germany that it was then fighting by itself. The United States
would not share either the responsibility or risks of preventing Japan
from taking what it wanted. Soon, it then seemed probable, France
would be governed by a group wholly subservient to Germany, and
British warships would be battling French. Why then, if Japan would
be satisfied with moderate gains in China and Indo-China, was Britain
called upon to deny them, and go under? Thus British official thoughts
ran for a brief summer spell.

Or so Welles thought, as Hull had thought a few days before, after
another review of the Far Eastern situation with Lothian on July 1.

Welles was as reserved as Hull had been (on the 28th). The American government, he said again, would not join in a program of either restraint or appeasement. Against the first, both the risks of war and public opinion were bans. Against the second, a sense of justice and pride rebelled.

If Japan were going to extend itself over the whole of Asia, both the President and Hull thought, let the nature of the deed be unobscured. To bargain with her would in some measure sanction her conduct. To settle with her at the expense of China or of lands that were part of the French Empire, would leave a smirch on all. Beyond such matters of sensibility and historic wisdom, there was a strong streak of confidence that no such sop to Japan was necessary. Japan could for the time being have its way in Asia—if it chose to use force. But, ultimately, Japan would have to reckon with American strength. Even in July 1940, the heads of the American government thought that Japan would be mindful of that fact. Or, anyhow, that it would wait till Britain was defeated and the United States stood alone, before it took what it craved.

On July 12 Lothian told Hull that pending a new effort to settle the Sino-Japanese war, the British government would close the Burma Road for three months.[5] When asked about these matters at his press conference, Hull said just enough to keep our position clear. He said this forced action was an unwarranted hindrance to world trade. The United States, he added, was maintaining its policy, pursuing its own separate and independent course.[6]

The divergence was caused by the contrast in the situation of British and American peoples. One was fighting for its life, the other was not. One had an empire to lose, the other had not. It lasted for some months. Then, as danger moved a little farther from Britain, and a little closer to the United States, the policies of the two governments towards Japan came together again. Both had the same primary wish and purpose: to maintain the situation in the Pacific without having to divert their main efforts from the war against Germany.

Such, then, was the outlook when in July the President had to decide what use to make of the power just given him to control or end the export of war materials to Japan.

[5] On July 17 the Japanese Foreign Minister, Arita, and the British Ambassador to Japan, Sir Robert Craigie, signed an accord providing for the suspension of transport of all war materials, including oil and trucks, from Burma and Hong Kong into China.

[6] This latter part of his remarks was not included in the circulated press release, as printed in *Foreign Relations: Japan,* II, 101.

## CHAPTER 9

# The American Government Forbears

THE National Defense Act was passed because of our own prospective needs. In May, after the German invasion of the West began, a program had been drawn up vastly to enlarge all branches of our military establishment. While it was before a still blinking Congress, the Army urged the insertion of a section that would permit the President to keep at home all products that might be needed for defense. The proposal was submitted to the State Department.

For Hull it was a mark of defeat: the very contrary of the trade policies through which he had sought to bring harmony in the world. If ever there had been a chance that nations might find peace through serving each other's wants, it was gone for the time being—even this most devout believer in the benefits of trade was at last forced to conclude. The essays on the theme to which so many glowing days and nights had been devoted were only dead files now.

In Japan, it could be foreseen, this law would ring alarm bells. Even if the control were used with restraint, that country would be hurt. For henceforth the United States would want to conserve for its own use and purposes many of the products which Japan was getting from us. No matter what we said or did, Japan would regard the measure as a blow and threat, as another proof that it must form a self-sustaining empire in the East. Even less than before would it like living within the boundaries of our tolerance.

But the accepted necessity outweighed such thoughts. In response to his request for some written word, on May 22 Hull had written to the Chairman of the Senate Committee on Military Affairs, in part: "I believe that the enactment of this legislation is highly advisable in the interest of national safety and defense of the United States."

On the 15th of June, as the law was being guided through Congress, the President had indicated publicly that he would probably stop the export of scrap iron as soon as he had the authority to do so. But Hull refused to confirm any such intention. Worried opinions were passed upon him by Grew, Sayre, and the Far Eastern Division of the State

Department. When Japan was wavering over how much to dare and demand in order to feel free, it would be, they all thought, foolish to take this cramping measure. Hull agreed. Thus, as already told, the proposal made on June 28 by the British Ambassador that the United States and the British Empire confront Japan with a joint embargo was turned down. Nor did the first Japanese forays against Indo-China, the Indies, and the Burma Road bring any change in judgment.

But the question abided—how could this power best be used to prevent this restless, sensitive, aggrieved nation from striking out against the West in its time of weakness? The answer given then, and during the next few months, was by using it hardly at all.

While the Defense Act was being made into law, several branches of the American government disputed for the chance to administer Section VI, the part which provided for the control of exports.[1] The State Department did not want the job. But it did want to be sure that it could govern the use made of the power; and, in order to be sure of this, thought it essential to occupy the command post.

Most eager of all to get the job of administering Section VI was the Treasury. There, of all places in the American government, the sense of crisis was most alive; the feeling that Hitler must not be allowed to win, the most ardent; and the will to act upon feeling, the most bold. By assignment of the President, Henry Morgenthau, Jr., Secretary of the Treasury, was in charge of the emergency aid for Britain. He had flung himself into that task with the utmost vigor. His energy propelled the movement of the weapons and ammunition needed by Britain to equip itself to resist invasion, to maintain the fight in the air and on the seas. Thus it was, perhaps, natural that he should want to have this additional power to manage the stock of vital war materials. In any case, his staff was most forward in producing plans connected with Section VI, and new ones to take the place of rejects.

But as regards Japan, Morgenthau's judgment seemed to the State Department rigid and rash. Time and again he had besought the President and others to restrict or end the flow of supplies to Japan. Thus it was feared that if charged with the administration of Section VI—despite promises to be obedient—he might provoke the crisis of decision which

[1] The name was "An Act to Expedite the Strengthening of the National Defense," (H.R.9850). The first sentence of Section VI was as follows: "Whenever the President determines that it is necessary in the interest of national defense to prohibit or curtail the exportation of any military equipment or munitions, or component parts thereof, or machinery, tools, or material or supplies necessary for the manufacture, servicing or operation thereof, he may by proclamation prohibit or curtail such exportation, except under such rules or regulations as he shall prescribe."

Hull wanted to avoid. Yet Hull shunned, as far as he could, any direct protest against Morgenthau's claims. Notes were dropped into the President's basket, memos were flung back and forth, stories were diffused to the press.

The President, after allowing the sullen contest to drag on, settled it in accord with the ideas of Harry Hopkins. He appointed a single administrator of export control, directly under the White House. But this official gave a confidential promise not to make any decisions affecting foreign policy, except on the advice of the Department of State. Colonel Russell L. Maxwell, an Army officer, was made administrator. He assumed the responsibility before the public, while the actual control of the policy and the actual issuance of licenses remained in the hands of the State Department.

The first Presidential Order (July 2) issued under the new law was of relatively small scope.[2] It placed under license three groups of items: first, all arms, ammunition, and implements of war; second, all raw materials then listed as "critical and strategic," including aluminum and magnesium; third, airplane parts, equipment, and accessories, optical instruments, and metal working machinery. Of none of these would the United States have a surplus to spare. Of many, the supply would be less than needed by ourselves and the countries opposed to Germany. Some were eagerly being sought and bought by Japan. But this order left out the items of which Japan was most in need—oil and scrap iron.

Invigorated by this show of will, Hull two days later (July the 4th, it was) dispatched to Grew a thirty-five-hundred-word syllabus to serve as guide for his next talks with the Foreign Minister. More, rather than less firmly, this held to every sector of our established line of argument—about China, about the New Order in East Asia, about economic matters. Any new trade accord was ruled out until and unless Japan ceased its attempts to secure, by threat of force, or force, a special economic position in Asia. Grew was also told to express our disapproval of what Japan was demanding of the Indies: the right to get minimum amounts of its essential products.

Grew, a week later, placed before Arita the basis for our claim for equal interest in the commerce of the Indies—to wit, that in "normal" years the Indies exchanged more goods with the United States than with Japan. This statement was like a headlight whose far beam reveals a

---

[2] Proclamation No. 2413, signed by President Roosevelt, July 2, 1940.

coming collision. The American government was not going to agree that its restrictions, such as those just announced, warranted Japan's efforts to acquire control of other sources of supply. The Japanese government was certain to think itself more entitled than ever to do so. This issue produced a clash of wills that lasted until Japan decided to settle it in war.

Grew ended his reports of this talk (the last one he was to have with Arita, for these were the last days of the shaky Yonai Cabinet) by observing that "The respective attitudes of the United States and of Japan having become deadlocked, my discussions with Mr. Arita with regard to the adjustment of our mutual relations have become a vicious circle." [3] He did not give up. But his attempts to find an exit from this circle (cables of July 11 and 15) seemed to the State Department to end in ambiguity. They reverted to the idea that the United States might announce its readiness to begin talks about a new economic agreement with Japan to be put into force—when, as, and if. About the "when," the "as," and the "if," Grew was found vague. But his main reason for urging Washington along this line was clear: that unless some counter inducement was offered, Japan would join the Axis.

This perception was correct. But his idea of how to prevent the liaison was—the record seems to me to show—by mid-July outdated. The Yonai Cabinet could not, even if it had wished, have obligated itself, in return, to drop the idea and program for a New Order in East Asia. Nor could it have managed (as Grew hoped) to stay in office merely because it got from us the prospect of a new trade treaty. The Army had already decided that it must go, and the Army had regained its power to destroy any cabinet. It is time, again, before going on with this narrative of American action, to review—out of the retrieved Japanese records—the crisis within that government.

[3] Grew to State Department, July 11, 1940. His report of this talk with Arita, and the texts of the so-called "Oral Statements" which he gave to Arita are printed in *Foreign Relations: Japan*, II, 94–100. But Grew's other advisory cable of this date—from which the quoted extract is taken—and the subsequent exchange of views with the State Department are not printed.

## CHAPTER 10

# Japan Selects a New Government

THE Yonai Cabinet had lived from the start in a state of transient tenancy. The lack of a treaty with the United States was like the lack of a lease. At any time its whole program, civil and military, might be disturbed by notice from Washington, while intrigue went on all around it.

May and June had gone, as has been told, in trying to splice together the fraying strands of friendship with the United States. But the attempt came to nothing; the American government could not be brought to take a consenting view of Japanese aims. After Holland and France fell, a tremor of expectancy ran through Japan; a clamorous hope of sharing in the turnover of power and wealth in the world which seemed ahead. The cabinet tried to govern these excited passions. It strove to keep the nation mindful that Britain was not yet beaten and the United States was strong. It tried to gain entry, without using soldiers, into Indo-China and the Indies. Thereby it sought to appease the more militant elements; to bring the war in China to an end; and to defeat any economic pressure that Britain and the United States might apply.

But these efforts did not quell the demand for bolder action. The impulse was too urgent, the belief too deep that the West would not yield what Japan wanted unless forced to do so. Arita tried to stave it off by proposing the issuance of a statement which would stress the wish of the cabinet to work with the Axis, but in terms which would not oblige Japan to go to war. The Army, not trusting him to make the sort of alliance it wanted, protested.

It was then, as recounted, that he had turned to the radio. On June 29 he made that speech about the New Order in Greater East Asia which aroused American opinion.[1] His statement that the program was to be carried out "by peaceful means," did not convince abroad. But it provoked the Army.[2] When the Chief of the Press Bureau of the Foreign Ministry revealed the dispute he was arrested by the military police.

The phrase itself, "by peaceful means," was, of course, a term of art.

[1] Text in *Far East Mil. Trib.*, Exh. No. 529.
[2] *ibid.*, Exh. Nos. 530 and 531.

To the unscrupulous it allows much leeway. Arita's thought is traceable: he hoped to exact consent to Japanese aims by using the pressure of circumstance and the threat of force. Thereby France, Holland, and Britain might be brought to accede to Japan's wishes. German consent, in contrast, would be bought by a promise to cause the United States to keep its fleet in the Pacific. All these are "peaceful means."

Thus, as Arita pressed his pleas to Grew to end American support of China, he sought at the same time to get useful promises from Germany. A special envoy, Sato, a former Foreign Minister, had been hurried to Berlin. On July 8 he asked Ribbentrop whether Germany would recognize Eastern Asia as a sphere of Japanese influence. Instead of answering, Ribbentrop asked questions. He wanted to know whether and on what terms Japan would enter the war against Britain. Sato promised to find out. But his remarks showed little relish for the idea.

Japan, he expounded, must weigh carefully the effect of its actions upon the United States. Relations were already, he said, very strained over China; and, contrary to the opinion held by some of the military, he did not think that Japan could conquer China by arms. He also was impressed by the American fleet and concerned with Japan's dependence upon the United States for vital war materials. "In particular," he explained, "after the entry of Stimson into the Government, Japan had to be very careful in regard to America in order not to provoke that country into taking severe measures against Japan."

Ribbentrop showed no patience with these excuses. At this time, early July 1940, he did not care much whether Japan promised aid against Britain or not, since he was sure that the war in Europe would be brought to a quick end. What he wanted was an agreement which would deter the United States from interfering with the outcome and settlement. Knowing what was afoot in Japan, he reserved any promises that might be sustaining to the Yonai Cabinet. He waited for control of the government to pass to others more ready to stand up against the United States.[3]

He did not have long to wait. The Japanese Army had decided to effect the change.

---

[3] This is only a slender summary and interpretation of the extensive exposition of Japanese and German attitudes to be found in the memorandum of the Sato-Ribbentrop talk, July 8, 1940, *Far East Mil. Trib.*, Exh. No. 524, and the exchange of messages between Arita and Sato, July 10, and 13–15, 1940, *ibid.*, Exh. Nos. 525, 526, and 1020.

Ott's messages during the whole previous month must have contributed to Berlin's prejudices against the Yonai Cabinet. For example, his cable of June 12, in which he said that Yonai and Arita were quietly hoping that the United States would go to war against Germany, as a result of the invasion of Holland, Belgium, and France, and thus relieve pressure on Japan. *ibid.*, Exh. No. 516.

[2]

Assassination was common talk, touching even the Emperor. Yonai had plans ready in case of an attack to hurry him from the palace to a battleship. One branch of the secret political police (the Shumpetai) organized in the first days of July a plot to kill all the leading advocates of friendship with Britain and the United States. Included were to have been the Prime Minister, Yonai; Ikeda, who was the liaison between the great banking families and the government; and several members of the court circle, among them Yuasa, Lord Privy Seal, and Matsudaira, the Household Minister. The government was warned; the attempt was defeated; the police acted loyally; the conspirators and weapons were seized; the Army did not intervene.[4] But the episode was a warning display of what might happen.

Changes of the cabinet in Japan are preceded by a time of a thousand whispers, which the members of the inner circle, the cabinet, the Army, and the court convey to one another with the industry and speed of bees. Such a period now reached its pitch. The whispers condensed into a purposeful message. On July 11 the Vice-Minister for War, Anami, spokesman for the Army, told leading figures around the Throne that in order to reorient foreign policy and military operations there would have to be a cabinet change. On the next day the Chief of the Military Affairs Bureau of the War Ministry, General Muto, and the head of the Asia Development Board, General Suzuki, said the same thing. The Prime Minister, Yonai, and the Minister of War, Hata, were just then in dispute as to whether the Army should move south. Hata was sending rude notes to Yonai, saying that he thought that the cabinet should resign, and also saying that he wished to resign. The General Staff of the Army demanded that he so act.[5]

[4] The account of this episode is based on the "Saionji-Harada Memoirs"; and on "Kido's Diary," entry for July 5, 1940.

[5] According to General Sawada, Vice-Chief of the Army General Staff at the time, the Chief of Staff, Prince Kan-in, sent Hata a letter stating that it was most urgent to end the China Incident; that to do so it was essential to have German help; that to obtain it a new and stronger cabinet was necessary; and demanding that the War Minister "take action in a manner appropriate to the situation." Deposition of General Sawada (Shigero), *Far East Mil. Trib.*, Exh. No. 3205. But copies of this letter could not be located.

The Prime Minister, Yonai, was convinced that Hata was forced to resign by elements whom he was powerless to control, and who wanted not only to get rid of him, but also to overthrow the cabinet. Deposition of Yonai (Mitsumasa), *ibid.*, Exh. No. 3198.

The Foreign Minister, Arita, was of the same opinion, attributing the Army's opposition to Hata partly as a result of his opposition to the idea of an alliance with Germany and partly because of his attempts to keep the Army out of politics and reach a moderate peace with Chiang Kai-shek. Deposition of Arita (Hachiro), *ibid.*, Exh. No. 3201.

The quarreling ministries arrived at a momentary truce. On July 12 at a special meeting of the Four Ministers (Foreign Affairs, Army, Navy, and Finance) it was agreed to advance preparations for mobilization for the purpose of a South China campaign.[6] These would take a month and a half, however; and it was further agreed that another cabinet decision would be had before any order to start actual operations was given. The time, it may be presumed, was to be used in watching the German fight with Britain.

On the same day, and over the next five days, officials of the three ministries—Foreign Affairs, War, and Navy—met with two connected assignments: first, to draw up the statement of Japanese policy which Ribbentrop had asked of Sato; second, to define what Japan should do if Britain surrendered to Germany. By the 16th, they had drawn up a program that was more comprehensive than clear. The long drafts over which they worked are confirmatory of the American impression that Japan, if it ever could, would extend its rule over Asia.[7]

The accepted first aim of Japanese policy, it was agreed, was to secure German recognition that Indo-China, the East Indies, and other island groups in the South Seas were within Japan's sphere of influence, and to secure German approval of Japanese political leadership in this area. All the conferees, especially those of the Navy, were afraid that Germany would claim these colonies, and wished to cut them away from Germany as soon as possible. In return, Japan was to support German policy in Europe and Asia, and to take steps, as far as possible, to check Britain in East Asia and thus facilitate its defeat. But for the time being, Japan was to resist proposals that it enter war in Europe; the Japanese Ambassador in England, Shigemitsu, was warning that Britain was not yet beaten. Japan was also to work with Germany to deter the United States from interfering in Europe. The final program was to be drawn up in accord with Germany, who was to be told the least possible about Japan's ideas of its future relationship with the United States and the Soviet Union.

But before the Yonai Cabinet could consult Berlin again it was expelled from office. For all this was not quick or conclusive enough for the Army. On the 16th, it forced the issue.[8] The Minister of War resigned. The Army chiefs refused to select a successor to take his place. The Prime

[6] *ibid.*, Exh. No. 534. This would have meant at the least military entrance into Indo-China. It was also preparation for taking over Hong Kong if Britain collapsed.
[7] The minutes of these interdepartmental meetings can be found, *ibid.*, Exh. Nos. 527 and 528.
[8] "Kido's Diary," entries for July 16 and 17, 1940, gives many details.

Minister, therefore, tendered the demission of the whole cabinet that evening.

The next day, July 17, former Prime Ministers and senior members of the Privy Council were summoned to arrange the succession. The discussion was short. Among all the Japanese public figures there were few deemed able to form a unified government. In fact, only one—Prince Konoye. So the meeting of the Senior Statesmen agreed. Family name, his many connections and past part in public affairs, all designated him. Konoye, who was thought to have been eagerly getting ready for this crisis, now did not rush to take up the burden. He said that he was not fit; that someone should be selected who was closer to the Army. But he was quickly persuaded by the Lord Keeper of the Privy Seal, Kido (who had on June 10 accepted this office on Konoye's advice). Kido's view was that it was better to have someone who could work with both Army and political circles; and that he would be able to manage "as having the consent of the Army and [being] close to them." [9]

Then Prince Saionji, the one surviving member of the Council of the Elder Statesmen (the Genro), was consulted. He would not give an opinion on the plea that he wasn't well enough informed. Either then, or very shortly afterwards, he is recorded by his secretary, Harada, as saying with a sigh of despair:

"Just as the Emperor Taiso of To was carrying out a very good government and improving the nation, the Empress Sokuten Buko appeared on the scene and assassinated the learned scholars and behaved in a brutal manner. She eventually destroyed society completely. In a way the military can be likened to the Empress." [10]

That the Emperor and the court circles were uneasy at what was happening is revealed by the tone of their talk, but not in any other way. The same evening the Emperor called Konoye and issued to him an imperial mandate to form a government.

Later, when on trial, Marquis Kido recalled that, on approving the selection, the Emperor asked him to advise Konoye "to be especially prudent in the choice of the Ministers of Foreign Affairs and Finance, in the light of conditions at home and abroad." [11] Especially prudent in the choice of a Foreign Minister! It was to be Matsuoka (Yosuke). Loose talking, always in a state of excited confusion, deceiving, and un-

[9] Kido explained himself at length in his defense deposition, *Far East Mil. Trib.*, Exh. No. 3340.
[10] I am informed that the gentleman of the old school was referring to the Chinese Emperor T'ai Tsung of the Tang Dynasty, who flourished A.D. 627–649.
[11] "Kido's Diary," entry for July 17, 1940, and Kido deposition, *loc. cit.*

stable, he was the chosen medium for Saionji's parable: "She eventually destroyed society completely." [12]

Matsuoka was the diplomat who had dismissed with contempt the American and British reproofs after Japan invaded Manchuria. It was he who had led the Japanese delegation, with an air of brutal defiance, out of the conference hall of the League of Nations. Stimson had been Secretary of State then, and his severe censure of Matsuoka's conduct stayed in his, and in the American memory.

What was known in Washington of the other chief members of the new cabinet did not alter the impression made by this appointment. Ohashi, who had run the foreign policy of the puppet government of Manchukuo, was made Vice-Minister for Foreign Affairs.[13] By selection of the heads of the armed services, General Tojo was made War Minister —a keen soldier (known as "Razor Brain"), but without breadth or feeling.[14] Hoshino was made Chairman of the Planning Board, in which office he was concerned with the industrial preparations for war. These men were without previous cabinet experience, but all had been prominent in Manchuria where they had worked closely with the Kwantung Army and must have pleased it.[15] The only figure found in the cabinet who might resist a violent course was the Minister of the Navy. Yoshida was continued on from the Yonai Cabinet—a concession to Navy opposition to a war with Britain and the United States.

About the Prime Minister, himself, and about the way in which he would try to manage Japan's foreign and military policy, there were in Washington several views. He was slightly known to the President, seemed to find American ways and ideas congenial, and had sent his son to college here. But he was said to be wavering, rather slack, dependent on advisers, and on good terms with the tough spirits in the Army.

His career gave no more reason for comfort than reports of his charac-

[12] Matsuoka as a youth went through Oregon University. Life in the United States may have encouraged in him the habit of candid and unguarded speech, so unusual amongst the Japanese. Also, perhaps, the wish to exert his will against us. After returning home he made his career first as director of the South Manchurian Railway, then in politics.

[13] According to Ott, the German Ambassador, Shiratori told him that the post was first offered to him, but that he refused. Telegram, Ott to Ribbentrop, July 17, 1940, *Far East Mil. Trib.*, Exh. No. 533.

[14] Noda, Chief of the Personnel Affairs Bureau, testified that he had recommended Tojo to the former Minister of War, Hata, who thereupon recommended Tojo to the Emperor. He also stated that this selection was made because of the wishes of the General Staff, and the officials of the War Ministry, particularly the Vice-Minister for War, General Anami. Transcript, *ibid.*, pp. 29394–29400.

[15] The Kwantung Army was the Japanese unit maintained in Manchukuo under the Portsmouth Treaty for the protection of Japanese interests, including the South Manchurian Railway. It was the ruler of Manchukuo.

ter. The war in China had started when he was Prime Minister before, in 1937. Though giving an impression of earnest regret about what the Army was doing, he had never brought it to a halt. What reason, then, to think that in this far more upset and tense time he could do so? This man did not seem made for the stern encounters that were ahead. Had the American government known of his ventures shortly before he became Prime Minister, it would have been sure of it. Konoye had sought the consent of the Yonai Cabinet and the Emperor to a mission to discuss with the heads of *all* the great foreign powers chances of peace; when this was refused he changed to the idea of visiting only Germany, Italy, and Russia for the purpose of improving Japan's relationship with them. The future was in this episode; he could be bent; Tojo could not be.

At times during his fateful term of office he was courted by the Army, at others he courted it. He was given to saying he did not want to serve as an Army tool, but allowed himself to be put in situations where he had so to serve. Harada relates a dialogue with Konoye which took place in the beginning of May when a one-party plan was being talked over by a group close to the Army. Konoye remarked to Harada: "If this plan is adopted, the Army may use it as a way to shake and overthrow the Cabinet. I presume they intend to use me as a tool for the Cabinet. I refuse."

Harada to Konoye: "You probably never appeared annoyed when they came to consult you."

Konoye to Harada: "I did not particularly appear annoyed, but I have no intention of complying."

These were the elements of nature that were to bring Konoye to the ultimate impasse, both with the American government and within himself.

Shortly after Konoye took office, Ambassador Grew wrote in his diary: ". . . at first sight the Konoye Government . . . gives every indication of going hell-bent towards the Axis and the establishment of a New Order in East Asia, and of riding rough-shod over the rights and interests, and the principles and policies, of the United States and Great Britain."

But another sentence in the same entry was more hopeful: ". . . in all probability, Prince Konoye, reflecting the presumable attitude of the Emperor and the Elder Statesmen, will exert responsible control over the 'wild men' and will endeavor to move slowly and with some degree of caution at least until it becomes clear whether Great Britain is going to win or lose the war."

As the nature of the program adopted by this new cabinet became known, the first impression proved the more correct.

## CHAPTER 11

# Japan Stencils Its Policy in Indelible Ink:
## July 1940

THE chief figures in the new cabinet began to confer even before they were formally invested with power. Germany might quickly accomplish the defeat of Britain or peace might be made between them. In either event Japan might find that the best chance to bargain had come and gone. This thought made for haste and zeal. On the evening of July 19 the Foreign Minister and the Ministers of War and the Navy met with the Prime Minister at his house at Ogikubo. There the ideas of those who wanted to move fast and the ideas of the more cautious ones were seamed together. But not without a taste of trouble. According to the account of the meeting which Konoye gave Harada: ". . . because Matsuoka spoke out as though he advocated war with the United States, the Navy Minister was aghast at first. However, he was placated when Matsuoka followed with moderate explanations. To say something out of line and scaring others, is one of Matsuoka's weak points."

A week of further talk within the cabinet, with the court, and with military men ensued. Each group had its chance to realign the program that had been sketched out on the evening of the 19th. The Army had its way in certain sections, not in others. And in composite the whole, as approved by the cabinet on July 26 and by an Imperial Liaison Conference on the 27th, contained a conflict between objects and means.[1] This stemmed probably from a mistaken estimate of what was about to happen in Europe.

The main lines of the diplomatic policy to be followed were set down in a paper called "Gist of the Main Points in Regard to Dealing with the Situation to Meet the Change in World Conditions."[2] Like almost all

---

[1] This Liaison Conference, the first of its kind, was attended by the heads of the civil government and the military forces. It came to overshadow the cabinet and lessen the influence of the court. Neither was able to reverse its decisions.

[2] *Far East Mil. Trib.*, Exh. No. 1310. Another document of great scope and importance called "Outline of Basic National Policy" was adopted at the same time. It summarized not only the essential points to be observed in the conduct of military affairs and foreign policy, but also a program for the "renovation" of the internal political structure. *ibid.*, Exh. No. 541.

Japanese official documents (and not only Japanese) of the sort, this was so composed as to allow different definitions by different persons at different times.[3] The ambiguity was useful. Gaps in meaning served to conceal secret purposes; obscurity of phrase permitted future twists of aim. Authority within Japan could become unified only in a haze. Therefore the student can never be sure of exact shades of intent, or even that he has culled out from the many parts and sections those that were most meant.

But the essential features of the diplomatic course which the new cabinet undertook to pursue can, I think, be summarized with confidence. Two of the main stated ends to be accomplished were (a) to hasten the end of the conflict in China; (b) to solve the problem of the south *within such scope as would not lead to war with other powers* (italics mine). To these ends Japan was:

(1) "To maintain a firm attitude toward America on the one hand; *to effect on the other hand a sweeping readjustment of Japanese relations with the USSR*, as well as a political combination with Germany and Italy. (2) To take stronger measures against French Indo-China, Hong Kong and foreign concessions in China looking to the prevention of aid to the Chiang regime . . . (3) To practise more vigorous diplomacy toward the Netherlands East Indies, in order to acquire vital materials."[4]

How did the makers of this program think to proceed with such moves and still escape the antagonism of the United States? The best surmise is that they counted upon German victory to cause the United States to

---

[3] A fuller version and different translation of the "Gist of the Main Points" is contained in the "Saionji-Harada Memoirs" (Chapter 373). The summary therein given of the decisions reached by the four Ministers (Konoye, Matsuoka, Tojo, and Yoshida) on July 19, is more blunt than the language used in the ultimate document approved by the cabinet on the 26th and the Liaison Conference on the 27th, especially in regard to (a) the alliance with the Axis and the detachment of European possessions from the mother countries, and (b) the possible use of force to prevent outside interference.

On this last point there was a difference of opinion between the majority of the International Military Tribunal for the Far East, and the Dutch Member, Mr. Justice Roling. The former held that the statement approved at the Four Ministers' Conference at Ogikubo, and the confirmatory resolutions were decisions that Japan would go to war if necessary to get control of Greater East Asia. Mr. Justice Roling argued to the contrary: that they were decisions only to resist if the United States used force to impede Japan's efforts.

I will not pursue this point—partly because of the lack of full texts and authoritative translations, partly because these meetings did not settle the question.

[4] "Gist of the Main Points in Regard to Dealing with the Situation to Meet the Change in World Conditions." Decision of Liaison Conference, July 27, 1940, *loc. cit.*

be quiescent, if not acquiescent. However that may be, this was the route which the second Konoye Cabinet during its year in office (July 1940 to July 1941) faithfully followed.

The concept of national self-defense has as many hues as a rainbow. Each country has its own filter, and each bends the rays to its own wants and fears. To the men who wrote Japanese policy in July 1940, national self-defense meant any action deemed necessary to place Japan in a position to win a war in case it could not achieve its aims without war. Thus Tojo later could argue with sincerity that the measures outlined in this program were justified acts of defense against American and British hostility.[5] The inner tenor of a hundred records, among them these decisions on July 26 and 27, belies this version. *It seeks to conceal agressive and threatening Japanese aims, by stressing the strategic justification of Japanese measures.*

The activities that Japan was about to begin can, indeed, be defended if the nature of Japan's ultimate aims is left aside. Some of them were influenced by the prospect that the United States might make it harder for Japan to achieve its ends. The Japanese government was well aware during the week of July 19–27 that the American government was likely at any time—and perhaps very soon—to reduce farther the flow of war materials to Japan. Virtually confirmed rumors reached it that plans for that purpose were being prepared in Washington that week (of which an account will shortly be given). This knowledge may well have stimulated the projects adopted, to put Japan in a position to avert or defy such pressure. In this sense they may be regarded as having a defensive aspect, but in this limited sense only. For it was only because Japan was pursuing threatening aims, that it was opposed and impeded. Basically, it was not on the defensive, but on the make.

Even before the new cabinet began to carry this program into action, the submerged differences of opinion reappeared. Of these the Emperor, who had been a confused and worried observer, spoke to his Lord Keeper of the Privy Seal. As recorded by the Marquis Kido: "I was received in audience and told by His Majesty his impression in regard to the execution of plans decided at the Imperial Headquarters Liaison Conference [of July 27]. The government body, Army and Navy cliques, all hold

[5] In his able defense deposition, *Far East Mil. Trib.*, Exh. No. 3655. The essence of this defense was that the two purposes of the program were (1) to cut off Chiang Kai-shek from foreign assistance and thus force him to make a just peace; (2) to make Japan immune from foreign pressure. Both these in his view were essential features of a satisfactory and safe national existence. Both were to be achieved by peaceful means until external pressure forced Japan to resort to other means.

different ideas in regard to the execution of the plan. Premier Konoye believing that the China incident cannot be settled easily, wants to try to reduce the area of occupation in China and start the southward operation. Thus he seems to be trying to divert the discontent of the people over the failure in China towards the South. The Army wants to leave the situation in China as it is, and to advance south if there is an opportunity. But the Navy seemingly does not wish to advance south until the war in China is settled." [6]

In Washington the reports received from Grew of his first talk on July 26 with the new Foreign Minister did not encourage the hope of any adjustment. The Ambassador felt in the whole manner of Matsuoka's entry into office an air of conceit and of confidence that Japan would have its way. And the Minister's words when read in Washington left the impression of a liar who boasted of his candor. He had ready a personal message which he asked Grew to send to the President. In this he wrote that his lifelong interest, like that of the President, was to preserve peace. But—and this was the core of the message—in his view this would only be done by making way for change, by accepting the emergence of an inevitable new order in the world.[7] Spoken by someone else, this thought might be regarded as wise and beyond dispute. But spoken by Matsuoka at that time it did not forecast quiet in our relations with Japan. The two governments, while continuing to aver that their purpose was to avoid war, were henceforth to quicken their stride toward war.

[6] "Kido's Diary," entry for July 30, 1940.
[7] The text of this message is printed in *Foreign Relations: Japan*, II, 105-6.

## CHAPTER 12

# Our First Firm Counteraction

ON THE same day (allowing for the time difference) that the Konoye Cabinet adopted plans to make the Empire independent, the American government brought home the fact that it was not. On July 25 (Washington time) the President announced that henceforth all exports of scrap metals and oils from the United States would be subject to license. No secret intelligence about Japanese affairs, of the sort that was had later, guided the timing of this statement. It was a swipe in a general direction, and not an exactly clocked and aimed blow. Its history is strange and worth the telling.

In the fore part of July concern over whether supplies of scrap iron would be enough for our own future needs became acute. The members of the Advisory Committee to the Council of National Defense, especially Leon Henderson, were actively pressing for restriction of export. But the uniformed spokesmen of the armed services on the Army and Navy Munitions Board were not insisting. And the State Department was still cool, still dubious whether the need justified the act.

During the first five months of 1940 Japanese purchases had greatly declined, while British purchases had grown much. The American government had not yet in the exercise of its export controls avowedly made a distinction between buyers of our products. The question was still to be faced—were we ready to refuse Japan so vital a product, while continuing freely to supply Britain? If we did not want Japan to take sides, could we so openly take sides ourselves?

In regard to oil, the situation was more pointed. Startling reports were coming in of Japanese attempts to buy great quantities of aviation gasoline and lubricants.[1] Of the latter, for example, according to word sent

---

[1] The reports were true. The official American statistics of this period do not distinguish between gasoline of aviation grade and other grades. But the record shows an immense increase in American exports of all kinds of gasoline and other motor fuels to Japan during the second half of 1940, as compared with any similar previous period. In barrels they were about 2.3 million, as compared with 600 thousand in 1937, 600 thousand in 1938, and 700 thousand in 1939. For the twelve months from July, 1940, they were to be about 4.5 million barrels, at least triple the amount in any previous twelve month period. The record of exports of lubricating oil to Japan tell the same story.

to the State Department by the Standard Oil Company of New Jersey on July 18, Japan was offering to buy any and all quantities. Furthermore, it was trying to secure these products not only in tanker loads but in metal drums, and was seeking to arrange for delivery at southern points in China. The American consuls at Kobe and Osaka were reporting their opinion that Japan was planning to accumulate stocks on Hainan Island, one of the natural starting points for a southern military expedition on the part of the Japanese.

This spurt of buying was to the watchers in Washington objectionable, in any and all of the meanings that might attach to it. Did it not portend the near start—while Britain was defending itself against invasion—of new military operations to the south? Or, if not that, the storing up of large reserve stocks which would later enable the Japanese Navy and Air Force to sustain a long war over all parts of the Pacific?

Hull well knew that such schemes were stirring—as they were—within the Japanese government. But could these be countered by embargoes? Would Japan suffer such restraint? Would it not more probably break out, not only along the fringes of China, but against the Indies? Then what would we do? No cheerful answer was to be had by asking the military. Thus, with an air of dejection, Hull refused assent to the proposals to cut the exports down to normal dimensions. Then (on July 19) he left for a conference of the American Republics at Havana. This was the day that the Four Ministers met at Ogikubo and settled Japan's policy.

On the evening before, Stimson, Knox, and Morgenthau dined with the British Ambassador and the Australian Minister. They had the same troubling reports as the American government regarding Japanese preparations to move south. Stimson was disturbed lest the British go further in an attempt to mollify Japan. He, as told in his diary, "brought out that we now had an opportunity under the new legislation of stopping the supplies of oil to Japan." Lothian suggested that Great Britain could also destroy the oil wells in the Dutch East Indies. If both of these things were done, Japan herself would be practically stalled for lack of oil. Morgenthau, Stimson noted, was struck by the thought.[2]

Indeed he was, and he hurried to pass it along next morning to the President.

"There is," Morgenthau wrote, "a possibility that a plan can be quickly developed with the co-operation of the British Government to stop oil and gasoline for Japan. Lord Lothian, whose proposal it partly is, is en-

[2] Unpublished diary of Henry L. Stimson, entry for July 18, 1940.

thusiastic about its possibilities and will ascertain his Government's reaction at once, should you deem the plan feasible."

This was the plan: The United States was, on the ground of national defense, to stop all exports of oil; Britain was to get all its oil from the Caribbean area; Britain and the United States were to buy up any surplus production in that area; Britain was to arrange with the Dutch government to destroy the oil wells in the Indies; and, finally, it was to concentrate bombing attacks on the synthetic oil plants in Germany. Where then, and how, would Japan and Germany get oil for war?

What a welcome change in fare this note must have been. For weeks the reports that had come to the President's desk had the same dull and disliked flavor; there was nothing to be done to save France; not a great deal that might help Britain; better mind and mend our own near-by defenses; better watch public opinion; better not arouse Japan and Germany too much. Here was a paper that said we might do something effective, something that might turn the course of the war. The President at once asked Stimson, Knox, and Welles to come to the White House to discuss it.

Stimson wrote an account of this meeting in his diary: "The President pointed to the map across the room and said that he had sat there day after day watching that map and that he finally came to the conclusion that the only way out of the difficulties of the world was by the starving of the people of Europe, particularly in regard to their supply of fuel to carry on the war . . . The President has ideas by which America could, acting under the recent legislation, prevent all of the petroleum supplies —particularly aviation oil—from going to the Nazi Axis powers. American oil could be stored in the ground and the cost of the Government buying it in that condition would be comparatively small. This would prevent oil from going to Spain and through Spain to the Germans. Great Britain would take care of the Venezuelan supplies, and so on. When they got to the Far Eastern side, Sumner Welles put in an objection that an embargo against Japan would cause Japan to make war on Great Britain. I ventured to doubt this and the question came up of whether or not the New Netherlands wells could not be put out of commission and thus Japan deprived of her objective for going to war with Great Britain. Altogether it was a long and interesting discussion but whether or not it was intended to be a factual one was left in the air." [3]

It was, the next few days showed, intended to be a factual one. But in the transition from idea to plan its features changed like a picture thrown

[3] *ibid.*, entry for July 19, 1940.

unsteadily upon a screen. Confusion arose in regard to both the purpose and the means. Welles prepared one program. Morgenthau at the same time prepared another. They were very different. The President did not seem clear as to which program he was about to carry into effect.

Welles, after the White House meeting, entered into a series of consultations with the President and Admiral Stark, Chief of Naval Operations. On the 20th, the President signed the bill for a two-ocean Navy, designed to make the United States able in time to deal with Japan without turning the Atlantic over to Germany. It seemed foolish to all of them to provide the means by which Japan could offset this program by increasing its Navy and Air Force.

Yet there were reasons to which Welles reverted for selecting with care the scope, time, and form of action. If the United States, he advised, did anything just then that bore vitally upon Japan's power to carry on the war in China, the result could not be predicted. A total ban on oil shipments would force it into a decision. Rather than desist, Japan, using our action as cause and reason, might move against the Indies. Should that happen it was doubtful whether the American people would support the government in any counter military action. Most of them would judge the oil embargo to have been an injudicious act towards war. This argument for not daring to try to prevent the calamity of Axis victory must have seemed arid. And so in a sense it was, for its only fruit could be time—time to prepare for defense in a world of enemies.

Yet the President was impressed. Or so Welles thought. In any case, the proclamation and orders which the staff of the State Department set about preparing were definitely limited in scope. Controls were to be established *only* over those kinds of gasoline and lubricants produced for use in aviation, and *only* over the very best grade of scrap iron and steel, not the rest. Papers adding these selected items to the list of controlled products were made ready. They lacked by the 25th only the initials of the Secretary of the Treasury.[4]

But Morgenthau, in touch with Stimson and Knox, who shared his impatience with the aura of anxiety which the State Department cast about the project, was busy too. While Welles was urging care, the others were urging boldness. Of the two, it was Morgenthau who spoke to the President's nature and inclination. He felt himself allowed, if not told, to prepare for the more decisive action.

Thus the Treasury staff also drew up a proclamation—placing export of *all* kinds of oil and *all* scrap metals (not merely iron and steel scrap)

[4] Notes of Joseph C. Green, Chief of the Division of Controls, State Department.

under control. On the 22nd, this was sent over to the President, with a note explaining that the orders would leave the President to decide later how to exercise the control; when, and to what extent to stop the export of the products named. While this paper was before him, the President, who was at Hyde Park, received (by relay from Washington at Stimson's behest) a telegram from General De Witt, Commander at San Francisco of the 9th Corps Area. This reported that tremendous Japanese purchases of aviation gasoline were being made and concluded: "Should the Army and Navy need it in quantity, during the next six to nine months there would be a shortage of aviation gasoline if these [Japanese] purchases are all consummated."

The President signed the proclamation which Morgenthau had sent. Whether or not he was under the impression that the State Department had approved it is unclear. In any case, shortly after lunch on the 25th, a White House messenger brought over to Welles—for countersignature and seal—this proclamation already signed by the President. It, as has been said, dealt with all kinds and grades of oil and all scrap metals.

Welles soon had a cluster of worried subordinates about his desk. He told nothing of his previous talks on the subject, as he listened to their earnest advice not to sign until he talked with the President. All agreed that if this order were issued, whether or not meant as an embargo, it would provoke a crisis with Japan sooner or later, and probably sooner. The members of the Far Eastern Division were the most agitated. They were all but sure that the controls in mind would incite Japan to join the Axis and the war against Britain. Impressed, Welles agreed to try to persuade the President to discard this proclamation in favor of the lesser one. That this might not be easy was indicated by word received while the meeting was on. The President had already informed the press of the contents of the paper he had signed, and in language that was read to mean "embargo." [5]

The President responded to Welles's first hurried telephone call (on the late afternoon of the 25th). He told the press that at the request of the State Department another order would be issued to make clear what kinds of oil and scrap were affected. On the next day, the President having returned to Washington, the cabinet met. There open argument broke out between Welles and Morgenthau. The President would have no part in it, would not decide what was to be done, and left the dispu-

---

[5] The story in the *New York Times* of July 26 was headed "Embargo Put on Oil, Scrap Metal, in License Order by Roosevelt." The story in the *New York Herald Tribune* on the same day was headed "U.S. Embargo Is Clamped on Metals and Oil."

tants to thrash the matter out. Hopkins was for discretion and Stimson was satisfied with a ban on the products used in aviation. Morgenthau yielded, but not without a sense that Welles had gone back on purposes for which he had shown earlier favor.

The signed proclamation was discarded; a new one was substituted. The regulations that were issued on the 26th dealt only with aviation motor fuel and lubricants, and No. 1 heavy melting iron and steel scrap.[6] The published notices were permitted to speak for themselves. The White House did not elucidate. The press, guided by the original White House announcement, had written of the step as an "embargo" on all oil and scrap. Only a few newspapers—mainly those printed for the business community—thought the correction of enough importance to place it where it would be surely seen.

The Japanese Embassy had, on the 23rd, inquired at the State Department about rumored American measures, and was put off. After the White House statement of the 25th, and the press comment, it could be assumed that Tokyo had been told that a total embargo of oil and scrap metals was in prospect. Welles therefore hastened to undo any effect such reports might be having in Japan.

Asking the Japanese Ambassador in Washington, Horinouchi, to call early on the morning of the 26th, he set out to soothe. The new export controls, he explained, were being imposed only because of our own needs. Details were still unsettled, but the action was not aimed at any particular foreign country, and would not discriminate between them. Part of the art of diplomacy is make-up; this answer was a false face for the facts.[7]

But the Japanese Ambassador did not then say so. He remarked only that the publicity had caused a sharp reaction in Japan and that he hoped the actual details, when learned, would modify the first impression. On the next day (the 27th), Welles asked the Ambassador to call again and told him what was about to be done. On this occasion Horinouchi was not so reserved. He said he was pleased to learn the facts, but questioned

[6] This grade of scrap iron was reckoned to be only about 15 per cent of the recent Japanese purchases.
[7] On July 31 the White House announced: "In the interests of national defense the export of aviation gasoline is being limited to nations of the Western Hemisphere, except where such gasoline is required elsewhere for the operations of American owned companies." Britain, it was understood, could draw as much as needed through Canadian companies. Not long after, the United States began to issue licenses for shipment anywhere in the British Empire.

whether the United States really had to enact such controls in order to assure its defense. Welles did not try to convince him. The Japanese government, he answered, had adopted many similar measures without protest by us.

Explanations also had to be given to the British. Lothian had heard from London. During the weekend that followed, members of the British Embassy called at the homes of their State Department colleagues to impress upon them the danger that Japan might at once take steps to insure control of the oil of the Indies. The Dutch government, while affirming that the Indies would defend themselves, expressed the same worry. Both pleaded for prudence.

But the President now took the position that he had been as prudent as he was going to be. The United States would not send any more aviation gasoline or top-grade scrap iron to Japan; it would send them to Britain. Japan was, he thought, more likely to be deterred by a firm, though not crushing, show of our will than by any sign of fear.

Thus bolstered by the White House, the State Department rejected the three formal notes of protest which the Japanese made during August. These asserted that Japan had been singled out for and subjected to unfair treatment, and reserved all rights to take future action. The State Department answered, as Welles had before, that the new controls were essential to national defense, and so not open to discussion. At the same time attention was invited to the great range of Japanese measures and restraints injurious to Americans in China.

At each successive talk with the Japanese Ambassador, the American answers grew colder. For the government, along with the country, was becoming aroused by the further demands which Japan was making upon Indo-China and the Indies, and by reports that an alliance with Germany was in the making. The grooves of action and of counteraction were becoming deep.

## CHAPTER 13

# Maneuver and Resistance

THE Konoye Cabinet read no lesson in the orders about oil and scrap iron. Or, if it did, only to the effect that there was still an area of action which could be entered without risk of war against either the local defenders or the United States. It still felt itself free to push on with the program for the New Order in East Asia, despite the injunction contained in the resolution of the Imperial Conference of July 26–27 "to solve the problem of the South within such scope as would not lead to war with other powers."

Other means, the strategists thought, should suffice: disguise of purpose, insincere treaties, the display of temper and, as might be needed, the threat of force.[1] In Indo-China, Japan need not appear as master, but as protector. To the Indies it could come as a seeker of raw materials and fair economic opportunities; and, perhaps if it suited, as advocate of native independence. For Thailand, there was the role of exponent of justice and mediator of the claims of that country against Indo-China. These tactics were aptly described by the Emperor, as "in the nature of a thief at a fire." [2]

The State Department knew roughly what Japan was about and guessed the means it would use. But how, without risking an unwanted war, could it be thwarted? How could the American presence and potential power be made to count at this time? Enough or not enough, there were three ways in which the United States could and did project itself into the situation: by supporting Britain; by hurrying on with the increase in its Army, Navy, and Air Force; and by displaying or using

---

[1] These tactics are defined and expounded in various resolutions and plans approved by the government. For example, see "Tentative Plan for Policies towards the Southern Regions," approved October 4, 1940, *Far East Mil. Trib.*, Exh. No. 628.

[2] "Kido's Diary," entry for February 3, 1941. The Emperor, upon being informed of the decision reached by the Liaison Conference of January 30 to enforce mediation on Thailand and Indo-China and exact payment from both, had remarked: "I do not approve of anything in the nature of a thief at a fire. However, in dealing with the fast changing world of today, it would not be gratifying to err on the side of benevolence."

its control over materials and machines needed by Japan. About the first two means there was full accord within the American government, but about the third there was much dispute.

On August 6 it was reported that Japan had demanded of France the right to send troops across Tonkin province (which bordered China) and the control of air fields in the region.[3] Matsuoka admitted to Grew on the 7th that the reports were true. He did not mention that he had already asked Germany to induce the French government to grant these favors. Nor did he inform Grew that the French Ambassador in Tokyo had already said that France would agree to the Japanese requests "in principle," if they were put in a form that did not injure French prestige. Grew, as instructed, expressed earnest concern over this upset of the situation. Another grudge, another entry against Japan in the black book kept by the man from Tennessee.

During the same first fortnight of August, the American government also learned about new demands on the Indies. In this act Matsuoka and the men he served showed themselves most clearly as they were: displaced villains out of nineteenth-century American melodrama, advancing upon the obstinate object of their affection with white words and black hearts. They belonged, and were, before the footlights.

The Japanese government had notified the government of the Indies as early as July 16 that it wished to talk over a comprehensive settlement of their relations and would send a large mission to do so.[4] The Dutch government replied that the mission would be welcome, but on no account would political questions be discussed. At the same time, it sought to propitiate by promising to do everything practical to see that Japan got what it wanted from the Indies. "The Netherlands Government,"

[3] The demand, virtually an ultimatum, had been made by Matsuoka on August 1. Baudouin, *op. cit.*, p. 187.

[4] The decision was hurried in order to get in ahead of Germany, and it was planned to offer Germany as payment aid in making existence impossible for the British anywhere in Asia.

There was much ado about the selection of the head of this mission. On Matsuoka's suggestion, General Koiso, a former garrison commander and vigorous advocate of expansion, was chosen. But he gave an interview to the press (on August 2), saying that the natives of the East Indies had long been oppressed and exploited. "We cannot," he declared, "tolerate such a condition—it is necessary to emancipate the oriental races." The Indies government said it would not receive him unless he retracted. Shortly afterwards he was replaced. According to the stories contained in the "Saionji-Harada Memoirs," the real reason was because Konoye grew scared of him. For he demanded unrestricted authority and insisted that he be sent on a battleship the better to enforce his demands. Harada says that Konoye suspected that he was engaged in a plot with Matsuoka and General Muto, Chief of the Military Affairs Bureau of the Army, to cause the fall of the cabinet. After some delay, the Japanese Government selected Kobayashi, Minister of Commerce and Industry, to head the mission.

this Dutch answer of July 26 read in part, "is prepared to stimulate and facilitate exports to Japan with all the means at its disposal—bearing in mind Japan's minimum demands . . ." Fear of what Japan might do if turned down, the Dutch government explained to the American, prescribed such compliance, and the fear was quickened by the prospect of an American oil embargo.[5]

Reports followed that the Dutch Minister for the Colonies, resident in London, was anxious that the oil companies in the Indies complete the deal with Japan; and that the British government was ready to cooperate. At this news the State Department showed restrained displeasure. Word was passed to the Standard Vacuum Oil Company that the American government did not favor the sale to Japan of unusually large amounts of oil from the Indies. If, the State Department added, the companies felt compelled to do so, it was hoped that they would limit their obligations to as brief a time as possible. The word, it was known, would be passed along to the Dutch Shell Company, which would in turn inform the British government.

Other branches of the American government sought more telling action of some kind. Morgenthau, Stimson, Knox, and the members of the Advisory Committee to the Council of National Defense were all vexed at the turnabout which Welles had persuaded the President to make on July 26—especially in regard to iron and steel scrap. They wanted to stop the whole trade in this killing metal—no matter what Japan might do. This wish governed the meeting of many departments, convoked by Morgenthau on August 14. But Hull, back from Havana, still demurred. Thus the junior officials of the State Department, sent to this meeting, spoke against doing anything more about scrap, except as needed for our own defense. While Morgenthau grumbled, the others agreed to weigh the evidence on this point longer. About oil, too, the opinion began to travel from the Treasury to the State Department that the controls should be extended. This commanded interest since, other instances showed, it might already have found a home in the White House.

The inflowing reports about the conduct of Japan did not, as the days followed, improve anyone's temper. They brought out in bold relief the course upon which Japan was set.

[5] Statement of the Governor General to Walter A. Foote, the American Consul at Batavia, August 5, 1940. It is improbable that news of the White House announcement of July 25th (Washington time) reached Batavia before the drafting of the quoted note to the Japanese government was completed, but advance rumors did.

Japan bullied the French government into complete acceptance of its demands upon Indo-China. Warning was served that if the French government continued to balk and bargain—in an attempt to protect French sovereignty—the Japanese Army would begin to move in anyhow.[6] After another fortnight of resistance France yielded. The American government would promise only moral support, and the same kind of aid that was being given to China. On August 29 an accord was signed in Tokyo which granted Japan the military facilities asked. In return for a promise to respect French sovereignty over Indo-China, Vichy recognized "the preponderant interests of Japan in the Far East in the economic as well as the political domain."

The Japanese government seemed to be preparing some similar entry into the Indies. Its mission, it announced, would be headed by a cabinet officer and contain Army and Navy officials of high rank. The Dutch authorities took this as a hint that they were to be led into spheres which they did not want to enter. Their answer made clear that they would not suffer any interference with Dutch control of the islands. This eminent mission, the reply of September 4 stated, would be received provided Japan understood that no political questions were to be raised. Further, the note went on, while the Governor-General of the Indies would want to greet the mission personally, his position would prevent him from taking part in the talks. Since they were to be about economic matters Van Mook would conduct them.

Though, as its records show, the Japanese government was displeased at this putting up of the guard, the mission was sent. It began at once to talk about oil. Japan's first purpose was to wean itself from dependence on the United States. The American government, which was kept informed of every turn of the talk, tried to see that it did not succeed. On the 16th of August, Hornbeck had met with representatives of the oil companies (Standard Vacuum and Dutch Shell) and the British government. He sought, as directed, to embolden the companies to stand out against the Japanese demands. He performed this task in a positive way —denying that the danger was sufficient to justify submission. Therefore, he urged, the companies should judge Japan's propositions on a business basis. To the sale of reasonable amounts of ordinary crude oil, he said, there could be no objection. But to the sale of large amounts of aviation gasoline there was much objection; all of this fluid produced in the

<hr/>

[6] Matsuoka had so informed the French Ambassador in Tokyo on August 10. And on August 12 the Japanese Ambassador in Vichy told Baudouin, the Foreign Minister, that "the Japanese Government expected a complete and rapid acceptance of its demands." Baudouin, *op. cit.*, p. 199.

Indies was being sold to Britain and if now it were diverted to Japan, the United States would have to replace it; further the American ban would be nullified.[7] Thus, he concluded, "it was for the interests themselves to decide . . . but that, if and in so far as they took any part of the proposed business, they would have to do so without assuming an authorization or blessing on our part."

This spout of cold water came at a good time. Churchill was at work. The British government advised the Dutch Shell to bargain hard and long on all features of the contract—quantities, grades, and length of obligation. In two talks (on August 25 and September 5) which Lothian had with Hull about the Burma Road, the situation in the Indies was reviewed. Even in the first of these talks—a new note of confidence in Britain's ability to win the battle of Britain and hold the situation in the Far East was to be detected. A proud and daring will had emerged from the shock of Dunkerque. Lothian remarked that the British government had been trying to give courage to the Dutch government and oil companies in the Indies, and urged that the American government do likewise. Hull said he would see to it.

On September 5 a spirited message was received from Van Mook which said that in dealing with the Japanese mission he would take "a reasonable attitude on reasonable things." But he would not permit the injection of political questions or admit any attempts of Japan to secure control of or special position in the economic life of the islands. The Indies, he said, would fight if necessary to maintain their position and asked us to hurry the shipment of the arms they had bought in the United States.

The American answer to Van Mook, sent on September 11, was wary. He was told (1) that the American government hoped it would be kept fully informed so that "it may be in a position to give appropriate consideration, within the framework of established policies, to problems of mutual and common interests"; (2) that in regard to oil, the American company operating in the Indies knew its ideas, and (3) that the government did not wish to intrude, or, unless the need for foreign assistance should appear, enter the picture. The same reserve was shown also in the comments made to the British government.

In short, while the American government was ready to see a test of its

[7] It was not then appreciated that faulty specifications in the American control regulations of July 26 opened a greater breach in the embargo on aviation gasoline than would have been made by shipments from the Indies. Japan was obtaining from the United States great amounts of high grades of both gasoline and crude oil, which with little trouble were converted into aviation gasoline.

judgment that Japan would not attack the Indies if the government bargained hard, it would not underwrite the test. American policy, then and later, was based on the hope that Japan would be restrained by the shadow that coming events are supposed to cast—while avoiding any advance engagement with the event.

~~~~~~~~~~~~~~~~~~~~~~~~~~~~~~~~~~~~~~~~~~~~~~~~~~~~~~~~~~~~~~~~~~~

## CHAPTER 14

# We Stop the Shipment of Scrap Iron

PROVOKING as the situation was, Hull thought it might be made worse. Until the outcome of the battle of the air above Britain was known, any decision as to whether or not to end the shipment of war materials to Japan seemed to him blind. If the Royal Air Force continued to do well, it would become safer, if not safe, to strike at the explosive center of Japan's position. If those brave squadrons were exhausted, it would, he thought, turn out to have been reckless to do so. So Hull wanted to wait. He asked time of the Secretary of the Treasury who thought action long since due, asked it of the Secretary of War who thought the same, asked it of the defense agencies who did not want to lose any more scrap iron, and of the directors of the Iron and Steel Institute who wanted an embargo.

Thus when, on September 13, the Japanese Ambassador called on Welles to inquire about reports that we were about to impose new restrictions on oil and scrap iron, he was told neither Yes nor No. After which the tutored Under Secretary spoke about the firm resistance of Britain, and said that he hoped the Japanese government would perceive the significance of the destroyer-naval-base deal between ourselves and Britain. The Ambassador nodded silently. The Japanese government also had its secrets. Matsuoka had by this day framed a conclusive alliance with Stahmer, Ribbentrop's special envoy. In the tempest of talk that was going on in Tokyo over the terms of this pact, oil and scrap iron were —as will be told—important items. But the American government knew nothing of that.

At this juncture a startling cable from Grew reached the State Department. Sent on September 12, the Ambassador came to call it his "green light" message. At the end of recent talks with Matsuoka, Grew reported himself to be possessed with a reluctant sense of complete frustration. Up to then he recalled that he had always said that the United States should not apply sanctions against Japan unless it was ready to support them by armed force. For, as he had written two years before (December 5, 1938), "They are a hardy race, accustomed throughout their history

[ 101 ]

to catastrophe and disaster; theirs is the 'do or die' spirit, more deeply ingrained than in any other people."

But now, after giving his reasons—which summed up to an opinion that the governing elements would use any means they dared to extend the Japanese realm of political and economic control—he forcibly came to the conclusion that: "If we conceive it to be in our interest to support the British Empire in this hour of her travail, and I most emphatically do so conceive it, we must strive by every means to preserve the status quo in the Pacific at least until the European war has been won or lost. In my opinion this cannot be done nor can our interests be further adequately and properly protected by merely registering disapproval and keeping a careful record thereof. . . . Until such time as there is a complete re-generation of thought in this country, a show of force, together with a determination to employ it if need be, can alone contribute effectively to the achievement of such an outcome and to our own future security." [1] This from the most patient and optimistic of diplomats.

Hornbeck gruffly expressed agreement with views he had long held. To Hull the analysis and forecast of Japanese policy seemed near the truth. But the advice tendered seemed to call upon the government to take risks which American opinion would not approve. The people still seemed to want to be sure of staying out of war more than they wanted anything else, and were being assured that they could. Only the night before, speaking in Washington, the President had said: "I stand, with my party, and outside of my party as President of all the people, on the platform, the wording that was adopted in Chicago less than two months ago. It said: 'We will not participate in foreign wars, and we will not send our Army, naval or air forces to fight in foreign lands outside of the Americas, except in case of attack.' " [2]

The Republican candidate was spreading promises of similar import over the land. [3]

[1] For the text of this important cable and a fuller explanation of the Ambassador's thought, see his testimony in *Pearl Harbor Attack*, Part 2, 634, *et seq.* His idea was that a quick and vigorous show of force might cause the Japanese government to be more careful and that, if then the war went favorably for Britain, the time might again come when diplomacy would get its chance to negotiate a settlement. As explained to the Committee, "My thought was that by taking these measures we would eventually bring at least the thinking, sane-minded statesmen in Japan to the realization that unless they stopped in their tracks they were going to have war with the United States and Great Britain and other countries."

[2] Address at Teamsters Union Convention, Washington, D.C., September 11, 1940.

[3] See, for example, Willkie's comment on September 7: "I believe that the United States should give all possible help to Great Britain, short of war. And when I say short of war I mean short of war." *New York Times*, September 8, 1940.

Suppose, then, that after the United States had made a show of force (if oil and scrap embargoes could be called that), Japan attacked the Indies or Singapore, could statements like these be discarded? Could they be considered outworn by events? Perhaps—but certainly not in time to prevent Japan from gaining its first objectives. And certainly not without diverting our too small naval and air forces, which would be most needed in the Atlantic if Britain should fall.

So Hull continued to ponder, and to count upon the assisted British to give the American people more time to change their minds. As he did, other elements within the government continued to nag. Morgenthau used stinging words at our failure to stop nourishing Japan. Stimson was convinced that much would be lost by delay. And while the President would not override Hull's judgment, he lent himself to initiatives which hurried it. Thus at the cabinet meeting of September 6 when Hull observed that a lot of people were messing around with oil, the President said that all materials on the subject should henceforth clear through Morgenthau.[4] This was a way of organizing the matter, but not the one most congenial to the Secretary of State. Morgenthau set up the Treasury as a statistical center from which material flowed to keep the President's interest alive.[5] But the British (Sir Andrew Agnew, Chief of the British Petroleum Board, was in Washington) proved to be elusive rather than responsive.[6]

During the next fortnight of waiting (September 12–26) news from the Far East confirmed Grew's impression of Japanese plans, while news from London confirmed the success of the British airmen.

The Japanese government answered the American protest against its entry into Indo-China by telling us in long language to mind our own business. Finding the Governor of Indo-China "obstructive," in carrying out the accord signed in Tokyo, the field commander, General Nishihara, on September 19 served notice that his forces would cross the border

[4] Unpublished diary of Henry Morgenthau, Jr., entry for September 6, 1940.

[5] The studies made of the Japanese oil position were useful. They brought out the fact that the current estimates of the American Navy of Japanese oil reserves (70–75 million barrels) were about double the estimates of the American oil companies and the British government. The actual fact, as later learnt from Japanese records, was about halfway between the two.

[6] On September 13 Lothian had told Morgenthau that in view of the delicacy of the situation, neither the Dutch nor British could be expected to antagonize Japan by interfering with the flow of oil from the Indies, unless they were able to count on American support in the Far East. ibid., entry for September 13, 1940.

on the 23rd—whether or not.[7] They did move in. The hapless French gave in after a short fight, and the Japanese soldiers took over Tonkin province.[8] Word was received, as well, that the Japanese government was pushing hard the claims of Thailand for the return of two of the border provinces of Indo-China: Laos, and Cambodia.

Upon the Indies no ultimatum was served. But the Japanese increased their demands for oil to upward of three million tons (roughly twenty-two million barrels) annually for five years. This was about five times the amount that the Indies had sent to Japan in previous years.[9] It would have been about three-fifths of Japan's usual total supply from all sources, and enough to let her struggle along even if American shipments ended. In addition large oil concessions were asked. The Governor-General politely referred both the mission and these requests to Van Mook and the oil companies. Angered, Kobayashi, head of the mission, reported to Matsuoka that "The Governor General . . . openly tried to do his utmost to evade political problems. He evinced not the slightest sign of fervor to try to sound out the true intention of the Japanese Government towards the Dutch East Indies. . . . It has made me feel that I have come all this way in vain." [10]

[7] The Japanese had increased their demands as the talks went on: from three to six airdromes, from the right to station twenty-five thousand troops in Tonkin to the right to station thirty-two thousand. For an account of the ups and downs of the negotiations and the clash between French and Japanese, see Baudouin, *op. cit.,* pp. 242–52.

[8] The ideas and purposes which the Japanese government had in mind when invading Indo-China were several and mixed together; and as time went on they changed.

The purposes officially advanced by the Japanese government were (1) to gain military advantage in the war against China, by preventing any movement of supplies into China, and by obtaining new points of attack; (2) to forestall any attempt by hostile French elements to gain control; (3) to eliminate any chance that any other foreign power would try to acquire control.

It is certain that in addition Japan hoped to secure much, if not all, the surplus supply of rice and raw materials produced in Indo-China. On September 3 the Japanese cabinet approved a plan for the economic development of Indo-China. This provided that the Indo-Chinese government should guarantee exports to Japan of minimum quantities of rice, rubber, manganese, zinc, industrial salt, tin, antimony, and other products. In the past most of these had been sold elsewhere—and the rivalry went on even after the Japanese occupation of Northern Indo-China; especially over rubber, tin, and rice—some of which the Indo-Chinese government continued to sell to the United States, France, and Britain.

The Japanese government pledged itself, in the agreements which it forced upon Indo-China, to respect its sovereignty and independence. But the Japanese records show that it had no intention of doing so. Certainly it would have retained permanent control of strategic points and a decisive voice in its political and economic affairs.

By the military elements, at least, there can be no doubt that the troop and air bases obtained were preparatory steps in a program of further movement south. See *Far East Mil. Trib.,* Exh. No. 628.

[9] This was about 40 per cent of the combined production of crude oil of Sumatra, Borneo, and Java.

[10] Cable, Kobayashi to Matsuoka, September 13, 1940. *ibid.,* Exh. No. 1312.

The Japanese government was on the point of defining its "true intentions" towards the Indies. The Liaison Conference of September 19 stated what was wanted there, and how it was to be had. The Indies were to be separated from Holland. Then Japan was to obtain from the new authorities recognition of its predominant political influence and economic interests. But these aims were to be achieved by indirect means. Fear that, in the event of attempted invasion, the Dutch might destroy the oil wells and refineries was a factor in the choice of tactics.[11]

The Dutch government, while showing no alarm before the Japanese, made its fears known to us. It earnestly asked (on the 24th) that nothing be done about American oil exports to Japan as long as their talks with Japan continued. Welles, after reaffirming the opinion that the situation in the Pacific would not be helped by supineness, gave the desired promise. Assured by this answer, the Dutch reaffirmed their intention to resist any form of aggression against the Indies.

The British government, though advising the Shell Oil Company not to give in, was not nearly as confident as the American that Japan would not attack the Indies, Singapore, and Hong Kong. It longed for surety that the United States would in that event join the fight. Hull, in talk with Lothian and Casey, the Australian Minister, on September 16, again ventured the opinion that no such attack was in sight. But he avoided any promise, or cousin of a promise, of military support in case his opinion was wrong. It proved to be right. The decisive reason why is to be read in the entry that Marquis Kido had made in his diary some time before:

"The Emperor told me what he and Prince Fushimi, Chief of the Navy General Staff, had talked about. The Prince said that 'The Navy at present want to avoid the use of force against Singapore and the Netherlands Indies, and that, since at least eight months will be required for preparations after a decision for war is made, the later war comes the better.' "[12]

On September 19, after hearing about the latest Japanese ultimatum to Indo-China, the President and cabinet agreed that the time had come to put a total stop to the export of scrap iron and steel. The defense agencies were getting out of hand in their opinion that the country should not export any more—except to Britain.[13] Hull, as the news came in day

[11] *ibid.,* Exh. No. 541.
[12] "Kido's Diary," entry for August 10, 1940.
[13] On September 4 the National Advisory Commission to the Council on National De-

by day of the fighting over England, grew less worried about what Japan might do. On the heels of this decision word came from Grew that the Japanese government had decided on some form of alliance with Germany; that on the previous day the matter had been settled in a three-hour conference in the presence of the Emperor.

Still it was judged best to wait until Japanese armies had actually marched into Indo-China. By the 24th they had, and reports of the projected alliance with Germany became confirmed. In haste another loan to China was arranged; and on the 25th it was announced. The next day the President ordered that the export of all grades of iron and steel scrap be placed under control. Without contradiction the press wrote that there was to be an "embargo." This time the statement stood.

Of oil nothing was said. Some might argue that the ending of exports of that most vital product would stop Japan and avert war. Hull and the Navy did not believe it.[14] Nor did the British or the Dutch.

The scrap embargo was both a reproof and a penalty. One which had practical effect in the scales of war strength, and as such a signal that the United States thought it might get into war with Japan. In retrospect it was, as Grew's "green light" message was, a crossing of the bridge from words to deeds. But even so, the measure brought only thin satisfaction to many in Washington. They thought it both little and too late. If the ban imposed in September had included oil, if it had been taken earlier, they thought that Japan would not have dared attack Indo-China, or enter into an alliance with Germany and Italy. Morgenthau, Stimson, and Ickes were among those of that view. As expressed in an entry in Morgenthau's diary on September 23:

"My own opinion is that the time to put pressure on Japan was before she went into Indo-China and not after and I think it's too late and I think the Japanese and the rest of the dictators are just going to laugh at us. The time to have done it was months ago and then maybe Japan would have stopped, looked and listened."

As to that, who is to know? But after study of the Japanese records, I think this a mirage. Had Hull not waited upon evidence that Britain would hold out, and had the President not borne with him, all our history

---

fense resolved to write to the President: "The Commission recommends, if other considerations are suitable, that a complete embargo on exports of iron and steel scrap be instituted."

[14] See Stark's letter to Admiral Richardson, September 24, 1940, *Pearl Harbor Attack*, Part 14, p. 961.

might have been different. My own best surmise is that stronger and earlier action would not have caused Japan to slow up, then desist from its course. More probably, I think, it would have caused it to move farther and faster. The Indo-Chinese expedition would probably not have stopped in the north. The terms of alliance with the Axis might well have been more clinching. Not improbably, Japan, despite the reluctance of its Navy, would have ceased to dally with the Indies. Or, in the coming January, when Hitler was greatly to want Japan to move against Singapore, it would have done so. In either event, the crisis in the Pacific might well have come during the winter of 1940-41, instead of the next one.

Such, rather than peace in the Pacific would have been, I think, the outcome of an earlier application of compelling sanctions. Unless, unless the United States had been willing (and sufficiently united in sentiment) at the same time to send the Pacific Fleet to Singapore, to make known that it would join Britain, France, and Holland in the defense of their Far Eastern possessions. That might have worked. If it had not, the United States would have been at war. But in all this I have let conjecture go free and far, and the opinions ventured are without benefit of notary or proof of legitimacy.

Of the soundness of the iron and steel scrap embargo as a measure of self-defense, there can be no doubt. The retained scrap was needed at home—though not vitally needed. While in Japan most of it was being used to build up war potential. Of the finished steel produced in Japan, about 40 per cent was being directly allocated to the Army and Navy, and another large part for shipbuilding.[15]

The embargo was a hard blow for Japan. But it was not a knockout. For four years at least she had been getting ready for it. She had planned and worked to change the base of the Japanese steel industry from American scrap to iron ore from areas under her control.[16] She had

[15] The allocation of finished steel for 1941 approved by the Planning Board for 1941 was, in anticipation of total production of 4.7 million metric tons, 950 thousand for the Navy, 900 thousand for the Army, 300 thousand for shipbuilding. Some of the rest was used to make products that went to the military forces.

J. B. Cohen, in his study of *Japan's Economy in War and Reconstruction* (Minneapolis, 1949), p. 48, estimates that in the year beginning April 1, 1940, 37 per cent of the production of finished steel was turned over to military forces and 5 per cent used in shipbuilding; in the year beginning April 1, 1941, 49 per cent went to the military forces, 7 per cent for shipbuilding.

[16] In the Four Year Plan, for example, adopted by a Cabinet Council on January 17, 1939, as part of an "Outline of Plan for the Expansion of Industrial Power" (*Far East Mil. Trib.*, Doc. No. 9021), it was planned to increase the production of iron ore in Japan,

accumulated a reserve stock of scrap to see her through the emergency. These measures made it possible for the steel industry to stand up under the blow. Even without further imports of American scrap, enough steel could be made for most essential purposes. Japan could still increase the supply of weapons for the armed forces, build most needed arsenals and industrial plants, and do much building of ships to keep the country supplied in time of war.

But it was costly and strength-reducing. To make up for the loss of each ton of scrap iron and steel, between two and three tons of iron ore and coking coal were needed. This was not to be had at once, or without high cost of labor, machinery, and materials.[17] Great new effort had to be made to increase production of iron ores within Japan and Korea, the Yangtze Valley, and Hainan Island off China, and of coking coal in North China; then also to build new smelting plants to make pig iron of the ore.

Nor was that the whole of it. Japan was at that time dependent on foreign countries, not only for scrap but for the substitute, iron ore. About half of its total supply of ore was then being imported from British Malaya and the Philippines.[18] This supply of ore could be, as it was to be in 1941, cut.

Nor was even that the whole of it. Japan's steel industry was very small compared to that of its possible opponents in war. Japan had since 1937 been using might and main to increase capacity. In 1940 the total production of ingot steel in Japan, Korea, and Manchuria combined was about 7.5 million tons. In the same year American production was almost ten times that amount. Now it became doubtful whether there would be enough raw materials to keep even the too-small industry in full production.

In summary, then, the American iron and steel scrap embargo (plus

---

Manchukuo, and China from 2.25 million tons to 5.7 million tons; and of pig iron from 3.3 million tons to 6.3 million tons. The goal was raised later.

[17] Japan had been using up some 1.5 million tons a year of imported scrap; thus some 4 million more tons of iron ore and coking coal would be needed.

Japan's imports of scrap iron and steel during the four years, 1937–40, inclusive, were almost 2 million metric tons per year; but during that period it added about 1.2 million tons to its reserve stocks. American exports of iron and steel scrap to Japan during the years, 1937–39 (i.e., before the embargo), averaged about 1.8 million tons per year. These estimates are derived mainly from the study of the subject—one of its many excellent ones—made by the United States Strategic Bombing Survey. They correspond roughly with the more detailed figures to be found in Cohen, *op. cit.*, p. 118.

[18] In 1940 the Japanese steel industry used about 7 million metric tons of iron ore. About 5.7 million tons of this were imported, of which about 2 million tons came from Malaya and 1.5 million tons from the Philippines.

the restraints on export to Japan of iron ore which were imposed later) hurt Japan in four ways. First, it compelled her to divert badly needed machines, materials, and men to increase production of iron ore, coking coal, and pig iron plants in areas under its control.[19] Second, it compelled her to draw heavily upon the hoarded stock piles of scrap iron and iron ore.[20] Third, it caused the Japanese steel industry to operate during the next critical year well below capacity.[21] Fourth, it took meaning out of the program to increase the capacity of the steel industry

One other result of the action was important. Japan, thereafter, would be more dependent than before on imported raw materials from China, Korea, and Manchuria—all water-borne. More ships would be needed and all be at the hazard of enemy attack in time of war.

These effects of the American ban were foreseen in the Japanese circles concerned. Among the more calculating they produced a spirit of caution and a wish for time. But few were in the mood to draw what would have been the saving conclusion or dared to do so: that Japan should give up aims that would bring her into war against the United States. The blow shook estimates but did not reform policy. It did not cause Japan to give up the program that had been adopted in July. The embargo failed as a lesson, since it was taken as a challenge. Japan had already engaged herself in a combination with the prime purpose of deterring the United States from bringing its power to bear.

[19] The increase achieved during the war in the production of iron ore and coking coal was remarkable. Thus, iron ore production in Japan proper rose from less than 1 million metric tons in 1940 to 4.4. million tons by 1944. Imports from China (including Hainan) rose from 1.2 million tons in 1940 to 4.8 million in 1942.

[20] The stockpile of scrap iron was about 5.7 million metric tons (over a year's supply) at the beginning of 1940. It was reduced by at least one-fifth before Pearl Harbor. The scrap pile of iron ore (55 per cent), which at its peak (1938–39) was over 4 million metric tons, was drawn on even more heavily. More detailed and precise figures are given in the reports of the United States Strategic Bombing Survey, and in Cohen, op. cit., pp. 48 and 118. But as both these compilers of the record are aware, the source material is hardly reliable enough to impart certainty in regard to the various estimates found for particular dates. The various estimates in the reports of the Cabinet Planning Board (September–October 1941) to Konoye differed from each other and cannot be interpreted with confidence.

[21] The production of ingot steel within Japan proper in 1941 was about 68 per cent of rated capacity.

## CHAPTER 15

# The Making of the Alliance with the Axis: September 1940

THE conclusion of the Tripartite Pact (as this agreement of September 27, 1940, among Japan, Germany, and Italy was called) was a best kept secret. American officials knew there was much chance some pact of the kind would be signed. Was it not plainly implied even in the published version of the Outline of the Basic National Policy adopted by the Imperial Conference on July 26? Were not the three countries already concerting their strategy? But all accounts of what was in the wind lacked convincing detail. None gave actual traces of the negotiation. In short, the project of such an alliance was no surprise to the American government, but its swift realization was.[1]

Of the various warnings received, all came from Tokyo—where the pact was written, even though it was to be signed in Berlin. Our diplomatic missions in Germany and Italy were wholly in the dark.[2] As far back as August 3, Grew had discussed, on the basis of press comment, the prospect of such an alliance. Then, on September 20, he had cabled that according to a reputable source, the Emperor at a three-hour conference on the previous day, in the presence of the entire cabinet and the highest military and naval authorities, had given his sanction to the conclusion of a defensive alliance with Germany.[3]

On the next day, Grew had sent along substantiating reports. But none could be confirmed or given precision. Almost up to the very hour

---

[1] This impression differs from that conveyed by Hull, *op. cit.,* I, 908.

[2] On the day after the signature of the pact, Grew asked the State Department whether it was possible that it had not received any pertinent information from Berlin or Rome or any other source. He said that his reports must have shown how the mission in Tokyo was groping, how it was shooting from the dark into the dark, and how helpful it would have been if it had received at the time even the briefest of clues from elsewhere. The State Department was compelled to inform him that it had not received any information from any other source. Exchange of letters, Hamilton-Grew, September 28–November 2, 1940.

[3] It is unclear to me whether this Liaison Conference of September 19 approved the actual text of the pact between Japan, Germany, and Italy or merely the program and principles that the four chief Ministers had already adopted on September 4. *Far East Mil. Trib.,* Exh. No. 541.

of signature, Grew was not entirely sure an actual accord had been reached. During the few previous months even the most brave and friendly of Japanese had become afraid of contact with the American Embassy.

The protective secrecy served the sponsors of the pact well. It permitted them to complete their work quickly and easily, avoiding such opposition within Japan as did remain. It eliminated the small chance that the United States might create a crisis by threatening war if the alliance were formed.

The pact was short and pregnant.[4] Japan recognized the leadership of Germany and Italy in the establishment of a new order in Europe; and they, in turn, recognized the leadership of Japan in the establishment of a new order in Greater East Asia. Article III then specified:

"Japan, Germany and Italy agree to cooperate in their efforts on the aforesaid lines. They further undertake to assist one another with all political, economic and military means when one of the three Contracting Parties is attacked by a power at present not involved in the European War or in the Sino-Japanese Conflict."

Thus the parties chose to point to the United States, not to name it.

Japan had not managed, alone, to break the broad front of American opposition. Neither had Germany, alone. Together perhaps they could. That was the magnetic hope that drew them together. The conjunction of purpose was tersely stated by Matsuoka at the Imperial Conference, which placed the final seal upon the pact (September 26): "Germany wants to prevent American entry into the war, and Japan wants to avoid a war with the United States."[5]

The Japanese records soon to be surveyed leave no doubt that the main authors of the pact expected it to be an effective servant of these wishes. They were confident that the United States would watch its step and give way rather than fight both Germany and Japan. This belief would have been shaken if they had been present at a talk between Hull and his staff on September 30. According to the notes of one who was: "The Secretary made clear that he had given no commitment to the British or Australians as regards co-operation in the use of the Singapore base or of the American Navy to resist Japanese aggression. He had explained that we must decide our own action in the light of developing circumstances. It was

[4] The text is given on pages 119–120.
[5] *Far East Mil. Trib.*, Exh. No. 550.

plain, however, in his own mind that if Japan did move in that quarter the United States could not afford to see the Singapore base fall into the hands of Japan, exposing Australia and New Zealand. He seemed convinced that nothing could restrain the combined attempt of Japan, Germany, and Italy to extend their power and nothing appease them."

Most Americans responded in the same way to this pact with hated Germany. Contrary to the conceiving hope, the attitude of the United States toward Japan hardened. The pact placed them definitely on opposite sides of the struggle. Hull, during the whole remaining period of peace, labored to dissolve it, but could not. All that followed can be better understood by reviewing the tale of its negotiation, as recorded in the Japanese documents.

## [2]

When an alliance with Germany and Italy was proposed before the war, it will be recalled that the dispute within Japan was interminable. Not so this time.[6] At the very first meeting of the key figures of the Konoye Cabinet it had been decided that Japan should no longer waver between Germany and the democracies of the West. A pact with the Axis was to be sought, to be extended by a non-aggression pact with Russia. The Liaison Conference on July 27 had endorsed the program.[7] The Germans were quickly told of Japan's inclination.

But tactics and terms puzzled. When should Japan sign the pact? What should it ask? What obligations should it accept? About all these points a reserve of caution remained. Not even this cabinet wanted to find itself at war with Britain and the United States. But it learned that Germany would not recognize Japanese desires in the Far East, except in return for definite Japanese aid. Thus, when Matsuoka, on August 2, asked Ott for German sanctions of "its economic great sphere plans," the Ambassador answered that Germany would in return expect "tangible and valuable advantages."[8] At that time the German government still felt no real need for help and no compelling reason to bless Japan's aspirations; if Japan would not pay for what it wanted in the Far East, others would.

The long lectures, which Grew, by direction, was giving Matsuoka

[6] Konoye wrote (in May or June 1945) an extensive account of the negotiation of the pact and the ideas shaping its terms, entitled "Concerning the Tri-Partite Alliance," which is printed as Exh. No. 2735A, *Far East Mil. Trib.* Stahmer, the German negotiator, gave a similarly comprehensive account in his affidavit, *ibid.*, Exh. No. 2744.
[7] *ibid.*, Exh. No. 1310.
[8] Telegram, Ott to Ribbentrop, August 2, 1940, *ibid.*, Exh. No. 622.

during August about Japan's efforts to change the situation in the Far East, merely bored him. He felt the tedium without harvesting the profit.[9] Hull's protests were left for others to read. The Japanese government, absorbed in its schemes and maps, did not worry over either. Whether it would have, had the scrap iron and oil embargoes then been imposed, is a point on which my allowance of conjecture has been spent.

At the end of August, Ribbentrop decided to send to Tokyo one of his close associates, Stahmer, to find out what the Japanese government really wanted and what it was really ready to promise Germany. In advance of his visit, the four chief members of the Konoye Cabinet met to define the answers.[10] Their decision was set down in a policy statement approved at a long meeting (September 4) among Konoye, the Prime Minister, Matsuoka, the Foreign Minister, Tojo, the Minister of War, and Yoshida, the Minister of the Navy. The program adopted on this occasion marks the farthest range to which Japanese dreams of empire reached: September 4, 1940, when the great German bombing squadrons were over London; when a German fleet was being assembled for the invasion of Britain; when the press was telling of the transfer of fifty old destroyers to Britain from the United States, but at the same time warning that this did not mean that the United States would enter the war.

This policy statement, approved by the Four Ministers' Conference of September 4, was the closely followed guidebook in the negotiations with Germany.[11] Being even longer and more tortuous than the usual

[9] To adopt the phrase in which Hawthorne in *The House of Seven Gables* describes the response of Hepzibah's brother to her reading of the "Happy Valley" in *Rasselas*.

[10] The drafting of the proposed pact was begun in Tokyo in early August. The original text was prepared by the Army and Navy, and revised in conference with the Foreign Office. A record of the texts drawn up before and during the negotiations is to be found in Exh. No. 3144, *Far East Mil. Trib.*, a Foreign Office memo prepared by Matsumoto (Shunichi), Technical Adviser to Matsuoka.

[11] This was entitled "Strengthening of the Japan-Germany-Italy Axis." It contained a statement of approval of a "fundamental agreement" between the three countries, and of the principles to govern the negotiation for the alliance, and four appendices of which No. 1, "Terms of Political Understanding forming the Basis for the Strengthening of Japan-Germany-Italy Collaboration," is the most important. *ibid.*, Exh. No. 541.

This statement of policy was one of the most difficult pieces of evidence for the defendants to controvert in the war crimes trials. They argued that nothing in it was of an aggressive character, and that it was only natural for Japan, like every other great power, not to lose sight of the possibility of war. It was said that the document was "never communicated to Germany," which was true. But the main reason seems to have been that the Japanese government did not want the German government to know how far its desires spread.

Of the four participants of this conference of September 4 only one, Tojo, was on trial. Konoye had killed himself; Matsuoka had died before he was tried. Yoshida was not accused.

register of Japanese official decision, no one would want the whole of it to be given. Dissection of a few of its main features will suffice to tell how far Japanese thoughts spread at this time.

The purpose of the agreement, the Four Ministers affirmed, would be to arrange for the cooperation of Japan, Germany, and Italy for a "new order" in Europe and Asia. Germany and Italy were to be asked to recognize and respect the Japanese "sphere of living" in East Asia; while Japan was to recognize and respect the German and Italian "sphere of living" in Europe and Africa. The parties to the accord were to work with one another to establish these spheres by all possible means: political, economic, and, if need be, by force of arms.

The boundaries of the prospective realm of Japanese authority were beyond the horizon: "The sphere to be envisaged in the course of negotiations with Germany and Italy as Japan's Sphere of Living for the construction of a Greater East Asia New Order will comprise: The former German Islands under mandate, French Indo-China and Pacific Islands, Thailand, British Malaya, British Borneo, Dutch East Indies, Burma, Australia, New Zealand, India, etc., with Japan, Manchuria, and China as the backbone." [12]

Not even the Germans were to be let know that Japan's longings ranged so far. In the talks with them, the South Seas region to be named by Japan was to be from Burma eastward, including the Dutch East Indies, and from New Caledonia northward. India might be recognized, for the immediate purposes, as being included in the sphere of living of the Soviet Union.

Just how each of these coveted parts was to be brought within Japan's sphere of living, and what place each would occupy within the whole, the Four Ministers did not specify. But in regard to the Dutch East Indies, one prime object of desire, the ultimate aim was to be concealed. The immediate objective would be "to secure recognition of Japan's position of political and economic predominance in that country."

Special interest attaches to the statements having to do with the possible use of armed force to carry out the aims of the alliance. For later the Japanese government tried to convince the American that the Tripartite Pact left it free to decide for itself whether or not to go to war against us if we got into war with Germany.

[12] As approved by the Liaison Conference on September 19, *ibid.*, Exh. No. 541. An answer of General Tojo's in response to a question on this point indicates the method of drawing the boundaries: Q. "Then both in Europe and Asia the sphere to be included in the New Order decreased or increased with the military situation?" A. "That was about the long and short of it." *ibid.*, Exh. No. 1157C.

"Japan should be resolved," this manual of policy reads, "if need be, to take any action, including recourse to armed force." And more particularly: "Concerning the possible use of armed force against Britain and the United States, Japan will make decisions independently in accordance with the following principles: (1) In the event that the China Incident has nearly been settled, Japan will use armed force by taking as favorable an opportunity, as may be afforded by the situation prevailing at home and abroad. (2) In the event that the China Incident has not been settled, it will be Japan's guiding principle to take action within limits short of war. If, however, diplomatic and foreign conditions take a decidedly favorable turn, or if it is deemed that, irrespective of whether our preparations are complete or not, the development of the international situation permits no further delay, Japan will resort to armed force."

To want, but not to admit; to decide, but still leave open; to promise, but not to set any time or date upon the pledge: these were the traits of this era of Japanese diplomacy. What could be said of Matsuoka at length was said by Hull in brief when he remarked that he was "as crooked as a basket of fishhooks." [13]

The talks with Stahmer began on the 9th of September. They were conducted by Matsuoka at his home in deep secrecy. The Japanese found Stahmer conciliatory. Germany, he explained, did not want Japan at that juncture to join the war against Britain, since it wished to end that war quickly.[14] Japan's help was sought in keeping the United States from entering and prolonging the war. The best way to do this was by an alliance whereby all the partners would be thoroughly prepared to

[13] Though the Japanese seem to have been able to assign him a place in a familiar cast of characters and thus understand him. "Mr. Matsuoka," Shinnosuké Abé wrote, "is neither so coarse nor talks so big as reported, but on the contrary he is very cautious in handling business, taking pleasure in his mental performance or acting as is done by *Kabuki* actors. The theatrical mental performance, or psychological interpretation, as done on the *Kabuki* theatre is intended to capture the fancy and imagination of the audience by acting as if he were an enemy when he is in reality a disguised friend or as if he were a rogue when he is in fact a good man. . . . Now, Mr. Matsuoka has a hobby in his mental performance, or 'abdominal performance,' in theatrical parlance. But he is too good by nature to stand being called a rogue and too talkative to remain silent at being abused as a scoundrel. His mental, or 'abdominal,' performance, therefore, used to be done openly instead of inside." Article on "Admiral Teijiro Toyoda, the New Foreign Minister," in *Contemporary Japan*, August 1941, pp. 1026-27.

[14] A summary of the Matsuoka-Stahmer talks is contained in the memorandum, "Some of the Salient Points in the Informal Conversations between Matsuoka and Stahmer," *Far East Mil. Trib.*, Exh. No. 549. Further information on the German ideas is to be found in Exh. Nos. 550, 552, and 553, and in No. 2774 (Stahmer's affidavit).

meet an emergency should it arise. Such an alliance would be an effective deterrent, especially if it were soon followed by betterment of relations between Japan and the Soviet Union. So ran Stahmer's presentation.

Whether or not this was the whole of the inner German calculation, it made agreement easy. For it provided a ready answer to the main objection made against the alliance; that Japan was not yet in a position to fight a major war. The answer was that Japan was not being asked to do so then, and the alliance would lessen the chance that it would ever have to. Many known figures in Japan, especially in the Navy and about the court, were worried about the liaison despite German victories. Among them, the Emperor. When on September 14 Matsuoka, in company with the chiefs of the Army and Navy staff, reported on the progress made in the talks with Stahmer, Kido noted that he showed gloom rather than pleasure.[15]

To Konoye, himself, the Emperor said on this day or shortly afterwards: "I believe that the signing of the German military alliance cannot be helped in the present situation. If there are no other means of dealing with the United States it may be the only solution. But just what is the Navy going to do in case of war with the United States? I am very concerned over what would happen if Japan is defeated. If that should happen I wonder if the Prime Minister would share the pains and toil with me."

Konoye replied by referring to Prince Ito's answer to the Emperor (Meiji) at the start of the war with Russia, "I would give up all my decorations and titles and go out on the battlefield and die alone." [16]

According to Konoye's account, when he told of this talk at the cabinet council, Matsuoka suddenly began to cry aloud in company with other politicians present. It was Matsuoka who most longed for and arranged the alliance; who, along with Tojo, wrested consent from the doubtful. He was persuasive, in part, because he promised peace, not war, dispelling fears with the answer that by this pact Japan was choosing the best way to avoid war with the United States. He was voluble in his promise to reserve Japan's freedom to decide its obligations in the "remote" chance that the United States entered the war.

Konoye adopted this view as his own.[17] Then he joined Matsuoka in

---

[15] "Kido's Diary," entries for September 14 and 15.

[16] As told in the "Saionji-Harada Memoirs."

[17] The "Saionji-Harada Memoirs" quote him as saying, "In regard to the American problem, if Wilkie [sic] should become President, Castle will probably become Secretary of State. A German-Japanese treaty is to be concluded for peaceful purposes; that is the

soothing the Emperor's qualms. The Emperor accepted the verdict. The Navy was last to consent. Then at once it asked for many more ships and planes. Apparently it was not wholly convinced by Matsuoka's assurances.

By September 16 the opposition was under control, though the Navy still did not like the pact. Then the official stamps were brought forth and placed against the ink. A Liaison Conference on that same day decided that "the time is now ripe to start quickly talks to strengthen the Axis." The terms which had been adopted at the Four Ministers' Conference of September 4 were endorsed without meaningful change. They were re-endorsed in another Liaison Conference in the Imperial Presence on the 19th. It was of this meeting that Grew learned. But only that an alliance with the Axis had been resolved upon; not of its text or that it was all but settled and would very soon be signed.

Matsuoka now had the fullest authority to convert the concert of minds into a conspiracy. The good news reached Berlin quickly for on the 19th (Rome time), Ciano wrote in his diary, "In the car Ribbentrop speaks at once of the surprise in his bag: a military alliance with Japan, to be signed within the next few days at Berlin." Ribbentrop said also that the alliance would have a double edge—against the Soviet Union and against the United States.[18]

A few days were enough. The date for signature was set for the 27th (Tokyo time). On the 25th Ribbentrop instructed the German Chargé d'Affaires to call on Molotov on the next day and inform him of the happy event. He was instructed to explain that "this alliance, . . . is directed exclusively against American warmongers. To be sure, this is, as usual, not expressly stated in the treaty, but can be unmistakably inferred from its terms." And further to point out that the three treaty powers are completely agreed that their alliance should in no way affect the relationship each of them has with the Soviet Union—as proven by a special article (Article V) of the treaty.[19]

---

object. There is no other way." I have not seen any evidence for a note that Grew entered in his diary, "We know that Konoye was against it [The Tri-Partite Pact] and even threatened resignation." Entry for October 1940.

[18] Mussolini in agreement with the plan for an alliance, said it would paralyze American action; that it must be remembered that Americans were very much afraid of Japan and of its Fleet, in particular. (Ciano memo of talk between Mussolini and Ribbentrop, September 19, 1940.)

[19] Message (September 25, Berlin to Moscow) printed in *Nazi-Soviet Relations*, pp. 195–96. Article V is given on p. 120.

Ribbentrop gave the same assurances to the Soviet Ambassador in Berlin on September 28. *Military Tribunal IV, . . . Final Brief . . . against Ernst von Weizsaecker . . .* (Nuernberg, 1948), Document No. NG-3074.

On the 26th (Tokyo time) the text of the pact was discussed in day and night sessions of the Privy Council at which the leading members of the civil government and military forces were present.[20] The government was able to inform the gathering that "The Emperor himself also with an unusual resolve has granted us his gracious words." An Imperial Rescript was to be issued—the first since Japan withdrew from the League of Nations.

The formality of question and answer at this meeting was ruffled by two anxieties—about the American Navy and the exhaustion of Japan's oil supply.

About the first, the Navy Minister (Oikawa had replaced Yoshida) expressed only qualified confidence: "Preparations of our ships for battle have already been completed. . . . For the time being, if we presume that the United States will challenge us to a short and decisive war, I have full confidence of victory. With regard to future plans, I wish to improve the quality of our Navy and expand our armaments as much as possible."

About the second, oil, no one offered a sure solution. It was realized that the United States might well express its dislike of the treaty by imposing new restrictions on exports to Japan—perhaps on oil. This was the risk assumed; by some because they thought the United States would not dare to be so severe, by others because they trusted that Japan would eke out its supply one way or another even without American oil, by still others because they already accepted the idea of war with the United States. The Minister of the Navy stated that its own reserves would last for quite a while, but if the war was prolonged the supply would have to be replenished. Tojo, Minister of War, agreed that reserves would not be enough for a long war. But he viewed this fact not as a reason for hesitation but as a problem to be solved in the course of the war if it came. The President of the Planning Board, Hoshino, said that despite the large stocks there would be trouble if the war were long. His vague references to synthetic production and overseas sources of supply were no solution. All the answers pointed to the oil of the Indies as a prime object of attention before war, or in war.

These answers did not put all minds to rest. The exponents of the alliance could not convince everyone it was safe. But they could and did reassert that it would improve the chance of avoiding a crisis with the

---

[20] The minutes of the meeting are given in the *Far East Mil. Trib.*, Exh. No. 552; the text of the resolution approved, in Exh. No. 541; an outline of the proceedings as written up in the Foreign Office, in Exh. No. 1030.

United States. As expounded by Matsuoka: "Our Empire should at this time ally itself with Germany and Italy, and adjust its relations with the Soviet Union, to bring about an international situation favorable to us, and thereby do our utmost to avoid the outbreak of war between Japan and America." Or as the thought was jointly put to the gathering by Konoye, Matsuoka and Tojo, "As to whether we shall be able to avert a crisis by courting America, such idea is wrong. In order to avoid a crisis, we must take a firm stand and nothing else. By this we will prevent an unfortunate situation from arising."

In words, tinctured with misgivings, the Privy Council added its endorsement to the others. Then after the final ritual before the throne, the waiting Ambassador at Berlin, Kurusu, was told to sign. Ciano has left behind a note about the occasion:

"The pact is signed. The signature takes place more or less like that of the Pact of Steel. But the atmosphere is cooler. Even the Berlin street crowd, a comparatively small one, composed mostly of school children, cheers with regularity but without conviction. Japan is far away. Its help is doubtful. One thing alone is certain: that the war will be long." [21]

In Japan the Imperial Rescript awed away all further questions. The Emperor said: "We earnestly wish that war be ended and peace be restored as quickly as possible." [22] Except in the barracks and the halls of the patriotic societies, there was no enthusiasm, no parades carrying flags and lanterns and portraits of heroes. On the morrow the newspaper, *Hocho,* felt constrained to comment, "The Tripartite Pact is a stirring march for Japan, not an elegy."

## [3]

The main articles of the pact were brief, compressing control of continents into short clauses: [23]

*Article I:* Japan recognizes and respects the leadership of Germany and Italy in the establishment of a new order in Europe.

*Article II:* Germany and Italy recognize and respect the leadership of Japan in the establishment of a new order in Greater East Asia.

*Article III:* Japan, Germany and Italy agree to cooperate in their efforts on the aforesaid lines. They further undertake to assist one another with all political, economic and military means when one of the three Contracting Parties is

[21] Ciano, *op. cit.,* entry for September 27, 1940.
[22] Text of the Rescript is to be found in *Far East Mil. Trib.,* Exh. No. 554.
[23] The English version may be read with unusual confidence because the text was first drafted in English and then translated into Japanese and German. This is the text as printed in *Foreign Relations: Japan,* II, 165–66.

attacked by a power at present not involved in the European War or in the Sino-Japanese Conflict.

*Article V:* Japan, Germany and Italy affirm that the aforesaid terms do not in any way affect the political status which exists at present as between each of the three Contracting Parties and Soviet Russia.

The Japanese and German governments had a rather explicit understanding as to the meaning of these brief sentences. But this was secret, and the American government had to grope for it. Searchers had to pierce through the fog of vague language and unreliable Japanese avowals. To three questions, in particular, answers were wanted. What was the nature of the "new order" recognized in the pact? What were the limits of "Greater East Asia," the Japanese sphere? Was Japan obligated to enter if war came between the United States and Germany? The Japanese records tell us something more than the American government could know then, but not all.

As for the first of these questions (the nature of the "new order"), even now the interpreter is left to dance with language in fancy dress. The Japanese intended to have it mean, at the least, effective political influence and control of chosen economic chances. These were to be got and kept in whatever way and form was found most practical for each country brought within the Japanese sphere.

As for the second question (the boundaries of the realm over which Japan had been recognized as leader), there is one definite description besides the extract already cited. The geography of the Greater Japanese Empire was to be like a chrysanthemum. At the Privy Council meeting of September 26, Matsuoka was candid. Asked about the sphere of the term, "Greater East Asia," he answered, "I mean the area which includes French Indo-China, Thailand, Burma, the Straits Settlements, and the Oceanic group comprising the Dutch East Indies, New Guinea, New Caledonia, etc. Regarding this we have made an understanding that this sphere could be automatically broadened in the course of time. This point is already stated in the minutes of the treaty negotiations." [24]

The word, "etc.," should be proof that Matsuoka was a man who could not be bothered by details. A comment which the last of the surviving Elder Statesmen, Prince Saionji, made to his secretary about this time has not lost point. Harada said to him: "there are some who say Matsuoka must be insane . . ." To which Saionji spoke, "It will improve him if he becomes insane."

[24] Minutes of the Meeting of the Investigation Committee of the Privy Council, September 26, 1940, *Far East Mil. Trib.*, Exh. No. 552.

But it is important to bear in mind that these were the ideas of September 1940. Then they defined a zone that Japan expected would soon fall in any strong outstretched hand. As British resistance grew, Japanese ideas shrunk and a later date was placed upon them. There is no place on Matsuoka's list over which Japanese soldiers did not walk after 1941, except New Caledonia.

As for the third question (the nature of Japan's obligation in the event that the United States and Germany went to war), there is also a helpful record. Ambassador Ott, presumably at Japanese request, affirmed in a letter to Matsuoka, bearing the same date as the pact, that the question of whether or not any of the three contracting parties had been attacked within the meaning of Article III was to be settled by consultation among them.[25]

When quizzed about the nature of the obligations of Article III, at the meeting of the Privy Council on September 26, Matsuoka was airy and evasive. He came nearest to precision when asked:

"In the event of the worse situation, will Japan be able to choose the time and place to let the Japanese Navy participate in the war?"

He replied that this opinion was correct.

Konoye and Matsuoka were not to be able to get away from this question in their talks with Hull during 1941. Their doctored answers implied that the pledge to join Germany in a war against the United States was *not conclusive*. But they refused *to cancel* whatever obligation did exist. They asked the American government to let the matter be settled in the future in a spirit of mutual trust. Events were to be permitted to decide whether Japan would turn out to be a hostile friend or a friendly enemy.

---

[25] This is one of the three letters written by Ott interpreting various points in the Pact. All are dated September 27, 1940, but were drafted earlier. *ibid.*, Exh. Nos. 555B and 555C.

## CHAPTER 16

# We Draw Closer to Britain

SECRETARY HULL took quick care to dispel any wisps of belief that the pact was a surprise, or that it would deflect American policy. After talking with the President, he made a statement to the press, which centered on the point that "the reported agreement of alliance does not, in the view of the Government of the United States, substantially alter a situation which has existed for several years." [1]

This was a permissible way of making the best of bad news. But it hid subdued regret. Despite the signs that the Konoye Cabinet wanted German easement for its ends, hope had lingered that no firm liaison would be formed. In the recesses of thought, it was known that the pact marked a dark turn in the prospect. War with Japan came plainly into sight. As before, the clash might come over Japan's marauding advances in the Pacific; but from then on it might also come in the course of our support of Britain. We were in the struggle against Germany—the response to the destroyer-base deal showed—to the end. Japan had set itself against us in a cause far closer to American hearts than the fate of China. [2]

[1] An illuminating, though undocumented account of the President's impression of the meaning of the pact, and of the course of his decision that it should not modify the policy of placing first stress on the struggle against Germany, is to be found in *How War Came* (New York, 1942), by Forrest Davis and Ernest K. Lindley.

[2] On October 14 one of the President's secretaries sent him a report on the turn of American opinion after the Tripartite Pact, made by the Princeton Public Opinion Research Project (using the Gallup facilities).

To the question, "Do you think the United States should let Japan get control of China, or do you think the United States should risk a war with Japan to prevent it from doing so?" the answers recorded (in percentages) were:

|                  | July 20, 1490 | September 30, 1940 |
|------------------|:-------------:|:------------------:|
| Let Japan control | 47           | 32                 |
| Risk war          | 12           | 39                 |
| Other             | 16           | 16                 |
| No opinion        | 25           | 23                 |

To the question, "Do you approve Roosevelt's embargo on scrap iron?" 88 per cent were in the affirmative on the later date. And to the question, "Should the United States take steps to keep Japan from becoming more powerful even if this means risking war?" 57 per cent of the answers were reported to be "Yes."

The validity of this survey was not tested by a vote on the issues.

The change was expressed in the trend of American policy during the next few months—in a direction quite the opposite to that which Konoye, Matsuoka, and Tojo had predicted the United States would take. The American government not only began to plan those measures of restraint of trade which the Japanese government had foreseen. It also began to consider, for the first time, the possible use of armed force in the distant reaches of the Southwest Pacific. In both thought and deed we drew closer to the British Empire.

On the day after his mild public statement Hull told the President that he thought that the alliance meant that Germany and Japan might quickly make a move that would force us into war. Both the State Department and the British Foreign Office, it should be noted, were almost sure that the published text of the alliance did not tell all; that there was a secret accord giving Japan free rein in Indo-China and the Indies. In substance this idea was correct. In the talks that crowded the next few weeks (October 1–15) the State Department came into the open; it let its basic belief be known, that nothing was likely now either to appease or restrain the Axis group, and that the United States could not afford to permit Japan to seize either the Indies or Singapore.

Among Hull's advisers, Hornbeck and Norman Davis were keen for some further use at once of our economic power as a deterrent. Hornbeck was sure that Japan could not and would not strike back. But the members of the Far Eastern Division, particularly Hamilton, advised otherwise—unless we were prepared to go to war. And as before, the issue flared up between Hull and his colleagues (Morgenthau, Stimson, and Ickes). They wanted at once to lower the grades of the permissible exports of oil and lesson the amounts. Morgenthau, in fact, refused clearance to a tanker which had 50,000 barrels of 86.9 octane gasoline in its holds.

Hull still edged away from this decision. Then, as to the end, he lacked faith in this kind of compulsion. He felt a need to go into the situation more thoroughly by talking with the British and the Army and Navy, and also by further parleying with the Japanese. While Knox seemed to favor the use of pressure, the admirals from Stark down were saying that the fleet was not ready to fight Japan. The Japanese government was warning us (of that more shortly) that further refusals to send them vital products would make future relations "unpredictable." The Japanese mission in Batavia was demanding more and more oil of the Indies, and muttering threats of what would happen if it were refused. The Dutch were still asking the State Department to refrain from any measure that would make their plight worse and danger greater. Torn this way and that, Hull went to the President; and the President turned upon the advocates of action, telling them that he and Hull—not they—were handling the foreign policy of the United States.[3]

The dissenters continued to think that the fueling of the very forces we might have to fight was foolish and the child of excessive caution. Stimson tried to persuade the President that any risk that Japan would enter the Indies to get oil could be met by sending a flying squadron of American warships to the point of danger. But the President promised only to study the maps.[4] The admirals, particularly Stark, Chief of Naval Operations, and Richardson, Commander in Chief of the United States Fleet, were opposed to such naval display.[5] The tactics of Theodore Roosevelt—who sent the fleet around the world in 1908 to impress Japan —were out of date.

But the Japanese government did not make it easier to maintain this restraint. Taking full advantage of the interim, it sought all the high-grade California crude and fuel oil for which tankers could be found. It prowled about for oil drilling equipment, a great variety of machine tools for armaments, excess tonnage of copper and lead, and iron and steel products of many kinds. Of some of these items, particularly the metals and iron and steel products, the defense agencies wanted none to be sent.

One other reason for looking before leaping should be mentioned—our still lagging production of everything needed for war. Willkie, during these weeks before election, was reproaching the Administration for the slow start. Lindbergh was using it as the basis of his pleas for isolation. Some visitors at the White House left with a sense that the President was unduly complacent about our progress in the production of weapons. He seemed unwilling to make hard demands of the country. The output of automobiles for civilian use was still at a record rate, while that of tanks was very small.

The country was not ready to make or meet an enemy. Most Ameri-

---

[3] The matter was argued out in the cabinet meeting of October 4—in which session Stimson found the President most serious and all agreed it was better to act than to talk (Stimson diary, entry for October 4, 1940). But Morgenthau thought the advocates of action were suppressed (Morgenthau diary, entry for October 4, 1940).

The President also appears to have told Morgenthau to permit the loaded tanker to sail. This particular argument ended when the ship struck the rocks or some other obstacle which put a hole in its bottom and caused it to be beached (*ibid.*, entry for October 10, 1940).

[4] Stimson diary, entry for October 8, 1940.

[5] *ibid.*, entry for October 12, 1940.

cans were still spending their days slackly, insulated from calls upon their energies, fortunes, or lives. Until they were brought to the cold hard drill ground only a foolish diplomacy would have hastened a crisis. But only a negligent diplomacy would have failed to get ready for one, if the United States intended to hold fast to the course it was on.

## [2]

Foot by foot, but with guard always up, the government began to plan for combined resistance against Japan in the Far East. We walked out with Britain but would not admit an engagement, nor permit our arm to be taken. At each step it was ritually repeated that no promise was being given as to what the United States might do if Japan attacked lands under the British or Dutch flags. Time and again bids were refused to go faster, further, and more openly. Now that the invasion season was passing and towns and factories still standing, the British government laid aside thoughts of conciliating Japan. Australia also grew calmer. Both began to line up with our sterner policy. But as they did so, they became all the more eager for assurances that we would stand by them if trouble came.

In the first talk between Hull and Lothian on the morrow of the Tripartite Pact, the Secretary revealed his enlivened wish for association by his questions, not his answers. Formerly he had turned aside proposals for conferences in regard to unified defense of the Pacific. He had said (as last expressed to Lothian on September 16) that Japan was assuming anyhow that all such steps were probable on short notice, whether or not they had actually been consummated. "I let," his memo of that talk had ended, "the matter rest there for the present." But now he asked Lothian to find out—since the Ambassador said he did not know—to what extent Britain and the Dominions were providing Japan with war materials. He also asked what forces the British Empire and the Dutch had in the Pacific, and whether they had discussed the pooling of them.

When, however, Lothian sought Hull's opinion as to whether Britain would be well advised to reopen the Burma Road, the Secretary was careful in his answer. He said merely that the United States government had been opposed to the closing of it, and that he doubted whether British decision one way or the other would change Japan's plans. Lothian agreed. Shortly afterwards Churchill announced in the House of Commons that the Burma Road would be reopened.[6] He also transferred most of the British ships stationed in the Far East to the Mediterranean, where they at once began to count.

The Secretaries of War and the Navy were consulted more seriously than before. Stimson's opinion was set down in a memorandum of October 2: "[Japan] has also historically shown that when the United States indicates by clear language and bold actions that she intends to carry out a clear and affirmative policy in the Far East, Japan will yield to that policy even though it conflicts with her own Asiatic policy and conceived interests." [7] As he was later to record, "The theory of that memorandum was not borne out by events."

On October 5 Lothian returned, along with the Australian Minister, to give the answers to the questions which Hull had put. When the visitors improved their replies by urging a conference in London among the British, Dutch, Australian, and American governments, including naval experts, Hull found the proposal too forward. He said that he thought it better for the British government merely to get in touch with the experts of these countries rather than have a conference. To make himself quite clear, he repeated, as recorded in his memo of this talk, "that our policy [was one] of aiding Britain all we could, while at the same time following the Far Eastern situation by a succession of words and acts, short of intending to become engaged in war in the East."

The proposal was altered to suit. On the 7th, Lothian returned to the subject. He asked whether the United States would take part in a conference of experts or others to consider, first, the size of the defense forces of those countries of the South Seas threatened by Japan; and, second, the ways in which a common defense against possible Japanese invasion could most effectively be presented without entering into any commitments. This time Hull was more responsive. He agreed that some kind of talks for the purposes of mutual instruction should be started as soon as possible.[8]

Knox on October 10, after talking with the President, asked Admiral

[6] Churchill informed the President of this decision on October 4. At the same time he urged the President to consider the dispatch of American naval units, including battleships, to reinforce the Asiatic Fleet and repeated the offer of Singapore as a base for American naval forces.

[7] Henry L. Stimson and McGeorge Bundy, *On Active Service in Peace and War* (New York, 1948), p. 385.

[8] On October 7 the British Chiefs of Staffs—taking Lothian's reports of the day before as reference—submitted to Churchill a memorandum outlining possible procedure, program and agenda for these talks. They were approved by Churchill and the War Cabinet. The telegram which instructed Lothian to present these plans to us crossed in transmission Lothian's telegram to London reporting on his talk with Hull on the 7th.

Stark and Admiral Richardson to draw up a plan to carry out counter measures against Japan, should it strike because of the reopening of the Burma Road. The President seemed to have been at this time playing in his mind a whole battery of measures: the reinforcement of the Asiatic Fleet, a complete trade embargo, and various patrols from Honolulu westward.[9] Over any and all of these, Richardson and Stark were uneasy.

And Hull had another brief lapse of extreme caution in regard to staff talks in Washington. He veered off the idea of starting them before the Presidential elections (November 5). Instead he urged that the British and Dutch proceed to examine the problems of cooperation in defense against a Japanese attack in the Far East, and then discuss the conclusions with the Special Naval Observer we had in London—Admiral Ghormley.

The British again altered their program and schedule to meet our wishes. On the 16th Lothian submitted another revision of the ideas as to how the talks might best be carried forward. The British commanders in the Far East and representatives from Australia, New Zealand, India, and Burma were to confer, and ask the Dutch to join them. At the same time Admiral Ghormley would be going over the ground with the British authorities. Thereafter the British planners might come to Washington to go on with the talks with us. In putting forward these ideas the British government observed "there is of course no suggestion of any kind of political commitment arising at the present stage and any conversations which take place must be purely hypothetical."[10]

While waiting to see the outcome of the election, the President and Hull reserved final approval of this program. But even before they

[9] Admiral Richardson so recalled Knox as stating, Testimony, *Pearl Harbor Attack*, Part 1, pp. 305–8, 317–20.

The Admiral was in Washington at the time and tried to persuade the President to return the fleet to the West Coast of the United States without success. He testified, also as follows:

"Later I asked the President if we were going to enter the war. He replied that if the Japanese attacked Thailand, or the Kra Peninsula, or the Dutch East Indies we would not enter the war, that if they even attacked the Philippines he doubted whether we would enter the war, but that they could not always avoid making mistakes and that as the war continued and the area of operations expanded sooner or later they would make a mistake and we would enter the war." *ibid.*, Part 1, p. 266.

Admiral William D. Leahy, who was present at this luncheon on October 8 did not recall any such statement by the President. *ibid.*, Part 1, p. 356.

[10] Memo transmitted by British Embassy to Welles, October 16, 1940. On one occasion, probably earlier, the State Department may have handed back to Lothian a memorandum about these staff talks, stating it would rather not have formal proposals in writing until after the election. The episode is mentioned in a British cable (of October 24) in Morgenthau's diary—Book 324, pp. 246–48—but I found no trace of it in the State Department files.

did so, American and British staff officers in London and Singapore were exchanging information and ideas of strategic cooperation.[11] While in Washington Stark and Marshall set their staffs to work upon a new estimate of American policy in the world and the new strategy for which it called. The studies then begun turned out to have great propulsive force. For their main conclusion ranged the Army and Navy firmly behind the judgments that the United States should not (must not) let Britain fall or Japan extend its conquests. But this view and the new supporting strategic concepts were not set down with authority or put before the President until after the elections.[12]

Thus, in shadow rather than open view, the American and British governments began to draw plans for a common front of resistance in the Pacific. In one way or another the Japanese government seems to have sensed what was under way. By the end of October the Japanese press was commenting angrily on the signs of joint activity. The word "encirclement" became official.

The speeches of the President in the weeks before election were rousing declarations that the country was in danger, and appeals to Americans to defend their freedom and security. They were defiant affirmations of our policy of support for Britain; as when at Dayton on October 12, he said, "No combination of dictator countries of Europe and Asia will stop the help we are giving to almost the last free people now fighting to hold them at bay." But he continued to deny the intention of taking any measures which would lead to the engagement of American forces in the fighting abroad. Or he was so understood by most.

[11] Admiral Ghormley had in fact begun to discuss these matters. In response to a request for instructions, Admiral Stark wrote him on October 17: "Your dispatch just received. Get in on any and all staff conversations you can—go as far as you like in discussions—with the full understanding you are expressing only your own views as what best to do—'if and when'—but such must not be understood to commit your government in any manner or degree whatsoever." Connected discussions were going on in Washington between Admirals Stark and Turner, and Captain Clarke, the Admiralty Plans Officer.

On or about October 23 arrangements were made to send Commander Thomas, U.S.N., to Singapore to discuss with the British naval strategy in the Far East, and to have an officer of the staff of the British naval commander in the Far East go to Manila later for the same purpose. Thomas was followed in November by Captain Purnell, who carried instructions from Admiral Stark. No written document resulted from any of these preliminary conversations.

[12] Stark approved the first draft of the plan prepared by the War Plans Division on November 5. Marshall thought that it committed the United States too far and too thoroughly. It was revised and on November 12 Marshall agreed with it. It was put before the President on the same day.

[3]

Matsuoka was, during this autumn interim, trying to convince the American government that its view of many things was wrong; that the Konoye Cabinet did not intend to submit to the dictation of the Army; that the Tripartite Pact was defensive and not directed against the United States; that the New Order was only a plan for economic expansion in which other nations would share equally. At the conclusion of a long talk (October 5) which Grew found hard to chronicle because of the Minister's volubility, he made a plea that Grew should urge the American government not to impose further embargoes. "They would not seriously handicap us," he said, "but they would intensely anger the Japanese people."

Three days later (October 8) Hull was given two notes, one called "formal," the other "informal." [13] In the formal one the Japanese government merely stated that our control of iron and steel scrap "cannot fail to be regarded as directed against Japan, and, as such, to be an unfriendly act." In the informal one, it observed that the unequal features of our control policy had "created a widespread impression in Japan that it was motivated by a desire to bring pressure upon her." The conclusion was intended to scare—stating that if our bans were carried further "future relations between Japan and the United States will be unpredictable." [14]

Hull, as has been seen, did not scoff at these warnings; they were, he told his colleagues, to be taken seriously. But he rejected both the protest and argument with lively words. The Japanese Ambassador was told that it was astonishing that a government with a record such as that of the Japanese should complain about discrimination, or feel entitled to call our defense measures unfriendly. Certainly, he asserted, the United States was not called upon to provide the means for Japanese acts of force and aggression.[15]

For matters in the Far East had not stood still while the American government, in ways just told, strove to adjust its policies to the Tri-

---

[13] At the same time (October 9, Tokyo time) the Vice-Minister for Foreign Affairs, at Matsuoka's behest, called Grew urgently back from the country to Tokyo to give him the same message regarding the effect of further sanctions upon future Japanese actions.

[14] The text of these notes and Hull's memo of this talk is printed in *Foreign Relations: Japan*, II, 224, *et seq.*

[15] The formal note of reply (October 23) was no less definite, though not as pointed. It merely said it saw no warrant for Japan's questioning of actions that we judged necessary for national defense—under international circumstances not of our own making. *ibid.*, II, 229.

partite Pact. As in a long paper chase, the trail of news gave guidance; it showed Japan on the move but not yet in the clear.

The entry into North Indo-China was turning into an occupation. Mention was being made of the Japanese wish for the use of Camranh Bay, further south, as an advance naval base. Thailand was being encouraged to press its claims against Indo-China.

Chiang Kai-shek was sending anxious messages telling of his difficulties in sustaining the war against both Communism and the Japanese, and asking positive American action. Nelson Johnson, the American Ambassador in China, was endorsing this request, stating bluntly that "all aid short of war was not enough." [16]

In the Indies, new trouble seemed in the making. The local government refused to be a broker between the Japanese buyer and the oil companies. Secretly guided, the companies dallied with the unwelcome customer. They offered about half of what was asked; and in that half there was to be very little aviation gasoline. The contract was to be for six months only. The Japanese government showed quick and sharp resentment against these terms. On October 22, the Chief of the Japanese Mission, Kobayashi, sailed for home, to sulk or plot, no one knew. According to the tales that reached Washington, he had tried to win at the last by stressing the political aspects of this oil question, and he attributed his defeat to our influence. The Dutch were not swayed that easily. But it is true that Washington had been telling them that acceptance of excessive demands would not buy safety against attack. And Washington had tutored the oil companies.

This was not the only rejected demand. Hardly less important in Japan's quest was the wish for rights to seek and develop oil in many parts of the Indies. In one of the early instructions Mukai, the top Japanese negotiator on oil, was told, "You must emphasize the acquisition of oil fields . . . . which is our main purpose." [17] In a note of October 29 the Japanese delegation defined their wishes; they wanted to be allowed to develop large areas in Borneo, Celebes, Dutch New Guinea, the Arroe Archipelago and Schouten Archipelago.[18] The Indies government was asked to acknowledge the whole of these sections as Japan's sphere of interest and to aid Japan's operations in them. It suspected that the selection was not guided entirely by hopes of finding oil. The

[16] Telegram, Johnson to Hull, October 20, 1940.
[17] *Far East Mil. Trib.*, Exh. No. 1314.
[18] The smallest of these was about 618 square miles, the largest nearly 35,000. The Japanese also asked that the government of the Indies sell part of the shares it owned in a large oil company to Japanese interests.

since read papers of the Japanese show there was some cause for these suspicions. In telling Matsuoka the reasons for demanding such extensive exploration rights, the delegation explained that its idea was to secure a chance to introduce into the areas planes and plain clothes troops, thus making them into strategic bases.[19] This may have been only a notion of the delegation (it contained military members), not sanctioned by the cabinet. Anyhow, the Indies government referred these and connected requests to the Mining Department for study, and refused to hurry the study.

Pushing, for a moment, ahead of the rest of the story, events in the Indies may be followed a little further. Unable to get more oil, but eager to begin to get even this much, the Japanese on November 12 signed an agreement with the oil companies. They accepted what was offered—about half of what had been asked.[20] The contract was valid for six months only and the Indies government did not guarantee the deliveries. The requests for concessions were unanswered. The discussion of other raw materials was in suspense. By the middle of November it began to appear that the Japanese government was not only balked but so undecided that the delegates were without instructions.

The Indies were sending, and would continue to send, greater amounts of raw materials to Japan than ever before—of oil, rubber, tin, bauxite, and other products.[21] But how far the promises gained fell short of Japan's hopes is shown by the record of the plans approved by the cabinet on October 25.[22] This is a diagram of the economic tendrils by which Japan hoped to embrace the Indies within Greater East Asia. All rights or interests of other foreign countries in the Indies likely to obstruct the expansion of the Japanese activities were to be ousted. Japan was to obtain (1) guiding control over the exchange and trade policies of the Indies (2) special place in the coastal trades (3) an influential say in the operation of the ports, submarine cables, inland communications, and the air services. If necessary, it was to lease or purchase suitable islands and territories. All these wishes were blocked by the stand of the Dutch.

Of this detailed diagram of desire, the State Department knew noth-

[19] *ibid.*, Exh. No. 1316.

[20] About 1.8 million metric tons instead of the 3.1–3.7 demanded by Japan.

[21] During 1940 the monthly average of exports to Japan of rubber was 2,410 metric tons, as compared with 1,812 tons in 1939; of bauxite 18,000 tons, as compared with 14,000; of tin 407, as compared with 93; of copra 1,610, as compared with 119; of nickel ore 5,000, as compared with 1,000; of scrap iron 5,600, as compared with 3,900.

[22] *Far East Mil. Trib.*, Exh. No. 1317. Document entitled "Measures for the Economic Development of the Netherlands East Indies." October 25, 1940.

ing at the time. But the cabled comment of Walter A. Foote, the American Consul General in Batavia, seemed to mark the situation well: "If the play is finished, the Japanese have lost face to an almost unbearable degree. If it is not finished, serious danger lies ahead."

The State Department was sure the play was not over. But the pause was very welcome. There would be more time. Time to show that Germany would not win, time to get ready. And now, the elections at home being past, the American government put time to fuller use.

## CHAPTER 17

# After Our Elections:
## Steps towards a Concerted Program

NOVEMBER 1940; the Roosevelt administration was safely confirmed in power. It could properly construe the election result as approval of its opposition to the Axis and its support of Britain short of war. But, because of the terms in which he had expounded these policies during the campaign, the President was obliged still to move warily and on the slant. The words spoken during the election contest lived on to complicate and confine decision for the times ahead.

Americans had been told that they need not take part in the battles then being fought in Europe and Asia and that the government would not cause them to do so.[1] They had been urged to provide weapons and resources to fend off the danger of having to go to war. British resistance, the expressed thought ran, was giving us time to become so strong that no country, or group of countries, would dare attack us. While if the Axis won, the United States would become exposed to its fury and forced to fight near or within our own land. This was a correct judgment of the meaning to us of the wars in Europe and Asia. It was a well founded basis for the program sponsored by the government and for the

---

[1] The most unguarded of these statements, amounting to a promise, was made by the President in a speech in Boston on October 30 when he said:

"And while I am talking to you mothers and fathers, I give you one more assurance.

"I have said this before, but I shall say it again and again and again:

"Your boys are not going to be sent into any foreign wars.

"They are going into training to form a force so strong that, by its very existence, it will keep the threat of war far away from our shores.

"The purpose of our defense is defense."

It can, of course, be well argued, that the question of what is or is not a "foreign war" is not to be learned from a map alone. But the manner in which it was used during the campaign seemed to give it a simple meaning of wars fought in and by foreign countries. The term was, unless I am mistaken, taken over from the opponents of intervention. A cousinly term was effectively used by Charles A. Beard in the title of a virulent article that he published in *Harper's Magazine* for September 1939, "Giddy Minds and Foreign Quarrels."

Willkie spoke in the same strain as Roosevelt; in fact he set the pace in providing assurance that the United States need not and should not enter the war. The isolationists were far more extreme, denouncing any and all acts of intervention.

acceptance of the connected risks. But it left the President open to a charge of blunder or bad faith if the United States found itself at war.

The government avoided all actions which could not be construed as defensive. It continued—and it was no easy thing to do—to refuse to enter into any accord which carried an obligation to go to war. But it shaped our policies in conference with other governments and fitted its action to theirs. We were about to form a common front against Japan without admitting it or promising to maintain it by force.

Before leaving the subject, a comment may be added about the information given the American people during the months after the election —the winter of 1940-41. Some things that were done were wholly told, some vaguely told, and a few, such as naval talks and movements, were hardly told at all. The President's utterances of this period did not provide all the explanatory knowledge that could have been wanted to follow and judge American policy in action. For they were not systematic statements of the situation facing the United States and the choice before it. They were emotional appeals to the American people to hurry along their military preparations and to stand firm and hard against the Axis. They were written as such, not by essayists but by political advisers and dramatists. They were pin-pointed explosives.[2] They were exertions of leadership in behalf of measures that were secretly in the making, or rather in the taking.

[2]

The American government was not left alone to find its way. The struggling opponents of the Axis were in dire need of our greater help.

In China, Japan was making a final effort to bring the war to an end. Air bombing had failed to subdue the Chinese government, or to end the resistance in the field. Now German diplomacy was being put to use. In Chungking, in early November, the German Ambassador was trying to persuade Chiang Kai-shek that the last chance had come for him to make peace with Japan before the war in Europe ended; and that once it did, all help from Britain and the United States would end. Germany would, he promised, guarantee the faithful observance by Japan of the peace terms arranged. Ribbentrop spoke in the same sense

---

[2] To adopt a description used by Robert E. Sherwood—*Roosevelt and Hopkins* (New York, 1948), p. 184—who writes that Willkie's radio speeches "sounded harsh, hurried and diffuse—short-range blasts of birdshot rather than pinpointed high explosive shells."

to the Chinese Ambassador in Berlin. One point in his talk, when repeated to Washington, aroused a query. He hinted that if China did
not make peace the Soviet Union would provide no more support. This
did not jibe with what the Soviet Ambassador in Washington was saying
to the American government.[3]

Chiang Kai-shek sent to the President full news of these offers bordered by black accounts of the misery of the Chinese people and of
their need for aid. Our Ambassador in China, Nelson Johnson, in a series
of blunt and warning cables confirmed Chiang Kai-shek's view of the
situation and claims. In the last of these (that of November 27), he said
that Chiang's appeals seemed to him to be those "of a man who has lost
confidence in his ability to contend further with the domestic situation
which he feels he cannot control, of a man in urgent need of help," and
that he (Chiang) "feels he has now virtually exhausted the strength of
his nation in resisting aggression, in an effort as much in the interests
of Great Britain and the United States as of China, and that it is now
time for the United States to come to its help." [4]

The President and Hull did not think that Chiang Kai-shek would
yield to any of the arguments or inducements if he could help it. But
they did fear that unless given aid and hope he simply might not be able
to carry on the fight.

The British, Australian, and Dutch governments also pressed for
more positive American action to deter Japan, and protect their fighting
positions in the Far East. Lord Lothian, buoyant and most bright, undertook to convert expressions of readiness to *plan* jointly into a program
for *acting* jointly. His advocacy of economic action was most ably sec-
onded by A. D. Marris, Counsellor of the Embassy, whose skilled
and dogged will was of the kind that wins. The official notes and
memoranda containing the ideas of the British government were with
propriety left at the State Department. But these two spokesmen of the
British (and our own) cause and need, turned for help wherever it
might be found. They often got it first outside the gray stone house of
care and caution. Richard G. Casey, the Australian Minister, a quick
and quickly-liked man, was just as persistent. And since Americans were
not as habituated to regard the aims of the Dominion of Australia with
the same respectful suspicion as those of Britain, he sometimes found
the path smoother than his British colleagues.

[3] Welles-Oumansky talk, November 27, 1940.
[4] Cable, Ambassador Johnson to Hull, November 27, 1940.

The whole range of methods of restraining Japan was, during November and December, again inspected in Washington. There were three main ways in which we might try to do so. Japan might be deprived of the means of sustaining a long war; ships and planes might be moved into the threatened regions; China might be so assisted as to be a continued worry and drain. Each of these measures had its advocates; each was in some measure deemed feasible. But each could turn out to be a blunder—that would take the United States into war, and maybe a losing one. The assignment was to use each in the right degree and at the right time.

Of the three, the further control of exports to Japan seemed the best justified. As already noted, the remaining trade was almost wholly a brokerage in war materials.[5] Prospectively we or Britain might need everything that was being sent.

On November 1 Lothian reported his government to be most seriously disturbed at this contribution to Japan's war power. It asked the American government to join the British Dominions and Empire in limiting the total export to Japan of all essential goods to what could be deemed "normal" amounts. There was a suspicion that some of the excess was going to Germany over the Trans-Siberian Railway. A few days later the State Department was notified that a proposal to this end had been put before the Dominions, India, and Burma, and was being discussed with the Dutch government. And a few days after that it was urged that oil shipments be similarly restricted if, as the British thought, Japanese war stocks were greater than the American government had reckoned.[6] This last suggestion was sent on to Admiral Stark with the request that if the Navy felt inclined to send an answer, it should please get in touch with the State Department before doing so.

The American agencies responsible for the production of weapons greatly wanted to act along this line. Stimson and Morgenthau also, as before, favored it. Knox seemed more than ready to go along, although Stark and other of the highest officers in the Navy still seemed of two

[5] As described by the President of the Planning Board to the Privy Council on September 26: "In our mobilization plan on materials the center of gravity is laid on the items for military purposes." Washington did not have to hear these words to know the fact; the trade statistics told the story.

[6] A British memorandum (of November 20) on this subject alluded to a supposed estimate of the American Navy, placing Japan's stocks as approximately 37 million barrels. This reference was a puzzle since the naval estimates known to the State and Treasury Departments were much higher, about 70 million barrels (Morgenthau diary, October 2, 1940). Perhaps there were several naval estimates in circulation; perhaps the figure cited in the estimate to which the British Embassy alluded referred only to stocks held by the Japanese Navy, and was misunderstood by it.

minds. It was the State Department, almost alone, which continued to hold off action.

The long and tired meetings within Hull's office ended in a different assessment of risks. On the one hand, American reports did not validate the sharp British fear that Japan was about to attack Singapore or the Indies. On the other hand, they warned anew that economic action would not avert war in the Far East; but, on the contrary (as Grew wrote to the President on December 14), "would tend to push the Japanese people onward in a forlorn hope of making themselves economically self-sufficient." [7]

This being so, Hull insisted that it was wise not to provoke Japan further until and unless American and British forces in the Far East were stronger. He would not, he retorted to critics, give assent to any step that might mean war in the Pacific until he knew the Navy was ready, until he knew that our ships were where they would be needed and prepared to fight. The Navy, or rather its senior admirals, were saying that they were not. And when Hull set about trying to get part of the fleet dispatched to the Far East—as he did—the Navy resisted.

The British government was eager to see our ships move. On November 23 word was sent of an intended reinforcement of Malaya by Australian and New Zealand soldiers. Would not, the query was transmitted from London, the American fleet in the Pacific use Singapore as a base, or at least send some ships there? [8] This was a proposal for the division of the Pacific fleet. Time and again during the coming months it was to be repeated with unrepressed anxiety. As it was by Lothian, who, just back from consultation with Churchill and the cabinet, told Hull

[7] Grew's many messages during November and December contained repeated statements of this conclusion, partly out of fear that the opposite one might have been drawn from his "green light" telegram of September 12. On November 3, for example, he cabled: "the view that war in the Far East can thus be averted by continuation of trade embargoes and, as proposed by some, the imposition of a blockade is not supported by what has thus far occurred."
But while his warnings were clear, his advice as to what policy the United States should follow was not clear. In some messages he seemed to approve further pressure on Japan despite the risk. Thus, for example, November 7 he cabled: "I believe that while the continuance of a firm policy by the United States would involve inevitable risks, nevertheless, a policy of laissez-faire would lead to dangers of greater magnitude." Nor does the explanation he gave to the Pearl Harbor Committee (*Pearl Harbor Attack*, Part 2, p. 617, *et seq.*) seem to me to make the intended purport of his advice during this period any clearer.
[8] As expounded by the First Sea Lord, Sir Dudley Pound, to the American naval mission in London, it was essential to hold Singapore at all costs. With the American fleet, or a substantial part of it based on Singapore, Japan, he argued, would be much less likely to risk war and if war came the Japanese fleet could be contained north of the long chain of islands comprising the Dutch East Indies.

two days later (on November 25) that his government definitely expected Japan to attack Singapore.[9] And as it was again by the Australian Minister on December 3.

These pleas came from knowledge that in the event that Japan did strike, Britain would not be able to protect the threatened colonies. All its ships and planes were needed in the Atlantic and Mediterranean, and even there were losing out. Unless the United States acted as shield, there was no shield.

Hull and Admiral Stark, to whom the British proposals were primarily directed, let them rest. The British government accepted the decision. But the same proposals about sending the American fleet to Singapore were waiting for Harry Hopkins in London when he arrived in January. This avoidance caused a temporary sag in the chain of resolution to confine Japan. The British would not give the Indies a promise to come to its defense. This caused the Indies government to state that it would oppose any further steps that would arouse Japan.[10] The Australian government also began to cool towards the proposals for joint economic action.[11]

The American government would not have the American fleet display itself in the threatened zones. It would not promise to join in their defense if they were attacked. But it was willing to plan in conference how the forces of all the opponents of Japan could best be used in concert or combination, *if* the United States should find itself fighting by the side of others. Staff talks for that purpose between the British and Dutch in Singapore and Batavia—with an officer of the American Navy in attendance—had thus far come to little.

On November 12 Stark recommended to the President that Army and Navy representatives be authorized to enter at once "upon an exhaustive series of secret staff conversations with the British, from which definite plans and agreements to promote unity of effort against the Axis and Japan could emerge."[12] Marshall concurred and the President ap-

[9] Hull's memo of this talk with Lothian is printed, *ibid.*, Part 20, pp. 4072–74.

[10] The Governor-General of the Indies sent word to this effect on Dec. 5 through the Dutch Ambassador in Washington, Loudon; he said he would not agree to the dispatch of American naval observers to the Indies or talk about possible naval bases.

[11] The Australian Minister for Foreign Affairs on December 10 pointed out that his country could not use economic sanctions with the same impunity as the United States. At the same time he brought up the possibility of an American naval visit to Australia.

[12] Samuel Eliot Morison, *History of United States Naval Operations in World War II, The Battle of the Atlantic* (Boston, 1947), I, 43–44.

proved. When on the 25th the British government said that "at once" was none too soon, Hull agreed. Upon doing so, he observed that "of course there could be no agreement entered into in this respect, but that there should undoubtedly be a collaboration with the view of making known to each other any and all information practicable in regard to what both might have in mind to do, and when and where, in case of a military move by Japan in the south or some other direction."

The invitation was sent off (November 30) in the form of a personal bid from Stark to the British Chiefs of Staff to send accredited representatives—before Christmas, if possible. They would, it was understood, work out further with our staff how all the opposed forces could be best used to sustain the battle against Germany, and prevent or defeat an attack by Japan. The military men were to be allowed to erect models for possible action. But they were forbidden to say whether their governments would use or follow the models. It was not going to prove easy for them, as the talks went on, to heed this injunction.[18] For it became more and more unreal in the face of what their governments were doing —by mutual accord—both in the Atlantic and Pacific.

While keeping the American fleet at American bases, while refusing to say what it would or would not do if Japan sailed into the Southwest Pacific, the American government—within a month after the elections —put together a program of subtly adjusted measures to hinder Japan.

---

This memorandum of Stark's was a lucid statement of the problems and burdens of an unlimited war with Japan and a convincing presentation of the opinion that the primary way to protect principal American interest was to assure the continued existence of the British Empire. Accordingly it recommended that even if forced into war with Japan, the United States should plan to avoid operations in the Far East and Middle Pacific that would prevent the Navy from moving to the Atlantic forces adequate to safeguard our interests and policies in the event of a British collapse. This judgment was adopted as basic American strategy and remained so.

As revised by the Joint Planning Committee of the Army and Navy it became at once the basis of the preparatory talks between our Special Naval Observer in London (Admiral Ghormley) and the British Admiralty in preparation for the Combined Staff meetings that opened in Washington in January 1941.

[18] The difficulty of avoiding misunderstanding was foreseen. Thus Admiral Hart, Commander in Chief of the Asiatic Fleet, wrote to Admiral Stark on November 13: "It should be possible, without making any political commitment, or without prejudging our final decision in each case to proceed on certain assumptions. For instance, that in the event of a Jap attack on the Netherlands East Indies we will intervene if the British do, and then carry on with the British (and the Dutch, if they are willing) the extensive conversations which that assumption necessitates. It is realized, however, that in practice there lies danger of certain implications of actually having made political commitments by the very fact of accepting such an assumption as having elements of possibility."

First came the decisions in regard to aid for China in response to Chiang Kai-shek's appeals. On November 30 the President announced that we would put another 100 million dollars at his disposal. Fifty modern pursuit planes at once were promised him, with as many more as possible. Steps were taken to issue passports to American citizens who wished to go to China to serve as aviators or aviation instructors. A plan for providing China with long-range bombers so that it could hit back at Tokyo was excitedly discussed with the British and Chinese. To the chagrin of all, it was found impractical.[14] These measures were the outcome of a tense effort to make sure that the Chiang Kai-shek regime would be able and willing to keep in the fight.

Ships and planes were sent out to the Philippines. Six submarines went, with more to follow. Plans were made to assemble the whole Asiatic fleet at Manila and to increase its size. Hull urged that the Navy send as well a whole squadron of cruisers to southernmost Philippine ports. The President was briefly for this, but changed his mind. He also wanted to publish the news of our naval movements, but he took Hull's advice to let them become known by reports that were certain to seep out, as the ships were seen. A public announcement, he thought, might cause trouble of two kinds: objection within the United States which would lessen the effect upon Japan; and excitement within Japan. Japan was not to be threatened publicly, but to be left guessing.

"I believed in letting them guess as to when and in what set of circumstances we would fight. While Japan continued to guess, we continued to get ready for anything she might do."[15]

The Japanese were not the only ones compelled to guess. The British were just as uncertain. A month later Harry Hopkins from London was reporting to the President that "Eden asked me repeatedly what our country would do if Japan attacked Singapore or the Dutch East Indies, saying it was essential to their policy to know."[16]

[14] This seems to have been inspired by a remark of the President, that it would be a good thing if the Chinese could bomb Japan. Morgenthau took it up, and talked it over with Lothian and T. V. Soong who enthusiastically cabled Chiang Kai-shek. Hull said he was for it, but it might occur to skeptical spirits who knew him that he saw no need to catch that arrow in his hand since it would soon fall to earth. Chiang Kai-shek answered that he would carry out the plan, provided the United States supplied not only the bombers but escort planes and the necessary ground organization. We, of course, had none of these to spare; the bombers would have had to be taken from the allotments destined for Britain, Hawaii, and the Philippines. The idea was dropped at a meeting on December 23, when General Marshall demonstrated how impractical it was. Morgenthau diary, entries for December 3, 7, 8, 10, 18, 20, 22, and 23, 1940.

[15] Hull, *op. cit.*, I, 915.

[16] Sherwood, *op. cit.*, p. 259.

The thought may be carried further. Not only did the British not know what we would do, but neither did Roosevelt or Hull know. Would the President ask Congress to declare war on Japan? Or would he merely take some lesser measures—such as turning submarines over to the British, or using American naval forces to maintain a patrol and convoy system in the Pacific? Or, because that might waste naval forces, would he not even do that?

He was spared the need of deciding. Most fortunately so. For grave uses for the fleet in the Atlantic loomed up more clearly than before, and a great need to face Hitler with unengaged forces. On December the 8, Churchill, by letter, put before the President (through Hull) a lucid and compelling summary of the situation faced by Britain and of the aid it would need to carry on. Among its parts were these: "The danger of Great Britain being destroyed by a swift, overwhelming blow has for the time being very greatly receded. In its place there is a long, gradually maturing danger, less sudden and less spectacular, but equally deadly. This mortal danger is the steady and increasing diminution of sea tonnage. . . . The decision for 1941 lies upon the seas. Unless we can establish our ability to feed this island, to import the munitions of all kinds which we need, unless we can move our armies to the various theatres where Hitler and his confederate Mussolini must be met, and maintain them there . . . we may fall by the way, and the time needed by the United States to complete her defensive preparations may not be forthcoming. It is, therefore, in shipping and in the power to transport across the oceans, particularly the Atlantic Ocean, that in 1941 the crunch of the whole war will be found." [17]

In drafting this, Churchill had before him Stark's memo of November 12. A copy had been sent on to him by the British naval representative in Washington, along with Stark's remark that it would be useful if the Prime Minister endorsed the basic suggestions therein contained. The advice was taken to heart. The Prime Minister's analysis left no doubt that the United States would have to do more than it had done.

While the President was still in the Caribbean—the problem drew together Hull, Knox, Stimson, Stark, and Marshall. They hunted for the response that would be sufficient yet possible. All agreed with the comment that Stimson wrote in his diary while these talks were on: "it is very apparent that nothing will save Great Britain from the starvation of her supplies, which Stark estimates will necessarily take place in six months except assistance from us by convoy in the Atlantic . . ." [18]

[17] Winston S. Churchill, *Their Finest Hour* (Boston, 1949) p. 560.
[18] Stimson diary, entry for December 16, 1940.

When Stimson so proposed in the cabinet (on December 19), "The President said he hadn't quite reached that yet." [19]

But, short of that, the resolve emerged from these December conferences to extend American naval protection over the Atlantic as far and as fast as might be necessary, and in the face of any risks of fighting at sea. This was enough (though not the sole) reason for refusing to promise to join the defense of Singapore and the Indies; enough reason why the President could not know or tell what he might do if Japan attacked them. A season was ahead in which the forces of the Allies were to be most wanly stretched.

## [3]

The steps just recounted—the support for China, the assembly of naval forces at the Philippines, the planned staff talks—turned the edge of Hull's judgment about the further use of economic restraints. Or perhaps it was only that the risk had to be taken; that the glide toward war could not be halted by the sand of diplomacy.

In any case, despite dislike for this "policy of pinpricks" as he called it, during December he gave assent to a widening of the ban on exports to Japan. This ended the flow, among other products, of iron ore, pig iron, steel, the main articles made of steel and many kinds of tools. It was promptly protested by Japan. Around the corner, impatiently awaited by the defense agencies, was another order dealing with such important raw materials as copper, brass, bronze, zinc, nickel and potash.

Now there occurred a strenuous attempt to displace the State Department as arbiter in this field. Several restless groups within the government urged the President to unify the direction of all economic warfare activities. These should be, they advocated, placed under the direction of a board or commission (to be created). On this the State Department would be one of many; perhaps the most influential among them, since all agreed that the Secretary of State would be the most appropriate chairman. But perhaps not. For the new board would probably turn out to be a loosely organized committee of officials whose primary duties were elsewhere; if so, the real power would fall to those who were day by day at the controls. Administration would make policy rather than the other way about.

Several groups were aspirants for the central job (as they had been

[19] *ibid.,* entry for December 19, 1940.

for the task of administering Section VI of the Defense Act). Among them the Treasury was most forward. It was tireless in the drafting of executive orders and of justifying briefs. A corps of earnest apprentices worked nights to provide the Secretary of the Treasury with drafts that could be at the White House in the morning.

The most seriously meant of these was an Executive Order given by Morgenthau to Hull on December 28. This had been sent directly to the President, probably with the hope that he would approve it first and tell Hull of it second. But the President had tossed it back. Under scrutiny, it turned out to be more than a relocation of administrative powers. Something had been added, and it was an item of great import in our relations with Japan.

This—the first of the two main features of the proposed Executive Order—was that the American government should at once take control over *all* funds which foreign countries and nationals possessed in the United States. Such practice was known as *freezing*. Morgenthau in talk with the Director of the Budget described it as "the kernel of the nut." [20] Which it was. Whoever governed the use of the funds belonging to the people and government of a foreign country governed all trade between the United States (at least) and that country.

The second main part of the order provided for the creation of an Economic Defense Board, to be composed of members of the civilian branches of the government concerned with economic controls. This was to direct the operation of the freezing program, as one part of its many wide powers. It was to have similar authority, under the President, over exports.

The draft nominated the Secretary of State as chairman of this Board. But the employment of the powers granted the Board were to be vested in the Secretary of the Treasury—who was to act in accordance with policies made by the Chairman and the Board.

In the abstract, this arrangement was not unsuitable. But few who had experience with the cohorts from the Treasury had any doubt as to what the plan would mean. As summed up privately by Welles, in the conduct of the economic foreign policy of this government, Morgenthau would become the works, Hull the front.[21]

Hull met the situation by glum silence—which to those who did not

[20] Morgenthau diary, entry for December 31, 1940.
[21] Or as expressed in another State Department memo: "Aggregate and interlocked, and in combination with other powers the Treasury has, this would result in a great concentration of power; great, perhaps decisive, influence in the United States foreign policy and diplomacy."

know him well could be misleading. In fact after calling upon him Morgenthau got the impression—to his surprise as he told his staff—that Hull was "practically ready to go along." [22] But Hull said to the President that he would not be Chairman; and that he wanted the Treasury to run the show. The President knew his man, and again sent the order back to him for an opinion. The consequent discussion between departments about both the freezing proposal and the organization of economic warfare was to drag on for many months.

Thus as Hull continued to ponder what steps might or might not be dared in the Far East, he knew that at any time this upsetting plan, or one like it, might be put into effect. The State Department was nearer the peril, but some of the advocates of change were nearer the President. To work under this challenge of the rights of office was hard. But perhaps the outcome was better than if the irritant had not been there. For it corrected Hull's tendency to be too aware of all the dangers of any decision, and thus to postpone and postpone—waiting for the answer to emerge out of the seas of events.

More time had been granted already than had been expected when the Tripartite Pact was signed. With the help of the Japanese records, it is now easier to know why.

[22] Diary entry for December 30, 1940. He later told the Director of the Budget; "As far as I know Mr. Hull is satisfied and Sumner Welles is satisfied." *ibid.*, entry for January 6, 1941.

## CHAPTER 18

# Matsuoka Pursues the Great Combination

MATSUOKA had wasted no time in pursuing the search for the grand combination which would hold the United States in check. The Soviet Union was the missing number. The quicker to make headway, Matsuoka had changed his Ambassador at Moscow, sending a jovial officer, General Tatekawa. This appointee announced before his arrival what his way of dealing with the Soviet government would be: "I will simply say, 'Tovarich, Molotoff!' and start getting acquainted with the Soviet big shots. I have no use for Communists but I like Russians. They are pure-minded and simple." [1] Perhaps it was those qualities which made Molotov so direct in the first talks with the Ambassador, so expectant that friendship should bring boons. For he asked at once what "present" Japan would give for the agreement wanted, remarking that Germany had given half of Poland. Matsuoka had thus learned that German help would be necessary.

This had been proffered when the Tripartite Pact was signed. Ribbentrop was glad to take the assignment for it fitted well with Germany's main current purpose. [2] This, as Ribbentrop explained to Ciano not long before Molotov's famous visit (of November, 1940) to Berlin, was "to confront the United States with a united totalitarian European bloc, which, linked with Japan, would make the United States most chary about intervening in the war." [3]

Hitler, in advance of Molotov's coming, sent a paper to Tokyo outlining the proposals he intended to make about the Far East. The

---

[1] *New York Times*, September 10, 1940.

[2] Though Hitler had even before then given thought to the obverse strategy—to restrain the United States by subduing Russia. Thus General Franz Halder, Chief of the German General Staff, records him as saying, "Britain's hope lies in Russia and the United States. If Russia drops out of the picture America, too, is lost for Britain, because elimination of Russia would tremendously increase Japan's power in the Far East." *Halder Journal*, IV, 144, entry for July 31, 1940. (This mimeographed translation of General Halder's private war journal was prepared under the supervision of the Office of Chief of Counsel for War Crimes.)

[3] Ciano, memorandum of talk with Ribbentrop, November 4, 1940, at Schonhof.

Konoye Cabinet were pleased by them.[4] They had in view an agreement in which the three partners of the Tripartite Pact should appear as one party while the Soviet Union appeared as the other. The Soviet Union was to recognize the spheres of influence designated in the Tripartite Pact. In return it was to have one of her own in the direction of the Persian Gulf and India. Pledges were also to be exchanged, providing for mutual respect for each other's territory, and refusal of help to enemies of any.

Hitler and Ribbentrop put these proposals up to Molotov. They tried to persuade him that Russia should be content with its assigned chances and duties in the new division of the world. They did not find him "pure-minded and simple." On the first day of talk (November 12) Molotov said the Soviet Union would, among other matters, "like to have an idea of the boundaries of the so-called Greater East Asian Sphere." Hitler answered in substance that Russia would itself have a chance to decide what these boundaries might be. "In no case," he said, "was a settlement to be made without Soviet Russian cooperation. This applied not only to Europe, but also to Asia, where Russia herself was to cooperate in the definition of the Greater East Asian Sphere and where she was to designate her claims there. Germany's task in this case was that of a mediator. Russia by no means was to be confronted with a *fait accompli.*"

It was a matter, he went on, of opposing any attempt on the part of America "to make money on Europe. The United States had no business in Europe, in Africa, or in Asia." [5] As set down in the notes of the German interpreter, Schmidt: "Molotov expressed his agreement with the statements of the Führer regarding the role of America and England. The participation of Russia in the Tripartite Pact appeared to him entirely acceptable in principle, provided that Russia was to cooperate as a partner and not be merely an object . . . But the aim and the significance of the Pact must first be more closely defined, particularly because of the delimitation of the Greater East Asian Sphere." At this point, the talk was broken off by warning of an air raid; it is neither

[4] Their substance is given in Konoye's paper "Concerning the Tripartite Alliance."
They were in accord with the policy approved by the Liaison Conference of September 26–27. This specified that the Soviet Union was to be persuaded to align itself with Japan, Germany, and Italy to divide the world into four spheres of influence; the Soviet sphere was to be in the direction of the Persian Gulf; Japan was to collaborate with Germany and Italy to restrain the Soviet Union on the east, west, and south. *Far East Mil. Trib.*, Exh. No. 541.
[5] German memorandum of talk, November 12, 1940, between Hitler and Molotov, *Nazi-Soviet Relations*, pp. 226, *et seq.*

seeming nor comfortable to divide up the world in a shower of shattered glass.

On the next day, November 13, the subject was resumed. Hitler in the flow of his discourse developed his idea of a working arrangement with Russia. "He wanted," he expanded, "to create a world coalition of interested powers which would consist of Spain, France, Italy, Germany, Soviet Russia, and Japan and would to a certain degree represent a coalition—extending from North Africa to Eastern Asia—of all those who wanted to be satisfied out of the British bankrupt estate." [6] Molotov neither repelled nor embraced the conception. As regards Russo-Japanese relations, he remarked with notable dryness that he anticipated improvement, and he thanked the Reich government for its effort in that direction. He also agreed that it was the task of Russia and Germany to aid in the settlement of the war in China. "But," he added, "an honorable solution would have to be assured for China, all the more since Japan now stood a chance of getting 'Indonesia.' " In short, before entering into an accord with Japan, the Soviet Union wanted a clear definition of what she would receive, as well as what Japan would receive; and it refused to toss China to Japan till then, if then.

The discussion was resumed after Molotov returned to Moscow. Schulenburg, the German Ambassador, had by then the draft of a treaty to submit. This was to pledge one and all to cooperate to oppose the extension of the war (to keep the United States out). In a Secret Protocol the territorial aspirations of each of the four powers were written out.[7] That of Japan was to "center in the area of Eastern Asia to the south of the Island Empire of Japan." How far from the center it was to extend was left vague. Molotov (on November 26) said that the Soviet government was prepared to accept the draft provided Germany got less and Russia more. Among the extras wanted was a renunciation by Japan of her rights to concessions for coal and oil in Northern Sakhalin.[8]

Hitler shortly afterwards threw away the book. Again Japan faced the prospect of having to pay a price even for paper security along its northern military frontier in Manchukuo and China.[9] The Soviet Am-

---

[6] German memorandum of talk, Hitler and Molotov, November 13, 1940, *ibid.*, p. 243.
[7] A draft found in the secret files of the German Embassy at Moscow is printed in *ibid.*, pp. 255–57.
[8] The substance of the Russian answer is printed, *ibid.*, pp. 258–59.
[9] Some reflections on the relations between Japan and the Soviet Union which the Lord Privy Seal, Kido, reports himself as speaking to the Emperor about at this time, have gained interest with the passage of time:

bassador in Washington, Oumansky, told the State Department that the attitude of his government towards China was the same as that of the United States; it would continue to aid Chiang Kai-shek.[10]

The failure of Germany's effort to act as broker forced the Konoye Cabinet again to change the basis of its address to Russia. The idea that they would become partners in a coalition to divide up the world was dropped. It was replaced by the idea of a simple pact between the two countries. This could at least safeguard Japan in the event of war with Britain and the United States. As a way both of enlisting German support for this move and of assuring Army assent, Oshima was sent back to Berlin as Ambassador, replacing Kurusu. Then Matsuoka decided to pursue the quest himself—to visit Germany, going via Russia. The Army encouraged this journey, and the projected pact with the Soviet Union. Konoye's consent was also quickly obtained. As explained by the German Ambassador to his government, Matsuoka's purposes were "to make a strong gesture in favor of the Tripartite Pact and, if possible, to overcome the deadlock in the negotiations with the Soviet Union and China." [11]

The records in hand do not tell whether Matsuoka knew, when in December he planned his trip, that Berlin and Moscow were at odds with each other. He may have, but still figured that something might be gained for Japan. If Germany and Russia were separating, there was need to preclude German protest against the accord he wanted. If Germany and Russia were still friends, help might be gotten. The one thing he could not do was to drop the attempt. For he had assured the Emperor and his colleagues that the Tripartite Pact would suppress

---

"Today, the U.S.S.R. is in the most favorable position in the world. As things stand now, the less she moves the better her position gets. The fact being so, she is haughty, and it is possible that she will not readily concede to negotiating with Japan. After the present war, there is little doubt that the only two uninjured countries will be the U.S.S.R. and the United States, while others will be exhausted.

"Then Japan will be placed between the two powers and subjected to an extremely enduring hardship. However, we need not be pessimistic because even these two powers, when they lose their strong rival countries around them, will automatically become relaxed, then inevitably deteriorate. So provided that we are prepared for ten years of hardship and cultivate a morale based on simplicity and virility, I believe it will not be so difficult to emerge well in the end."—"Kido's Diary," entry for December 3, 1940.

But Japan did not wait to see it happen.

[10] Oumansky's way of stating this to Welles on December 16 was that the Soviet relations with China were those of a "good neighbor," guided by the spirit of the Chinese-Soviet nonaggression pact of 1937.

[11] Telegram, Ott to Ribbentrop, December 19, 1940. *Far East Mil. Trib.*, Exh. No. 567.

American interference with plans for Greater East Asia. Five months had passed since the Imperial Liaison Conference (July 27), called by this cabinet, had resolved "to hasten the end of the conflict in China" and "to solve the problem of the South." Germany had not made it easy by beating Britain into submission. The alliance with the Axis had not made it safe by forcing the United States to cease its machinations.

Yet, as has been seen, the Japanese government persisted in its program of southward penetration. The advent of winter found it busily engaged in trying to find the way.

## CHAPTER 19

# At the Same Time Japan Continues
# to Seek the Best Road South

THE scheme and schedule of Japanese operations showed up in the Indies, Indo-China, and Thailand.

In the Indies, the Japanese mission did not accept the rebuff, earlier recounted, as final. On January 16 it again advanced with vigor all the requests made the previous autumn, and added some new ones.[1] The Indies authorities were still without assurance that they would be helped if the Japanese sent ships and troops to enforce their wishes. They knew that even if Britain wished to aid, its forces in the Far East were of small account and tied down to the defense of Singapore. Still they decided, and so informed Washington, that the Japanese requests were entirely unacceptable. The American government did not comment.

Standing up for itself, the Indies government (February 3), through Van Mook, stiffly rebutted Japanese insinuations (as contained for instance in some remarks of Matsuoka's to the Diet) that the Indies belonged to any new order in East Asia. The Dutch were having none of Matsuoka's talk, allies or no allies. The effect of their attitude upon the chief of the mission, Yoshizawa, is recorded in a gloomy report, since found, which he sent for the attention of the Vice-Minister of War and the Vice-Chief of the General Staff. Its conclusion was:

"Therefore it can be considered that unless our Empire adopts determined resolutions or measures, not only the progress of the Japanese-

---

[1] Japan now asked, among other things, (1) an unconditional promise that the Indies would provide designated quantities of war materials; (2) admission of a much greater number of Japanese; (3) permission to explore for oil and minerals in many areas, including some reserved for the Indies Government; (4) all necessary assistance required to create joint Indo-Japanese enterprises; (5) permission to the Japanese fishing fleet operating in the territorial waters of the Indies to operate land establishments for fishing operations; (6) permission to increase the number of Japanese ships engaged in coastal navigation and the right to use closed harbors. *Far East Mil. Trib.*, Exh. No. 1309A.

These were, it may be surmised, the first main segment of the plans for acquiring control over the economic life of the Indies, as formulated by the cabinet on October 25, 1940 —of which an account has been given in Chapter 16.

Netherlands negotiations, but also the development of Japanese-Netherlands relations would be extremely difficult." [2]

The Japanese showed they were still not ready to use force by again accepting the rebuke and reducing their demands. When the negotiations were resumed at the end of February, "the discussion," according to a memorandum given the State Department by the Dutch Legation in Washington, "was generally characterized by a remarkable lack of strength on the part of the Japanese representatives. Several exaggerated and far-reaching proposals were reduced to much more modest requests."

Such reports confirmed the opinion of the American government that Japan would pause longer before points of real resistance. They imparted offsetting calm to British anxieties, of which more will be told shortly, that Japan was on the point of launching an attack upon Singapore.

But it would apply the wedge further to the weakest and undefended points. Japan thrust itself further forward (January–February 1941) as mediator in the dispute which it had encouraged between Indo-China and Thailand. The latter was now threatening to invade Indo-China unless border provinces, once part of its domain, were given back. The British Foreign Office, and particularly the British Ambassador in Japan, Sir Robert Craigie, were afraid that if the French did not compromise, Thailand would enter the embrace of Japan. If that happened the Japanese armies would be installed close, not only to Indo-China, but to Burma, Malaya, and Singapore. The British urged the Vichy government to negotiate. They asked the American government to do the same, and also to soften its reproofs. Hull on January 13 had warned Thailand to remember that in accepting Japan's aid it was taking a ride upon a tiger.

But the Thai government denied that Japan was seeking special favors, and accepted Japanese mediation (January 20 to 26). The State Department prepared for bad, perhaps dangerous, news. The motives it attributed to Japan were akin to those which (it has since been learned) were being conveyed to the German government. Thus Ribbentrop was told by Matsuoka that the Japanese Army could not advance south in the direction of Singapore without using the Malacca peninsula as a land bridge, to do which it would have to pass through Thailand

[2] *Far East Mil. Trib.,* Exh. No. 1318.

as well as Indo-China. If the mediation was successful Japan would, it was thought, be allowed to do so.[3]

The methods to be used to open this path south were defined at a Liaison Conference held in Tokyo on February 1.[4] It was then decided that both Indo-China and Thailand should be compelled to accept the settlement Japan would propose. Force should, if necessary, be used to compel Indo-China to do so. Japan would proceed to conclude economic, political, and military accords with both countries. It was to secure from Vichy air bases (near Saigon), port facilities (the use of Camranh Bay), and the right to station Japanese troops. All this was to be accomplished by March or April.

Quite different was the version which, on February 15, Matsuoka gave to Craigie. The Japanese government, he avowed, would neither expect nor demand a price for its work as mediator. Service and peace were to be their own reward. "He wished me," Craigie reported to the Foreign Office, "to believe him when he said that even though a strong section of opinion demanded that Japan take advantage of her present opportunities in every way possible, he and Prince Konoye were thoroughly opposed to any adventurous or aggressive schemes, and, if necessary, they would enlist the Emperor's support for their policy. They would have to resign if this step proved inadequate."[5]

The man had as much faith in his powers of deception as his Axis colleagues; when they met each other as they were soon to do, their words formed a perfect hooked cross.

On March 11 Vichy, succumbing to the combined pressure of Japan and Germany, accepted Japan's plan of mediation.[6] It promised also that Indo-China would not enter into any agreement with any other country which provided for political, economic, or military cooperation directly or indirectly against Japan's interests. This was taken in Washington to presage further trouble. But it did not bring any major crisis of decision.

[3] Memorandum from Weizsaecker (of the German Foreign Office), January 23, 1941. *ibid.*, Exh. No. 629.

[4] *ibid.*, Exh. No. 564, and "Kido's Diary," February 3, 1941.

[5] Probably since Matsuoka perceived that Craigie was skeptical, he cabled a long report of his statements to Craigie to the Japanese Ambassador in London, Shigemitsu, for repetition to the British Foreign Office. Telegram, Matsuoka to Shigemitsu, February 18, 1941, *Far East Mil. Trib.*, Exh. No. 1046.

[6] On that date—March 11 (Tokyo time) Matsuoka gave the French Ambassador in Tokyo a note stating in part "The Imperial Government has drafted a mediation proposal as per enclosure, which we expect the French government to accept unconditionally." *ibid.*, Exh. No. 633. On the 12th the Japanese Vice-Minister for Foreign Affairs sent to Ribbentrop a message of gratitude for "valuable and effective support." *ibid.*, Exh. No. 376.

## CHAPTER 20

# Diplomacy by Gesture and Signal:
## American Policy in the Winter of 1940-41

THE face which the American government showed Japan, while it weighed these events in the East, is well exemplified by extracts from two of Hull's statements. Appearing before the Foreign Affairs Committee of the House of Representatives on January 15, 1941, in connection with the Lend-Lease Act, he said, in part: "It has been clear throughout that Japan has been actuated from the start by broad and ambitious plans for establishing herself in a dominant position in the entire region of the Western Pacific. Her leaders have openly declared their determination to achieve and maintain that position by force of arms . . ." [1] And on January 22, in a press statement issued to answer Matsuoka's criticisms of these remarks: "We have threatened no one, invaded no one, and surrounded no one. We have freely offered and now freely offer cooperation in peaceful life to all who wish it. . . . Our strategic line must depend primarily on the policies and courses of other nations. . . ." Matsuoka was not squelched. A few days later, speaking to the Budget Committee of the Diet, he called Hull's statement erroneous and Hull's language violent.

There was a new and most definite reason for being careful in these early months of 1941. A crisis might imperil the passage of the Lend-Lease Act. Opposition to that measure in Congress was, as Ernest K. Lindley wrote, "rooted chiefly in the fear that it will enable the President to take us into war." [2] Nothing, both the President and Hull felt, must be done or said while this act was under debate, which might quicken that fear. Once it was law, the President would be able to place

---

[1] The Lend-Lease Bill ("A bill to further promote the defense of the United States, and for other purposes," H.R.1776) was introduced into Congress on January 10, 1941. Hull's statement is printed in the *Department of State Bulletin* January 18, 1941.

[2] *Washington Post*, January 27, 1941. As voiced by Senator Taft: "More dangerous perhaps than any other authority is the power given the President by this bill to make war on foreign nations. . . . Unless Congress is prepared to approve a declaration of war, it cannot and should not authorize the President to engage in acts which are in fact warfare." Radio address, January 25, 1941.

his own construction on it. So, it may be interjected, he did: as when on March 15, speaking to the White House Correspondents Association, he said: "This decision is the end of any attempts at appeasement in our land; . . . the end of compromise with tyranny and the forces of oppression." [3]

At the beginning of the year, Harry Hopkins was in London with a letter of authority from the President which began: "Reposing special faith and confidence in you, I am asking you to proceed at your early convenience to Great Britain, there to act as my personal representative." There, as recorded by one of his English auditors, he "left us with the feeling that although America was not yet in the war, she was marching beside us, and that should we stumble she would see we did not fall." [4]

From London, along with reports upon the help that Britain would need to meet Germany in the spring, he sent back at the end of January, messages from Churchill and Eden to the President and Hull in regard to the Far East. These complemented what the new British Ambassador, Lord Halifax, was saying to Hull; that Japan under German influence would probably move against British territory in the Far East; if not at once, then in the early spring, to coincide with the German advance upon Greece and the Balkans and attacks along the Mediterranean. All the ships and planes the British had were being sent to fight in these areas; there were none at all for dispatch to the Far East. Churchill and Eden were anxious that the United States express its will to deter Japan, and urgently asking what we would do if Japan attacked Singapore and the Indies.[5] To these queries Hopkins had no answer, nor was there a definite one in Washington.

British fears did not abate with the passing of the weeks. On February 7 the British Embassy gave the State Department another message from London: "Evidence is accumulating that the Japanese may already have decided to push on southward even if this means war." On the 11th, Lord Halifax reaffirmed this statement on the basis of the estimates of the British Chiefs of Staff.[6] He urged, and Churchill did so again

[3] *New York Times,* March 16, 1941.
[4] Sherwood, *op. cit.,* p. 249.
[5] *ibid.,* pp. 258-59.
[6] This estimate of the British Chiefs of Staff is reprinted in *Pearl Harbor Attack,* Part 19, pp. 3445-49. It ends as follows: "It is essential, therefore, in the interests not only of the British Empire but of the United States, to take steps which will prevent the Japanese from taking the plunge."

a few days later, that the American government find still further means of deterring Japan from moving south and raiding British trade routes across the Pacific and Indian Oceans.[7]

Grew had the same impression of the situation as the British. He cabled on February 7 that Japan's actions, such as the presence of Japanese naval vessels in the southern waters of Indo-China and Thailand, seemed to point to some Japanese plan of attack, perhaps to synchronize with the next German offensive. This cable had an unusual ring of action: "It is axiomatic that an ounce of prevention is worth a pound of cure. . . . I have expressed the opinion that the principle question before us is not whether we must call a halt to the Japanese southward advance, but when. . . . The moment when decisive action should be taken, if it is ever to be taken, appears to us to be approaching."

What further action? The President read Hopkins' messages, the notes of the Hull-Halifax talks, the reports of events in the Far East, and reviewed them all with Hull, Stimson, Knox, Stark, and Marshall. The Far Eastern specialists at the State Department continued to doubt whether the compelling crisis was as close at hand as the British (and Grew) thought. They remained convinced that Japan had not yet made up its mind to go to war, and would do so only as an unhappy last resort. The program pressed upon the President from London might lead into quick trouble; for instead of causing Japan to desist, it might harden and hasten her will to advance. Further it might imperil the Lend-Lease legislation, and thus the whole program of support for Britain.

This judgment of necessities and risks prevailed. The government did not do what Britain asked. Instead it resorted to signals of possible later action; signals that would seem to be clearer than they were, that

_____

The British Admiralty had also officially informed the American Military Attaché in London that it believed Japan was planning a large scale offensive, presumably against Indo-China, the Malaya Peninsula, and the Indies, to be coordinated with an attack on Britain—approximately February 10. The Navy so advised the State Department by memo of February 4. But shortly thereafter the Admiralty revised this opinion and said that action might not be immediate.

The sources of the intelligence which so alarmed the British government were obscure at the time, and remain so. Craigie's cables may well have been one source. But it is also likely that the British were in part misled by reports originated in, perhaps by, the German Government. For this was the time when Hitler was doing his utmost to persuade Japan to attack Singapore. See Chapter 23.

[7] This message of February 15 from Churchill to the President began, ". . . many drifting straws seem to indicate Japanese intention to make war on us or do something that would force us to make war on them in the next few weeks or months."

It then proceeded to analyze with convincing clarity the "awful effect upon the British war effort of Japanese naval action in the Indian and Pacific Oceans." A paraphrase is to be found in *ibid.*, Part 19, pp. 3452–53.

would be studied more intently in Japan than in the United States. Three kinds were used: the shifting about of our fleet, the extension of American controls on exports to Japan, and earnest talk.

And, if I may interpose, the British fears turned out to be ill-founded. They fitted, as will be seen when we revert to the other side of the story, Hitler's urgent advice. But the Japanese government was disregarding that advice; it had no plans, then, to attack either Singapore, or the Indies. But this is later knowledge.

Naval cruises were made to do the work of the naval dispositions which the British asked us to make. Hull now became an active proponent of plans to send naval vessels all around the threatened area— even on a visit to Singapore. Admiral Stark's anxiety found outlet in a letter to Admiral Kimmel, the new Commander in Chief of the Pacific Fleet on February 10: "I continue in every way I possibly can to fight commitments or dispositions that would involve us on two fronts and to keep from sending more combatant ships to the Far East. I had a two hour struggle (please keep this absolutely secret) in the White House this past week and thank God can report that the President still supports my contentions. . . ."

In a postscript he added: ". . . I had another hour and a half in the White House today and the President said that he might order a detachment of three or four cruisers, a carrier and a squadron of destroyers to make a cruise to the Philippines; perhaps going down through the Phoenix and Gilbert or the Fiji Islands, then reaching over into Mindanao for a short visit and on to Manila and back.

"I have fought this over many times and won, but this time the decision may go against me. Heretofore the talk was largely about sending a cruise of this sort to Australia and Singapore and perhaps the N.E.I. Sending it to the Philippines would be far less objectionable from a political standpoint but still objectionable. What I want you to do is to be thinking about it and be prepared to make a quick decision if it is ordered." [8]

In March, to anticipate a bit, the Navy sent two cruisers and accom-

[8] *Pearl Harbor Attack*, Part 33, pp. 1196–97. The admiral did not remain entirely constant in his views. On March 28 in a memorandum to the President he said he liked Admiral Hart's idea of a cruise to the Indies if it was properly timed—since it was in line with American war plans and the most positive move we could make. But at a meeting in Hull's office on April 3 it was decided that such a visit was not just then advisable.

panying destroyers on a visit to Australia and a similar group to New Zealand. They were to signify solidarity with the British Commonwealth.[9] Few ships ever were as cordially welcomed.

The movement of ships was one way of showing, or showing off, American interest and power. The denial of war materials was another. It also was used during the period as a constraining signal. Hull, after consulting with the President, assented in early January to an extension of control to six other materials: copper, brass and bronze, zinc, nickel and potash, and the products into which they were made. The ban on copper and brass was of real moment. Japan had a reserve stock equal to about a year's imports, but would be in great trouble if that were used up.[10] Almost every week thereafter other items were added to the list, each of which was much needed for Japanese industrial production —lead, jute, burlap, borax, phosphate, carbon black, cork, and all animal and vegetable fats.[11] One of these items listed in the order of February 4 caused no comment at the time—uranium. Japan was not to have any until it was transformed into the missiles which ended the war.

For weeks before each of these lists was approved, the defense agencies of the government pressed to have it done on the score of our own military needs. The resistance of the State Department was lapsing; it, too, was coming to think it more important to prevent Japan from obtaining war stocks than to avoid offense. Less heed was paid than in the past to the aggrieved protests from Tokyo. Both Konoye and Matsuoka warned publicly and privately that Japan was being forced to secure its economic lifeline within the area of East Asia.

Even assuming that their warnings were only half-meant, how much farther could the United States and Britain curtail Japan's essential supplies without adding the missing half? Thus far the Secretary of

[9] At about the same time the British, Dutch, and Australian governments took further defensive measures which were quickly noted by Japanese officials. Additional troop formations were sent to Malaya, mining of the waters about Singapore was begun. Dutch ships were recalled from Japanese and Chinese waters. We were sending more planes to Hawaii and the Philippines.

[10] Imports fell from about 105,000 metric tons in 1940 to about 38,000 in 1941. The reserve stock at the beginning of 1941 was about 130,000 tons. During the war supplies were short, and affected the production of wire cable and sheet brass for cartridge cases.

[11] In the case of some, no export to Japan was henceforth permitted, in the case of others, usual or diminishing quantities. Ordinarily there was an interval of two to three months before a new order began to produce its full effect because of the usual period of grace, or the permitted use of uncancelled licenses, or the arrival of cargoes afloat.

State was willing to have the economic screws turned upon Japan, but no further. In regard to the most vital product, oil, he continued to oppose the imposition of new restraints.

The advocates of restriction could, and did, cite many troubling facts. The existing embargo on aviation fuel was of no avail. Japan was still able to buy slightly poorer grades of gasoline and high grades of crude for conversion into a usable fuel for airplanes. Some of the gasoline was being shipped in metal drums, easily moved to military centers. While the total imports of all kinds of oil and oil products from the United States was less than before, they were still large, and judged by some to be more than required for current needs.[12] We were also making it easy for Japan to retain its reserves; during 1940 alone we exported to that country storage tanks (in knocked down form) with a capacity of over a million barrels.

The British government had not allowed its proposals for curtailment of this trade to lapse. No answer had been given to the memorandum turned in to the State Department on November 20. On January 6, 1941, the Chargé d'Affaires of the British Embassy, accompanied by his oil expert, had served a reminder. This again urged concerted action to bring about a reduction of the flow from the Indies (by having the companies reject their quotas) and from the United States (by taking tankers out of the trade). Hornbeck stressed the delicacy of the question, and recalled, according to his notes of this talk, "the fact that the British government on more than one occasion, and the Netherlands authorities on at least one occasion had begged us to go lightly and to think long and hard in relation to petroleum and other embargoes lest we produce repercussions in the Far East which would be unfortunate for all concerned, but particularly for them."

Having thus made the point, Hornbeck as authorized by Welles had got in touch with the Standard Vacuum Company. An understanding

---

[12] The amount of gasoline which Japan was trying to obtain and was obtaining had risen. Between July 26, 1940 (date of the embargo on aviation gasoline), and January 15, 1941, licenses had been issued for 7 million barrels of gasoline, of which about 3 million barrels were actually exported during this period, compared with 1936-39 average rate of exports of about one third that amount.

But the amount of crude oil exported from the United States to Japan in 1940 was much less than in certain earlier years. In millions of barrels:

$$1938—21.2$$
$$1939—16.1$$
$$1940—11.5$$

In the middle of January, 1941, however, Japan still had unused export licenses for a huge quantity of crude oil; and under its recent accord the Indies was obligated to provide about 14.5 million barrels a year, much more than before.

was reached that the company should accept the proffered Japanese quota, and then later find it hard to make full or prompt deliveries.

But this had not disposed of the situation. New reports came in that Japan was asking licenses for large amounts of gasoline for the use of its Navy. Was this wanted for the squadrons and the transports which the British then thought would set themselves against Singapore before the spring ended? Hull, busy with the Lend-Lease Act, harassed by moves to take authority to control exports out of his hands, listened while his subordinates wearily argued. Discretion won again, and he refused assent to any direct restrictive orders. But he did give the nod to some new halfway and half-invisible measures. The export of metal drums, containers and storage tanks, of oil drilling and refining equipment was stopped. Tankers under American control—even those under foreign flags—were kept out of the routes to Japan. The new restrictions were put into effect during February and March.

They did not satisfy either the American or British advocates of strangling action. During the rest of the spring, the British Embassy persisted in its efforts to have the flow still further reduced.[13] Its proposals regarding oil were influenced by estimates of Japanese stocks—including one by the American Navy—that were too high; and by an opinion that they were still increasing, which is now seen to have been wrong.[14]

Later on Hull yielded a little further to these dubious statistics. But not much. For we were, in his judgment, brushing close to the limits of tolerance—if a settlement without war was still to be sought.

In the disturbed realm of diplomacy which the United States and Japan had entered, the language used is in part symbolic, in part spoken. Battleships and economic controls are the symbol of power in reserve, symbols used to give edge to verbal warnings, a way of saying "Do you see what I mean?" without saying it. But at the same time the American government were giving secret spoken warnings to Japan.

Dooman, the experienced Counselor of the American Embassy in

[13] The effort culminated in a comphrensive group of memoranda which Halifax gave Hull on March 3. These urged an immediate decision to deny all excess supplies to Japan, and proposed the establishment of a joint centralized unit to make recommendations in regard to the action necessary to carry out this basic policy.

[14] The Division of Naval Intelligence, in a report which reached the State Department on March 12, 1941, reckoned total stocks to be (as of January 1, 1941) about 10 million tons (70-75 million barrels) equal to Japan's current requirements for at least 18 months. The United States Strategic Bombing Survey, after examination of the Japanese records, reckoned them to have been 50 to 55 million barrels. It states also that by the spring of 1941 stocks had begun to fall.

Tokyo, had been on leave in the United States. He was known by the Japanese to be a firm and straightforward friend. So it was thought that his report of the state of American opinion might be accepted as advice rather than as a threat. On February 14 (Tokyo time) he put before Ohashi, the Vice-Minister for Foreign Affairs, the "philosophy" of the American position. The Vice-Minister was told that the American people were determined to support Britain even at the risk of war; that if Japan or any other country menaced that effort it "would have to expect to come into conflict with the United States"; that if Japan were to occupy Dutch or British areas in the Pacific it would create havoc with the British situation in the war; and that the United States had abstained from an oil embargo in order not to impel Japan to create a situation that could only lead to the most serious outcome.

On the same date, February 14 (Washington time), the President had his first talk with the new Japanese Ambassador, Admiral Nomura. He made no such blunt affirmations. By being affable and eager, the President sought to show that he wished peace not war. He spoke as though the danger of war lay in a chance error or incident rather than because of any basic clash of interest. The purpose was to encourage the Japanese government to talk with us. If, as was thought, and correctly thought, in Washington, there was still a division of opinion in the Japanese government, an engagement to talk with us would help the proponents of peace. The light touch was chosen for heavy work, for critical work.[15]

In summary, then, American policy during this winter period of alarm (January–February) was a compound of warning gestures, slowly spreading coercion, earnest advice, and an invitation to talk.

The reports that came back from Tokyo were taken to mean that this policy was, at least for the time being, effective. Grew reported on the 18th of February that the Japanese officials were much disturbed by the reactions abroad; and that Matsuoka was being compelled again to defend himself against criticisms of the Tripartite Pact. The Japanese Foreign Office denied in a calm note on the 20th to the British that there was any basis for their alarm; nor for the warlike preparations which the British and the Americans were taking to meet unreal contingencies in the South Seas.

On February 20, or thereabouts, it became confirmed that Matsuoka

[15] Hull's memorandum of this talk is printed in *Foreign Relations: Japan*, II, 387-89.

was about to leave for Moscow, Berlin, and Rome. "For the purpose," Churchill informed the President, "of covering the failure of action against us." [16] This was not an adequate explanation. But about the direction of Matsuoka's mind at any given moment any guess seemed to be as good as another—so like a twisted rope was he. As when told by Grew that everything that Dooman had said to Ohashi had his (Grew's) entire concurrence and approval, he answered that he entirely agreed with what Dooman had said.[17] To Craigie at about the same time he said that Japan's motto was "No conquest, no oppression, no exploitation."

Matsuoka's words were not trusted. But the allowance of time was a great relief. And beyond that a great chance—both to strive further to avert war with Japan, and to get ready for the fight if war came. Projects for each purpose were in secret course. Two ladders were being built for history; no one knew which would be used.

Within the white marble Public Health Building on Constitution Avenue a bevy of American and British military officers were hard at work. They were writing plans for cooperation, both in measures short of war, and against the event that the United States might get into war with the Axis. At the same time, within the granite walls of the State Department a start was being made in the drafting of terms on which the United States and Japan might compose their quarrel. Let us tell first of the military planning.

[16] In this message of February 20, reprinted in *Pearl Harbor Attack*, Part 19, p. 3454, Churchill attributed the postponement of the attack to fear of the United States. He was doing his best to keep the fear alive, as when on the 24th he remarked to the Japanese Ambassador in London that it would be a pity if Japan, already at war with China, should find itself at war with Great Britain and the United States. But he took occasion also to assure the Japanese government that the measures taken by Britain were only for defense, that no attack would be made upon Japan or Japanese forces.
[17] *Foreign Relations: Japan*, II, 143.

# PART THREE
## ENMITY

## CHAPTER 21

# We Reach a World-Wide Strategic Accord with Britain: March 1941

MILITARY cooperation between the British Commonwealth and the United States up to this spring of 1941 was only a favored concept.[1] It was about to be converted into a plan and program.

This was the natural issue of our foreign policy. The critic, to merit attention, must quarrel not with it but with the decision to uphold Britain and resist the expansion of Japan—at the risk of war. Three purposes deriving from these policies called for the joint military planning which was now begun. First, to devise ways by which, without actual American entry into the war, essential sea lanes to Britain could be kept open. Second, so to allocate and station the combined forces as to present a defense to Japan and Germany everywhere, and hence discourage them from extending the war. Third, to provide a ready basis of coordinated military operations, should the United States get into war in either the Atlantic or Pacific or both.

The formal Joint Staff Conferences started in Washington on January 29. The American delegation represented the Chief of Naval Operations and the Chief of Staff of the Army.[2] The British delegation represented the British Chiefs of Staff, and with them were associated representatives of the Dominions of Canada, Australia, and New Zealand. The visitors had come over from England with the arriving English Ambassador, Lord Halifax, on the great new British battleship, *George V.* While the President went aboard the ship at Annapolis to greet the Ambassador, they stayed in their cabins. Their presence was a close secret.

---

[1] As it was in reality also between Germany and Japan. The cooperation visualized in the Tripartite Pact was not realized even as regards exchange of technical information; each partner was afraid the other would betray it. See "Japanese-German Naval Collaboration in World War II," by John W. Masland, *United States Naval Institute Proceedings,* February 1949.

[2] The Joint Army-Navy Planning Committee suggested that the British delegation should be received at the first meeting, not only by Stark and Marshall, but also by the Under Secretary of State, Welles, who was Chairman of the State-War-Navy Liaison Committee. The President decided, however, that Welles was not to attend.

Dressed in civilian clothes, they accounted for themselves about town as technical advisers to the British Purchasing Mission.

Of the meetings, and of the conclusions reached thereat, nothing was publicly told. But in one way or another the knowledge that they were taking place seeped into and through world-wide news channels.

The guiding idea on which the delegations drew up their report shows how broad was its scope:

"The Staff Conference assumes that when the United States becomes involved in war with Germany, it will at the same time engage in war with Italy. In those circumstances, the possibility of a state of war arising between Japan and an Association of the United States, the British Commonwealth and its Allies, including the Netherlands East Indies, must be taken into account." [3]

The chief points of divergence between the American and British delegations was in regard to the method of holding a defensive position against Japan in the Pacific.[4] The British thought that the defense of Singapore was essential and wanted the United States to divide its Pacific fleet for the purpose. The American delegation, under Admiral Richmond Kelly Turner, War Plans Officer for the Chief of Naval Operations, in Morison's phrase, "doubted the premise and resisted the demand." The President backed them up.

[3] *Pearl Harbor Attack*, Part 15, p. 1489. The use of the word "when" in this paragraph of the report is puzzling, since it seems to suggest an agreement between the planners, if not between their governments, that the United States would enter the war. There was no such agreement. The word "if" or the expression "if and when" would have been more consonant with the instruction given to the American delegation by Stark and Marshall. This read "should the United States be compelled to resort to war." *ibid.*, Part 3, p. 998.
This latter form of words was, in fact, the President's own. It was one of three changes made by him in the language of the draft of the text of the opening American statement to the Conference which was submitted to him on January 26 for approval by the Joint Army-Navy Planning Board, after approval by Stimson and Knox. JB 325/674. This opening statement, as made to the Conference, affirmed that all military plans envisaged would "remain contingent upon the future political action of both nations."
[4] This issue, which became entangled with current British pleas that the United States send part of the Pacific fleet to Singapore almost disrupted the conference. For Halifax, who, as a member of the British War Cabinet was in close touch with the British delegation, appealed to Hull. He, while having knowledge of the general purpose of the meeting, seems to have seen none of the papers which Halifax (or Casey or both) brought to him and he complained to the President. The American delegation, on learning of Halifax's talk with Hull, protested to their British colleagues, reminding them that the conferences were not to involve any political commitment or supervision. The British delegation expressed regret and agreed that no further papers would be passed to the State Department, though it insisted that Halifax had to be kept informed.
Hull and Halifax continued, in fact, to discuss the current situation; and on April 10 Halifax delivered to him, through Welles, a secret memorandum containing information about the British forces at Singapore which he prepared at Hull's request.

No accord was reached in this field. As stated in the minutes: "It was agreed that for Great Britain it was fundamental that Singapore be held; for the United States it was fundamental that the Pacific Fleet be held intact." [5] As explained in a letter which Admiral Stark sent to the commanders in chief of the Pacific, Asiatic, and Atlantic Fleets after the conference disbanded:

"The difficulties are our present uncertainty as to Japanese action, and British insistence on the vital importance of holding Singapore, and of supporting Australia, New Zealand, and India. Their proposals, which I rejected, were to transfer almost the whole of the Pacific Fleet to Singapore to hold that position against the Japanese." [6]

Later, it may be observed, it was agreed that Britain should send more ships to defend Singapore, while the American Navy would, if necessary, assist the British in the Mediterranean.

The joint conclusions of the delegations were expressed in a group of documents that became known as the "ABC—1 Staff Agreement." [7] This was a world-wide agreement covering all areas, land, sea, and air, of the entire world, in which it was conceived that the British Commonwealth and the United States might be jointly engaged to act against any enemy.

The main elements of the plan, as bearing on American strategy and obligations (in contemplation of possible war against Germany and/or Japan), were:

1. That the principal American military effort was to be exercised in the Atlantic Ocean and in Europe, since Germany was the predominant member of the Axis and these were the decisive theaters of combat.

2. That the United States would increase its forces in the Atlantic and Mediterranean areas so that the British Commonwealth would be in a position to release the necessary forces to defend British territories in the Far East.

3. That the tasks assigned to the American Pacific Fleet were in the main defensive—the protection of Hawaii, the Philippines, Guam, Wake, etc. But it was counted upon to undertake a diversion towards the Marshall and Caroline Islands, in order to relieve pressure on the

[5] Morison, *op. cit.*, III, 50.

[6] Letter, Admiral Stark to Fleet Commanders, April 3, 1941, *Pearl Harbor Attack*, Part 17, pp. 2462–63.

[7] Published in *Pearl Harbor Attack*, Part 15, pp. 1485–1550. The documents, approved by the Conference, March 27, 1941, consisted of (a) the Joint Letter of Transmittal to the United States and British Chiefs of Staff; (b) the basic report—"Short Title ABC-1"; (c) five annexes to ABC-1, of which Annex 3 was the "United States-British Commonwealth Joint Basic War Plan."

Malay Barrier, and to attack Japanese communications and shipping (mainly a task for submarines).

The plan, it will be noted, provided for connected, but not joint or jointly commanded operations in the Pacific. This made little difference. For the main preliminary naval dispositions in that area visualized in ABC-1 could be and were put into effect by the separate action of the countries concerned.

The report of these Joint Staff Conferences in Washington was submitted by the two delegations, subject to confirmation by both military and civil authorities. It was to be passed upon first by the Chief of Naval Operations of the United States Navy, the Chief of Staff of the United States Army, and the Chief of Staff Committee of the British War Cabinet; and, second, by the government of the United States and His Majesty's government in the United Kingdom.

The named American and British military authorities approved it quickly. Then it was endorsed by the Secretary of the Navy on May 28 and by the Secretary of War on June 2. The President did not approve it formally and explicitly. This fact, however, is not conclusive as bearing on the American obligation to carry it out. To all effects and purposes, the President permitted it to be understood that he approved; and he allowed American military plans and arrangements to be guided, if not governed, by the plan.[8] The Navy at once set about the making of a new basic war plan based on the joint reports, and soon it was issued (Rainbow No. 5).[9] The operation plans of all three main American fleets were revised to fit. The President knew everything that was being done in this, his natural field of interest.[10]

[8] See Admiral Stark's letter of April 3, 1941, to the commanders in chief of the Pacific, Asiatic, and Atlantic fleets notifying them that copies of the ABC-1 plan were being sent by officer messenger. This letter was, according to Stark's testimony, read by the President and sent with his assent. *ibid.*, Part 5, p. 2391. See also Stark's letter to Admiral Kimmel on April 4, which states that he reviewed the agreements with the President on April 2 and April 3 and got the President's "general assent." *ibid.*, Part 16, pp. 2160–61.

Beard (*President Roosevelt and the Coming of the War*, p. 420) states that although a copy of Stark's letter of April 3 (Serial 038612 ONO to commanders in chief of the United States Pacific, Asiatic, and Atlantic fleets) was presented in mimeographed form to the Congressional Committee, it was not included in the printed record. It is to be found, however, in *Pearl Harbor Attack*, Part 17, pp. 2462–63.

[9] Stark's letter of April 3 stated that the "Navy Basic War Plan Rainbow No. 5, founded on the United States-British plan, is in preparation and will be distributed at an early date."

[10] But when on July 2 Stimson and Knox sent him a copy of Rainbow No. 5, he sent it back without signifying either approval or disapproval. Through his military aide, General Watson, he informed General Marshall that he was familiar with both ABC-1 and Rainbow No. 5, but since the first had not been approved by the British Government

Beyond that, American participation in these staff conferences had consequences—practical and moral. To give effect to the jointly approved strategic conception, warships were moved over the seven seas, and planes were shifted between combat points. Scarce fighting forces and weapons of other countries were distributed in accordance with its terms.[11] Had the American government refused to play its part in their execution, loss and trouble would have followed. The British and Dutch would have felt themselves wronged. The problem is not peculiar to this instance. If once a nation (or individual) enters deeply, as adviser or sharer, into the troubles or dangers of others, it must accept the duties of partner or name of shirker. Public figures in their public statements and memoirs do not usually enter into subtleties such as this. But the President and Secretary of State were perceptive men; and I think it safe to conclude that they appreciated this point.[12]

In summary then, the situation at the end of March 1941 in this area where strategy and diplomacy merge was—as regards the Pacific—as follows: The American government had refused to obligate itself to enter the war or even to specify the circumstances in which it might do so. It had refused also to station part of its fleet at Singapore or to promise to join in the defense of Singapore or the Indies. However, it had moved naval vessels out to the Philippines. It had entered into conferences with the British which were likely to come to the knowledge of the Japanese government. American and British military authorities had agreed upon the basic lines of their strategy, both while the United States was stop-

he would reserve approval of both papers. In case of war they were to be returned to him. Memo of Colonel W. P. Scobey, *ibid.*, Part 3, p. 995.

But Stark felt authorized to go ahead. As he said later, "I do know the President, except officially, approved of it. . . ." Testimony, *ibid.*, Part 5, p. 2391.

[11] As later (September 17, 1941) succinctly stated in the report of the Planning Sub-Committee of Joint (U.S.–Great Britain) Staff Planners on "Overall Production Requirements for Victory."

"2. . . . the ultimate object is to produce a statement of the production requirements for the defeat of enemies and potential enemies. It had been agreed that these requirements should be based on the strategic needs of the situation.

"3. . . . the strategic defense policies of the United States and the British Commonwealth have been clearly defined in paragraph 11 of ABC-1 and agreed between the American and British Chiefs of Staff. They remain the foundation of our joint strategy."

[12] Thus I think Sherwood missed the full significance of these planning conferences and agreements in quitting the subject with the comment that "the plans drawn up at the staff conferences bound nobody. They could have been altered or renounced at any time 'in the light of subsequent events' . . ." *op. cit.*, p. 274.

ping short of war in its support of Britain, and in the event that it became engaged in war with Japan, Germany, Italy, or all three of them. The American Army and Navy were amending their own basic war plans to fit the strategy set down in ABC-1. Further meetings were about to begin (April 1) at Singapore, for the purpose of making a combined plan of battle operations in the Pacific.

And here, for a moment, I must outdistance the rest of the narrative. The meeting at Singapore (which brought together military delegates of Britain, the Indies, and the British Dominions in the East, with American attendance) failed in its set purpose. Its report, called "A.D.B.," has been aptly described by Morison as "A combined operating plan of local defense forces." [13]

The obstacles to agreement upon anything more were several and conclusive. Japan had the choice between any one of a dozen good striking places in the Southwest Pacific; her selection rather than any prior plan would determine what measures were best. Then divergence of interest caused a variation in strategy between the United States and the rest. Each of them felt compelled to think first of the defense of its own territories, while the United States was looking for some larger plan to force the Japanese Navy north and east.

Stark and Marshall both found the ADB report poor and rejected it. They did not like either its strategic features, or what they correctly took to be its excessive political implications.[14] And yet this Singapore report left one lasting mark on American official thinking and planning. The conferees defined the geographical limits on land and sea beyond which Japanese forces could not be permitted to go without great risk to the defenders. They drew the line at which, in their judgment, military resistance against Japan was dictated. When in December next, Japanese warships and troop transports were reported on their way south to an unknown destination, Stark and Marshall advised the President to declare these limits, and to warn Japan that we would join the fight if they were passed. Had not the Japanese struck at Pearl Harbor and the Philippines, this line would have become the boundary between war and peace.

[13] Morison, *op. cit.*, III, 55. The plan is printed in *Pearl Harbor Attack*, Part 15, pp. 1550, *et seq.*
[14] Their objections, as summarized for the British Chiefs of Staff, are printed, *ibid.*, Part 3, pp. 1542–44. See also statement of Admiral Turner, *ibid.*, Part 4, pp. 1931–33.

## CHAPTER 22

# Hull and Nomura Begin the Search
# for Formulas of Peace

IN A letter which Admiral Stark sent to his fleet commanders just after the Washington conferences ended, he wrote, "The question as to our entry into the war now seems to be *when,* and not *whether.*" [1] But this was not accepted as a foregone conclusion either by the President or the State Department. They were at the same time trying to build another ladder for history. That one would lead back to peace and order in the Far East, and friendship between the United States and Japan.

Hull and Nomura began work upon it in their first earnest talk of March 8. The two men were to meet some forty or fifty times, almost always at night in the Secretary's hotel apartment. There, in the air, which like all hotel air, seems to belong to no one, they exchanged avowals of their countries' policies. And there, among furniture which, like all hotel furniture, is neutral, they sought formulas which would make them friends. The talk was always quiet but it was never free. Each idea and sentiment was carefully composed in advance. It was like the Japanese game of "go"—in which the players with solemn and reflective air move about armies of pieces, toy soldiers really; the game is won when one player manages to place his own pieces in such a sequence as to surround his opponent's pieces, and thus obtains an admission of defeat.

During the nine months of talk the texts of a great number of possible accords, parts of accords, supplements and interpretations, were passed from one to the other, crisscrossed, added, and subtracted. Bright staffs were at work, trying either to define or conceal meaning, as suited the end.

The divergence between what the Japanese government wanted and what the American government wanted defined itself soon and remained late. To foretell, only two important changes of position occurred in the long consultations. First, as the British, Russians, and

[1] *Pearl Harbor Attack,* Part 17, p. 2463.

Chinese stayed on their feet, the Japanese offered to renounce plans for pushing further south, and to accept something less than full victory in China. Second, when towards the end of 1941 both governments realized that war was near, thought veered from a firm permanent settlement to a brief truce. The game of "go" ended with the pieces on the floor, because those elements controlling Japan in the days of ultimate decision preferred fatality to frustration.

Of the impression left by Admiral Nomura, Hull has written: "He was tall, robust, in fine health, with an open face, . . . He spoke a certain—sometimes an uncertain—amount of English. His outstanding characteristic was solemnity, but he was much given to a mirthless chuckle and to bowing. I credit Nomura with having been honestly sincere in trying to avoid war between his country and mine." [2]

The much-esteemed admiral was acquainted with many Americans, including the President and Admiral Stark. He had not been eager to come. Matsuoka had not had an easy time to get him to accept the Washington errand; to take on himself the task of bringing the Americans to grasp the "true" (and as Konoye and Matsuoka conceived it "ultimately peaceful") nature of Japanese intentions. His refusal reflected mistrust of both Matsuoka and Japanese policy. In explaining his hesitation to Harada, he said: "[Matsuoka] only observes the external appearance of matters" and "while the Japanese Army continued to insist on military power, the relations between Japan and the United States will never be amicable." But his former naval colleagues had earnestly pleaded with him to go; and had given him some kind of promise that the Navy would not allow war with the United States. So he had consented. He seems to have arrived in Washington with no instructions except to persuade the American government to accede to what Japan was doing.

As for the Secretary of State, years of Senate committee hearings had trained him to endure prolonged and watchful talk. A viscosity of speech covered, as those who dealt with him long enough found out, insight and set purpose. No leaf turned over outside the room, no look travelled within the room, of which he was not aware.

Throughout the talks Nomura had an uneasy knowledge that his government might be planning very different things from those of which he spoke. This was his secret, which he did not always keep secret. Hull had his secrets, also, of which he gave not the smallest sign. Some time before the event, he knew it likely that Germany would attack Russia,

[2] Hull, *op. cit.*, II, 987.

and could guess that it would be calling for Japanese help. Thereafter, he usually knew in detail what Nomura was being told to say to him before it was said, and with what purpose. He could even, in fact, compare what Nomura was saying with what the Japanese government was thinking and doing.

Nomura thus entered Hull's apartment exposed to a knowledge which rendered his errand needless. This was derived from the cables between the Japanese government and its diplomats abroad which the American and British governments were intercepting and decoding. "Magic" was the name given to this filched information, this radar of diplomacy.[3] Never, by a single phrase or hint during the many hours of talk, did Hull give any token of knowing more than he was supposed to know. His care matched his sensitivity. In the center of the web of strategy he sat, patient, downcast, poring over principles, and undeceived.

The task of talk was heavy for all after the ordinary day's work. Much of it fell upon the small group of State Department officials who prepared and recorded the discussions. Of these there were four—Stanley K. Hornbeck, Adviser on Political Relations, Maxwell M. Hamilton, Chief of the Far Eastern Division, and Joseph W. Ballantine and Max Schmidt, Foreign Service officers with a thorough knowledge of the Japanese language and affairs.

Of the four, Hornbeck was seldom present at the talks. He was an unrelenting judge of Japan's attack on China and convinced it would in the end fail. A confirmed foe of compromise, inclined to lay down the law, he was little suited for this touchy and circuitous business. In the background his incisive analysis caused many vague Japanese proposals to crumble into dust. Any tendency to by-pass some disputed point or to leave it in the mists of language was routed by him.

Hamilton was present at some of the talks and usually consulted after them. He was patient, gentle, and eagerly on the search for something in the Japanese proposals which might form the basis for a settlement. Within him the Japanese plight aroused worry, sympathy, rather than reproof—which led to a wish to give them all the chance possible to amend their course.

Ballantine was the language scholar and the industrious draftsman. Behind the pale impassive face, a nimble mind kept account of every corner of the talk. His drafts were monotonous and exhaustive. They left

[3] The Japanese were also intercepting and deciphering certain American codes. It was the belief of members of the American Embassy in Tokyo that the Japanese had managed to break four of the five American codes in use; but had failed completely with the fifth in which messages of an important or secret kind were sent.

no spaces in which the Japanese might hide their intentions. There was a dull evenness in his speech which made him a good interpreter, and it was he who wrote most of the official records of these meetings.

Schmidt was the youngest and most tireless in trying to find words for policies; and, like Hamilton, a believer in a chance of a just compromise if it were really wanted. With these four men to help him, the Secretary of State could have worn out even the voluble Matsuoka, had he been there.

## [2]

The talks were propelled into being by volunteers: at the American end, by two Catholic priests, Bishop James Edward Walsh, Superior General of the Catholic Foreign Mission Society at Maryknoll, New York, and Father Drought from the same group.[4] The two priests had been in Japan where they had talked to influential Japanese, among them Matsuoka. The Foreign Minister had, in one of his gyrations, asked them to report to the President that he wished to improve relations with the United States. Upon returning to this country in January, they duly sought to deliver this message through Postmaster General Walker. Further, they brought word that various elements in the Japanese government wanted an agreement with the United States. If one could be devised, they said, that would give Japan "security" these elements would prevail and change Japanese policies.

Walker brought the priests to talk with the President and Hull. They received Matsuoka's message with discreet politeness. Both were disbelieving and a little bothered lest official diplomacy be confused. But they stimulated the visitors to pursue their talks with their Japanese contacts.

Meanwhile, a strangely impassioned member of a Buddhist sect, named Hashimoto, was playing a similar part in Japan.[5] With the secret

[4] Bishop Walsh's account of these talks is given in his deposition, *Far East Mil. Trib.*, Exh. No. 3441.
[5] S. Hashimoto was one of the original members of the Amur Society (those who had operated as spies behind the Russian lines during the Russo-Japanese War—mainly in Amur province), which became known to foreigners as the Black Dragon Society, that name being the Chinese name for Amur province. Upon reaching the conclusion that Japan was being led into trouble, he left the Amur Society. Thereafter he sought to further the cause of international cooperation under the anonym, Shi-Un-So, which means the Purple Clouds Society—the allusion being to clouds lighted by the dawning sun as an augury of good weather. He was reputed to be a confidant of some of the leading figures of the Japanese government, particularly of Baron Hiranuma. His steadfastness to the cause was proved by the fact that he continued to call on members of the American Embassy in Tokyo after all other Japanese friends had been frightened off. Memorandum of Eugene H. Dooman to the author.

support of some members of the Japanese government and industrialists, he had visited Washington in January. There officials of the State Department had convinced him that the United States would not appease or condone further Japanese advances. Upon his return to Tokyo he had so reported—contrary to Matsuoka's view—that the risk of war was very real.

Thus, the ground was prepared for the messages from Walsh and Drought suggesting a continuance of the talks begun in Tokyo. Two Japanese emissaries hurried to the United States. Not too much was known of their connections. But both were believed to be in touch with Konoye and other elements in the government mistrustful of Matsuoka. One was Colonel Iwakuro, a leading member of the young officers clique in the Army, having, it was said, Tojo's confidence. The other, Wikawa, President of the Cooperative Bank, an active go-between who spoke fluent English and was married to an American. Upon their arrival a start was made towards reducing to writing ideas that had been talked over by the priests in Japan.[6]

This, remember, was in February, when the British were most afraid of an attack on Singapore, and when the Americans were most worried over British prospects in the Atlantic and Near East. Official diplomacy was in a state of suspense—since neither government was willing to come forth with any offer attractive to the other. The President, in his first reception of Nomura on February 14, 1941, had, as already told, put himself out to convey a feeling of cordiality, both for his old acquaintance, Nomura, and for the Japanese people. This, national differences aside, was genuine, and the expression of it was natural. But the hint he gave towards the end of the talk was not as casual as it was made to sound.

". . . it occurred to him," the President said, "that the Japanese Ambassador might find it advisable and agreeable as he, the President, does, to sit down with the Secretary of State and other State Department officials and review and reexamine the important phases of the relations between the two countries, . . . to see if our relations could not be improved."[7]

Nomura said he thought it a good idea. But he did not take it up until March 8—after three weeks of effort to find out what his government

[6] Iwakuro was given diplomatic status as Assistant Military Attaché. Wikawa was described on his visa application as "Extra Secretary of the Ministry of Foreign Affairs." Their reports were seen by Konoye, Tojo, Kido and Hiranuma. *ibid.*

[7] A memorandum of this talk is to be found in *Foreign Relations, Japan*, II, 387–89.

wanted him to say. Then, at this very first rub of the iron, emerged the pattern of the half hundred talks that were to follow. Hull earnestly lectured on the way Japan was abandoning the principles of peace, law, and order, and wooing fake gods. The Ambassador denied that this was the true view or inner meaning of Japanese policy. He tried to make the point that Japan's campaigns for expansion were caused not by a wish to conquer other countries but by a need to offset foreign unfairness and pressure. As summed up in Hull's memo of this talk, Nomura "sought to play down the view that such military conquest was really in the mind of his Government and he then said that embargoes by this country were, of course, of increasing concern, and that he did not believe there would be any further military movements unless the policy of increasing embargoes by this country should force his Government, in the minds of those in control, to take further military steps." [8]

This talk ended with Hull's criticism hanging in the air and Nomura's warning regarding the effect of embargoes hanging alongside of it. So did a similar one between the President and the Ambassador about a week later.

Both Nomura and Hull were keeping in touch, however, with the discussions which were going on outside the government. Ballantine twice visited the striving volunteers in order to show interest and to learn what was going on. By the end of March a draft emerged of which both the Secretary of State and Ambassador were willing to take notice, while still not admitting kinship. Born in a private nursing home of parent unknown, it was introduced into official society on April 9.[9]

The proposed agreement turned out to be of great scope and many parts—the meaning of some of which was far from clear. But its main points can be briefly summarized. The Japanese government would have, according to its terms, given two pledges of importance; first, to use only peaceful measures in the Southwest Pacific, and, second, to come to the support of Germany only if that country were the object

[8] *ibid.*, II, 387–96.

[9] *ibid.*, II, 398–402. It is printed under the title "Proposal Presented to the Department of State Through the Medium of Private American and Japanese Individuals on April 9, 1941."

Thereafter Hull assumed charge of the discussions. But Postmaster General Walker continued to exchange views and ideas about the situation with Nomura from time to time. Brief allusions to these talks with Walker are given in an unpublished manuscript which Ambassador Kichisaburo Nomura prepared, based on his notes, entitled, "My Mission to the United States," of which a translation (partly in summary) was made for the International Prosecution Section of the International Military Tribunal for the Far East.

of an aggressive attack. In return for these promises, the American government was to do several things, among them: to restore normal trade with Japan in so far as the wanted products were available; to assist Japan to obtain the raw materials it wanted from the Southwest Pacific area (that meant oil, rubber, tin, and bauxite); and to ask Chiang Kai-shek to make peace with Japan on terms specified; his regime was to coalesce with the rival created by Japan; if Chiang rejected the request the United States was to end its support of China. Among the other items was a suggestion that the American government give friendly diplomatic assistance "for the removal of Hongkong and Singapore as doorways to further political encroachment by the British in the Far East."

Talk was to roam for many months over each and every one of these matters. The items were resorted so often that at times the negotiators became unsure of the connections between them. Nomura once or twice seemed to lose track of which were in and which were out. The phrases were varied as often as a rich dowager changes costume, and the object was usually the same—to enhance the impression without changing the article.

As the skeptical students in the State Department assayed this April text, they found it poor—too poor to use as payment for protection against a Japanese move south. The United States would have been obliged, not only to end aid to China, but to coerce it into accepting permanent Japanese influence in its affairs. It would have been pledged to provide Japan with the means of maintaining whatever size army and navy it wanted. And even then, if Japan should have decided to join in the war against Britain, it would have been free to do so; the Axis connection was not severed.

Yet no purpose, Hull thought, would be served by an unqualified rejection of this child of chance. It was wise to keep the opinion alive within the Japanese government that the issues dividing the two nations might be settled by talk. It was essential to ward off the conclusion that no path except that of war could take Japan towards its ends. Who knew what turn of battle or new estimate of chances might change the outlook? Thus Hull decided to deal with the proposals gently, to show himself ready to discuss them, and to try to modify them.

Then when he saw Nomura on April 14 he said merely that he would like to know whether the Japanese government wished to present the document which had found its way into the State Department as a first step in negotiations—it being understood both governments could propose changes. Nomura said he was so disposed.[10] Two days later, the news of the Japanese-Soviet neutrality pact having just arrived, the Secretary made a detour of the sort for which he had special talent. Ushering the action in by one octopus-like sentence which it would take a whole chapter of print to dissect, he gave the Ambassador a piece of paper.[11] On it four points were jotted down, about which he invited the comment of the Japanese government as a "paramount preliminary" to the start of the discussions.

In weighing all that came after, these four points should be borne in mind. For they marked out the ground on which the American government stood. In some phases of the talks with Japan, it was deemed discreet to leave them in the background. But they were never forgotten. In order they were:

"1. Respect for the territorial integrity and the sovereignty of each and all nations.
2. Support of the principle of non-interference in the internal affairs of other countries.
3. Support of the principle of equality, including equality of commercial opportunity.
4. Non-disturbance of the *status quo* in the Pacific except as the *status quo* may be altered by peaceful means."

The Japanese government did not want to argue principles; abstract principles, which took no account of place, time, or degree. It wanted an end to American aid to China, a lifting of the embargoes, economic independence, a commanding place in the Far East. Thus, the Japanese records verify, it studied this list of commandments glumly. They made a cavern in which Japan could become lost and delayed. But the Japanese government was to find that there was no way round them. Or, as the matter was regarded by the heads of that government (and so stated in their later defense), American insistence that Japan subscribe to these four principles was "symptomatic of a doctrinairism which was to exercise a baleful influence throughout." [12]

Ambassador Nomura conveyed Hull's query (of April 14) and this list of principles to his government at Tokyo. The American officials

[10] Hull's memorandum of this talk is printed, *ibid.*, II, 402, *et seq.*
[11] *ibid.*, II, 406–7.
[12] *Far East Mil. Trib.*, Defense Document No. 3100.

"sat down to await the Japanese reply." [13] To wait, but not, as will be seen, with hands in lap.

The wait was to be almost a month, for Nomura's message evoked great disputes within the Japanese government. It arrived while Matsuoka was on his way home from Moscow with his head full of other plans, and as the Japanese Army and the Navy were getting ready to take over the rest of Indo-China. Now the separate strands of Japanese diplomacy which ran east and west, south and north, became tangled with one another.

The answer was received on May 12. Before telling of that, it is illuminating to trace back what had been happening within the Japanese government during those months of 1941 so far traversed.

[13] Hull, *op. cit.*, II, 996.

## CHAPTER 23

# Matsuoka Goes to Berlin and Moscow, and Returns with a Neutrality Pact

THE first three months of 1941; but in the other part of the forest. It has been told how Britain, preparing for the onsurge of the German armies (over the Balkans, and at the east and west ends of the Mediterranean) greatly feared Japanese intentions. An attack on Singapore was, in fact, closely contemplated—in Berlin with ardor, in Tokyo with qualms. The Nazi war leaders were most eager to have Japan strike at the British position in the Far East. This action, they reckoned, would help Germany whether or not the United States joined the defense. If it did, American naval forces would be diverted and American aid to Britain would fail. If it did not, vital connections of the British Isles would be lost.

As reasoned out by the Naval Staff for Hitler, early in January, "It must and can be assumed that if America's entry into the war is provoked by steps taken by Japan, the United States will not commit the main part of her fleet to the European theater. She is far more likely to keep it in the Pacific as protection against the danger from Japan, which she considers great." Thus the report concluded: ". . . it is in our interest to encourage Japan to take any initiative she considers within her power in the Far Eastern area, as this would be most likely to keep American forces from the European theater in addition to weakening and tying down British forces.

"We can accept the risk that such action by Japan might bring about America's entry into the war on the side of Britain, since, so far as naval warfare is concerned, the total advantages outweigh the total disadvantages." [1]

---

[1] These are extracts from the report called "Observations on the Question of Japan and the Tripartite Pact," submitted by Admiral Raeder as a basis for discussion between Hitler and his supreme military commanders, January 8–9.—*Germany, Kriegsmarine, Oberkommando, Fuehrer Conferences on Matters Dealing with the German Navy, 1939–[1945]* (Washington, U.S. Navy Department [1947]), 1941, I, 12, *et seq.*

The German military staff in Tokyo, under the orders of Ribbentrop and Ott, busied themselves with a study of the problems of the capture of Singapore. Activist circles of Japan contributed to this effort, which was completed by the end of January.[2]

The tormenting questions of whether and where to act drew the civilian and military leaders of Japan together in almost constant conferences. At a Liaison Conference on January 30 it was decided, as already told, to enforce mediation upon both Indo-China and Thailand, and to get payment from both of them. The State Department was correct in its estimates of what these exactions were to be. Of Indo-China the use of air bases, ports, and the right to station and transport troops were to be demanded under threat of seizure.[3] The Navy had in mind, particularly, the use of Camranh Bay and air bases near Saigon.[4] These transactions the Army insisted should be completed by April 1. But Matsuoka asked, and was granted, more time so that he could first reach an understanding with Germany and Russia. The idea of a possible attack on Singapore was deferred until these advance points in Indo-China and Thailand were secured.[5]

The Emperor, Cabinet, and Army had all approved Matsuoka's visit to Berlin and Moscow. On February 3, another Liaison Conference passed upon the ideas by which he was to be guided in his tour. They were set down in a reference paper rather than a firm instruction.[6] It was a reversion to the ideas of dividing up the world in four spheres with which Matsuoka had bemused his colleagues when the Tripartite Pact was first signed in September, 1940. He was to secure recognition of Japan's supremacy in Greater East Asia, and reach an accord with the Soviet Union, under which the latter would act in harmony with the Tripartite powers. No murmur had yet reached Tokyo of Hitler's secret plans. Some of Matsuoka's colleagues had a leaning to make sure that Matsuoka would not, without further consultation, obligate Japan to

[2] *Far East Mil. Trib.*, Exh. Nos. 562 and 572.
[3] "Outline of Policies Towards French Indo-China and Thailand," *ibid.*, Exh. No. 3658.
[4] *ibid.*, Exh. No. 1303.
[5] As explained to the Emperor and retold by the chief aide-de-camp to the Emperor to Kido on February 1: "The 'Outline of Operations in French Indo-China and Thailand' is intended to establish Japan's leader position in the south so as to prepare the ground for her southern advance; taking advantage of their acceptance of Japan's mediation in their border dispute. The Navy intends to use Camranh Bay and also the air base near Saigon, but its objects cannot be boldly expressed. . . . In case armed force is resorted to, it is arranged that Imperial Sanction be obtained afresh." Kido's deposition and diary entry for February 1, 1941.
[6] Decision of the Liaison Conference: The Outline of the Plan for Negotiations with Germany, Italy and the Soviet Union. *ibid.*, Exh. No. 3657.

use force north or south or both. But he managed to avoid having this explicitly stated.[7]

To Ott, the mission was explained in a way to ensure a hearing in Berlin. He was told by Matsuoka with obvious joy that his mission was approved; that he would talk first of all with Hitler and Ribbentrop about the attitude of the partners of the Tripartite Pact towards the United States. He wished, if possible, to prevent American entry into the war by diplomatic influence; but, if that came to appear impossible, Japan was considering a preventive attack on Singapore. This question, the advance word went on, Japan would decide only in ˄ccord with the Reich. Meanwhile, it was preparing for war and hoping to conclude accords with Russia and China.[8]

Hitler saw no need or sense in the delay. Oshima was at hand to reflect his visions. He was the mica in the rock which came alight under the German beam, no matter how bent the angle of impact. "Japan in its own interest," Ribbentrop ended a long essay in persuasion on February 23, "would be right to enter the war as soon as possible. The decisive blow would be an attack on Singapore . . . it must be carried out with lightning speed and if at all possible without a declaration of war . . ." Japan would be better, he advised, to leave the Philippines alone, while striking at Singapore. For, if the job were quickly done, the United States would stand aside, not yet being armed, and unwilling to risk its fleet west of Hawaii.

Oshima agreed. But still he asked a few questions—in particular, about the relations with the Soviet Union. Ribbentrop's answer left much to be learned. He said that Molotov "had indicated readiness" in principle on certain conditions "to adhere to the Tripartite Pact . . ." This meant that "The political discussion with the U.S.S.R. was still in the balance." [9]

Thus Ribbentrop tried to win the decision before Matsuoka's arrival.[10]

[7] General Tojo, when on trial before the International Military Tribunal, said that he did not trust Matsuoka's traits and personality and feared he might commit Japan to military operations. The Chiefs of the Army and Navy General Staffs spoke in the same vein. They were, to hear them, rivals in the wish to keep peace unbroken.

[8] Telegram, Ott to Ribbentrop, February 10, 1941, *ibid.,* Exh. No. 569.

[9] German official memorandum of talk, Ribbentrop-Oshima, at Fuschl, February 23, 1941. *ibid.,* Exh. No. 571. This long, disorderly, and deceptive talk found Ribbentrop at his silliest; but he sent full reports of it to the heads of the German Foreign Office and the German diplomatic missions abroad, as being of "fundamental significance for orientation."

[10] Also by exertions in Tokyo. "You are to work with all the means at your disposal," he instructed Ott on February 27, "to induce Japan to take possession of Singapore as soon as possible by surprise." *ibid.,* Exh. No. 572.

Tempted but unsure and unready, the Japanese government refused. It waited longer to see how the war in Europe went, hoping still that the lands to the south could be scooped up like a widow left adrift by the death of a great man.

Hitler's intention to attack the Soviet Union was by now fixed. All the more useful, he thought, Japan could be. As set down in a Military Directive issued from his headquarters on March 5: "It must be the aim of the collaboration based on the Three Power Pact to induce Japan as soon as possible *to take active measures in the Far East.* . . . The Barbarossa operation [attack on Russia] will create most favorable political and military prerequisites for this.

"The seizure of Singapore as the key British position in the Far East would mean a decisive success for the entire conduct of war of the Three Powers. In addition attacks on other systems of bases of British naval power—extending to those of American naval power only if entry of the United States into the war cannot be prevented—will result in weakening the enemy's system of power in that region. . . ."

Thus Japan must act at once, but in ignorance.

"The Japanese must not be given any intimation of the Barbarossa operation." [11]

Admiral Raeder advised Hitler to let Matsuoka know of the plans regarding Russia.[12] So did Weizsaecker, who in a memorandum of March 24 reminded Ribbentrop that:

"Matsuoka is still following the line of an understanding with Russia and claims German encouragement for this. A clear statement which course our relations to Russia may take is unavoidable in order to protect him from surprises, and in order to control Japanese policy through him after his European journey." [13]

But Hitler was afraid to trust the Japanese government with this vital information. He feared that it might be used to strike a bargain with Russia, or even with Great Britain and the United States. Japan was not

[11] Basic Army Order, No. 24, regarding collaboration with Japan, issued from the Fuehrer's Headquarters, March 5, 1941.—Nuremberg Doc. C-75.

[12] *Fuehrer Conferences,* 1941, I, 33. The German Navy seems to have revised its opinion as to the relative advantages and disadvantages of American entry into the war. Its approval of Japanese attack had been unqualified, now it became conditional. But Hitler remained convinced of the advantages. The minutes of a conference on March 18 between him and his military chiefs record the conclusion that "Japan must take steps to capture Singapore as soon as possible, since the opportunity is more favorable than it will ever be again: The entire British fleet is tied down; the U.S.A. is not prepared to wage war on Japan; the U.S. fleet is inferior to the Japanese fleet." *ibid.,* I, 32.

[13] Memorandum of Weizsaecker to Ribbentrop, March 24, 1941. *Far East Mil. Trib.,* Exh. No. 575.

to be regarded as a reliable partner.[14] There were, when Matsuoka travelled from Moscow to Berlin and back, scores of German divisions on the frontier between. He passed through them without looking out of the window. Probably he was too busy talking.

## [2]

Matsuoka took to the rails, tossing behind him an assortment of assurances; to his colleagues that he would return with Greater East Asia in his brief case, to Grew and Craigie that all he was after was peace with the Soviet Union, in order the better to settle the war in China.

In his first stop at Moscow on March 5 he offered Stalin and Molotov a non-agression pact.[15] Molotov proposed, instead, a neutrality agreement. Matsuoka said he would give an answer upon his return from Berlin—where, no doubt, he hoped for help.

The essential features of Matsuoka's long talks with Hitler and Ribbentrop (March 27–April 4) may be briefly told.[16] The Germans tried to convince Matsuoka that the battle against Britain was in its final phase and that Germany was complete master of the situation in Europe. Britain would have long since quit if it had not been for American support. Japan was now in a position to make a decisive stroke, one that would hasten Britain's collapse and prevent United States' aid from being effective. It ought to, it must, occupy Singapore at once and by lightning measures. Thereby, and thereafter, Japan would secure the positions it needed for the New Order in Greater East Asia. It was in one of these talks (April 4) that Hitler said:

". . . if Japan got into a conflict with the United States, Germany on her part would take the necessary steps at once. It made no difference with whom the United States first came into conflict, whether it was with Germany or with Japan."

To all of this Matsuoka responded with a gushing eagerness that con-

[14] Memorandum of Ott to Ribbentrop, March 25, 1941. *ibid.*, Exh. No. 576. Ott had returned to Germany to participate in the talks with Matsuoka.

[15] As contemplated in the Decision of the Liaison Conference of February 13, he was also to propose (1) that Japan would recognize the Soviet Union's position in Sinkiang and Outer Mongolia in return for Russian recognition of the Japanese position in North China and Inner Mongolia; (2) that Soviet Union end its aid to Chiang Kai-shek; and (3) to secure a five-year guarantee of oil deliveries from Sakhalin. *ibid.*, Exh. No. 3657.

[16] German records of these five talks (March 27, 28, 29, and April 4) are reprinted in *Nazi-Soviet Relations*. When afterwards Matsuoka, through Ott, asked for copies the German government refused on the ground that as a matter of principle, no records were kept, and that Interpreter Schmidt took note only of catchwords and phrases for purposes of translation.

densed into nothing solid. As he talked, it became plain that he had come to Berlin without either the authority or confirmed will to engage Japan. Hitler wished to have Japan in the war before or as soon as his armies entered Russia. All he got was an avowal of Matsuoka's intention to do his utmost to bring Japan into the struggle sometime soon. The invited guest, it had been hoped, would be a man of radiant action; the arrived guest turned out to be a man of excusing talk.[16a]

He expressed himself as convinced that war between the United States and Japan must come sooner or later, and in favor of having it come sooner, rather than later. He agreed that the lightning seizure of Singapore was essential and should be undertaken. But in Japan there were many, he explained, who would like to capture the tiger cub but were not prepared to go into the den to take it away from the mother. (How often this figure of speech appeared in his talk!) There were the wavering intellectuals, the persons of pro-British and pro-American sentiments, inside and outside the government, and, most important of the lot, the naval people who feared a long war with the United States. By all these he "was considered to be a dangerous man with dangerous ideas." Over all these he would surely at some time prevail. "But," in summary, "at the present moment he could under these circumstances make no pledge on behalf of the Japanese Empire that it would take action. . . . He could make no definite commitment, but he would promise that he personally would do his utmost for the ends that had been mentioned."

So Singapore still was threatened only by Matsuoka's intentions, not by his government's decision. The shadow of the United States lay in between, and the ritual phrases of Hitler and Ribbentrop did not dispel it.

In regard to Russia, the talk went even more awry. Matsuoka told of his dickering with Stalin and Molotov; of how he had proposed a non-aggression pact to them, and they a neutrality agreement to him. It was arranged, he said, that the subject should be settled when he stopped in Moscow again on his return journey. With emphasis that grew heavier it was explained to him how greatly relations between Germany and the Soviet Union had changed since September 1940. Then Russia was thought of as a likely partner in the Tripartite Pact. Now it was a menace

---

[16a] Churchill seems to be of the opinion that Hitler and Ribbentrop in these talks showed clear anxiety lest the United States enter the war, even while they were urging Japan to attack Singapore. He attributes Matsuoka's evasion of their demands and his signature of the neutrality pact with the Soviet Union as due in no small measure to this display of worry by the German leaders. The records do not seem to me to support these conjectures. Winston S. Churchill, *The Grand Alliance* (Boston, 1950), pp. 189–191.

who might become an enemy; a pushing power and a dangerous diffuser of Communism throughout all Europe and Asia.

Hitler, himself, avoided any hint of a decided and planned attack against Russia. He thought it enough to paint the sky dark, to point to the lightning, and let Matsuoka deduce that a storm was brewing. But when the visitor did take notice, Hitler pretended vagueness. Thus when Matsuoka asked about the chance that Russia might enter the war on England's side, Hitler answered that Germany "did not fear such a possibility in the slightest and would not hesitate a second to take the necessary steps in case of danger. He (the Führer) believed, however, that this danger would not arise."

Ribbentrop's remarks were plainer. Thus (to choose one of a dozen examples) on March 29, he "expressed the opinion that in view of the general situation it might be best not to go into things too deeply with the Russians. He did not know how the situation would develop. . . . He (the Reich Foreign Minister) in any event wanted to point out to Matsuoka that a conflict with Russia was always within the realm of possibility. At any rate, Matsuoka could not report to the Japanese Emperor, upon his return, that a conflict between Germany and Russia was inconceivable. On the contrary, as matters stood, such a conflict, though not probable, still would have to be designated as possible."

Both Hitler and Ribbentrop spoke as though the uncertain question was whether Russia would attack Germany, never of the opposite turn. Despite this disguise it is hard to believe that Matsuoka did not grasp that the Soviet Union was in German eyes no longer a friend and quite possibly an enemy. It is easier to believe that he would not allow what he learned to disrupt his plans, to rob him of his triumph.[17] There is another interpretation of his conduct not to be dismissed; that his mind, by then, was in disorder.

Whichever of these surmises is correct, back in Moscow Matsuoka was no less eager than before to sign some sort of pact. The knowledge he gained in Berlin may have been used, in fact, to obtain it. What could have been as likely to cause Stalin to come to terms as word that Hitler

[17] Matsuoka's talent for duplicity was well displayed in the variety of statements he made on this point then and later on. Thus, he told the American Ambassador at Moscow, Steinhardt, on April 8 that Hitler and Ribbentrop had urged him to come to some agreement with the Soviets, and he had said he wished to do so, but would not pay the excessive price Molotov asked. He told the German Ambassador in Moscow (Schulenburg) on April 13, after the pact was signed, that when in Berlin he had told Hitler and Ribbentrop he would show no eagerness for a pact, but would be compelled to sign one if Russia met Japanese terms; and that Ribbentrop had agreed with this point of view. He told Konoye, on his return, that Ribbentrop had said that there would be no objection to such an agreement, although he saw little use in it. (Konoye paper "Concerning the Tripartite Alliance.")

and Ribbentrop thought war with the Soviet Union by no means unlikely? The Director of the European Department of the Japanese Foreign Office, Sakamoto by name, and close companion of Matsuoka on this trip, was making no secret of this fact. According to a report which reached the American Ambassador in Moscow he was expressing the belief that "Germany wished and was capable of destroying the Soviet Empire, would attack as soon as the Balkan campaign was over, or as soon thereafter as German armies were in shape; further that he was under the impression that the Russians were well informed about the Germans' designs." [18]

Stalin, it may be surmised, was not disturbed by the thought that this way of securing protection would cause Japan to feel more free to move south; he may even have relished the idea. In any case, with dramatic abruptness, he dropped the conditions which had been previously attached to Soviet assent. The neutrality pact was signed in the last hours before Matsuoka's departure (April 13). In order to authorize Matsuoka to sign in time, Konoye sought an instant audience with the Emperor. Imperial sanction was given without consulting either the Cabinet or the Privy Council. By behavior well understood in these circles, i.e., reverse behavior, Stalin made it clear that he had Germany in mind. On the railway platform after hugging Matsuoka, Stalin sought out the German Ambassador and, throwing his arms around his shoulders, remarked: "We must remain friends and you must now do everything to that end!" [19]

The pact provided that Japan and Russia would maintain peaceful relations and respect each other's territory. If either became "the object of hostilities on the part of one or several third Powers, the other . . . will observe neutrality throughout the duration of the conflict." [20]

Neither government, of course, trusted the other to stand by these promises if the strain or temptation was great. In the diplomatic bazaar where such treaties were transacted, the rule was "Let the buyer beware." The goods had become degraded, the coin false.

[18] Steinhardt so informed Washington by cable April 15. Of course the Russian government had had other advance intimations of a possible attack—some conveyed by the American government. The German Embassy in Moscow was sure that Russia had more than an inkling of German plans; on April 22 the German Chargé in Moscow reported to Berlin that between March 27 and April 17, there had been 80 cases of violation by German forces of Russian frontiers, and discovery inside a fallen German plane of evidences of German military photography of Russia.

[19] A description of this scene of muddled, sinister joviality is given in Schulenburg's cable to Ribbentrop, April 13, printed in *Nazi-Soviet Relations*, p. 324. Matsuoka's description of the departure, as remembered by one of the advisers in the Foreign Office, is to be found in the deposition of Saito (Toshiye) *Far East Mil. Trib.*, Exh. No. 3143.

[20] *New York Times*, April 14, 1941.

## CHAPTER 24

# The Two Faces of Japanese Diplomacy Glare at One Another: April 1941

WHEN Hitler was told that Japan had signed this pact with Russia, he put on a mask.[1] He was extremely angry; but he half hid the feeling from both the Japanese and his own circle. In a meeting with his military leaders on April 20, he told them that the Russo-Japanese pact had been concluded with Germany's acquiescence.[2] The fact, he added, that it was known that Matsuoka consulted him shortly before signing would cause Russia to be off guard and to act with great correctness. Further, it was to be expected that, having gained this protection, Japan would soon proceed to attack Singapore. For this operation, he continued, both Matsuoka and Oshima had assured him that all preparations would be completed by May.

Who can tell how much of this was self-protection, and how much self-deception? Did he really count upon Matsuoka's cloudy forecasts? Or—as seems more likely—did his discretion spring from another thought: that when the German march upon Russia began to succeed, Japan would find a way to join him anyhow?

The Japanese government was jubilant over the new pact with the Soviet Union.[3] Konoye, who, as has already been told, had secured the Imperial sanction in the greatest of hurry, welcomed it with the rest. For it tempered the Army's chronic impulse to war with Russia, brought hope that Chiang Kai-shek would come to terms, and make the way

---

[1] According to the Konoye paper on the Tripartite alliance, Oshima reported that both Hitler and Ribbentrop showed pained surprise and perplexity at the news. This is confirmed in Ribbentrop's telegram to Ott of July 5, 1941, recounting his version of what had occurred when Matsuoka was in Berlin and after: "What I said to Matsuoka at the time unmistakably revealed that I did not consider the conclusion of a Japanese-Russian Treaty of Non-Aggression or Neutrality Pact to be suitable. The news of the conclusion of the Pact therefore came as a surprise to me. However, I refrained at the time from making this known to Matsuoka." *Far East Mil. Trib.*, Exh. No. 792.

Ribbentrop repeated his protests to Oshima, who cabled that the German leaders were showing "extreme antipathy" to the Japanese-American talks. *ibid.*, Exh. No. 1075.

[2] *Fuehrer Conferences*, 1941, I, 53.

[3] Report of the German Chargé Boltze to the Foreign Office, April 14, 1941. *Far East Mil. Trib.*, Exh. No. 584.

south safer. Perhaps, even, the American government would become more lenient.[4]

However, Konoye's satisfaction was brief, indeed. Within a very few days bewildering troubles beset him.

Hardly had the pact with Russia been signed, when the Japanese Army and Navy met again at Imperial Headquarters to consider what, if anything, could be done to hasten the movement south. In some respects their earlier plans had gone well; in others badly.

With their program of acquiring economic and strategic control of the Dutch East Indies, no progress had been made. The government of the Indies was continuing to deny Japan special place or opportunity. It was also refusing to discuss an increase in oil and rubber shipments. The oil was wanted more than ever as the inflow from the Western Hemisphere was being reduced; the rubber was needed to meet promises given to Germany.[5] Konoye, himself, had found it necessary to instruct the Japanese mission in Batavia not to quit in discouragement, "to push pertinaciously our original demands for the time being, to direct your main effort to the acquisition of resources, and to await further developments in the situation. (Decision reached in concert with the Army.)"[6]

Some, though not all, of the desired benefits from the mediation between Thailand and Indo-China were being gathered. The government of Thailand was arranging to send Japan greater amounts of rice, rubber, tin, and other materials; but it was avoiding all political and military demands. In Indo-China the Japanese Army and Navy had installed themselves at points well beyond those specified in the agreement with Vichy. But they still did not have the use of the naval bases, ports, and air fields at the southern points commandingly close to Singapore; vigorous elements were urging that the sphere of occupation be extended.

As it struggled to decide what to do next, the Japanese government followed intently the movement of the American, British, Dutch, and Australian forces in the area. It counted the increase in American troops

[4] In the statement he gave to the Press (April 14), Konoye interpreted the Pact as a step towards peace. "This treaty is not only an epoch-making event in the diplomatic relations between Japan and the Soviet Union, but also I believe that it will contribute to the realization of world peace."

[5] Reich Marshal Goering had singled out this subject to discuss with Matsuoka on March 29. "Each day on which Germany could receive these deliveries earlier and every increased quantity she could receive were of the utmost importance." German official memorandum of Goering-Matsuoka talk, March 29, 1941, *Far East Mil. Trib.*, Exh. No. 581.

[6] *ibid.*, Exh. No. 1320.

in Hawaii and the Philippines, the movements of American ships, and, plane by plane, charted the growth of aviation strength at each point in the Pacific. It studied every scrap of intelligence or gossip regarding the naval discussions held in Washington, Singapore, and Batavia. The Japanese Foreign Office, at least, seems to have become sure that a definite military understanding had been conceived between the United States and the British Commonwealth and the Netherlands.[7]

This the President and Hull were willing to have the Japanese government suspect. But only to suspect; not to be sure, and not to feel publicly challenged. Thus, when on April 16, 1941 the Australian Minister, Casey, and the British Minister, Neville Butler, separately informed Welles that the British Commander in Chief of the Far East was urging that the British and Dominion governments give publicity to the approaching staff conferences at Singapore, they were told that the effect might be prejudicial. Such an announcement, Welles said, would be regarded by the Japanese government as unduly provocative and would arouse the more hot-headed elements in the Japanese Army and Navy. His notes of this talk continue: "I said it seemed to me that through their intelligence organization the highest ranking officers of the Japanese Army and Navy would know in any event that these staff conferences were going to take place, and that if the holding of these conferences was going to have any deterrent effect upon them, that effect would be created without publicity."[8]

[7] Evidence of the care with which Japan followed these military movements is found in two memoranda prepared in the Foreign Office. One in April 1941 was entitled "On the Formation of the Anti-Japanese Joint Encirclement by Great Britain, United States and the Netherlands." *Far East Mil. Trib.*, Exh. No. 3566. The other, dated July, 1941, was entitled "The Anglo-American Policy of Encirclement against Japan in the Southern Pacific Ocean." *ibid.*, Exh. No. 3567.

Both summarize press, radio, and other reports upon the meeting of diplomats of the ABCD powers, movements of the American fleet, the dispatch of American naval advisers and military observers, military conferences at Washington and Singapore, and American military preparations in the Southern Pacific. They were both a hodgepodge of correct and wrong facts and statistics. But it is clear that the compilers were convinced that a joint ABCD defense understanding existed and was being implemented.

[8] The *Investigation of Pearl Harbor Attack, Report, Senate Document 244, 79th Congress . . .* (Washington, 1946), p. 171, states: "There is no evidence to indicate that Japanese knowledge of the 'ABC' and 'ADB' conversations was an inducing factor to Japan's decision to attack the United States . . ." The real question would seem to be not whether *actual* knowledge of the contents of these plans affected Japanese decisions, but rather whether what the Japanese *thought they knew* affected them. Certainly they knew the talks took place; Japanese officials mentioned them to Grew and Craigie. They also assumed that it was probable that joint plans resulted. This presumed knowledge may well have had a deterrent effect during the spring and summer of 1941. Later, it probably influenced the Japanese Navy to accept the view that unless Japan took the initiative and took it soon, it could not win. This matter is discussed on pages 217, 264-265. Compare Beard's *President Roosevelt and the Coming of the War*, pp. 450-51.

The Japanese Navy always tended to think that if Japan attacked Singapore or the Indies the American Navy would sooner or later enter the war. But it was hardly less bothered by the thought that we would keep the main Pacific fleet out of the Southwestern Pacific, until we could use it tellingly in a flank attack. This was the reason why, as early as January 1941, the Commander of the Combined Fleets, Admiral Yamamoto, took up the project for attacking Pearl Harbor.

At the end of a special meeting of the Army and Navy at Imperial Headquarters on April 16 all ultimate decisions were deferred. It was resolved merely to proceed with the already approved program for extending relations with Indo-China, Thailand, and the Indies; this visualized the use of economic and political means before resorting to force. The final section of the resolution shows that those elements that wanted to avoid war with Britain and the United States were still strong enough to force the more reckless ones to temporize:

"III.    In executing the foregoing measures resort to arms in the interest of self-existence and self-defense will be taken only when the following instances should occur and when no means for solution of the same can be found:

"1. In case the self-existence of the Empire should be threatened by the embargoes of the United States, Great Britain, and the Netherlands.

"2. In case anti-Japanese encirclement by the United States, Great Britain, the Netherlands, and China become so tense that it cannot be tolerated in the interests of national defense." [9]

This, then, was the contingent (the "in case") statement of Army and Navy judgment which Konoye had before him when called upon to decide between Matsuoka, who was on his way home from Berlin and Moscow, and Admiral Nomura, who was cabling from Washington. The one was returning with promises strewn behind him that he would try to bring about an attack on Singapore. The other was seeking to maintain peace with the United States. He was urgently asking answers to the two questions which Hull had asked on April 14 and 16. Would the Japanese government subscribe to the four general principles which Hull had written down? Was it disposed to use the draft which had emerged from the talks between Fathers Walsh and Drought and

[9] "Gist of Imperial Headquarters Army and Navy Department Policy concerning Measures to be Taken in the South." *Far East Mil. Trib.,* Exh. No. 1305. This meeting was probably held on April 16—but it may have been a little earlier.

the Japanese emissaries as a basis for official discussions? The two faces of Japanese diplomacy were glaring at each other.

## [2]

Nomura's cables transmitting Hull's queries reached the Japanese Foreign Office on the evening of April 17. They were sent directly to the Prime Minister, Konoye. On the same day ominous word came from Oshima: Germany was nearing war against Russia. Konoye was thus confronted with the greatest packet of hard decisions in his wavering career. Should Japan just watch events, or move north, or south? What was it to say to Germany and the United States?

He summoned at once (April 18) another Liaison Conference of all high government and military leaders. With them he reviewed the long Washington text containing terms of settlement. Hull's request for an affirmation of hard general principles of conduct was mentioned only briefly and obliquely.[10] Konoye, it may be presumed, did not want the talks with the United States to go aground on this rock. He was ready to assent to them—as generalities which Japan would by and by, and with flexible adaptations, observe.

With speed most unusual in that circle, a program was adopted. But it had one great defect: the two main parts cancelled each other. One part resolved to accept conditionally the terms of a possible accord with the United States, as transmitted by Nomura. The conferees seem to have thought that the (so-called) Walsh-Drought draft was well regarded, if not approved, by the American government. Whether Nomura failed to make clear that Hull took it merely as a starting point for discussion, or whether Konoye failed to make clear what Nomura had made clear, I do not know.

The Prime Minister in his "Memoirs" summarizes the reasons for the decision to proceed with discussions with the United States. All were of a practical kind: the depletion of Japan's national strength which

---

[10] The available Japanese records, particularly the "Memoirs of Prince Konoye . . . ," Exh. 173, *Pearl Harbor Attack,* Part 20, pp. 3985, *et seq.,* "Kido's Diary," and Tojo's defense deposition, *Far East Mil. Trib.,* all encourage this inference.

The text of the Konoye memoirs cited throughout this narrative is a translation by American authorities of the version completed in the spring of 1942, and corrected by him. It consists of a main text; appendices, and supplement. Another version turned out with Konoye's consent two years after the war began, cut down, and partly revised by him, was printed in Japan. Then in May, 1945, he wrote the note entitled, "Concerning the Triple Alliance," to which reference has been made. Deposition of his private secretary, Ushiba (Tomohiko), *ibid.,* Exh. No. 2737.

made it desirable to end the war in China as soon as might be; the wish to get war materials from the United States once more; and the fact that the supreme military command was neither prepared for, nor confident of, success in a southward advance. Thus, what Washington had surmised, the enemy records show to have been so. One strong faction was pulling towards Germany, another was still holding back. Our export controls were hurting. The Japanese Navy was not yet ready to risk a long war. The unguessed item was the smoldering idea of eliminating the American fleet at Pearl Harbor. For that more time, training, and special equipment was needed.

But other sections of the program adopted by this April 18 conference were not compatible with a friendly American settlement. For example, the conference also resolved that nothing must be done that would affect Japan's obligations under the Tripartite Pact. Thus the United States must be kept in a state of worry over Japanese intentions, since, the record states, if it were relieved of the need of keeping guard in the Pacific and so enabled to increase aid to Britain, Japan would be breaking faith with Germany.

Konoye had asked Matsuoka to hurry back to Tokyo. While waiting for him, the heads of the government, civil and military, in several more joint conferences confirmed these opposites. Konoye was authorized to proceed with the Washington talks. An Army and Navy memorandum of the 21st stated the opinion that "Japan must turn the American scheme to good advantage and by embracing the principles embodied in the proposal, attain the objectives of the China Incident, restore the national strength, and thereby attain a powerful voice in the establishment of world peace." [11]

When Matsuoka arrived on April 22, the Prime Minister drove to the air field to meet him. But the excited diplomat hurried away to see the Emperor. When later he was brought into conference with Konoye he showed himself much upset by and utterly against negotiating with the United States. The spell of Hitler and Ribbentrop was still upon him. He said the proposal from Washington contained 70 per cent ill will and 30 per cent good will. What percentages would he have used had he known Mr. Hull's full thoughts about it? He stormily recalled that during the First World War the United States had induced Japan to sign an agreement (the Lansing-Ishii Agreement), which, he said, the United States had scrapped as soon as the war was over and had forced Japan out of China. This was only the start of his tantrums.

[11] "Konoye Memoirs," *Pearl Harbor Attack*, Part 20, p. 3987.

He asked two weeks to study the question. Then he took to his bed with bronchitis, where he saw only those he wanted to see.

The German Ambassador, Ott, was among those seen. At the end of his visit he had a copy of the text that had come from Washington. Not long after, Matsuoka told Ott that it was his opinion that if Germany fought Russia, Japan would be compelled to join.[12]

Konoye pulled this way and that, also took to bed and there he stayed until the first of May. From his house in Ogikubo he let it be known that he wanted to resign. Neither the Emperor nor the cabinet paid attention to his wish. By May 3 both the Prime Minister and the Foreign Minister were out of bed and the conferences were resumed. They centered on the production of a counter proposal to that which had come from Washington. It was agreed that Japan should be reticent about the terms of the peace with China (one of the points which had most bothered Hull); and also to extinguish the most real obligation in the text—that Japan should not advance southward.

Even with these changes, Matsuoka was not appeased. He insisted that *before* submitting any accord of this kind the American government should be asked to enter into a treaty of neutrality: that is, one which would obligate the United States to be neutral even in the event of a war between Japan and Britain. Further, that Hull be told that Japan could never act in any way injurious to the position of her allies, Germany and Italy. The conference gave in to him and those who were behind him. Nomura was advised accordingly.

Nomura swallowed hard and divided his assignment. On May 7 he placed the idea of a neutrality treaty before the Secretary of State. Hull's response is described in Konoye's memoir: ". . . Mr. Hull showed no interest whatever. . . . in a tone unusually strong for him, [he] urged commencement of the negotiations themselves as speedily as possible."

Thereupon Nomura judged it best to request alteration of the rest of his orders. He informed Tokyo that any further statement in regard to Japan's relations with the Axis would do more harm than good. Japan, he counselled, ought to avoid argument about this and also about the questions of principle which Hull had posed. It should, rather, proceed to discuss the identified issues on a practical basis.[13] Nomura was supported by the Japanese Military and Naval attachés in Washington, who called Matsuoka's attitude "gesture diplomacy."

But Matsuoka did not mean to be gesturing. He was really bent on

[12] Telegram, Ott to Ribbentrop, May 6, 1941, *Far East Mil. Trib.*, Exh. No. 1068.
[13] Telegram, Nomura to Matsuoka, May 8, 1941, *ibid.*, Exh. No. 2872.

bringing Japan into the war on the side of Germany. Matsuoka did not have the habit of keeping his thoughts off his tongue even in the Imperial Palace. On May 8 he aroused great alarm in the Emperor's mind by his talk of the prospect. First he said that if Japan inclined too much to the United States he would resign. Next he said that if the United States entered the war against Germany, Japan would have to attack Singapore; and that if war came between Germany and Russia, Japan would have to attack Siberia. The Emperor hurried to consult Konoye. Konoye hurried to talk with the leaders of the Army and Navy about the best way to deal with Matsuoka. He reported to the Emperor on May 10 that the eventualities which Matsuoka had discussed would be the worst that could happen; and he reminded the Emperor that before any decisions were taken that might result in war the military high command would have to be consulted.

Konoye thought himself able at last to pursue the talks in Washington. But Matsuoka was still scheming to undo the decision of the cabinet. He had invited German advice on the reply to be sent to Washington, and deferentially promised to wait for the German comment, until May 14, Tokyo time (the 13th, Washington time).[14]

But the rest of the cabinet would not wait that long. Word had come from Washington that a speech which the President was scheduled to make on the 14th, Pan-American Day, might be of unusual importance. In London, also, according to Hopkins, the rumor spread that the President was about to announce that the United States was going to war with Germany. So despite Matsuoka's discontent, Nomura was told to present the Japanese comments on the "American proposal" at once.

Nomura did so on May 12 (Washington time). At last, after almost a month, Hull had some written basis on which to judge the state of Japan's intentions. The American government had not been inactive during this month of waiting. It was assuming guardianship of the Western Atlantic and extending the restraints upon the flow of supplies to Japan.

[14] Telegrams from Ott to Ribbentrop, May 10 and 11.—*Weizsaecker Brief*, Documents No. NG4454 (b) and No. NG4422 (c).

## CHAPTER 25

## Would Japan Stand Still While We Extended Ourselves in the Atlantic? The Spring of 1941

THE line of our drive was still in the Atlantic, the line of watch in the Pacific. American policy was being shaped to fit, edge to edge, fighting Britain's needs. At times during this spring of 1941 it seemed that our help was neither bold nor great enough to save Britain. This might have proven to be the case had Hitler, instead of turning upon Russia, acted with full strength in the Eastern and Western Mediterranean. But the President was confined by his own evasions, beset by opposition, and faced by accusations that he was wilfully leading the country into war. While outside observers might urge unguarded use of our forces, the men in office felt compelled to choose measured ways. Even in these there was risk of war.

The government was no longer yielding to the wish to leave our peacetime economy undisturbed. It was now trying hard to hurry on the conversion of the country to an arsenal, and the flow of arms to Britain was growing fast. Sector by sector the American Navy and Air Force extended their protective activities over the Atlantic waters through which ships moved to Britain. By the end of April the Navy was operating a "neutrality patrol" over the Western Atlantic (west of the median line drawn between the bulge of Africa and the bulge of Brazil). American warships and planes patrolled the waters and escorted convoys, reporting to the British movements of enemy vessels.[1] These operations

---

[1] According to Sherwood, *op. cit.*, p. 291, Roosevelt on April 2 ordered the Navy to draw up a defense plan which provided for combat action by United States warships against German submarines and surface raiders in the Western Atlantic. But Hull counselled caution and the news of the neutrality pact between Japan and the Soviet Union caused the President to be so concerned that the plan was revised (Hemisphere Defense Plan, No. 2, *Pearl Harbor Attack*, Part 5, p. 2293) to provide that American ships were merely to *report* movements.

This plan seems to have been adopted at a meeting at the White House on April 10. As recorded in Stimson's diary (entry, April 10), the President's idea was that "by the use of patrol planes and patrol vessels we can patrol and follow the convoys and notify them of any German raiders or German submarines that we may see and give them a chance to escape. Also notify the British warships so they can get at the raider."

were not formally announced by the President, but became known through casual stories.

We were in the course of taking over from Britain the defense of Greenland and Iceland. These would give us bases in the Middle Atlantic. The move into Greenland had been in the President's mind since February; he had waited for the Lend-Lease Act to pass, for the season of heavy ice to end, and for diplomatic arrangements to be settled.[2] On April 10 the government announced that, in agreement with the Danish Minister in Washington and the British and Canadian governments, we would thereafter include "Greenland in our sphere of cooperative hemisphere defense." A few days later (April 14) Hopkins and Welles began secret talks to arrange for the occupation of Iceland by American troops. But this was not consummated until early in July.

The probability was foreseen by Roosevelt and others that American warships would soon have to engage in more positive activities than those of patrol and report in the guarded waters; that patrol would turn into convoy; and reporting into prevention of actual or threatened attack by German ships.[3] And so it happened between April and July. Thereupon if German submarines or raiders got in the way of merchant vessels en route to Britain they risked a fight with American warships. If the German government chose to turn these encounters at sea into war, then war it would be. That was the anxiously assumed risk. So was the amendment of the limits of the "combat zone" in and around the Suez Canal, permitting unarmed American merchant ships to enter the Red Sea and Persian Gulf. This was the supply route to Egyptian and other ports and to the British armies in the East.

As these measures were put into effect, about a fifth of the Pacific fleet was moved into the Atlantic. Stimson and Knox favored the transfer of the whole main fleet, as needed to make sure that the American weapons and food were not sunk at sea. Marshall imparted confidence to their views, since at this time he was of the opinion that with our new heavy bombers and defense planes we would be able to put up such a fight that the Japanese would not dare attack Hawaii.[4] But both the President and Hull were reluctant to reduce the striking force based

[2] Morgenthau diary, entries for February 7 and 13, 1941; Stimson diary, entry for February 14, 1941.

[3] Stimson thought the President was trying to conceal the meaning and character of the patrol program by calling it a defensive and reconnaissance action. *ibid.*, entry for April 24, 1941.

[4] *ibid.*, entry for April 23, 1941. A few weeks later the Army flew a squadron of twenty-one Flying Fortresses from the West Coast to Hawaii.

on Hawaii—which, by its mere presence there, they thought protected the Southwest Pacific.[5] Hull, always on guard against the possible worst, was also worried about the position in which the United States would be left if the British were beaten in the Mediterranean (and perhaps Far East) and our fleet was not in location to stop Japan.[6] Churchill was consulted and at first thought the shift would be a great help. But after review with Australia and New Zealand, the British government asked that at least six capital ships be kept at Hawaii. When in a "showdown" meeting at the White House on May 6 Stark veered towards Hull's opinion, the decision was made to move only a small part of the fleet.[7]

Thus, the striking force was left in being at Hawaii, a deterrent for some months longer, and then a magnet.[8] It was correctly surmised that Germany would not declare war upon us unless it could draw Japan into the struggle.[9] More feared was a decision by Japan that American and British forces were so stretched that it could safely advance; particularly if Germany won another great victory, either the capture of Suez or of Gibraltar and the Straits.

To keep Japan from breaking across the danger line, the American government relied upon the same combination of measures as before. And the same familiar dilemma had to be faced. The more telling these measures became, the greater the chance that Japan would dash into war. Could the situation be held until the odds against Japan became so openly bad that it would give in? Here was the narrow passage between peace and war which the American government tried to keep.

[2]

During this whole period (April through June) the argument went on within the American government over the restriction of Japanese oil supplies and the freezing of Japanese funds.

Japanese buying was still being concentrated on those grades of gasoline and crude oils which could be converted into aviation fuel, and on

[5] *ibid.*, entry for April 24, 1941.
[6] *ibid.*, entries for May 5, 13, and 14, 1941.
[7] *ibid.*, entry for May 6, 1941.
[8] In the middle of June, Stimson and Knox tried to persuade the President to move a second section of the fleet from the Pacific to the Atlantic. But the admirals objected. *ibid.*, entries for June 6 and 19, 1941.
[9] The German government, of course, longed to do so but dared not. It did not want to be at war simultaneously with the United States and the Soviet Union unless Japan was certain to enter also. In a study of the American measures, prepared by the Navy for a meeting between Hitler and the military commanders on June 21, it was observed: "We have deliberately put up with American violations of neutrality and acts of provocation." *Fuehrer Conferences*, 1941, II, 8.

high-grade lubricants.[10] Much of the Japanese funds in the United States was being used to pay for this oil, and some of the rest was being taken out of the banks to escape possible United States control.

Still Hull would allow no extension of our controls. Now to the Secretary of the Treasury his answers grew brusque. Nomura in every talk cited the existing denials of vital materials as the prod which might set Japan off for the south. If, Hull said over and over to his more impatient colleagues, the American government stopped oil, any remaining influence of the Japanese advocates of peace would vanish.

On May 11 and 12 Nomura at last brought in the answers to Hull's queries of a month before.[11] They bore marks of the tension with which they were conceived. Nomura brought papers, took them back, left others, and was not able to answer questions about their meaning. The Japanese government took notice of Hull's four principles. It submitted a draft basis of agreement in amendment of that which had been received from Washington. One word, the State Department thought, described it, "scheming," or as Hull expressed his impression, "Very few rays of hope shone from the document." [12]

They would, it was judged, permit Japan to pull out of the Pacific Ocean whatever was wanted; not all at once, but haul over haul. Oriental fishermen put rings around the necks of cormorants and send them out to fish; the bird gulps the fish out of the waters; the ring prevents him from swallowing it; the fisherman takes the fish out of the gullet. These proposals, the State Department concluded, were the rings by which the United States would help to catch the fish.

There is little to be learned by inspecting the secondary details or turns of phrase in this Japanese answer of May 12, or the variants and annotations of it which were argued back and forth during the next ten weeks.[13]

---

[10] These were being bought and exported under licenses issued months before the regime became stricter. The State Department reckoned in the middle of April that if Japan used the already issued licenses for 5 million barrels of gasoline, got licenses for 2 million for which applications were in, and received the 4 million barrels scheduled under the accord with the Indies, it would obtain (including 1 million already shipped from the United States) 12 million barrels during 1941. This would be about three times the normal amount. For crude, licenses were still outstanding for 15 million to 16 million barrels—also for lubricants.

[11] Nomura gave Hull on May 12 two documents. One was called a "Draft Proposal," that being a revision of the (so-called Drought-Walsh) text which had originated in Washington. The other was called an "Oral Explanation for Proposed Amendments to the Original Draft." These and the American memoranda of the conversations held in Washington, are printed in *Foreign Relations: Japan*, II, 415, *et seq.*

[12] Hull, *op. cit.*, II, 1000.

[13] Between May 12 and July 23, when Hull temporarily suspended the talks because of the Japanese invasion of Southern Indo-China, there were some twenty-six lengthy talks in Washington alone.

Of all points that of keenest interest at that time to Hull—as it had been to Matsuoka—was the question of what Japan would do if we began to fight Germany in the Atlantic. A shooting war, if not a declared war, might start there any day. Much of Hull's talk from then on was directed toward getting Japan to accept the view that our activities in the Atlantic were defensive; and, that being so, it need not feel obliged to support Germany in the event of a clash. The Japanese proposal reversed this. The United States was asked to recognize the Tripartite Pact as defensive; and—so the text seemed to mean—suspend its activities in the Atlantic in aid of Britain.[14]

On the other main points the answer was judged adversely, not so much because of what was plainly stated, as because of what was obscurely stated or left unstated. In regard to China, the President was to ask Chiang Kai-shek to make a peace with Japan based on a list of broad principles. The American government was to enter into a separate and secret agreement to end aid to his regime if he refused to do so. On their face the Japanese terms of peace seemed to offer a fair settlement which would leave China whole and independent, though obligated to cooperate with Japan. But their meaning in actuality would be settled, it was thought, by whether China was weak or strong.[15] The Japanese military units that were to remain in China would be the interpreter. Japan had used similar veiled terms to force its rule upon Manchukuo.

Konoye had lost his good name as an author of peace proposals. In any case, the American government was not disposed either then or later to trust any general formula in regard to China that was prepared

[14] The language on this point is so turgid that it is impossible to be sure whether the United States was called on to refrain from such measures or merely deny that it was doing anything of the sort. "The Government of the United States maintains that its attitude toward the European war is, and will continue to be, directed by no such aggressive measures as to assist any one nation against another." But in the light of what is now known of Matsuoka's aims and wish to satisfy Germany, there can be little doubt that this was its intended meaning.

[15] A good summary of their probable intended meaning is given in the majority decision, *Far East Mil. Trib.*: (1) Japan, Manchukuo, and China should unite with the establishment of a New Order in East Asia as their common object, and, in order to realize this, China would abandon resistance to Japan and hostility to Manchukuo; (2) Japan considered it essential for the readjustment of Sino-Japanese relations that there be concluded an anti-Comintern agreement between the two countries in consonance with the spirit of the anti-Comintern agreement among Japan, Germany, and Italy; (3) In view of the circumstances prevailing in China, Japanese troops should be stationed at specific points; (4) Japan did not desire economic monopoly in China or limitations of interest of other foreign powers. But she demanded that China should in accordance with the principle of equality between the two countries recognize freedom of residence and trade on the part of Japanese subjects in the interior of China to promote the economic interests of both, and should extend to Japan facilities for development of China's natural resources, especially in North China and Mongolia.

in Tokyo. It wanted to know precisely what Japan was going to do; and at bottom it wanted Japan entirely out of China, and maybe out of Manchukuo as well.

One other feature of the May 12 answer was sharply noted. The language of the Washington draft had been so changed as to eliminate the pledge to refrain from force in the Southwest Pacific area. When asked by Hull about this point, Nomura gave as reason that the United States and Britain were not required to accept the same obligation.[16] Whereupon we offered to do so.

In return for these scarred outlines of Japanese policy, the American government was to resume normal trade with Japan, and to cooperate in the development of the natural resources of the Pacific which Japan needed.

The first stage of talk thus reduced the hope of finding a basis for agreement. Hull was at the time despondent. There was a downbeat in his thoughts, not only about the news from Japan, but also about the prospects of Britain. This found words in the refrain, "everything is going hellward," which visitors were apt to hear. But he doggedly went on with the talks with Nomura. It was more urgent than ever to try to counter the exertions of Germany and its responsive friends within the Japanese government.

[16] In the Oral Explanation it was stated, "The words . . . 'without resorting to arms' have been deleted as inappropriate and unnecessarily critical. Actually, the peaceful policy of the Japanese Government has been made clear on many occasions in various statements made both by the Premier and the Foreign Minister."

## CHAPTER 26

# Japan Chafes and Germany Invades
# the Soviet Union: May–June 1941

MATSUOKA was being offensive. On May 14, on seeing Grew for the first time since his sojourn in Berlin and Moscow, his jumbled candor turned into insult. Hitler he thought patient and forbearing in not declaring war on the United States. If war came because of our naval activities in the Atlantic, the United States, in his judgment, would be the aggressor; and he had no doubt that, under Article III of the Tripartite Pact, Japan would be compelled to fight us also. To make the charge complete, he added that he thought that the " 'manly, decent and reasonable' thing for the United States to do was to declare war openly on Germany instead of engaging in acts of war under cover of neutrality." [1]

Before Grew could put these words on the cables, Matsuoka tried to wash his adjectives away. All that he had really meant to say, he professed in a note to Grew, was that the United States should be more cautious and careful. Another letter two days after, revealed a most upset and wandering mind. [2]

What was Matsuoka up to? Did he himself know? In another Foreign Minister such words would have been taken as a considered threat. But with this man, who staggered among contradictions, it was impossible to tell. In Washington no one made much ado about his words. Hitler had hardened statesmen to the whole vocabulary of abuse. Or so it was thought at that time before Moscow enriched it. Besides, it was known that Matsuoka was talking only for a faction. As soon as word of his statements to Grew spread in Tokyo, the Lord Privy Seal sent Grew a message that he should not become too troubled. Both the Prime Minister and the Minister of the Navy wanted him to know that care was being taken to prevent any hasty action by the Foreign Minister.

---

[1] Grew's report on this talk is in *Foreign Relations: Japan*, II, 145–48.
[2] The first letter is included in the text of Grew's cable of May 14, printed, *ibid.*, II, 148. The second letter, sent on May 16, in which he predicted that the day of doom was approaching, has not been printed.

They were, it seemed, genuinely alarmed that the United States might strike back at Japan—perhaps by an oil embargo.

We can now, with the help of enemy records, put our fingers upon the reasons for Matsuoka's agitation. By his words he thought to do one of two things: either to bring an end to the talks, or to exact a promise from the United States that it would not join in the defense of Singapore. For he was being pursued by vows exchanged during his Berlin visit. Hitler was making a great stir. He was pressing Matsuoka to tell the American government that its operations in the Atlantic were regarded as intended to provoke a war with Germany into which Japan would be forced to enter. He was insisting that any agreement with us should contain a promise not to interfere in the war against Britain, and recognition of Japan's conclusive obligation to the Axis. Further he was demanding as due the right to pass upon the answers made to the United States.[3]

Matsuoka had spoken his piece to Grew pretty much as it was spoken to him. Stung and frustrated, he poured out to Grew the feelings and threats he had been compelled to omit from his instructions to Nomura. By doing so, he could prove to his German friends that he had not betrayed the faith and connection.

So much for Matsuoka. No matter what he intended, his unbalanced antics could end only in war. But what did the rest of the Japanese government mean? Was there still chance that if the United States remained patient Japan might recede from its present purposes? Spurred on by Lord Halifax, Hull made the utmost effort during the following weeks of May and June to find out. The utmost effort, that is, short of agreeing that Japan might retain place in China, or acquire an economic realm of its own. Courteous in words, but unbending in judgment, he plodded on. The offers that were placed before the Japanese contained nothing extra or guaranteed; only a chance to live at peace, and by hard and patient work earn the means of living on their crowded islands.

[3] Matsuoka, as related, had given Ott a copy of the "American proposal." Ribbentrop and the German Foreign Office were noisily indignant and wanted Tokyo to be forbidden to proceed with any talks of this kind with Washington. But Hitler decided it was more practical to try to turn them to advantage in this way.

Ribbentrop's reaction is expressed in his statements to Oshima (*Far East Mil. Trib.*, Exh. No. 1075), Weizsaecker's views, in Document No. 4422 (d), *Weizsaecker Brief*. A record of the instructions sent to Ott, of Ott's talks with Matsuoka, and of Oshima's talk with Ribbentrop, and his messages to Matsuoka, is provided by Document No. NG 4454 (c), *ibid.*, and by Exh. Nos. 1073, 1075, 2758, 2759, 4060, *Far East Mil. Trib.*, and the "Konoye Memoirs."

In the swap of texts that now ensued, the corps under Hull had full employment for their talents. They phrased suave questions to expose the ambiguity of Japanese proposals. They inserted words into Japanese formulas which turned their sense, as the touch of the brush can change the effect of a portrait.

In summary, these things were asked of Japan: to refrain from acts of force in the Southwest Pacific area; to concur in the view that the United States in aiding Britain was acting only in self defense, and, therefore, to promise that, if we got into war with Germany, Japan would not join; to withdraw, on a schedule to be agreed upon, all its forces from China.[4]

When on the 27th of May the President declared an "unlimited national emergency" he dispelled any remaining notion that the United States could be induced to leave the Atlantic to Germany. He said, "all additional measures necessary to deliver the goods [to Britain] will be taken. Any and all further methods or combination of methods, which can or should be utilized, are being devised . . ." But he omitted all mention of Japan, as a way of signifying that it was not regarded, like Germany, as a confirmed opponent. Opponent or friend, however, the American terms for a settlement remained fixed: no premium, no consolation prize, for returning to the company of peaceful and orderly states and accepting a place below the salt.

Nomura and his associates went on with their earnest efforts. In the middle of June, their statements on some points seemed to begin to bend towards ours.[5] This turn coincided with reports from Grew that the Japanese government was badly divided, and that a sudden change in Japan's diplomatic policy was possible. But Hull and his assistants found that hard to believe. They were afraid of being tricked by ambiguity. Matsuoka's words caused doubt as to whether the Japanese government could really mean what Nomura seemed to be saying. So Hull continued to probe.

He passed back to Nomura on June 21 a revision of the terms of accord that were being discussed. On doing so he handed over a statement (to be taken as spoken) which struck the raw center of the dispute within the Japanese government. This said that recent public utterances

---

[4] This is, to repeat, only a summary of the intended meaning of some of the main features of the terms placed before Japan, first in the form of draft suggestions given to Nomura on May 31. See *Foreign Relations: Japan*, II, 446–54.

Details and language were revised and reshuffled often in the course of later talks.

[5] Particularly as indicated in a draft document that the associates of Nomura gave the State Department informally on June 15th, which is printed *ibid.*, II, 473.

of certain influential members of the Japanese government which stressed Japan's obligations to Germany could not be ignored, and caused doubt whether any agreement with Japan was worth pursuing.[6] Both men knew that Matsuoka was first in mind.[7] Hull's purpose may be guessed though there is no record of it. Matsuoka was the spokesman for the Axis connection. If his fervor for that cause was shown to be a hindrance to an accord with the United States, he might be suppressed. Especially, since that connection was about to receive a sharp cut. For, it must be recalled, this was the eve of the German invasion of the Soviet Union on June 22.

[2]

Knowledge that this might happen had eased the fears of the American government that Japan would smash the fragile peace, though chafing under our economic punishment.

For by then the American and British restrictions were greatly affecting the inflow of supplies on which Japan depended. There was scarcely a basic industry in Japan that was not having to scrimp, substitute, or limit production because of the need to conserve some raw material, machine, or part that could no longer be imported. Moreover, on May 28, by Act of Congress, Section 6 of the National Defense Act (the export control provision) had been extended to all territories, depend-

[6] This was, of course, put in more clothed language: "The tenor of recent public statements gratuitously made by spokesmen of the Japanese Government emphasizing Japan's commitments and intentions under the Tripartite Alliance exemplify an attitude which cannot be ignored. So long as such leaders maintain this attitude in their official positions and apparently seek to influence public opinion in Japan in the direction indicated, is it not illusory to expect that adoption of a proposal such as the one under consideration offers a basis for achieving substantial results along the desired lines?" *ibid.*, II, 485.

Churchill also had had his guns trained on Matsuoka. When in April it had been thought that the Japanese Ambassador in London, Shigemitsu, was going to meet Matsuoka in Berlin, Churchill wrote a letter for delivery to the Japanese Foreign Minister, posing eight hard questions. One of them was, "Did Japan's accession to the Triple Pact make it more likely or less likely that the United States would come into the present war?"

Since Shigemitsu could not get to Berlin, Churchill had sent the letter to Sir Stafford Cripps, British Ambassador in Moscow. Steinhardt had arranged that Cripps and Matsuoka should meet at the theater, where Cripps handed over the letter. The letter is given in *Far East Mil. Trib.*, Exh. No. 1062.

Churchill's enjoyment of the posers he phrased was lasting. In telling of this letter in his memoirs, he remarks, "I was rather pleased with this when I wrote it, and I don't mind the look of it now." *The Grand Alliance*, p. 190.

[7] Nomura informed Matsuoka on June 25 of rumors that Grew had told Hull that Matsuoka was saying that his (Nomura's) efforts were unsanctioned, and that he (Matsuoka) would "torpedo any accord reached in Washington." Nomura manuscript (*op. cit.*).

encies, and possessions of the United States.[8] The President had applied it at once to the Philippines. Japan would no longer be able to get needed iron and chrome ores, manganese, copper, copra, and abaca from that source.

The official as well as the public appreciation of the meaning of the controls had become duller. They tended to be taken for granted, to fall out of mind. A year had passed since the first significant ones were imposed (on No. 1 scrap iron and aviation gasoline) and no crisis had been provoked. The risk had become familiar—and thereby, perhaps, somewhat forgotten. The State Department, along with the country, rested in the attitude that what was done was done, and that it was up to Japan, not to us, to undo it.

In June domestic scarcity touched the product most wanted by Japan. Mainly because of lack of transport, oil supplies in the eastern seaboard regions of the United States became short of demand. American users could not get enough, even for essential purposes. To continue to ship oil from these areas would have been a tribute not a trade, and an unpopular tribute.

Hence on June 20 the American government announced that thereafter no oil could be exported from eastern ports (including the Gulf of Mexico), except to the British Empire, Egypt for the British armies, and the Western Hemisphere. Though aware that Japan would resent and protest the discrimination, Hull (on June 6) had given assent. There had been a short scuffle with Ickes, who (as Petroleum Administrator for National Defense) wanted to suspend the issuance of all licenses for the export of oil to Japan. This Hull would not consider, and the President upheld him. Ickes gave in, but not without a volley of argument and an aggrieved letter of resignation.[9]

One paragraph in the President's later (July 1) answer to this letter of resignation is a map of his thoughts at the time: "the Japs are having a real drag-down and knock-out fight among themselves and have been for the past week—trying to decide which way they are going to jump —attack Russia, attack the South Seas (thus throwing in their lot definitely with Germany) or whether they will sit on the fence and be more friendly with us. No one knows what the decision will be but, as you know, it is terribly important for the control of the Atlantic for us to

---

[8] Public No. 75.

[9] His view that all exports of oil to Japan should be stopped grew even more confirmed after the German invasion of Russia. For it was his opinion that Japan would be too preoccupied with what might happen in Siberia to attack the Indies; and when Germany smashed Russia, as he anticipated, Japan would move north, not south; and then would go after the Indies whether or not the United States continued to send oil.

help to keep peace in the Pacific. I simply have not got enough Navy to go round . . ."

The ban of oil exports from eastern ports was imposed because of a genuine local scarcity. Still, the reason did not change the effect upon Japan—one more supply route closed. Would it not now decide that its position was being made unbearable, and advance upon the nearby sources of supply—Borneo and the East Indies? The fear that it might was sharpened by news from Batavia.

The Indies government had stood fast. On some points it had been yielding but not on those which would have enabled Japan to gain a special economic position in the Indies, or conduct preparatory military or political activities there. The request for a larger quantity of oil had been again referred to the oil companies; the request for concessions had been deferred. Export permits were promised for somewhat increased quantities of rubber, tin, bauxite, and nickel ore. But of rubber, only half what Japan sought, and of tin, only about a quarter. These quantities, it may be remarked, were quite enough along with what would be received from other sources to meet the usual Japanese needs.[10]

Thereupon (June 17) Japan had broken off the talks and fetched the delegation home. But care had been taken to make the break seem without portent. A joint communiqué drafted by the Japanese was issued, saying it was needless to state that the ending of the talks would bring no change in relations between the two countries. The Japanese cabinet, its since published papers reveal, had decided to talk softly—so that the flow of supplies from the Indies would not be jeopardized.[11] Matsuoka had also made a real effort to minimize the public effect of

[10] The Indies government offered 15 thousand tons of rubber. It based its refusal to grant more on the ground that Japan was in a position to get almost all, if not all, of the rubber and tin it needed from Indo-China and Thailand. So it was, according to the American figures of the situation; of rubber Indo-China and Thailand were producing at least 100 thousand tons and Japan's needs were estimated to be about 50 thousand. Matsuoka insisted, however, that Japan would get only 35 thousand tons from these sources. It may be recalled that he had promised Goering that he would procure rubber for Germany.

Later the Japanese government was to allege that the difficulty of assuring itself enough tin and rubber was one reason why it had to occupy the rest of Indo-China. The available Japanese records regarding actual imports during 1941 are greatly at variance with one another. Those presented to the *International Military Tribunal for the Far East* (Exh. No. 2834) contain an estimate of 70 thousand tons. But the sets of figures found in the reports of the United States Strategic Bombing Survey, also from Japanese sources, vary from 36 to 67 thousand. Almost none was received after September.

[11] See exchange of telegrams between Yoshizawa and Matsuoka June 7 and 14, *ibid.*, Exh. Nos. 1322 and 1323.

the rupture. His politeness was bred of the knowledge that Germany was about to attack Russia.

So had ended a critical negotiation. This defeat, the experts in the Far Eastern Division of the State Department thought, might well sway the balance of decision within the Japanese government towards Singapore and the Indies. Or would Japan ignore it and march against the Soviet Union? We can now follow the argument that took place in Japan over the issue.

## CHAPTER 27

# Japan Makes the Crucial Decision: July 2, 1941

THE Japanese government had many hints that Germany and Russia were at odds—some as broad as Ribbentrop's subtlety. In Berlin, it had been dinned into Matsuoka that war was not out of the question as a necessary step of defense against Russia. Maybe he was misled by this manner of statement, or maybe not. Before his arrival in Tokyo he does not seem to have worried much about the event—either because he did not believe it would happen or because he did not mind its happening. Other members of the government, including Tojo, were inclined to think the early reports were feints to screen German plans to invade England.

But when the event came on the horizon, all, even Matsuoka, were much put out. The Army and Navy felt fully engaged in the war in China and plans for Greater East Asia. On May 28 Matsuoka, on behalf of the government, informed Ribbentrop that in view of the external and internal situation which it faced, the Japanese government wished Germany to avoid war with Russia by any and all means.[1] The appeal was ignored. Oshima reported on June 6 that both Hitler and Ribbentrop now told him that Germany had decided to attack the Soviet Union.[2] Oshima added that the highest German military authorities were saying that the war would probably end within four weeks; that it could more properly be called a police action than a war.

The American government made up its mind quickly and in advance as to what to do if war came between Germany and Russia. All possible assistance would be given Russia. The Japanese government found it far harder both before and after the event to decide its course. The strategists were thrown into confusion. They had been betting, though not without hedge, on quick German victory over Britain. Now Hitler, with barely a nod in their direction, changed the game.

[1] *Far East Mil. Trib.*, Exh. No. 2735A.
[2] "Kido's Diary," entry for June 6, 1941.

One of the reasons the Japanese government was so upset was that by early June, if not before, the Army was firmly bent upon advancing south, not north, and the Navy was consenting. On June 10 Oshima informed Ribbentrop that he wanted to discuss the wish of the Japanese Army to get bases in the southern parts of Indo-China.[3] He was acting on word sent by higher Army authorities in Tokyo. On this day, it may be recalled, the government of the Indies formally refused to accede to the "peaceful" Japanese demands for greater economic and political privileges within its territories. Three days later, the Minister of War, Tojo, brought this southern project before a Liaison Conference. Matsuoka would not assent to a decision that looked only south. He argued that Japan should be prepared rather to follow Germany if it got into war with Russia. And at his request the final decision as to whether or not to move south was postponed.

He began at once to find out through Oshima and Ott whether the German government would aid Japan in causing the Vichy government to yield to Japanese demands. The bases were needed, he explained, for prospective attacks upon Singapore and the Indies.[4] Perhaps he thought that if the French government could be scared into consent, he would be able to induce Washington to regard the Japanese advance as a peaceful one. If so, a crisis with us would be avoided and Japan would be free to join the war against Russia.

Word that the attack on Russia was about to begin came from Berlin before any response to this query about Indo-China. The friction between Konoye and Matsuoka grew worse. The Prime Minister resented Hitler's "perfidious act" which, he thought, reflected on his wisdom and ruined his policy.[5] Therefore, as in every crisis, his thoughts turned to resignation. But he was assured by Kido, the Lord Privy Seal, that what was about to happen was no fault of his and not necessarily harmful to Japan, and that he need not and should not resign.

When Germany crossed the Russian frontier on the 22nd, the Foreign Minister rushed to see the Emperor. Before his coming, Kido advised the Emperor to ask him whether he had consulted Konoye, and, if he had not, to suggest that he do so. The Emperor might also, the advice continued, say that it was his wish that Matsuoka should present matters of foreign policy only through the Prime Minister. The Emperor drew

[3] Memo made by Woermann of German Foreign Office of talk with Kase, Secretary of the Japanese Embassy in Berlin, June 10, 1941. *Far East Mil. Trib.*, Exh. No. 586.

[4] "Kido's Diary," entry for June 18, 1941, and telegram from Ott to Ribbentrop, June 21, 1941, *Far East Mil. Trib.*, Exh. No. 635.

[5] "Konoye Memoirs."

back from any such self-assertion. He did not deny Matsuoka access to the Throne. Throughout the crisis of decision that was ahead, the Foreign Minister continued to report to the Emperor directly, alone, and almost every day.[6]

Matsuoka was in his most prophetic mood this day of invasion— June 22. He told the Emperor that in his view Japan must cooperate and attack Russia. To do this he thought that any advance in the south should be postponed for the time being. But he predicted that sooner or later Japan would have to fight the Soviet Union, the United States, and Great Britain, simultaneously. The Emperor was not elated by this prospect. He remarked that it was doubtful whether the government and the Supreme War Command would agree to dual wars north and south, and also whether Japan was strong enough to fight them.

Thus reproved, Matsuoka visited Konoye well after midnight to explain that in talking to the Emperor he had roamed from the present to the future; he had not meant to advise that Japan should fight both north and south *right away*.[7] The question of what he was up to can be left with the conclusion that Konoye reached after searching inquiries—that Matsuoka's policy summed up to this: "First, we must attack the Soviets. Although we must try to avoid war with America, in the event that America does enter the war, we must fight her too." [8]

Konoye was of quite a different mind. He wanted to strike a bargain with the United States; to seek American assent to the maintenance of Japanese influence over China and Indo-China, in return for Japanese neutrality in Europe. He talked with the Ministers of the Army and Navy about dissolving the Tripartite Pact. But the leaders of the Army, among them General Tojo, Minister of War, were opposed. They foresaw a quick and great German victory, bringing Japan the awaited chance to acquire the Russian Maritime Provinces.[9] However, they eased Konoye's fear that the Kwantung Army (the Japanese army in Manchukuo) might march without orders from the cabinet—promising that this unruly force would take a calm and prudent attitude.

At this juncture the cabinet received Nomura's report of Hull's latest

---

[6] This is to be seen from the later entries in "Kido's Diary," and the "Konoye Memoirs" —the chief sources for the events just related.

[7] If the report which Ott sent to Ribbentrop on June 23 is accurate, Matsuoka spoke to him in a similar vein. Ott reported that Matsuoka said that he was of the opinion that Japan could not remain neutral in the long run; and that, if the United States entered the war against Germany as a result of the war with Russia, the Tripartite Pact would apply for Japan. Further that he would propose that Japan take counter measures against Russian troop withdrawals from the East. *Far East Mil. Trib.*, Exh. No. 795A.

[8] "Konoye Memoirs."

[9] *ibid.*

comments and rewrite of the proposal for an accord.[10] There were no plums in them. But there was a dart—the reference to those members of the Japanese government who were being spokesmen for the Axis.

## [2]

Nothing in the American proposal drew Japan half as much as the chances south and north. These beckoned the unresting Army to march on; we asked it to turn back. They gave glimpses of a continent to govern; we offered a prospect of sparse living in small space. The government put aside the briefs from Washington, and met to adjust Japanese plans to the new chances.

Liaison Conferences of June 25 and July 2 made decisions of the utmost consequence; decisions which doomed Japan to a later choice between dismal retreat and war. The policy statements, plans, and programs adopted by these Conferences are long and involved. But the Army estimates which shaped them are short and simple. Three rules were laid down: first, that Japan should not join in the attack on Russia for the time being—or, as expressed in "Kido's Diary," "Army policy towards the war between Germany and the U.S.S.R.—[was] that the attitude of the Kwantung army should be calm and careful"; [11] second, that Japan, however, should not separate itself from Germany: third, that Japan should secure control over all of Indo-China. No combination of policies could have been more certain to bring Japan to ultimate defeat.

The first of the two Liaison Conferences—that of June 25—set down the program for the south.[12] Japan was to hasten to obtain air bases, the

[10] This had been given to Nomura on the 21st (Washington time). Probably to test out the effect upon the Japanese government of the German attack on Russia, Hull submitted on the 22nd a draft of an exchange of letters between the American and Japanese governments, which would in essence mark Japanese retirement from the Tripartite Pact. Nomura said he found it difficult to recommend approval of these letters.

[11] Entry for June 28, 1941.

[12] "On Matters Relating to Expediting the Southern Policy," Far East Mil. Trib., Exh. No. 1306. The text of its operative parts was:

"1. In view of the various existing conditions, the Empire shall, in accordance with its fixed policy accelerate its measures towards FRENCH INDO-CHINA and THAILAND. Especially in connection with the return of the JAPANESE Delegate from the Dutch Indies, a military union shall be established with FRENCH INDO-CHINA as soon as possible for the purpose of the stability and defense of EAST ASIA.

"Concerning the establishment of joint military relations with FRENCH INDO-CHINA, the essential factors which the EMPIRE should lay stress upon are as follows: (a) The establishment or use of Air Bases and Harbour Facilities in specified areas in FRENCH INDO-CHINA, and stationing of the necessary troops in the southern part of FRENCH INDO-CHINA. (b) Furnishing of facilities in connection with the stationing of IMPERIAL troops.

use of specified harbors, and the right to station troops. The government at Vichy was first to be asked for these privileges. But in case of refusal the resolution stated: "We shall attain our objective by force of arms." The Army and Navy were to get ready to act swiftly.

The authors of this project realized that the United States and Britain would be provoked. Some foresaw that they would react by imposing further restrictions on oil. But others were more hopeful, thinking that as long as Japan did not help Germany by attacking Russia, they would let the action pass. So Konoye's rather rambling comments in his "Memoirs" may be construed. In any case he did not combat the move, either before the Liaison Conference of June 25, or during it. By his failure to do so the Army had its way. As later affirmed by General Tojo, then Minister of War, "The responsibility in connection with the movement of troops into Southern Indo-China was mine as War Minister." [13]

Konoye, accompanied by the Chief of the Army General Staff, Sugiyama, and the Chief of the Navy General Staff, Nagano, reported the decision of the June 25 Liaison Conference to the Emperor. Although fuming a little over the dangers into which his Ministers were leading the country, the Emperor made no objection now. Compared with Matsuoka's talk of war at one and the same time against Russia, the British Empire, the United States, and China, the measures proposed may have seemed a sober enterprise.

As soon as word of the Japanese program reached them, Hitler and Ribbentrop angrily protested. The messages exchanged with Ott show that they did not care to be reminded that Japan had entered the Tripartite Pact with the thought that a great group, including Russia, was being formed. This was dead and decried. These German leaders buried their promises without getting an official certificate of natural death and without playing taps.

Oshima had conveyed the impression before June 22 that Germany did not expect Japan to enter the war against Russia at once. Ott also thought himself informed by Berlin to that effect. As late as June 28 he asked Ribbentrop whether his orders to work first of all to get Japan to move southward, while ignoring the Soviet Union, still stood. [14]

---

"2. To open diplomatic negotiations for the purpose of the preceding paragraph.

"3. In case the FRENCH Government or the FRENCH INDO-CHINA authorities do not comply with our demands, we shall attain our objective by force of arms.

"4. In order to deal with such circumstances as mentioned in the above paragraph, preparations shall be commenced beforehand for the dispatching of troops."

[13] Extract from interrogation of General Tojo.—*Far East Mil. Trib.*, Doc. No. 2502B.

[14] Telegram from Ott to Ribbentrop, June 28, 1941, *ibid.*, Exh. No. 1097.

The answer, conveyed through both Oshima and Ott, dismissed the thought.[15]

Hitler had merely been postponing a blunt exposition of his desires. Now he intensely wanted Japan to attack Russia right away. His reasons were the usual heavy blend of cunning and contempt for the enemy. What Japan should and must do, he insisted, was first solve the Russian problem and thereby protect its rear for the later movements south. The time to do this was at hand; for if Japan should delay until Russia was beaten to the ground its moral and political position would be prejudiced. This last statement could be taken to mean that unless Japan went to war with Russia at once, when (there was no *if*) Germany won it might not grant Japan's claims in the south.

Ribbentrop repeated the arguments with more daring in a personal message to Matsuoka on July 1. After the usual assertion that Russian resistance was practically ended, he went on: "It seems to me, therefore, the requirement of the hour that the Japanese Army should, as quickly as possible, get into possession of Vladivostock and push as far as possible toward the west. The aim of such an operation should be that, before the coming of cold weather, the Japanese Army advancing westward should be able to shake hands at the half-way mark with the German troops advancing to the east, . . ."

When this occurred, Germany, Japan, and Italy together could strengthen the pressure on England enormously and bring about its final destruction. "In respect to America, I hope that, after the defeat of Russia, the weight of the Three Power states, Germany, Italy, and Japan, and the powers allied to them, . . . will suffice to paralyze any rising tendency in the United States to participate in the war."[16]

Matsuoka, during the next two days, did his best to convince his colleagues that German strategy was sound. He failed. Those elements in the Japanese government which had never liked or wanted the alliance with Germany opposed union in war. The Army, stalled in China, did not want to use up forces and supplies in the vast plains of Manchukuo and Siberia. The Navy saw no chance for oil or glory in a north-

[15] Telegram from Ribbentrop to Ott, June 28, 1941, *ibid.*, Exh. No. 1096; and memorandum by Ribbentrop, June 28, for "department heads," *ibid.*, Exh. No. 587.

[16] This message was reprinted in full in the *Department of State Bulletin* for June 16, 1946. The German military heads were at this time truly confident of quick victory. Thus General Halder recorded, "It is thus probably no overstatement to say that the Russian campaign has been won in the space of two weeks." *Journal* VI, 196, entry for July 3, 1941. Three weeks later he was quoting Hitler as saying, "You cannot beat the Russians with operational successes . . . because they simply do not know when they are defeated." *ibid.*, VI, 272, entry for July 26, 1941.

ward attack, and knew that the United States and Great Britain would use the interval to strengthen their defenses in the south.

The Japanese government rejected the German pleas. But, counting upon the triumph of German arms, it took a no less fateful course.

## [3]

On July 2 there came together in the presence of the Emperor the chief figures of the civil and military governments of Japan. These included the Prime Minister, Prince Konoye; the Foreign Minister, Matsuoka; the Minister for War, General Tojo; the Minister for the Navy, Admiral Oikawa; the Chief of the Army General Staff, General Sugiyama; the Chief of the Naval General Staff, Admiral Nagano; the President of the Privy Council, Hara; and the Minister for Home Affairs, Hiranuma. The plans ratified at this Imperial Conference set into determined motion the acts and responses that six months later resulted in war between Japan and the United States. The tail of the serpent wound round to its mouth.

From the text of the resolution adopted at this conference the course of events that followed can now be clearly traced. It is not very long and the reader, I think, will want to have most of it: [17]

### AN OUTLINE OF THE POLICY OF THE IMPERIAL GOVERNMENT IN VIEW OF PRESENT DEVELOPMENTS

*(Decision reached at the Conference held in the Imperial Presence on July 2)*

#### I. POLICY

1. The Imperial Government is determined to follow a policy which will result in the establishment of the Greater East Asia Co-Prosperity Sphere and world peace, no matter what international developments take place.

2. The Imperial Government will continue its effort to effect a settlement of the China Incident and seek to establish a solid basis for the security and preservation of the nation. This will involve an advance into the Southern Regions and, depending on future developments, a settlement of the Soviet Question as well.

[17] I have selected the translation of this "Outline of the Policy of the Imperial Government in View of Present Developments" contained in the "Konoye Memoirs" (as printed in *Pearl Harbor Attack*, Part 20, pp. 4018-19), in preference to that contained in the text presented to the *International Military Tribunal* (Exh. No. 588). Between these two translations there are points of difference, both in the order of exposition and in the tone, though no basic difference in meaning. The translation presented to the *International Military Tribunal* reads as though the Japanese government were virtually determined on war with the United States, while the one herein used seems to regard that event as a possibility against which Japan was to prepare but still seek to avoid.

3. The Imperial Government will carry out the above program no matter what obstacles may be encountered.

## II. SUMMARY

1. Steps will be taken to bring pressure on the Chiang Regime from the Southern approaches in order to bring about its surrender. Whenever demanded by future developments the rights of a belligerent will be resorted to against Chungking and hostile concessions taken over.

2. In order to guarantee national security and preservation, the Imperial Government will continue all necessary diplomatic negotiations with reference to the southern regions and also carry out various other plans as may be necessary. In case the diplomatic negotiations break down, preparations for a war with England and America will also be carried forward. First of all, the plans which have been laid with reference to French Indo-China and Thai will be prosecuted, with a view to consolidating our position in the southern territories.

In carrying out the plans outlined in the foregoing article, we will not be deterred by the possibility of being involved in a war with England and America.

3. Our attitude with reference to the German-Soviet War will be based on the spirit of the Tri-Partite Pact. However, we will not enter the conflict for some time but will steadily proceed with military preparations against the Soviet and decide our final attitude independently. At the same time, we will continue carefully correlated activities in the diplomatic field.

. . . In case the German-Soviet War should develop to our advantage, we will make use of our military strength, settle the Soviet question and guarantee the safety of our northern borders. . . .

4. In carrying out the preceding article all plans, especially the use of armed forces, will be carried out in such a way as to place no serious obstacles in the path of our basic military preparations for a war with England and America.

5. In case all diplomatic means fail to prevent the entrance of America into the European War, we will proceed in harmony with our obligations under the Tri-Partite Pact. However, with reference to the time and method of employing our armed forces we will take independent action.

6. We will immediately turn our attention to placing the nation on a war basis and will take special measures to strengthen the defenses of the nation.

7. Concrete plans covering this program will be drawn up separately.

The main lines of this policy were set and most stubbornly held by the forces who spoke through General Tojo. They did not get their whole way, but a ruinous share of it. They thought that if Japan acquired a self-sufficient base of operation in the south it could wear down China, and stand, if need be, a long war against Britain and the United States. The Army and Navy were to get ready for such a war. But the hope remained that it would not have to be fought. It was expected that

JAPAN'S CRUCIAL DECISION

if Germany defeated Russia, the United States and Britain would give way; that they would allow Japan to establish the New Order in East Asia at the expense of others.

To Matsuoka this course of action was a rebuff and a mistake. But he buoyed himself up with the belief that his views would prevail later. Thus he busied himself with excuses, assuring Ribbentrop that Japan was preparing for all eventualities and when the time came would turn against Russia; in the meantime the advancing vigil in the Pacific was no less a contribution to the common cause.[18] To Konoye and the Imperial Household the resolution of July 2 was at least a temporary respite from the disputes with which they were surrounded. All gambled on the chance that the German armies would bring both the Soviet Union and the British down before winter came. Then there would be only one strong possible enemy left—the United States. This was the strategy that failed. But it might have won.

Japan's actions during the next few months followed this plan:

The economic resources of the country were organized for war.

The entry into Indo-China was begun. Before July ended the demands were served upon Pétain, and the Japanese Navy and Army moved into Indo-China.

The Army hastened its operational plans against Malaya, Java, and other points in the Netherlands East Indies, Borneo, the Bismarck Archipelago, and the Philippines.[19]

The Navy developed corresponding plans—among them one highly secret tactic. It began to practice the Pearl Harbor attack, conceived first in January. The fleets went into Kagoshima Bay and there the planes practiced coming in low over the mountains, dive bombing, and the use of torpedoes, specially designed for shallow waters.[20]

The Japanese government gave the government of the Soviet Union on July 2 formal assurances that it would observe the neutrality pact.[21] The size of the Kwantung Army was increased (from some 300 thousand men to about twice that number). But troops were withdrawn

[18] ibid., Exh. Nos. 636, 796, 1113.
[19] Testimony of General Tanaka (Shinichi), Chief of the Operations Section, General Staff of the Army. The studies were ordered by General Sugiyama, Chief of the General Staff, with the approval of Tojo and General Muto, Chief of the (so-called) Military Affairs Bureau of the War Minister.
[20] Interrogation of Admiral Nagano, ibid., Exh. No. 1127 (a).
[21] When first asked about this by the Soviet Ambassador, Smetanin, on June 25, Matsuoka evaded and left the matter doubtful. Extract from Smetanin's diary, entry for June 25, 1941. ibid., Exh. No. 793.

from the borders of Manchukuo and concentrated at interior points. Orders were given to avoid border troubles with Russian forces and compose any incidents as quickly as possible.[22] At the same time a new plan of operations against Siberia was prepared; in contrast to former ones it contemplated simultaneous attacks on several fronts.[23]

All these items of preparation looked towards war. And yet most of the Konoye Cabinet still eagerly wished to avoid war with the United States. If persuasion and the use of the least offensive forms could keep the United States quiet, they would not be economized.

[22] Testimony of General Tanaka.
[23] Testimony of General Tominago (Kijoji), Section Chief, War Ministry, *ibid.*, Exh. No. 705; of General Yanagita (Genzo), Chief, Army Special Service Agency, Harbin, *ibid.*, Exh. No. 723: of General Otsubo (Kazuma), Chief of Staff, Third Front of Kwantung Army, *ibid.*, Exh. No. 837.

## CHAPTER 28

# The Konoye Cabinet Resigns—
# to Get Rid of Matsuoka

But, alas, the American government had even less faith than before in the formulas presented. For it learned the gist of the decisions made on July 2 through an intercepted circular message from the Japanese Foreign Office.[1]

The screen of Japanese diplomacy was now down. Through the lenses of "Magic" the American government watched what was going on behind it. Only the pure of heart and honest of mind could qualify well under such exposure. The government of Japan did not.

This secret knowledge enabled the American government to foresee the advance into Indo-China and to trace its execution. But it did not lead to the finding of any way of averting the event. No means short of a promise to fight Japan, it was thought, would suffice; and even that might not; and if it did not, the United States would be at war in the Pacific. Besides the unreadiness of our military forces and the opposition of public opinion, there was special reason for not taking that risk at that time. All available transport, arms, and naval strength were needed for two other tasks which the American government was assuming: aid for the Soviet Union and the extension of the guarded Atlantic frontier.

The American military authorities, as is well known, did not regard Russian chances as bright. Stimson, after consultation with the Chiefs of Staff and War Plans Division of the General Staff, reported to the

[1] Diplomatic Circular, No. 1390, Tokyo, July 2, 1941, to the Japanese Embassies in Washington, Berlin, Moscow, and Rome. *Pearl Harbor Attack*, Part 12, pp. 1–2. The text of this was available to the heads of the American government by July 8 at the latest. The language of this summary is vaguer than the actual resolution; and that version which was obtained by the American government did not contain specific mention of preparations for a war with England and the United States.

President that the Army estimated that Germany would be thoroughly occupied in beating Russia for a minimum of one month and a possible maximum of three months.[2] Knox, after consultation with the Chief of Naval Operations wrote him that the best opinion he could get was "that it would take anywhere from six weeks to two months for Hitler to clean up on Russia." [3] Both urged that the interval should be used vigorously to improve the situation in the Atlantic.

Proof of our will to support Russia would, it was thought, have more effect on Japan than any words or sanctions. The news brought by "Magic" was to the effect that Japan would stay on the sidelines in the north until the Russian armies in the east were used up. Still, on July 3, Grew was instructed to convey directly to Konoye the President's hope that Japan would not intervene. Grew was not able to do so. The Foreign Minister, he found, could not be by-passed. On the 8th, Matsuoka gave a written answer, dry and flavored with malice. The Japanese government, it said, had not thus far considered the possibility of joining the war against the Soviet Union, and had already made its position clear to the government of that country. Then it asked a question in turn: was it really the American intention to intervene in the European war? [4]

While Grew and Matsuoka were engaged in this *tu quoque* exercise, the State Department was quizzing Nomura. His answers (July 5) were taken as virtual proof of the scheduled move to the south. He said that Japan had prepared for all eventualities. He named some: the signs of American plans to encircle Japan—as indicated by the shipment of planes and pilots to China, the movements of forces and supplies to Malaya and the Indies, the visit of American naval vessels to Australia, and reports that the United States was going to aid Russia in the Far East and perhaps even to acquire air bases in Siberia. He alluded also to rumors of orders to stop the export of oil to Japan, remarking that in

[2] Letter, Stimson to President, June 23, 1941. This opinion was soon revised.

[3] Memorandum, Knox to President, June 23, 1941. This opinion, also, was soon revised. The British military staffs also originally thought the fight would be very short. But a British military mission that had been hustled to Moscow at the end of June reported that the stubborn Russian resistance and the competent organization of the Russian retreat made it probable that the struggle might go on longer, and urged their government to give all available help. However, at the end of July the British staffs still thought Germany might dispose of all organized Soviet military resistance within two or three months.

[4] As Walter Millis remarked, "Clearly Mr. Roosevelt had asked for that one." *This is Pearl!* (New York, 1947), p. 101. This is a narrative of events, diplomatic and military, preliminary to and bearing upon the Pearl Harbor attack. Considering the date at which it was written, and the fact that the study was made only from material published up to that time, the treatment of the complex events reviewed is skillful as well as interesting.

that event Japan would have to get oil somewhere. Hence, he concluded, "it was necessary for Japan to take appropriate preparatory measures."[5]

If the Japanese government was seeking a parallel for the advance into Indo-China, we were now about to provide one that could be construed as close—to the Japanese people, at least. The plans to have American forces occupy Iceland had been completed some time since. The final formality had been settled in an exchange of letters between Churchill, Roosevelt, and the Prime Minister of Iceland, Jonasson, on July 1. American transports had left almost at once. On July 7 the President informed Congress in a special message that, at the invitation of the local government, American forces were in Iceland to stay. This step, he explained, had been taken in order to thwart possible German occupation, which would be a threat to North America, to Atlantic shipping, and to the flow of munitions to Britain. Thus he informed Congress that "As Commander-in-Chief I have consequently issued orders to the Navy that all necessary steps be taken to insure the safety of communications in the approaches between Iceland and the United States, as well as on the seas between the United States and all other strategic outposts."

Iceland was less than seven hundred miles from Scotland and about nine hundred from German-occupied Norway.

The Navy on July 11, as directed by the President, issued a new order —to make this policy effective. American warships were (beginning July 26) to protect American-flag and Iceland-flag ships against hostile attack by escorting, covering, patrolling, as required by circumstances; and by destroying hostile forces which threatened such shipping.[6] As a result of the way in which travel and convoy arrangements were made, British merchant vessels were also in effect to be given the same protection.[7]

[5] The memorandum of this talk is printed in *Foreign Relations: Japan*, II, 499–502. Two days before (July 3) Nomura had cabled Matsuoka, "If you are resolved to use armed forces against the Southern Regions at this time, there seems to me no room at all for adjusting Japanese-American relations." Nomura manuscript (*op. cit.*).

[6] Hemisphere Defense Plan, No. 4 (W.P.L. 51). This is Admiral Stark's summary of the order. Stark had recommended to the President on June 24 that the American government begin naval escort of convoys in these waters and announce that it was doing so. He wrote to Admiral C. M. Cooke, Jr., on July 31 that he had told the President that such action "would almost certainly involve us in the war [i.e., in the Atlantic] and that I considered every day of delay in our getting into the war as dangerous, and that much more delay might be fatal to Britain's survival." *Pearl Harbor Attack*, Part 16, pp. 2175–77.

[7] According to the original plan (W.P.L. 50) the order was to have openly included British-flag vessels (Morgenthau diary, entry for July 10, 1941; Stimson diary, entry for July 21, 1941). But instead it was arranged that departures of American vessels from

These measures had long been preceded by hints and rumors. As Arthur Krock wrote at the time, "the step which occupied Iceland was forecast to informed persons here at least four months ago." [8] Japanese observers must have been torpid, indeed, if they had not forewarned Tokyo. Surely the German government knew it was in the wind.

But there is no sign in the Japanese records that foreknowledge of our action in Iceland was a spur to the Indo-China venture. It was, however, a reason why the Japanese government thought the United States neither fair nor justified in protesting its own project. If the United States needed Iceland for its defense, was not Japan excused for feeling it needed Indo-China, and perhaps places beyond?

So the spokesman for the Japanese Navy, Admiral Mayeda, said at once that "if such moves could be taken by Washington an equal occupation of new bases in the Pacific must be considered a possibility." [9] The spokesman for the Army, Major Akiyama, said "Just as the United States did not announce the Navy was in Iceland until it was occupied, we cannot make an announcement about future matters. . . ." And, when asked about possible Japanese occupation of the Indies, he answered, "If Japan ever does, it would be as important as the occupation of Iceland and would be regarded by the United States in the same light Japan regards Iceland, that is as a stride toward war." [10]

Against this darkening talk the State Department waited for an answer to its latest proposals. Hull, being sick, was in White Sulphur Springs. Nomura went down there on July 13, but Hull had not seen him, observing later, "I was not well and Nomura had nothing new to offer." This was shown to be so when Hamilton and Ballantine talked with him. For two days later Nomura presented himself again to ask that Hull take back the paper in which he had hinted that the pro-Axis statements of some of the Japanese leaders were keeping the two countries apart. This was, it turned out, Matsuoka's last fling. For at that very time he was in the center of a wrangle over what was to be said to us, which ended with his ejection from office. A better grasp of what

Halifax would coincide with those of British convoys and they would move in company.

On July 19, the Commander in Chief of the Atlantic Fleet issued an order, organizing Task Force, No. 1, with the duty of supporting the defense of Iceland "to escort convoys of United States and Iceland flag shipping, including shipping of any nationality which may join such United States or Iceland flag convoys, between United States ports and bases, and Iceland." This task force was "to provide protection for convoys in the North Atlantic Ocean as may be required by the strategic situation" (Morison, *op. cit.*, I, 78). Canada made Shelburne and Halifax available as operating bases for the American Navy.

[8] *New York Times*, July 8, 1941.
[9] *ibid.*
[10] *ibid.*, July 9, 1941.

happened after can be had by reviewing what the Japanese documents tell of this quarrel.

## [2]

The Japanese government still had—after the Imperial Conference of July 2—to decide how to deal with the American proposals before it (the papers given by Hull to Nomura on June 21). They had made up their minds to go on their way regardless of what the United States might say or do; but they still hoped to avoid war. The German ally continued to argue the case against the southward advance, and for an immediate attack on Russia, but with civility, being a little afraid still of a secret deal with the United States at its expense.[11]

Liaison Conferences were held on July 10 and 12. Matsuoka took the center of the stage. He spoke harshly, going so far even as to distribute among his audience leaflets stating his views. They were in essence that the American proposals were from first to last based on ill will, and designed either to subdue Japan or to throw it into utter confusion. Hull's allusion to the outspoken pro-German attitude of certain members of the Japanese government he took as an insulting attack on himself. He compared it with the Kaiser's famous demand for the resignation of the French Foreign Minister, Delcassé. He insisted that Japanese honor required rejection of the oral statement and termination of the talks with the United States.

This did not appeal to any of his colleagues—civil or military. They saw no use in throwing away any chance to convince the United States and Britain that Japan really wanted peace and order in the Pacific—once its leadership in the area was granted. None was as prone as Matsuoka to accept the idea of inevitable war. Konoye in his "Memoirs" writes, with acceptable sincerity, that he "was determined to do [his] utmost, and would work for the success of negotiations even at the cost of some concessions." Even the Army wanted the talks with the United States to go on, at least until after Japan had completed the occupation of Indo-China and the outcome of the fighting in Russia was clear. The Liaison Conference on the 10th adjourned without decision to allow two days for private consultations.

[11] Ribbentrop wondered whether such a deal might account for Roosevelt's boldness in occupying Iceland. (Telegram, Ribbentrop to Ott, July 10, 1941, *Far East Mil. Trib.*, Exh. No. 771.) But Ott reassured him that any agreement between the United States and Japan was almost out of the question—especially since "the economic strangulation measures of the United States" were increasing the tension. Telegram, Ott to Ribbentrop, July 14, 1941, *ibid.*, Exh. No. 867.

The breach was as great as before when it met again on the 12th. The Army and Navy presented a joint statement confirming their wish to continue the talks with the United States, and outlining the future basis for them.[12] In this there can be detected a disposition to satisfy the United States that Japan was not likely to join Germany in an Atlantic war. As revised in the Foreign Office, this Army-Navy draft was turned into an answer for Washington of which all the conferees save Matsuoka thought well.

The Foreign Minister would not give in. At first he refused to read the statement. Then he insisted that Hull be asked to withdraw the offending oral statement (of June 21) before talks were resumed on any basis. Thoroughly aroused, he also confided in the German and Italian Ambassadors—which was a way of asking for another German protest. This defiance angered the Army and Navy. They shared Konoye's feeling that if Japan served any such demand, as a condition for the resumption of the talks, the American government would choose to let them lapse.

On that same day (July 12, Tokyo time) Kato, the Japanese Ambassador at Vichy, was ordered to ask of Pétain, himself, the right to occupy eight air fields, and the use of Saigon and Camranh Bay, as naval bases. He was to say that if consent was not had by the 20th Japanese forces would enter anyhow. "This decision," Kato was told, "was made by the Japanese Government with the firm determination that it would be carried out despite any hindrances by Britain and America or even if the French or Indo-French authorities oppose it." So little time was allowed Vichy, it was explained, because delay would make it more likely that the United States and Britain would make a fuss "which we must avoid to the utmost." [13]

For a day, after much running back and forth, Konoye thought that Matsuoka would give in. But on the night of the 14th (Tokyo time) he went ahead on his own. He ordered Nomura to ask Hull to withdraw the offending oral statement before submitting the Japanese answer.[14] Nomura sent a junior to perform the errand. The Secretary agreed without ado to take the statement back, disavowing any intent to interfere in Japanese internal affairs or to force Matsuoka's expulsion from the cabinet.

[12] Its chief authors were General Muto, Chief of the Military Affairs Bureau of the War Ministry, and Admiral Oka, Chief of the Naval Affairs Bureau in the Navy Ministry. "Konoye Memoirs."

[13] Telegram, Matsuoka to Kato, July 12, 1941. *Far East Mil. Trib.*, Exh. No. 640.

[14] "Kido's Diary," entry for July 15, 1941.

But it fell out—because of the way Matsuoka behaved—that he was expelled anyway. For, on learning of Matsuoka's disregard of the cabinet, Konoye concluded that the situation could no longer be managed. The decision may have been in part precipitated by cables from Nomura to the Japanese naval authorities, warning of the danger of war, and to Matsuoka, asking to be allowed to resign and come home.[15] When the Minister of War, Tojo, nodded, the final signal was given for a change.

Should the whole cabinet resign or should Matsuoka alone be asked to retire? There was much worry over the idea of a total cabinet resignation. Many of the figures concerned with the question shared the qualms that Kido expressed in his "Diary" on July 15: "At this time when popular tension is so great that even the higher schools closed lest disturbances should arise, the resignation of the whole cabinet for a secret reason which cannot be told to the people should be avoided by all means." There was another fear, too. If the cabinet just dropped Matsuoka he might, by posing as a victim of American pressure, so arouse public feeling that the cabinet would be forced to end the talks in Washington.

Thus after consultation with the Emperor the whole cabinet, on July 16, resigned. Konoye, it was then found, was the only one who could get on with both the Army and political circles. Thus two days later he was again given a mandate to organize the government. The only real difference between the new cabinet and the old was the omission of Matsuoka. He was succeeded by Admiral Toyoda, who, it was thought, would be trusted by the United States. Tojo remained War Minister.

The American government paid little heed to this cabinet crisis. For it correctly surmised that the scrap was over strategy rather than basic attitudes. Matsuoka was being faithful to the vows he had given in Berlin. His colleagues did not want to enter the war against Russia then, and wanted to avoid a break with the United States. But all remained set upon the execution of the advance to the south. If Konoye's readiness, recorded in his "Memoirs," to give up this advance was genuine, he did not make an issue of it—during the cabinet crisis. Perhaps among the many ideas that battled within his wavering spirit was the thought that he could presently reverse the action.

But the first diplomatic actions of the new cabinet were quite of the opposite import. That most active agent of Axis collaboration, Oshima,

---

[15] Nomura manuscript (*op. cit.*). He was dissuaded from resigning by cables received from the Navy Minister and Chief of the Naval General Staff on July 15.

was kept in Berlin as Ambassador. The new Minister for Foreign Affairs hastened to assure the German and Italian governments that Japan's policy would continue to rest on the spirit and aims of the Tripartite Pact, and that Japan intended to go on with its advance into Indo-China, as planned.[16] Berlin, in fact, was asked again (July 19) to support the ultimatum that had been served on Vichy. All this and more was learned through "Magic." In Washington, plans were being made to strike back.

[16] "Most Urgent" telegram from Ott to Ribbentrop, July 20, 1941. *Far East Mil. Trib.*, Exh. No. 1118.

## CHAPTER 29

## The United States and Britain
## Prepare to Impose Sanctions

IN WASHINGTON, one passage in the intercepted summary of the program adopted on July 2 had been underscored: *"Preparations for southward advance shall be reenforced and the policy already decided upon with reference to French Indo-China and Thailand shall be executed."* [1]

Until this occurred the government had continued to reject all proposals for anticipatory action in the Pacific. Thus when, on June 27, Halifax and Casey urged that events be no longer left to drift, no direct answer had been given. Hull had sidled away from the alternatives they broached: either to awe Japan by joint embargoes and sending our fleet to Singapore, or to quiet Japan by arranging peace in China. But as the confirming news of the portended Japanese advance poured in, the restraint was relaxed.[2] Hull, ill and discouraged, remained at White Sulphur Springs, from where he sent advice in equal parts of fire and foam. With him away, the advocates of action had easier going.

On July 10 Welles, Acting Secretary, informed the British Ambassador, Halifax, that the President authorized him to say that "If Japan now took any overt step through force or through the exercise of pressure to conquer or to acquire alien territories in the Far East, the Government of the United States would immediately impose various embargoes, both economic and financial, which measures had been under consideration for some time past and which had been held in abeyance for reasons which were well known to the Ambassador." [3]

---

[1] Diplomatic Circular, No. 1390, July 2, 1941, Tokyo, already cited.

[2] It came from several sources. One of them was Eden, the British Secretary for Foreign Affairs, who wrote Winant on July 4 that the British government had secret information that the Japanese had decided to acquire bases in southern Indo-China.

[3] Indeed they had been held in abeyance. The Secretary of the Treasury had been urging that Japanese funds in the United States be frozen since December 1940. Hull had withstood attrition over many months, as he had also in regard to the imposition of severe additional restrictions on the export of oil.

In March 1941, Grew had joined the Washington advocates of the freezing of Japanese funds, but for different reasons. On March 10 he reported that the Japanese government was about to force all American business in Japan to accept Japanese management and

The use of the word "embargoes" (complete cessation of trade) may have been intended or careless. Later the President found it hard to make up his mind what he meant by it. On the same day (the 10th) the President told the Soviet Ambassador, Oumansky, that the United States would undertake to supply the Soviet Union with such products as it might wish to order in this country, to the extent that they could be shipped.

On July 14 discussions were begun between the American and British governments as to how best to put the intended restraints into effect. Halifax, after giving an account of the measures which the British government were thinking of taking if Japan moved into southern Indo-China, suggested joint work upon a correlated program. This would include not only Great Britain and the United States, but the Dominions, India, and the Colonies. Welles agreed on the basis that such an effort should be purely informal, exploratory, and entirely confidential. How, in view of what Welles had told Halifax on the 10th, this planning could be regarded as "informal," is a riddle of subtlety. It was taken to mean that the American government would not feel bound to carry out the program which the subordinate officials, in conference, devised.

The assignment was turned over in the first instance to Stanley Hornbeck of the State Department and Noel Hall, Minister in the British Embassy representing the Ministry of Economic Warfare. They made not too easy a combination. Thus, after the first few days, direction of this work was passed over to Dean Acheson, an Assistant Secretary of State. Though the American and British groups met often from then on, the limits and lines of combined action did not become wholly clarified up to the end. It was not the fault of the staff; the heads of their governments could not quite make up their minds how far and fast they wanted to go.

Each newspaper and each intercept from "Magic" gave further details of the Japanese actions towards Indo-China. By the 12th the Ameri-

---

control, without allowing them to sell out for dollars. The only effective remedy, he advised, would be to freeze, and, as necessary, to liquidate Japanese assets in the United States. This recommendation caused a flurry of excitement in the State Department. Hornbeck supported Grew, but it was plain that his mind was not upon injury to American business. The Far Eastern Division thought the action likely to precipitate Japan into an all-out accord with Germany, or (and) into war to get raw materials for which it could not pay. It also prophesied, and correctly, that if Japanese funds were frozen, there would be a tendency, no matter what the announced policy, to end all trade with Japan. Hull allowed the competing drafts of answers to Grew to remain in the hands of their authors.

On June 14, after a long period of hesitation, German and Italian funds in the United States had been frozen, but the Japanese had been permitted to continue to use their funds freely.

can government knew of the demand for bases, to be met by the 20th, under threat of forcible entry.[4] By the 15th it knew the details—eight strategically located air bases and two great naval ports (Camranh and Saigon).[5] These facts, which showed how menacing a position Japan was about to acquire, whetted the wish to end the shipment of war materials. Nomura had little with which to counter the wish. He waited to get orders from the new Foreign Minister, Toyoda—who had taken office on the evening of the 17th (Washington time). There was an air of baffled pessimism in his presentations.

On the 17th Secretary Hull telephoned to Hamilton from White Sulphur Springs to say that he thought that if it became plain that the new Japanese cabinet intended to stay hooked up with Hitler, the American government should increase its economic and financial restrictions against Japan. But, he added, "always short of being involved in war with Japan."

With this somewhat intangible counsel from the Secretary of State, the cabinet in Washington discussed the situation on the 18th. All were in favor of some action or combination of actions against Japan. Divisions of opinion among the members as to exactly how far to go were left unsettled. After this cabinet meeting Welles instructed Hornbeck to have prepared by Monday, July 21, three sets of orders: the first, to freeze Japanese and Chinese funds in the United States; the second, to prohibit or restrict imports into the United States of silk and, if so decided, other items; the third, to restrict the export of oil to Japan to "normal" quantities and to lower the grades of gasoline and lubricants that could be sent.

The officials who were called upon to prepare these orders were in a snarl. They did not know, nor could they find out, whether the President understood that if all Japanese funds were frozen it was likely that all trade with Japan would be halted, if not ended. But by the 21st, an agreement was reached between the State and Treasury Departments. It contemplated the freezing of Japanese funds, but the issuance of licenses for strictly limited quantities of oil, cotton, and other exports to be paid for, in effect, by an equivalent import of silk.[6]

By July 20 "Magic," as well as other sources, supplied the answer as

[4] This ultimatum date was later changed to 6 p.m., July 22, and then later still to the 24th.

[5] Marshall on July 15 sent a special memorandum to the President calling attention to this "Magic" message, and upon the rescheduling of Japanese merchant shipping under way. *Pearl Harbor Attack*, Part 20, p. 4363.

[6] Memorandum of July 21 from E. H. Foley, Jr., to the Secretary of the Treasury. Morgenthau diary, entry for July 21, 1941.

to whether the reformed Konoye Cabinet would renounce its attachment to Germany or its plan to occupy Indo-China. It did not intend to do either. A message which Toyoda had broadcast on July 19 (Tokyo time) to various Japanese diplomatic missions was intercepted. This stated "that although the Cabinet has changed there will be no departure from the principle that the Tripartite Pact forms the keystone of Japanese national policy." Another intercepted message of July 20 (Tokyo time) revealed that Toyoda told Kato (the Japanese Ambassador in Vichy) that the Japanese Army was ready and would advance into Indo-China on the 24th, whether or not the French government consented.

By now Admiral Nomura was distraught. He knew that the American government would pay no heed to the latest set of proposals in his hands (those prepared just before Matsuoka resigned). He resorted to his friends in the American Navy in the effort to find out what was going on, and to avert trouble if he could. Failing to find (on the 20th) either Admiral Stark or his deputy, Admiral Ingersoll, at home, he called on Admiral Richmond Kelly Turner, the head of the War Plans Division. To Turner he explained that he was seeking to talk with Stark, because if the United States and Japan could not stay at peace, a devastating naval war would ensue. Then he put before Turner a somewhat apologetic defense of the Japanese policy, informing him that the action against Indo-China would start within the next few days.

On one important matter he seemed to imply that Japan would meet our wishes. He stressed the fact that the decision as to whether and how to act under the Tripartite Pact would be settled by Japan alone; and he conveyed the impression to Turner that if the United States acceded to the Japanese ideas in the Pacific, Japan would not concern itself greatly over American actions in the Atlantic.[7]


The narrative may be interrupted to say a bit more about this. Matsuoka, just before his dismissal, had passed on to Berlin new verbal formulas to be put before the United States regarding Japanese obligations under Article III of the Tripartite Pact. Ribbentrop had not liked them. He had not liked them at all. He had ordered Ambassador Ott to say that they were very different from previous understandings, and to ask that they be withdrawn. Ott did so, and got a soothing answer.

[7] A memorandum of this talk is printed in *Foreign Relations: Japan*, II, 516 ff.

On the 20th (Tokyo time), Toyoda gave him a message for Ribbentrop which read in part:

"I request you particularly to take note of the fact that the policy of Japan will continue to rest on the spirit and object of the Tripartite Pact . . . There will be no change in the attitude of Japan towards Germany and Italy, based on the Cabinet decision of July 2nd, of which you were notified . . ."

Toyoda went on to remind Ribbentrop that he was personally active in the Navy when the Tripartite Pact was signed, and had a part in bringing it about, and that he intended to continue Matsuoka's policy and to stress the close unity among Japan, Germany, and Italy.[8]

In short, the Japanese government was trying to persuade the American government that it probably would not support Germany in the event of a clash in the Atlantic and to reassure Germany that it would. This double talk was the natural child of the resolution of the Imperial Conference of July 2. What Japan wanted was to keep both the United States and Germany calm until it was in control of Indo-China, and had further chance then to estimate the military situation.

There is another point in Japanese-German relations at this time worth a passing comment. The Japanese government had thrice asked the Germans for help in getting Pétain's consent to the occupation of Indo-China. In the papers, since open to scrutiny, there are indications that Germany held back—waiting to see how Japan's talks with the United States would evolve.[9] But on the 24th, Toyoda through both Ott and Ribbentrop thanked the German government for the cooperation given by Germany in bringing the Vichy government to sign the accord.[10]

But to return to Nomura's call upon Admiral Turner on the afternoon of July 20. A memo of this talk was sent to Stark, who, on the morning of the 21st, passed it on to the President. At the same time he sent along a report (dated the 19th) by the War Plans Division of the Navy, entitled "Study of the effect of an embargo of trade between the United States and Japan."

The conclusions set down in this study reflect the Navy's absorption in the battle of the Atlantic, and its belief that Japan was not likely to

[8] *Far East Mil. Trib.*, Exh. No. 1118.

[9] Telegram, Ribbentrop to Ott, No. 678, July 19, 1941, *ibid.*, Exh. No. 642. Japan also solicited Mussolini's help in getting Vichy to give in, *ibid.*, Exh. No. 2753.

[10] Cable, July 24, 1941, Ott to Ribbentrop, *ibid.*, Exh. No. 1121; cable, Oshima to Toyoda, July 24, 1941—intercepted by "Magic."

move beyond Indo-China in the near future unless we embargoed oil: [11]

"7 (c). An embargo would probably result in a fairly early attack by Japan on Malaya and the Netherlands East Indies, and possibly would involve the United States in early war in the Pacific. If war in the Pacific is to be accepted by the United States, actions leading up to it should, if practicable, be postponed until Japan is engaged in a war in Siberia. It may well be that Japan has decided against an early attack on the British and Dutch, but has decided to occupy Indo-China and to strengthen her position there, also to attack the Russians in Siberia. Should this prove to be the case, it seems probable that the United States could engage in war in the Atlantic, and that Japan would not intervene for the time being, even against the British.

"8. *Recommendation.*—That trade with Japan not be embargoed at this time."

This study was signed by Admiral Turner. Underneath Turner's signature Admiral Stark wrote on the copy he sent to the President: "I concur in general. Is this the kind of picture you wanted?" [12]

The Navy, particularly Secretary Knox, was still inclined to wish to transfer more of the fleet from the Pacific to the Atlantic for its expanding tasks there. It was on this day, the 21st, that Knox got off final orders, already mentioned, to convoy both American and British ships (when in company with American) between the United States and Iceland. [13]

It was the day also on which Washington learned that Darlan had given an answer to Japan. "The French Government," the answer was, "cannot but submit to the demands of the Japanese Government."

"Magic" also picked up the report which Kato, the very pleased Ambassador to Vichy, sent to his superiors: "The reason why the French so readily accepted the Japanese demands was that they saw how resolute was our determination and how swift our will. In short they had no choice but to yield."

Hull, fretting at White Sulphur Springs, could see that the situation was reaching a climax. Over the telephone he asked Welles to make one last try to cause Japan to realize how grave was the step which it was about to take. Even though no good came of the effort, he added, it would keep the record clear. Welles asked Nomura to call. To his sur-

[11] See Turner's testimony, *Pearl Harbor Attack,* Part 4, pp. 2013-14, and Stark's letter to Admiral Hart, July 24, 1941, *ibid.,* Part 5; p. 2114, and his letter to Admiral Cooke, July 31, 1941, *ibid.,* Part 16, p. 2175.

[12] This memorandum is printed, *ibid.,* Part 5, pp. 2382-84.

[13] Stimson diary, entry for July 21, 1941.

prise he found that the Ambassador had left by automobile to visit an old naval friend in Maine, leaving word that he would be back on the 26th. Plainly he had made up his mind that he could do nothing more to influence either his own government or the American government and wanted a respite from statesmen.

Wakasugi, the Minister in charge of the Embassy when Nomura was away, was summoned to the State Department. Welles asked him about the reports that Japan was about to occupy Indo-China. The answer is set down in Welles's memorandum of the conversation: "Mr. Wakasugi looked me squarely in the eye and said that the Japanese Embassy had no knowledge whatever of any intention on the part of the Japanese Government of occupying Indochina . . ." [14] He then asked Welles whether such an action would interfere with the successful conclusion of the talks with the American government. Welles said it would be hopelessly at variance with the assumptions on which the American government was conducting the talks. With the aid of "Magic," the American government was able to be sure that Wakasugi was a faithful reporter, making it clear to Tokyo that Welles had said that if Japan moved into Indo-China further discussions with the American government would be in vain. By the time this statement reached Tokyo, the troops were already crowding into the transports off the island of Hainan.

Nomura had been caught in New York and called back. It was arranged that he should see Welles at three o'clock on the afternoon of the 23rd. The talk followed its expected course. Nomura made several points in defense of the Japanese advance. It was, he said, necessary to provide Japan with an assured supply of rice and other raw materials, to defeat the schemes of supporters of De Gaulle, and to protect it against encirclement. He said also that Japan could not pursue a do-nothing policy in the face of the embargoes to which it was now subject; that if it merely submitted to them it would be committing national suicide. [15]

The Japanese leaders, it may be remarked in passing, continued even before the International Military Tribunal to pretend that their prime reason for occupying Indo-China was to make sure of getting its rice, rubber, and tin. This did play a part in the decision, though not a leading or compulsive one. Japan was failing to induce or force the Indo-Chinese government to sell to it, and to it alone, the local surpluses of

[14] Welles's memo of this talk is in *Foreign Relations: Japan,* II, 520–22.
[15] This feature of Nomura's remarks is more definitely and fully reported in Nomura's message to his Government (as revealed by "Magic") than it is in Welles's memorandum of the talk which is printed, *ibid.,* II, 522, *et seq.*

these and other products. The United States and Britain were still active rival buyers.[16] But, as the Japanese records show, strategic and political purposes were the really moving ones. If they had not been, Japan could have obtained assent to its economic demands without taking naval and air bases.

Welles refused absolution. He said that the American government could construe the move only as the last preparatory step for the conquest of other lands in the South Seas.[17] Then slowly he remarked that Secretary Hull had asked him to say that he could not see that any further basis remained for the talks in which he and the Ambassador had been engaged.

Shortly before this talk, or within a few hours after, the American government learned what Nomura and the Japanese government were saying to each other. Nomura, recalling earlier advice, was telling Tokyo that he thought the case now so serious as to create a danger that diplomatic relations would be broken. The new Foreign Minister, Toyoda, was explaining to Nomura that the advance into Indo-China had been decided before he took office and could not be undone. He was asking Nomura to do all he could to lessen friction and to let the American

[16] During 1940, after the fall of France, the American government actually managed to obtain about 29 thousand tons of the total Indo-Chinese production of rubber of about 60 thousand tons. In bargaining, the American government had the advantage of being able to promise to supply Indo-China in turn with goods which were wanted—particularly oil. The rivalry for rubber and metals continued during the early months of 1941. On the one hand, the United States and Britain were threatening to end all oil shipments, unless Indo-China sold us a substantial share of its rubber and metals. On the other hand, the German Armistice Commission was insisting that the Vichy government give instructions that all the rubber must be sent to Japan, and Japan was offering a high price for it. As late as the beginning of July 1941, the Governor General of Indo-China, Decoux, an independent man, was offering to sign a contract to continue to send some rubber to the United States in return for American goods. In short, it was true that Japan could not be certain of getting all the Indo-Chinese production of rubber and tin.

In regard to rice the situation had been somewhat similar. Britain, not the United States, was the rival buyer, and its control of the supply of products needed by Indo-China, e.g., jute bags for the rice crop, gave bargaining influence. The War Ministry reckoned Japan's annual rice needs to be 400 million bushels, of which domestic production was about 300 million. Of the 100 million bushels imported, about 50 million were from Thailand and Indo-China.

On May 26, 1941, the governments of Japan and France signed a Convention on Navigation and Trade between Japan and Indo-China which granted preference to Japan in purchasing Indo-Chinese products and allowed her to secure rice for deferred payments. This Convention had not yet become fully effective in operation.

[17] This general judgment was supported by a "Magic" intercept of a message (July 14) from officials of the Japanese Southern Army in Canton to military attachés, which read in part: "The immediate object of our occupation of French Indo-China will be to achieve our purposes there. Secondly, its purpose is, when the international situation is suitable, to launch therefrom a rapid attack . . . next on our schedule the sending of an ultimatum to the Netherlands Indies. In the seizing of Singapore the Navy will play a principal part."

government know that retaliatory action, such as freezing Japanese funds, might create an extremely critical situation.[18]

On the same afternoon (the 23rd) Butler and Hall of the British Embassy brought further word of the action planned by Britain if Japan occupied Indo-China. The Treaty of Commerce and Navigation which had bound the two countries since 1911 would be denounced.[19] Further, the British government had recommended to the Dominions that all Japanese funds be frozen, and had no doubt of their response; and it was in touch with the governments of the Netherlands and the Belgian Congo, and the Free French leaders concerning the taking of similar measures. Acheson, by order, took care lest Britain be led into action before the American government was ready to act, or be led into some variant or more severe action. He stated that the exact situation in Indo-China was still not clear to the American government and that the timetable, the order and extent of the restrictions, would depend upon the facts as they developed. His prior exploration with them of all available modes of action was not, he added, to be taken to mean that this government would use all the controls right away or at the same time. He promised ample notice.

These cautionary comments, despite Welles's stern words to Nomura, reflected the fact that the President had not, by the evening of July 23, finally made up his mind precisely how far to go.[20] The Navy favored prudence; the Treasury wanted freezing; the State Department did not object to freezing, but was not clear as to what would follow; the British government seemed ready for anything; and the Secretary of State, from White Sulphur Springs, was telephoning that he thought it best to leave the decision to those on the ground.

[18] Telegram, Toyoda to Nomura, No. 397, July 23, 1941.

[19] Also sundry other important accords, including the Trade Convention between India and Japan, signed in 1934, and the Treaty of Commerce between Japan and Burma, signed in 1937.

[20] Both Acheson and Welles were still uncertain as to whether the President appreciated the full weight of the freezing action and had decided how it was to be administered. Several of the State Department officials concerned seem to recall that either on the 22nd, 23rd, or 24th, a small chit, pencilled in hand, had come over from the White House. This listed the possible alternative forms of action, and opposite the entry, "freeze Japanese funds," the President had made a check. I have failed to find any such chit, however, in the State Department archives or elsewhere. Further, according to their memory, this chit left unanswered the core question—whether licenses were to be issued to enable Japan to draw on the frozen funds to pay for oil or other products.

## CHAPTER 30

# We Freeze Japan's Funds

ON THE next day, the 24th, the radio reported that Japanese warships had appeared off Camranh Bay, and that twelve troop transports were on their way south from Hainan.

In the morning a home defense group, the Volunteer Participation Committee, was brought to the White House by Mayor La Guardia. Great men make great occasions of small visits. Now the President chose to talk about a subject upon which the probing reporters had been unable to get him to comment—oil for Japan. Adopting the tone of a primary school teacher, he seemed to be chatting for the sole purpose of making his company understand. But his words were read around the world.

"Here on the east coast, you have been reading that the Secretary of the Interior, as Oil Administrator, is faced with the problem of not having enough gasoline to go around in the east coast, and how he is asking everybody to curtail their consumption of gasoline. All right. Now, I am—I might be called an American citizen, living in Hyde Park, N.Y. And I say, 'That's a funny thing. Why am I asked to curtail my consumption of gasoline when I read in the papers that thousands of tons of gasoline are going out from Los Angeles— west coast—to Japan; and we are helping Japan in what looks like an act of aggression?'

"All right. Now the answer is a very simple one. There is a world war going on, and has been for some time—nearly two years. One of our efforts, from the very beginning, was to prevent the spread of that world war in certain areas where it hadn't started. One of those areas is a place called the Pacific Ocean—one of the largest areas of the earth. There happened to be a place in the South Pacific where we had to get a lot of things—rubber—tin—and so forth and so on—down in the Dutch Indies, the Straits Settlements, and Indo-China. And we had to help get the Australian surplus of meat and wheat, and corn, for England.

"It was very essential from our own selfish point of view of defense to prevent a war from starting in the South Pacific. So our foreign policy was— trying to stop a war from breaking out down there. At the same time, from the point of view of even France at that time—of course France still had her head above water—we wanted to keep that line of supplies from Australia and New Zealand going to the Near East—all their troops, all their supplies that they have maintained in Syria, North Africa, and Palestine. So it was essential for Great Britain that we try to keep the peace down there in the South Pacific.

"All right. And now here is a Nation called Japan. Whether they had at that time aggressive purposes to enlarge their empire southward, they didn't have any oil of their own up in the north. Now, if we cut the oil off, they probably would have gone down to the Dutch East Indies a year ago, and you would have had war.

"Therefore, there was—you might call—a method in letting this oil go to Japan, with the hope—and it has worked for two years—of keeping war out of the South Pacific for our own good, for the good of the defense of Great Britain, and the freedom of the seas." [1]

These remarks were without clear issue. Neither the American nor the Japanese readers could tell whether or not the President intended henceforth to cease supplying oil. Was he, perhaps, trying to find out whether the American people, now having been told that it might mean war, would support him in doing so?

That afternoon the cabinet met. The President ruled that the order to "freeze" (i.e., subject every use to license) should be all-inclusive. This would enable the government, he thought, to make up its mind later as to whether, and on what terms, to permit Japan to use these funds to pay for oil, and to change its mind as often as it wanted. Queried as to whether so unqualified a first order might not cause the Japanese government to jump to the conclusion that no more oil was to be had, and hence move against the Indies, the President answered that he thought not. He was inclined, he added, to have applications to pay for oil passed on as they were presented to the Treasury rather than by formula. In any case no further exports of gasoline that could be converted into fluid suitable for aviation use would be permitted. As he was leaving for Hyde Park that evening, the pertinent order and regulations were to be sent over to the White House before he left, or speeded after him by plane. For he wanted to issue them on the morning of the 26th. [2]

While these papers were being completed, the President received Nomura again. Welles and Admiral Stark were asked to be present to emphasize the gravity of the talk. The President related to Nomura what he had said to the Volunteer Participation Committee in the morning, but added a warning. If Japan, he said, "attempted to seize the oil supplies by force in the Netherlands East Indies, the Dutch would, without the shadow of a doubt, resist; the British would immediately come

---

[1] Excerpt from Radio Bulletin No. 176, issued by the White House on July 25, 1941.

[2] Memorandum of Acting Secretary Bell of the Treasury. Morgenthau diary, entry for July 24, 1941. It was also decided, at this cabinet meeting, in accord with Chiang Kaishek's request, to freeze all Chinese funds in the United States at the same time.

to their assistance, war would result between Japan, the British, and the Dutch, and in view of our own policy of assisting Great Britain, an exceedingly serious situation would immediately result."

The President, after listening to Nomura's exposition of the views of the Japanese government in regard to the advance into Indo-China, then said he had a proposal to make. It might be, he remarked, too late, but he still wanted to use every possible chance to prevent trouble. The essence of this proposal was: ". . . if the Japanese Government would refrain from occupying Indochina with its military and naval forces, or, had such steps actually been commenced, if the Japanese Government would withdraw such forces, the President could assure the Japanese Government that he would do everything within his power to obtain from the Governments of China, Great Britain, the Netherlands, and of course the United States itself a binding and solemn declaration, provided Japan would undertake the same commitment, to regard Indo-china as a neutralized country . . . . this would imply that none of the powers concerned would undertake any military act of aggression against Indochina, and would refrain from the exercise of any military control within or over Indochina." [3] The President kept this talk, with its wrapped warning, secret, in order to make it easier for the Japanese government.

The morning of the 25th the President was at Hyde Park. The reporters found him in a genial shirt-sleeved mood, but unwilling to talk about oil. The press carried the item that Willkie had said that the United States should place an embargo on oil shipments to Japan, and that in his opinion it should have done so long ago. But when the President was asked whether his talk of the day before marked the swan song of a policy, ". . . he insisted that he had said nothing about that and would say nothing about it." [4] He was similarly unwilling to be drawn into any discussion about freezing Japanese funds.

At eight o'clock in the evening the President's office at Poughkeepsie passed out to the press a release which stated that, in view of the unlimited national emergency, the President was issuing an Executive Order freezing Japanese assets in the United States. "This measure," the press release continued, "in effect, brings all financial and import and export trade transactions in which Japanese interests are involved under the control of the government . . ." [5]

[3] Welles's memorandum of this conversation is printed in *Foreign Relations: Japan,* II, 527, *et seq.*
[4] *New York Times,* July 26, 1941.
[5] Press release issued at Poughkeepsie, N.Y., by the White House at 8 p.m., July 25, 1941.

The step had been taken which was to force Japan to choose between making terms with us or making war against us. No longer would the United States be providing the resources which left her better able to fight if she should so decide.

On the next morning, the 26th, the requisite official orders were issued.[6] The first quick response within the United States was approval, while the subdued comment in the Japanese press seemed to show dismay. That afternoon, in cabling to Hopkins that he consented to his going to Moscow to see Stalin, the President asked that the Former Naval Person be told that "our concurrent action in regard to Japan is, I think, bearing fruit. I hear their Government [is] much upset and no conclusive future policy has been determined on."[7] Not much reason can be found for this buoyant note, for in the same cable the President asked that Churchill also be informed that he had as yet received no reply to his suggestion that Indo-China be neutralized, but thought that when it came it probably would be unfavorable. No dew fell from "Magic" to freshen the belief that Japan would heed the proposal or the warning.

Events were to show that the freezing order shook the Japanese rulers. But they did not change their course. They were soon to decide to rush full speed ahead, lest they would not have enough oil to reach those distant ports which were marked on the Imperial chart.

## [2]

To what extent were the heads of the military forces of the United States consulted about the order which the President issued on July 26? What views did they express? These questions were often asked in the course of the Congressional investigation of the Pearl Harbor attack. A somewhat more systematic, if still incomplete, answer may now be given to them.

The decision was, as has been recounted, discussed at the cabinet meetings of July 18 and 24. There is no record of any dissent by Stimson and Knox; they had long since favored some such action.

[6] Executive Order, No. 8832, signed by President Roosevelt, July 26, 1941. This amended Executive Order, No. 8389, of April 10, 1940 (as amended) to include Japan and China. Executive Order, No. 8389, prohibited, except when licensed, all transactions: (1) "by, or on behalf of, or pursuant to the direction of any foreign country designated in this Order, or any national thereof." (2) which "involve property in which any foreign country designated in this Order, or any national thereof, has at any time on or since the effective date of this Order had any interest of any nature whatsoever, direct or indirect."
[7] The message is printed in *Pearl Harbor Attack*, Part 20, p. 4373.

The Chief of Staff of the Army, Marshall, knew that the government was on the point of subjecting all trade with Japan to rigorous control. Stimson kept him well informed about all matters that affected the chances of war. After the cabinet meeting of the 18th he was consulted by Welles as to whether the Army had any objection if the import of silk was forbidden, in view of its possible need of silk for parachutes. Marshall replied by letter that from a military point of view there was no objection. His knowledge of what was about to occur is further suggested by the fact that on July 24 he sent Welles a copy of a letter to the President that was waiting Stimson's signature. In this letter it was recommended that, in view of the situation in the Far East, all practical steps be taken to increase the defensive strength of Singapore.

If General Marshall made any objection during the July fortnight when the freezing action was being matured, it is not of accessible record. Later he testified before the Pearl Harbor Committee: ". . . our state of mind in that period—I am referring now to both Stark and myself —was to do all in our power here at home, with the State Department or otherwise, to try to delay this break to the last moment, because of our state of unpreparedness and because of our involvement in other parts of the world." [8] This was so. But he either thought the freezing action outside his province, or that it would not cause a break.

As for Admiral Stark, his view in regard to an oil embargo was often expressed. He was against it. As phrased in a letter to Admiral Hart on July 24, "This question of embargo has been up many times and I have consistently opposed it just as strongly as I could." [9] If the oil supply was cut off, he thought, Japan was likely to go to war to get it, and he did not want war with Japan yet. The Navy had all the work it wanted in the Atlantic. I must leave to others the task of reconciling his anxiety about an oil embargo with the view which he expressed in his letter to Admiral Cooke on July 31, after the freezing order had been issued. He wrote that after the German invasion of Russia he advised the President to take action in the Atlantic that would almost certainly involve us in war; "and that I considered every day of delay in our getting into the war as dangerous, and that much more delay might be fatal to Britain's survival." [10] Can he have thought that we could get into the war against Germany in the Atlantic without facing a crisis in the Pacific?

[8] *Pearl Harbor Attack*, Part 32, p. 560.
[9] *ibid.*, Part 5, p. 2114.
[10] *ibid.*, Part 16, pp. 2175–77.

The President does not seem, in the final days or hours of decision, to have talked the question through with either Marshall or Stark. A message which he sent to Stark on the 22nd may have seemed to the Admiral to mean that the President was more or less of his opinion. Through Captain Beardall, the President's Naval Aide, he sent back word that he liked Admiral Turner's study and asked Stark to send copies to Hull and Welles.[11]

But anyhow, the President did not worry over the outcome of an embargo as much as some of his military aides. He seemed fairly sure that the United States would get more time, that Japan would await the outcome of the battle against Britain and Russia before it crossed the boundary. Churchill, in contrast to his fears of February past, felt the same way for a time.[12] In a meeting on July 24, convoked by him with the British Chiefs of Staff and Army and Navy observers, with Hopkins present, he said that he was convinced the Japanese would not enter the war until the British were beaten; that it did not want to fight the United States and the British Empire together. As Sherwood has written: "This conviction, shared by Roosevelt, was of enormous importance in the formulation of policy prior to Pearl Harbor." [13]

[11] Stark so informed Welles when sending him a copy of this study, *ibid.*, Part 5, p. 2382.

[12] Churchill was, I think, mistaken in his belief that the responsible officers of the State Department (with the possible exception of Hornbeck) shared this judgment, as stated in the third volume of his history of World War II, to wit: "The State Department at Washington believed, as I did, that Japan would probably recoil before the ultimately overwhelming might of the United States." *The Grand Alliance*, p. 587.

[13] Sherwood, *op. cit.,* p. 316.

## CHAPTER 31

# Was Japan to Have Any More Oil?

But this belief fluctuated. It alternated with its opposite—that Japan would fight no matter what. Hence weeks of wavering about the line to follow in applying the freezing order. Should the American government be lenient or severe in the issue of licenses to use "frozen" dollars to pay for Japanese purchases? Should Japan be allowed to get some oil? It was decided that it should be left to hope and guess, and that we would be guided by its further behavior.

The Acting Secretary of State did not clarify our intentions. Nor did the other officials of the Treasury and State Departments when on the evening of the 25th they met the press together. Asked whether licenses would be issued under the freezing order, Foley, General Counsel of the Treasury, answered that the Hyde Park statement seemed to speak for itself. He then ventured the opinion that the effect of the freezing order would "probably be to restrict American-Japanese trade." [1] Assistant Secretary of State Dean Acheson protested the description of the action as an "embargo." But he did not explain how far short of one it would be.[2] He had made himself a nuisance to Welles and the White House during the previous day or two, but had been unable to find out. The President was—as he had hinted he would to the cabinet on the 24th—leaving the matter in obscurity. One remains master of an intention as long as it is not disclosed.

It is not to be wondered that persons outside the circle differed in their guesses. Thus, in an informative message which Admiral Stark sent to the Commanders in Chief of the Pacific, Asiatic, and Atlantic Fleets on July 25, he said, "It is anticipated that export licenses will be granted for certain grades of petroleum products, cotton, and possibly some other materials . . ." [3] While, in contrast, Crider began the lead story in the *New York Times* on the following morning by writing, "President Roosevelt tonight froze all Japanese assets in the United States,

[1] *New York Times,* July 26, 1941.
[2] *ibid.*
[3] *Pearl Harbor Attack,* Part 5, p. 2115.

thus virtually severing trade ties with the empire and dealing it the most drastic blow short of actual war." [4] Most of the American and British press and radio interpreted the order in the same way, without official contradiction.

In Washington and London there was a clear appreciation of the meaning of a combined American-British-Dutch trade embargo. It would be almost equivalent to a world-wide embargo. Transport between Europe and Japan was cut. Exports of all war materials from the Central and South American countries to Japan had already been reduced to a few occasional cargoes. The American and British governments had by then acquired the exclusive right to buy almost all the supply of such materials produced in that region. [5]

All informed observers, inside or outside the government, agreed that despite Japan's progress toward self-sufficiency and despite its reserves, the impact of a total embargo would be very serious. The commercial effects would be quick and strickening. Goods would pile up in warehouses, while storage and insurance bills climbed. Factories producing for export would have to shut down. Businesses dealing in imports would have to quit. Shipping would become idle, available for military transport. Government tax revenues would be certain to suffer.

The effects on Japan's military position, while more slowly felt, would be no less certain. Within a short time, some months, the production of the industries which formed the basis of a modern army and navy —iron, steel, chemical, machine, and electrical—would decline. The turnout of new weapons would be limited. Enough, it still might be, to add some to the number of ships, guns, tanks, planes, and bombs for the armed forces; but not much, and very little compared to the climbing American production. And actually, because of the lack of two things—oil and bauxite—the program of naval and aviation expansion might be arrested. All of this was reviewed in the press and radio of the

[4] *New York Times,* July 26, 1941.
[5] By then the American and British governments had arranged to buy the total export surpluses of all important war materials produced throughout Latin-America, with the exception of some Argentine and Peruvian supplies, despite persistent and generous Japanese bids, especially for copper, lead, tungsten, and mercury. They had similarly contracted for all or most of the production in neutral countries—as, for example, of Portuguese and Spanish wolfram, Turkish chrome, part of the rubber and tin of Thailand, the graphite and mica of Madagascar. Only a small margin of a few products was outside their control.

world, as well as in the memoranda that were distributed in government departments.[6]

Oil was vital. There was no way, no uncontrolled source of supply, from which Japan could get as much as it would have to use even with the most rigid economy. Ton by ton, it could be foreseen, Japan would have to empty the tanks which had been filled with such zealous foresight. The Navy was the envied custodian of most of this reserve supply. Every time a ship moved there would be less, and soon it would be asked by other branches of the government to share its hoarded stocks. Would the Navy, which hitherto had been the chief opponent of any reckless venture, consent to this suction? Would it insist that the government make terms with the United States and Great Britain? Or would it also begin to favor, no matter what the odds, an effort to get control of the sources of supply in the Southern Pacific?

And, if the Army was uncertain as to whether to move north against the Soviet Union or southward, might not this question of oil fix the answer? The more severe the control over Japan's oil supply, the less likely that it would dare join the attack on the Soviet Union; the more likely that its soldiers would go where there was oil.

It took only the daily press and an open mind to locate this sensitive spot in history. The dispute between Japan and the United States had been slowly moving toward a crisis ever since 1931, the invasion of Manchukuo. From now on the oil gauge and the clock stood side by side. Each fall in the level brought the hour of decision closer. It was in the power of the American, British, and Dutch governments to decide how fast the gauges should drop. It was in the power of the Japanese government to decide how much more time was spent in the search for peace; and whether the ultimate choice would be peace or war. The American government wanted it to be peace, but a lasting one not a patched-up truce; a peace that would end Japan's attempt to rule the Orient.

### [2]

The administration of the freezing order was assigned to a committee of the State, Treasury, and Justice Departments: Acheson for State, Foley for Treasury, Shea for Justice. All three were adroit lawyers, disposed

[6]An extensive review of the situation cabled from London, for example, appeared in the *New York Times* of July 26, the morning after the event. The officials of the British Ministry of Economic Warfare then and later showed more inclination to discuss this subject than their American counterparts. The Australian government was even more loquacious—as it was on most aspects of the Pacific situation.

to ask thorough proof of the reasons for allowing the dollars under their control to be used. As agreed, they took the position that the Executive Order would be construed only when and as particular requests were placed before them.

The governments of Great Britain, the Dominions, India, Burma, and the Colonies, swiftly took action parallel in effect to our own.[7] Within a week after the issuance of the American freezing order, all the funds which Japan might use to secure goods in the British Empire and Commonwealth were under strict control; and no one knew whether, when, or for what purposes their use might be authorized. The authorities of these countries followed our enigmatic example. They refrained, in the same fashion as we, from statements of policy, and met inquiries by saying that individual cases would be decided as they came along.

To the government of the Dutch Indies, the haze over American and British intentions was worrisome. It was nearer to the danger than either. The decision—whether or not to go along with Britain and the United States without quite knowing where they were going—might well, it knew, settle the fate of its great domain and the lives of all the people in it. An official promise had been given to Japan, though against the grain, to supply definite quantities of oil, bauxite, rubber, tin, and other raw materials. If this promise were kept, the Indies would be separated from its companions in defense, and the Japanese ships and planes fueled for attack. If it were broken, the Japanese government would be resentful and almost sure to try to seize the oil, and quickly.

The government of the Indies by then could feel fairly sure that if their land was attacked Britain would fight Japan also. What the United States would do, it was still compelled to guess. The American government would not say. True, American military strength in the Pacific was being built up. On the very day, July 26, that the freezing order was issued, the President, as Commander-in-Chief, placed the Philippine Army in American service and under an American commander. An American military mission was established in China, and American fliers, known as Chennault's Flying Tigers, were beginning to fight the Japanese in China.[8] True, also, coordinated use of naval and air forces of all powers opposed to Japan was visualized in the strategic

[7] They also served termination notice, as they had informed the American government they would, of their trade treaties with Japan.

[8] This force grew. By the end of September the Chinese government had hired 100 volunteer American pilots and 181 American ground personnel to man and service 100 P-40 airplanes provided under Lend-Lease.

plans drawn up in Washington, and discussed in Singapore and Batavia. But even if these were acted on, the local Dutch forces could expect little quick help in battle.

On July 27, the day after the freezing order, an effort was made to find out whether or not we intended to maintain a complete embargo. The Counsellor of the Dutch Embassy, Van Boetzelaer, consulted Acheson. But Acheson at that time was not able, even if he had wanted, to help the Indies government make up its mind. Later Van Mook, the stubborn negotiator who had withstood the Japanese demands, complained that he had received no advice regarding the American freezing order until four days after it went into effect, and that what he learned then was unclear.

The first official response to the President's proposal for the neutralization of Indo-China, received on the same day, stiffened feeling within the American government. Grew had done his utmost to persuade the Japanese government to accept. To Toyoda in a long Sunday talk he made, in the words of his diary, "the strongest appeal of which I was capable and perhaps the strongest representations that I ever made." The Foreign Minister, while reserving his final answer for further study, said that he was afraid that the idea had come too late and that in any case nothing could be done until Japanese anger at our freezing action had waned.[9]

During the next two days (July 28 and 29) the restraining band became broader and tighter. Nomura came in to plead for a relaxation of controls. Welles, having talked with the President and Hull, answered that we could not see the slightest grounds for compromising with the policy that Japan was now pursuing.[10] By Hull's telephoned direction, our missions in the other American republics were told to induce the governments to which they were assigned to follow our example.

After a conference lasting day and night (July 28, Batavia time), the Indies government decided to require special permits for all exports to Japan, and for all payments to or receipt of payments from Japanese subjects.[11] This still left the way open for some trade. But Van Mook —as the American government learned from an intercept—warned the Japanese Consul General that if the Japanese did not conduct them-

---

[9] Grew's report on this talk of July 27 is printed in *Foreign Relations, Japan*, II, 534 *et seq.*

[10] Welles's memo of this talk of July 28 is printed, *ibid.*, II, 537–39. Japanese ships then hovering off the Pacific coast were, however, permitted to enter, discharge cargo, and obtain dollars to pay for fuel and supplies.

[11] No exports of tin or rubber were to be allowed whether previously paid for or not.

selves in an acceptable way in the future, the Indies would exercise a complete economic blockade. Its period of semi-appeasement was over. The Indies government was stoutly confronting the fate ahead, rather than trying to buy dubious safety.

The Japanese government had not been surprised by the American and British repressive measures. But this edict of the Indies was not foreseen. Ending the inflow of oil, by means of which Japan might have managed despite the American and British ban, it produced shock.

Once again (on July 29) the Dutch tried to find out what the United States would do if the Indies were attacked; and once again it had to be satisfied with something less than an answer. The Ambassador, Loudon, explained to Welles, still Acting Secretary, that the Indies government had now made it plain that it would not "appease" Japan. If Japan, he continued, should as a result attack the Indies, he trusted that the American government would bear in mind what had been done to present a firm, united front by all powers concerned in the Pacific. Welles answered only by alluding to the past talks between our military authorities and those of Britain and the Netherlands, and by saying that careful note would be taken of Loudon's statement.

But was Japan to have any more oil from the United States or was it not? The President had still not answered. The Secretary of State, still at White Sulphur Springs, suffused advice throughout the State Department. But his words curled around the issue without settling it. As, for example, when he advised: "I think we need to keep a stiff rein and consider making it just as stiff as possible short of actual military activity."

By this time some applicants for licenses to pay for oil, as well as foreign diplomats, were begging for answers. During the last days of July concerned men rushed from office to office trying to teach each other reason and strategy; the diligent young lawyers who surrounded Acheson, the assertive young advocates who came from the Treasury, the financial and trade specialists from the office of the Economic Adviser, and the diplomats of the Far Eastern Division. They were excited, for they perceived that the schedule and geography of war might be in their keeping. Acheson managed to get this platoon of talent to agree, more or less.

Welles welcomed their recommendations, and on the 31st submitted them to the President. They were stiff, but not a complete embargo. Licenses (both export and the right to draw on frozen dollar balances) might be issued, national defense needs permitting, for as much low-grade gasoline, and crude oil and lubricants, as Japan bought in 1935–36—considered to be a normal period. Virtually no other trade, except in cotton and food, was to be allowed. On August 1 the President approved this program. The main points were announced by the White house.[12] But, in fact, no licenses to export and pay for oil from the Western Hemisphere were issued. New objections were found.

As the days passed the American and British public concluded that the ban was to be complete, and apparently they wanted it that way. This impression had consequences; the issuance of licenses would have seemed a reversal of policy, a return to appeasement. And within Japan, as the meaning of the combined "freeze" became plainer, the sense of crisis grew deeper. Grew reflected the mood about him in Tokyo when he wrote in his diary at the beginning of August: "The vicious circle of reprisals and counter reprisals is on. *Facilis descensus averni est.* Unless radical surprises occur in the world, it is difficult to see how the momentum of the down-grade movement can be arrested, or how far it will go. The obvious conclusion is eventual war."

## [3]

Hull was no more cheerful. He returned from White Sulphur Springs, gray, and still having trouble with his throat. Wearily he had permitted the circle of economic confinement to contract about Japan. But he still clung to the wish to avoid a showdown. Thus, despite the message he had sent when Japan moved into Indo-China, he resumed his talks with Nomura.

But from now on, these talks were turns in front of the footlights, while the real play went on behind. The curtain of diplomacy was becoming more and more transparent. Less and less it concealed the military preparations made by each side to cause the other to yield, before or in battle. Speaking on the telephone to one of his staff on August 2, Hull expressed his inner thoughts, "Nothing will stop them except force. . . . The point is how long we can maneuver the situation until the military matter in Europe is brought to a conclusion. . . . I just don't want us to take for granted a single word they say, but appear to

[12] White House Press Release, No. 1892, August 1, 1941. This stated (1) that no motor fuels or oils suitable for use in aircraft or raw stocks from which they derived could be exported, except to the British Empire and Western Hemipshere; (2) export of other oil products would be limited to "usual or pre-war quantities." The order (No. 19), issued by the Administrator of Export Control, conformed.

do so, to whatever extent it may satisfy our purpose to delay further action by them."

How could a man have much hope when the tubes of "Magic" yielded up such messages as the one which Toyoda sent to Oshima on July 31, and repeated to Nomura. Oshima was told to explain why Japan was moving south and leaving Russia alone. "Commercial and economic relations between Japan and other countries, led by England and the United States, are gradually becoming so horribly strained that we cannot endure it much longer. Consequently, the Japanese Empire, to save its very life must take measures to secure the raw materials of the South Seas. It must take immediate steps to break asunder this ever-strengthening chain of encirclement which is being woven under the guidance of and with the participation of England and the United States, acting like a cunning dragon seemingly asleep." [13]

On August 6, Nomura gave the tardy formal answer to the President's proposal that Indo-China (and Thailand) be neutralized.[14] The Japanese government offered instead a promise not to station troops in Southwest Pacific areas aside from Indo-China, and to withdraw from Indo-China after the settlement of the war in China. The United States was, in return, to (1) suspend all military measures in the Southwestern Pacific areas; (2) restore normal trade relations with Japan; (3) co-operate with Japan so that it might obtain the raw materials needed from the Southwest Pacific, especially the Indies; (4) use its good offices to get Chiang Kai-shek to make peace with Japan, and (5) recognize that Japan was entitled to a special status in Indo-China even after the Japanese forces might be withdrawn.[15]

The American government, as Hull said, orally and in writing, did not find Japan's answer responsive and did find its theme of "encirclement" false. "There is no occasion," he emphasized, "for any nation in the world that is law-abiding and peaceful to become encircled by anybody except itself." [16] When Nomura in this talk remarked that the President might meet with Prime Minister Konoye to settle the gaping

[13] Cable, No. 708, Tokyo to Berlin, July 31, 1941. In this cable to Oshima, the Japanese government again assured the Germans that it was preparing to attack Russia when it could. It was available in Washington, August 4.

[14] The American and British governments were alarmed by reports that Japan was bringing or was about to bring pressure on Thailand to obtain privileges similar to those secured in Indo-China. On August 1, Welles, at the President's request, told Nomura that we would be willing to extend the neutralization plan to Thailand. *Pearl Harbor Attack*, Part 4, p. 1697.

[15] This is a summary of the main points of the proposal printed in *Foreign Relations: Japan*, II, 549 et seq.

[16] Memorandum of conversation, Hull-Nomura, August 8, *ibid.*, II, 551.

issues, Hull seemed hardly to hear. He did not tell the Ambassador that the President was about to join Churchill off the coast of Maine, and that the question of how to deal with Japan was high on their agenda. "Magic" had ended belief in Konoye's power to settle Japanese policies. About his unhappy turnings and twistings at this time we now know more. It is of interest to glance at them before following Roosevelt and Churchill to Argentia Bay.

## CHAPTER 32

# The Choice Before Japan Is Defined; and Konoye Seeks a Meeting with Roosevelt

THE freezing order propelled the Japanese authorities into another urgent round of conferences. All thought that the United States was being wilfully unjust; none advocated that Japan give in. But all, except Tojo and the Army heads, were worried; despite their bitter feeling they were glad to have Konoye keep on trying to change our attitude.

On July 28 the Privy Council met, first alone, and then in the Emperor's presence, to consider the Protocol that had been forced upon the Vichy government for the joint defense of Indo-China. This ruled out Roosevelt's proposal that the country be neutralized. While the Council talked, they could hear power shovels at work around the Imperial Palace, digging shelters. The sounds of war were crossing over the Imperial moat and wall. Old trees, planted when Japan held itself apart, were being dug out to make holes for gun-mounts.

The Cabinet gave the Privy Council the same reasons for the advance into Indo-China as had been given the outside world. It gave no hint of planning any more beyond. But then, as Tojo admitted, the Privy Council when asked to pass upon the resolutions of July 2, had not been told that the government was going to occupy Indo-China by force. In other words these sessions of the Privy Council were only a ceremony, a way of involving all respected Japanese political figures in official decisions. So in this case, by late afternoon the qualms of the Privy Council were met and the agreement with Vichy was unanimously approved.[1]

The real tissue of policy—of peace or war—was treated in talk among Konoye, the Army, and the Navy. The Army, through Tojo, refused to consider any accord with the United States which would limit its freedom to move either north or south. At this very time the Kwantung

---

[1] Summary minutes of this meeting are given in *Far East Mil. Trib.*, Exh. Nos. 649, 650. The formal Protocol was supplemented by a letter of July 29, defining in detail the various rights accorded Japan, *ibid.*, Exh. No. 651. They were to be valid as long as the causing circumstances were deemed to exist.

Army was perfecting its plans for the government of areas in Siberia that were, it was hoped, soon to be taken. The Navy, hitherto a firm negative influence, began to waver.

Admiral Nagano, Chief of the Naval General Staff, was asked by the Emperor to advise as to what course should be followed towards the United States. His answer was a crossroads marker. Japan, he said, should try hard to avert a war with the United States, retiring from its alliance with Germany, if need be. If the effort to adjust relations failed, there would be no other way than to take the initiative in war. One main reason was Japan's need for oil. If the embargo continued all Japanese reserves would be used up in two years. When the Emperor asked whether Japan would win a sweeping victory as in the war with Russia, Nagano said he was doubtful whether Japan would win at all.[2] Kido had intervened to prevent this gloomy report from having too agitating an effect. He advised the Emperor that if Japan annulled the Tripartite Pact it would earn American contempt, not friendship.

Another opinion was asked of Suzuki, the President of the Planning Board. He was even less hopeful about the stretching of the oil supply. He confirmed the estimate that if the embargo continued, Japan would collapse within two years.[3]

Now the choice was narrowly defined. Either an agreement with the United States, prolonged scrimping, or a defiant war. Konoye hurried to compound out of his talks with the Army and Navy the offer which was presented to Hull on August 6. This, the reader will recall, fell flat. Konoye found our response "sharp." By the Japanese military leaders the promise offered not to advance beyond Indo-China was regarded as a main concession. Why, they asked, if Japan gives that pledge and also stipulates that it was not obligated to follow Germany into a war against the United States, should not the American government be satisfied?

But Nomura's reports made clear that it was not. The American government would not swap oil and its position in regard to China for these limited assurances. And—though this point was not thoroughly discussed—it would not suspend the military measures under way to strengthen the Philippines.

Konoye made up his mind that the only way out of the impasse would be a meeting with Roosevelt. No one, no matter what papers come to

[2] "Kido's Diary," entry for July 31, 1941, and Kido's deposition.
[3] Deposition of Suzuki, *Far East Mil. Trib.*, Exh. No. 3605.

light, will be entitled to be sure about his train of purpose. To find a way past both the man of rigid doctrine, Hull, and the hard and threatening Japanese generals; and thus to achieve a compromise that would save both "peace" and "face"? To escape by guile, out of the trap of circumstance in which Japan was caught, now that Germany had failed to release the catch? To gain time and strength for later ventures?

To each he gave the reasons best suited to win assent. Thus, perhaps, the arguments used to convince the Army and Navy give a misleading version of his real thought.[4] When talking with Roosevelt he would, he promised, insist upon the firm establishment of the Greater East Asia Co-Prosperity Sphere. This aim, he assured them, he would not give up; but it could not be achieved all at once; and for the present Japan would be wise to compromise. However, he went on, if the President failed to understand Japan's true intentions he would break off the talk and return home. Even if that happened, the mission would have served a good purpose, since it would solidify the determination of the Japanese people.[5] But, he stressed, the conference must be held *soon,* for if the German attack on Russia should lag, the American attitude would stiffen.[6]

The Navy agreed to his going at once. But Tojo, Minister of War, remained opposed on the score that no matter how the meeting was managed and what was said, relations with Germany would be hurt. But he did not impose an absolute veto. He wrote Konoye that if it was his firm intention to support the basic principles of the existing Japanese plans, and to carry out a war against the United States if the President failed to grasp the true intentions of the Empire, then the Army would suspend objection.[7] "However," Tojo's letter concluded, "you shall not resign your post as a result of the meeting on the grounds that it was a failure; rather, you shall be prepared to assume leadership in the war against America."[8]

[4] As recounted in his "Memoirs."

[5] He drew a comparison: "Although outwardly Chamberlain of England appeared to have been deceived by Hitler on his several trips to the Continent prior to the European War, it is believed that they were effective from the standpoint of solidifying the determination of the British people." *ibid.*

[6] Oshima was reporting that it was lagging, that Keitel admitted that it was two or three weeks behind schedule. Interrogation of Oshima, *Far East Mil. Trib.,* Exh. No. 776A.

[7] "Konoye Memoirs." The actual phrases used in the letter were "with determination to firmly support the basic principles embodied in the Empire's Revised Plan to the 'N' Plan . . ." I have not identified the "N" Plan.

[8] Konoye had been saying to the Lord Privy Seal, Marquis Kido, that if the Army and Navy could not agree on fundamentals of foreign policy, the Cabinet would have to resign and the armed forces assume responsibility for the destiny of Japan. *ibid.,* and "Kido's Diary," entry for August 2, 1941.

A report made by the Navy to the Emperor brought the permission which Konoye sought. This restated what Admiral Nagano, the Chief of Staff, had said—that the choice before Japan was among negotiation, collapse, or war; and it favored negotiation. The Emperor, therefore, told Konoye, "I am in receipt of intelligence from the Navy pertaining to a general oil embargo against Japan by America. In view of this, the meeting with the President should take place as soon as possible." For whom was Konoye to speak, for the Army, the Navy, the Emperor, or himself? It is most doubtful whether he knew.

Still, he asked Nomura to remind the American government again that he was eager to meet with Roosevelt, and the sooner the better. When Nomura did so, Hull did not directly dismiss the idea. But in his own roundabout way he made clear that he saw no purpose in such a meeting until Japan changed its policies.[9] Nomura so advised Konoye on August 9, saying that he would ask the President upon his return to Washington.[10]

While Konoye convoked other Liaison Conferences to decide what more could be said to Roosevelt, the latter was talking with Churchill. When these two men parted there was less space than ever left for Konoye's distressed movements.

[9] Memorandum of Hull-Nomura talk of August 8, 1941, *Foreign Relations: Japan*, II, 550–51.

[10] In some way or other Nomura had found out that the President was about to meet Churchill. He reported to Tokyo that there were rumors that a joint statement would be issued on Far Eastern problems. Nomura manuscript (*op. cit.*).

## CHAPTER 33

# Roosevelt Meets Churchill;
# Argentia and After: August 1941

THE rendezvous in a Newfoundland bay had been arranged by Hopkins in London. Though Roosevelt and Churchill had drawn close in the conduct of the war, this was the first time they met as President and Prime Minister. The Far Eastern situation was one of the main items in their talk.[1]

Churchill brought along an incisive opinion and proposal. Only two weeks before he had thought, so Hopkins reported, that Japan would not risk war unless Britain seemed about to be beaten. Now he again seemed alarmed lest it would. Perhaps the change was the aftermath of the freezing action; a perception of the critical dilemma which was being defined in Tokyo. In any case, he told the President and Welles, he was convinced that only a clear warning could prevent Japan from expanding further south. That must not be permitted to happen, he asserted. For if, as a consequence, war occurred between Britain and Japan, all British shipping in the Pacific and Indian Oceans could be destroyed and the lifelines between the British Island and the Dominions would be cut.

"He pled with me," Welles recorded after a first talk with Churchill on the 10th, "that a declaration of this character participated in by the United States, Great Britain, the Dominions, and the Netherlands Indies, and possibly the Soviet Union would definitely restrain Japan. If this were not done, the blow to the British Government might be decisive."

The President agreed to the idea of serving some kind of parallel or concerted warning. But he found the text which the British prepared too plain and clutching. The American government, for its part, was to announce that if Japan advanced further in the Southwestern Pacific,

---

[1] This account is drawn mainly from the two long memoranda prepared by Welles, *Pearl Harbor Attack*, Part 14, pp. 1275, *et seq.*; Sherwood's narrative based on the Hopkins papers, *op. cit.*, pp. 356, *et seq.*; and the British official records of the conference. A memorandum prepared by Commander Forrest Sherman for the Chief of Naval Operations August 18, 1941, summarizes the discussions between the military staffs on strategic questions.

it would be compelled to take countermeasures even though these might lead to war between the United States and Japan; and that if Japan attacked any third power as a consequence of such measures the President would ask Congress for authority to aid the country attacked. The British and Dutch governments, and perhaps the Soviet, were to make parallel declarations.

So forceful a warning, Roosevelt told Churchill, all by itself, might be regarded as an insulting threat, and arouse Japan to war to save its pride. Therefore he suggested that it be toned down, and coupled with an offer to go on talking with Japan. Even if the President had favored the more positive form, the news from Washington might well have caused him to doubt whether he could back it up. As he was discussing the matter (August 12), the House of Representatives all but failed to extend the term of the Selective Service Act; the bill was voted by a majority of one. The American people seemed warmly to approve all measures of support for Britain and all economic sanctions against Japan. But there was a gap between feeling and will which could be ruinous.

The President had one other change to propose—that the awning be put over the Soviet Union as well as the southern regions of the Pacific. Molotov had implied to Hopkins, when he was in Moscow, that a statement that the United States would aid Russia in the event of an attack by Japan would be liked.[2]

Welles rushed back to Washington with a text that conformed to Roosevelt's preferences. Even so Hull and his staff looked over this sea-born statement with a worried gaze, with a sense that the President, away, had forgotten the divisions of opinion at home. The dome of the Capitol cannot be seen from Argentia, nor can the speeches made under it be heard there. Grew's current advice was also against severe talk at this time. In fact, it might be read as urging that, in order to assist Konoye to deal with the extremists, the American government should be more lenient. More explicit certainly, he thought, should

[2] Military dispositions in the Far East were also discussed at this Argentia conference. The British Chiefs of Staff presented a new version of a report on American-British military cooperation in the Far East, ADB-2, to take the place of the rejected Singapore draft, ADB-1. But Stark and Marshall stated that the subject would require further study. Tentative arrangements were made for a later meeting of the naval commanders in the Far Eastern area. The British agreed to send stronger naval forces to the Far East than had been contemplated before. The Americans agreed to use the new battleships, U.S.S. *Washington* and *North Carolina,* in the Atlantic, while retaining in the Pacific three older ones which under ABC-1 were to have been transferred to the Atlantic. Report of Commander Goodenough R.N. on discussions at the Atlantic Conference from the Minutes of the Admiralty Liaison Meeting, August 22, 1941.

be our proofs of just how, when, and where Japan would benefit from the rules to which it was being asked to subscribe as a condition of friendship.

Thus advised, the President varnished the statement still more.[2a] He had gone a long way and back again to compose a caution but little different from those spoken before. Nomura was asked to call at the White House at once. In response to the President's query about the situation, he read a paper which set forth Japan's wish for good relations and Konoye's wish to meet with the President to talk the troubles out in a peaceful spirit. The President in response read out the prepared admonition of which the telling section was: ". . . this Government now finds it necessary to say to the Government of Japan that if the Japanese Government takes any further steps in pursuance of a policy or program of military domination by force or threat of force of neighboring countries, the Government of the United States will be compelled to take immediately any and all steps which it may deem necessary toward safeguarding the legitimate rights and interests of the United States and American nationals and toward insuring the safety and security of the United States." [3]

While so speaking, the President took pains to indicate that the United States would rather be Japan's friend than its enemy. His manner was affable, impressing Nomura as being "thrilled at the reception given by the British people to the joint British-American peace terms, which he had succeeded in getting from Churchill. . . ." [4] And after a pause he read a second statement which in effect said that we were willing to resume the informal talks that had been going on.[5] This warning, which had figured so largely during the meeting with Churchill, thus turned into little more than a diplomatic tryst. It kept Konoye trying. But it did not change the stance of things between Japan and the United States, long since grown rigid.

A few days later Churchill made a radio address which roughly matched Roosevelt's statement to Nomura. This ended by stating that

2a Churchill was aware of this possibility. Informing Attlee on the 12th about his talks with the President he said, "We have laid special stress on the warning to Japan which constitutes the teeth of the President's communication. One would always fear State Department trying to tone it down; but President has promised definitely to use the hard language." Churchill, *The Grand Alliance*, p. 446.

3 *Foreign Relations: Japan*, II, 556–57.

4 Nomura's cable, No. 709, to Tokyo, August 18, 1941, printed in *Pearl Harbor Attack*, Part 17, pp. 2749, *et seq.*

5 In effect, though the statement itself was made up mainly of our conditions for doing so. It is printed in *Foreign Relations: Japan*, II, 557–59.

if the patient efforts of the United States to reach fair and friendly settlement should fail, Britain would range itself "unhesitatingly at the side of the United States." Churchill probably at the time felt that he had failed to get the President to do what he wanted. Still he carried away the impression, more important than any words, that if the Japanese attacked, the United States would fight. After we were in the war he told the House of Commons: "On the other hand, the probability, since the Atlantic Conference, at which I discussed these matters with Mr. Roosevelt, that the United States, even if not herself attacked, would come into a war in the Far East, and thus make final victory sure, seemed to allay some of these anxieties. . . . It fortified our British decision to use our limited resources on the actual fighting fronts. As time went on, one had greater assurance that if Japan ran amok in the Pacific, we should not fight alone." [6]

For a short time after the Argentia meeting Tokyo became a second center of diplomatic effort. Toyoda (on the 18th, Tokyo time, and before receiving a report of the Nomura-Roosevelt talk) made a fervent plea to Grew that the American government show greater trust of Japan, moderate its economic pressure, and that the President agree to meet with Konoye. [7] All that could be clearly learned from this plea was that Japan wanted if not the whole of its own way, much of it without war.

Terasaki, Chief of the American Section of the Foreign Office, added in almost as many words that this was the last try of the Japanese government to reach a peaceful solution; that if Konoye failed no other Japanese statesman could succeed. Grew said the same thing. In messages to the President and Hull he urged with all the force at his command "that this Japanese proposal not be turned aside without very prayerful consideration." [8] The Prime Minister would, he understood, probably be prepared to give far-reaching undertakings in regard to China. If the proposal were rejected or the Konoye-Roosevelt meeting ended in failure, Japan's destiny would probably be placed in the hands of the Army and Navy for an all-out, do-or-die effort to extend Japan's rule over all of East Asia.

These grave words were weighed in the White House and the State

[6] January 27, 1942. See Winston S. Churchill, *The End of the Beginning* . . . (Boston, 1943), p. 33.

[7] *Foreign Relations: Japan*, II, 560, *et seq.* Admiral Toyoda asked to be regarded not as a diplomat, but as a naval officer. There seems to have been a general assumption that naval officers and lovers of the sea were more given to favor peace and truthful talk than diplomats. That is probably true—as long as they remain in uniform and do not have to deal with the problems of the diplomat.

[8] Grew's telegram to Hull, August 18, *ibid.*, II, 565.

Department with care.[9] But doubts, both those drawn from a study of Japanese proposals and those dredged out of "Magic," poured over them. Was Konoye in a position to adjust Japan's policies to the fixed American ideas of justice, even if he wanted to? The terms then being advanced by Tokyo (substantially the same as presented to Hull on August 6) did not attract. All they seemed really to offer was a promise not to go further south. They would still have left Japan, during an indefinite period, in the strategic position acquired by force; they might break Chinese resistance; they would enable Japan to obtain war materials.

In summary, Hull concluded that while a meeting between Konoye and Roosevelt might bring the semblance of peace, it could not bring either a good or lasting peace. This judgment was not governed solely by the particulars of the offers which Japan made. It was strongly tinged by mistrust of what Japan really meant and planned. Hull shared the opinion which Stimson had entered in his diary on August 9, "The invitation to the President is merely a blind to try to keep us from taking definite action."

Konoye's record was bad; he had too often been either the author or tool of deception. The Japanese promises seemed born of design, not of desire. They had something of the same hand-to-heart touch that Hitler had used upon Chamberlain at Munich.[10] In short, there was no faith—and, as has been said, without faith there can be no works.

Was this mistrust allowed to have its full sway because it suited some hidden wish to punish Japan? Because it was in line with the momentum of American policy? The sanctions could not have been cancelled, the dispatch of forces to the Far East halted, without a struggle inside and

[9] Konoye's proposal that the President meet with him was kept most secret. The White House went so far as to issue (on September 3), through Secretary Early, a denial. Beard, *President Roosevelt and the Coming of the War*, especially pp. 187, *et seq.*, and p. 496, dwells upon this concealment, without mentioning one, if not the main reason; that Konoye besought it. He and Toyoda feared they would be accused of negotiating under pressure, and stopped by German-Italian interference. See [e.g.] Grew's report of talk with Toyoda on August 18th, *Foreign Relations: Japan*, II, 560, *et. seq.*, Toyoda's instructions to Nomura, August 7, *Far East Mil. Trib.*, Exh. No. 2887, and Terasaki's plea on August 29 (Grew, *Ten Years in Japan*, pp. 422–25).

Konoye stubbornly refused to keep Germany informed as to what was being said to and by the American government. Thus, to anticipate, when on August 29 Ott did his best to find out the contents of the President's note to Konoye (which was mentioned in a communiqué which the Japanese government had been forced to issue because of a leak) the Vice-Minister of Foreign Affairs, Amau, evaded. The American government knew through the intercepts how reticent Japan was being. See Ott's talk of August 29 with Amau, published in *Nazi Conspiracy and Aggression* (Washington, 1946– ), VI, 548–49.

[10] Secretary Hull made the comparison in the statement he made before the Congressional Investigation, *Pearl Harbor Attack*, Part 2, p. 426.

outside the American government; a struggle uncongenial to the men who would have had to bear its brunt. Who is to know?

In any case, the next fortnight of back-and-forth talk brought the meeting no nearer. Konoye addressed himself personally to the President. The message (deciphered by "Magic" before it was delivered on August 28) was just an expression of an eager wish to meet in order to exchange views "from a broad standpoint" about the questions that divided the two countries. Competent officials, Konoye suggested, could settle "minor items" after leaders had talked.[11] A steamer (the *Nitta Maru*), secretly commandeered and outfitted with special radio equipment, was standing by in Yokohama harbor, ready to sail at a moment's notice.

Tempted, but afraid that the meeting could bring only confusion into the whole of American foreign policy, the President still avoided either a refusal or an acceptance. He continued to give the impression that he wanted the meeting almost as much as Konoye; that he was held back by his other duties.[12] But when, on September 3, the President saw Nomura again, he seemed farther away from Honolulu or Juneau than before. He said that while he appreciated the Prime Minister's expressed wish for peace in the Pacific, he had to have first a clearer idea of what the Prime Minister had in mind on the disputed points. These must be settled, he said, before, not at the conference.[13] He might have expressed his thought by quoting Confucius: "Utterance is only a guest of fact."

Konoye and his circle were, it is now known, measuring each degree of warmth and coolness shown by the President. He and Toyoda, at the Foreign Office, were resting their hopes on the belief that the President's "statesmanlike way" would prevail over Hull's "theoretical diplomacy." Now the President, too, to their chagrin, began to turn into a disciple of principle. Not only that. Both he and Hull were placing more stress upon the need for British, Dutch, and Chinese assent to any accord that might be reached.[14] Within and without, Konoye's project of persuasion was encircled with vetoes.

[11] The text of the Konoye letter is printed in *Foreign Relations; Japan*, II, 572–73.

[12] Hull's memorandum of this talk, August 28, between Nomura and the President is in *ibid.*, II, 571–72. Nomura's intercepted report is in *Pearl Harbor Attack*, Part 17, p. 2794, *et seq.*

[13] Memorandum of this talk and text of Roosevelt's reply, September 3, are printed in *Foreign Relations: Japan*, II, 588 *et seq.*

[14] *ibid.*

# The Japanese High Command Demands
## That the Issue with the
## United States Be Faced and Forced

FEW days passed that the Japanese did not speak bitterly to Grew or Hull about the American freezing order—particularly because it deprived Japan of oil.[1] The Secretary's way, and Roosevelt's also, was to make as little as possible of this ban.[2] When the reproaches did not end, Hull answered that Japan had forced the United States to do what it was doing in its own defense. Japan could, he insisted, undo the situation by behaving like a peaceful and law-abiding nation.

There was still no formal or obligatory accord between the American and foreign governments about the maintenance of this embargo. Parallel and coordinated action worked as well, and left the American government freer. Freer, that is, to change its policy should some turn in the talk with Japan warrant; freer also to decide for itself what to do if Japan tried to break the embargo by force. The American, British, and Dutch worked in close harmony. By then the government of the Indies was openly refusing to allow the export of oil to Japan (or of any other raw materials specified in the Batavia agreement). Its terms for trade—the Dutch Minister told the Japanese government on August 23—were withdrawal of the Japanese forces from Indo-China and a public promise not to attack the Indies.[3]

[1] All requests for permission to use frozen funds were kept in suspense. The Japanese government had abstracted some million dollars in cash from American banks before the freezing, and had suspended customary remittances to American banks from South America. The Japanese Embassy neither denied these facts nor explained the use made of these funds. The State-Treasury-Justice Committee decided that if Japan wanted oil, it should have to use these abstracted dollars to pay for it, before being licensed to use any others. On this point (and variations of it) all attempts to arrange licenses went aground. A multitude of details regarding the operation of the freezing order are to be found in the Minutes of the Tripartite Committee for the Application of Executive Order No. 8389; and a multitude of details about the other controls enforced by us, the British, and Dutch are in the State Department files.

[2] The President on August 28 was still saying to Nomura that Japan was in a position to get a quota of oil. See memorandum of their talk, *Foreign Relations: Japan*, II, 572.

[3] As reported in a cable from Grew to Hull, August 26, 1941. The termination of ex-

Hull's answers soothed all the less because tankers loaded with American oil were moving closely past Japan on their way to Vladivostock. "Under its nose," as Grew said. Against this the Japanese government protested.[4] This oil, it said, would enable Russia to maintain large forces near Japanese lines. Hull replied that our only concern was to supply the Russian armies fighting Hitler in Europe. Turning ironical, he added that in view of its pact with Russia, Japan should not be worried. The Japanese government hinted that the shipments were contrary to international law and friendly practice. Hull replied that they were just as valid acts of commerce as our former great oil shipments to Japan. The Japanese government then implored us to recognize that the shipments would arouse strong hostile feeling among the people of Japan, who were reduced to using charcoal instead of oil. To which Hull asked by silence rather than by words—whose the fault?[5]

The American government refused either to end the trade or to recall the tankers that were on the way to Vladivostock.[6] But presently it arranged that the tankers should take a longer northern route, so as to avoid passing through Japanese waters. Even so they remained an irritant to the Japanese officials who observed the shrinkage in their own reserves of oil. Time was not only reducing their size, but making harder the tasks for which they might be needed.

For all the possible opponents of Japan were improving their military positions in the Pacific. Many little additions were being made to the British naval and air forces at Singapore, American forces in the Philippines, and the Dutch forces in the Indies. Far too small and unbalanced they were, as the Japanese staff experts knew them to be. But would they still be so after many more months? How much longer before

---

ports of bauxite from the Indies and Malaya was of almost as critical importance to Japan as that of oil. Japan had been receiving about 90 per cent of all the bauxite used in making aluminum from these sources. As of December 1941, it had a reserve stockpile of about 254,000 metric tons, reckoned to be nine months supply at the current rate of use; seven months, under the program for increased airplane production. These figures are derived from the report of the United States Strategic Bombing Survey.

[4] As much, if not more, at the behest of the German government as at its own. Ribbentrop kept prodding Ott, and Ott kept prodding Toyoda to make a great issue of the matter, e.g., Telegram, No. 1654, Ott to Ribbentrop, August 28.

[5] The memos of Hull's talks with Nomura on this subject, August 23 and 27, 1941, are to be found in *Foreign Relations: Japan*, II, 567, *et seq*.

[6] Though no one knew what would happen if Japan sank them. Stimson diary, entry for August 19, 1941.

these wardens of the West became so strong that any advance would be too risky? Or even strong enough to join up with China?

These same questions were, of course, being studied in Washington. And a new and hopeful answer which was to influence American diplomacy was emerging. This is well explained in Stimson's later memoir: ". . . there occurred in this same month of August [1941] an important change in the thinking of the General Staff with regard to the defense of the Philippine Islands. For twenty years it had been considered that strategically the Philippines were an unprotected pawn, certain to be easily captured by the Japanese in the early stages of any war between the United States and Japan. Now it began to seem possible to establish in the Philippines a force not only sufficient to hold the Islands but also, and more important, strong enough to make it foolhardy for the Japanese to carry their expansion southward through the China Sea. For this change of view there were two leading causes. One was the contagious optimism of General Douglas MacArthur . . . The second . . . was the sudden and startling success of American Flying Fortresses in operations from the British Isles. Stimson found his military advisers swinging to the belief that with an adequate force of these heavy bombers the Philippines could become a self-sustaining fortress capable of blockading the China Sea by air power. . . . Both the optimism of General MacArthur and the establishment of an effective force of B-17's were conditional upon time. . . ." [7]

General Marshall was attaching a definite date to this hope; by December 5-10 he thought the Philippines would be able to defend themselves. Admiral Stark thought the Navy would not be as well situated till somewhat later—January or February.[8]

The Japanese government did not know the schedule of the American and British program. But it knew what was under way and could estimate the reckoning behind it. The Japanese Army was determined

[7] Stimson and Bundy On Active Service, p. 388. A squadron of Flying Fortresses had completed the flight to Manila, via Hawaii, Midway, and Wake. Stimson diary, entry for September 12, 1941.

[8] These estimates were explained by General Marshall, Pearl Harbor Attack, Part 32, pp. 560–62.

On September 11 the Joint Planning Committee of the Army and Navy submitted a report to Stark and Marshall which included among the major strategic objectives of the United States the retention of the Philippines, Malaya, the Netherlands East Indies, Australia, Burma, and China. This marked a change of judgment about the Philippines. Stark and Marshall approved this report and used it as the basis of their recommendations to the President in regard to the programs for increase of American military forces and production and distribution of weapons.

that it should not succeed. Thus, as September came, and Konoye could show nothing for his exertions, the call to arms was spread throughout Japan.

## [2]

Tojo and the senior Army commanders demanded that the talks with the United States be dropped, and that war be begun as soon as Japanese forces could be placed in position. The Navy called together its senior staff and combat officers at Tokyo. Admiral Yamamoto, the Commander in Chief, explained to them on September 2, that the games about to begin were truly practice for war. The assembled ships rehearsed a series of great battles with the British and American fleets.

As they did, the Prime Minister and Foreign Minister met with the heads of the armed forces every day, and almost every hour every day. Beset, Konoye bent before the demand that the issue between Japan and the United States be faced and forced. He agreed that the Army and Navy should make all dispositions for war. But he struggled for consent to keep on talking with the United States, while they were doing so. Furthermore, he opposed the naming of any day for the commencement of war.[9]

Konoye won only a short reprieve—six weeks or so more. The argument before which he yielded was that if Japan did not *soon* fight for what it wanted (what he was pledged to get) it would not be able to fight with fair hope of victory, for the defense of its enemies would be too strong and its oil would be short. As later put by General Tojo, the Minister of War, when on trial: "The elasticity in our national power was on the point of extinction." [10]

The cabinet and the High Military Command, having reached agreement on September 4-5, Konoye arranged for a conference before the Throne on the 6th. The program of dual initiative that was prepared for submission to this conference—and adopted by it without change— could only mean war unless there was a reversal in the American attitude. The machinery of war was to be placed in gear; it was to be stopped only if Konoye managed to win American assent to terms which up to then had been rejected.

[9] As summed up by General Suzuki, Head of the Planning Board: "The Supreme Command was in favor of making a decision then and there for war; calling off negotiations with the United States; but Konoye opposed, suggesting that no time be set when war was to be commenced, only war preparations." Deposition, *Far East Mil. Trib.,* Exh. No. 3605.

[10] *ibid.,* Exh. No. 3655.

The first segments of this agenda [11] tell their own story:

"1. Determined not to be deterred by the possibility of being involved in a war with America (and England and Holland) in order to secure our national existence, we will proceed with war preparations so that they be completed approximately toward the end of October.

"2. At the same time, we will endeavor by every possible diplomatic means to have our demands agreed to by America and England. Japan's minimum demands in these negotiations with America (and England), together with the Empire's maximum concessions are embodied in the attached document.

"3. If by the early part of October there is no reasonable hope of having our demands agreed to in the diplomatic negotiations mentioned above, we will immediately make up our minds to get ready for war against America (and England and Holland)."

The substance of the most important among Japan's minimum demands can be briefly summarized.

As regards China, the United States and Britain were not to obstruct a settlement along lines specified. They were (presumably as soon as the accord was signed) to close the Burma Road and end help of every kind to the Chiang Kai-shek regime. Japan was to "rigidly adhere" to the right to station troops in various points or areas within China.

As regards current military measures, the United States and Britain were not to establish any bases in the region or increase their Far Eastern forces.

As regards Indo-China, Japan would withdraw when a just peace was made in the Far East, but it was to retain the special relations set down in the agreement which had been forced upon Vichy.

As regards economic matters, the United States and Britain were to restore trade relations. They were also to engage themselves to see that Japan got the raw materials wanted from the Southwest Pacific.

In return, Japan was to promise not to use Indo-China as a base for southern operations, and to observe the Neutrality Pact with the Soviet Union.

[11] There are differences of some importance between the text here quoted from Appendix V, "Konoye Memoirs," *Pearl Harbor Attack,* Part 20, pp. 4022–23, and that submitted to the *Far East Mil. Trib.,* Defense Document, No. 1579. The version here given is contained in the text completed by him in the spring of 1942, and carefully reviewed and corrected by him at the time. The other version was turned out with Konoye's consent two years after the war began, and was cut down and revised in part by him. This was printed in Japan. For the history of the several versions and parts of the "Konoye Memoirs," see the testimony of Ushiba (Tomohiko), his private secretary, *ibid.,* Exh. No. 2737.

In the event that the United States entered the European war, Japan was to decide independently on the meaning and applicability of the Tripartite Pact.

These were the terms set down by Japan as the price of peace in the Pacific, if not tranquillity. They expressed the same fixed purpose which had taken Japan into Asia years before—to acquire a pliant and self-sustaining empire, to be the "stabilizing" authority throughout the Far East.

On the 5th—the day before the ceremonial conference—Konoye went over this program with the Emperor. Thereupon the Emperor observed that war preparations were mentioned first, diplomatic negotiations, second. "This," he said, "would seem to give precedence to war." Konoye said that was not the intention; it would be war only if the diplomatic effort failed. The heads of the Army and Navy were called into the Emperor's presence to answer the same, rather pointless, question. They gave the same answer. The rest of the examination, as recorded in Konoye's "Memoirs," shows that the Emperor did not feel it prudent to ask for more than half a loaf of truth and logic:

". . . the Emperor asked the Army Chief of Staff General Sugiyama what was the Army's belief as to the probable length of hostilities in case of a Japanese-American war. The Chief of Staff replied that he believed operations in the South Pacific could be disposed of in about three months . . . . the Emperor recalled that the General had been Minister of War at the time of the outbreak of the China Incident, and that he had then informed the Throne that the incident would be disposed of in about one month. He pointed out that despite the General's assurance, the incident was not yet concluded after four long years of fighting. In trepidation the Chief of Staff went to great lengths to explain that the extensive hinterland of China prevented the consummation of operations according to the scheduled plan. At this the Emperor raised his voice and said that if the Chinese hinterland was extensive, the Pacific was boundless. He asked how the General could be certain of his three months calculation. The Chief of Staff hung his head, unable to answer.

"At this point the Navy Chief of General Staff [Admiral Nagano] lent a helping hand to Sugiyama by saying that to his mind Japan was like a patient suffering from a serious illness . . . the patient's case was so critical that the question of whether or not to operate had to be determined without delay. Should he be let alone without an operation, there was danger of a gradual decline. An operation, while it might be extremely dangerous, would still offer some hope of saving his life. The stage was now reached . . . where a quick decision had to be made one way or the other. He felt that the Army General Staff was in favor of putting hope in diplomatic negotiations to the finish, but that in case of failure a decisive operation would have to be performed. To this extent, then, he was in favor of the negotiation proposals. The Emperor, pursuing the point, asked the Chiefs of the Supreme Command if it was not true that both of them were for giving precedence to diplomacy and both answered in the affirmative." [12]

The Emperor asked the heads of the Army and Navy to be present at the final conference on the 6th, so that they might be quizzed again. But he yielded to Kido's advice not to stir up trouble by putting questions himself. It was arranged that Hara, President of the Privy Council, should do so in his stead. Again the query was put—was diplomacy or war to come first—so that the whole assembly might hear and note the answer. The Navy Minister, Admiral Oikawa, spoke up: "Diplomacy." But the Chiefs of the Army and Navy General Staff remained silent. The Emperor waited, then out of the pocket of his robe he drew a piece of paper and read a poem by the great Emperor Meiji:

> "Since all are brothers in this world,
> Why is there such constant turmoil?" [13]

"Everyone present was struck with awe, and there was silence throughout the hall." Admiral Nagano rose to explain that he thought that the Navy Minister had spoken for all; that the Supreme Command concurred in what he had said, and that force would be used only when there seemed no other way.

The Emperor Meiji's spirit thus received its homage. Konoye was granted time to continue his effort to persuade Roosevelt to save Japan from war. The Army and Navy secured Imperial permission to assume the posture of war, to get ready for attack.

## [3]

The schedule adopted at the Imperial Conference of September 6 was, in Tojo's words, "Initiated by the Imperial High Command and based on its anticipated requirements." [14]

The American Army and Navy were, for reasons explained, seeking time. The Japanese High Command were even more intensely concerned with time, for reverse reasons. They knew that opposed forces

---

[12] "Konoye's Memoirs." The account given in "Kido's Diary," entry for September 5, 1941, is substantially the same.

[13] The translation as given in "Konoye's Memoirs." The version offered in "Kido's Diary," entry for September 6, 1941, is probably more in accord with the poetic language of the original:

> "Over the four seas prevails universal fraternity.
> I think why turbulent waves wage so furiously."

[14] Defense deposition, General Tojo. *Far East Mil. Trib.*, Exh. No. 3655.

in the region, particularly naval and air, could from then on be built up more effectively than their own. They thought that there was only a short season ahead of good fighting weather; after that it would hinder or prevent the kind of operations they planned. And they knew that the reserves of materials for war—particularly oil—would grow less with each day that was allowed to slip by. These were the reasons why they found long delay intolerable.[15] To them the face of time was getting pock-marked.

Despite every device of economic control, and every twist of diplomacy, the Japanese oil position had not been secured.[16] The total result of all its efforts and outlays was much poorer than Japan hoped or wished. Together natural and synthetic production (Inner Zone of Japan) in 1941 provided only some 3 million barrels, or 10 to 12 per cent of Japan's estimated minimum needs.[17] The other 30 to 35 million barrels, the other 90 per cent, had been obtained from the United States, the Caribbean, and the Indies.[18]

The Japanese government during the thirties had imported far more than required for current use. Much had been put into reserve. Towards the end of 1939, the reserve stock had been highest—about 55 million barrels, enough to last a year and a half or longer. But thereafter use—especially for military operations and training—had grown, while it had

[15] See, in particular, "Konoye's Memoirs" and the defense depositions of General Tojo, General Tanaka, Chief of the Operations Section of the General Staff, and Marquis Kido.

[16] The civilian consumption of motor gasoline, for example, was cut from some 6 to 7 million barrels per annum in the past to 1.6 million in 1941. The tanker fleet was increased from 230 thousand tons in 1937 to about 575 thousand tons at the end of 1941.

[17] These estimated needs were indeed minimum both for any training period for war, or for war. They allowed for almost no civilian consumption of gasoline, and greatly reduced amounts of fuel oil.

[18] Japanese imports had been (in millions of barrels for fiscal years beginning April 1):

|      | CRUDE OIL | REFINED PRODUCTS | TOTAL |
|------|-----------|------------------|-------|
| 1931 | 6.4       | 13.3             | 19.7  |
| 1935 | 12.8      | 20.6             | 33.5  |
| 1937 | 20.2      | 16.6             | 36.9  |
| 1939 | 18.8      | 11.8             | 30.6  |
| 1940 | 22.0      | 15.1             | 37.1  |

Of which total the following portion came from the United States:

| 1937 | about 29 million barrels, about 80 per cent |
| 1939 | " 26 " " " 85 " " |
| 1940 | " 23 " " " 60 " " |

Totals of Japanese imports derived from reports of the United States Strategic Bombing Survey, those of American exports from unpublished statistics of the Bureau of Foreign and Domestic Commerce. The latter include the figures for crude oil, gasoline, and other oil motor fuels, gas, fuel and residual fuel oil, and lubricating oil. Owing to the time interval between import and export entries and other factors, these estimates are only approximate.

become much harder to import. The reserve had shrunk—probably to less than 50 million barrels by September 1941.[19] The fuel oil stocks held by the Navy had shrunk from some 29 million to some 22 million. But the reserve of aviation gasoline had been increased from 1 million barrels to about 4 million; the early American hindrance had been completely overcome. The inflow from both the Western Hemisphere and the Indies was at an end. Japan could no longer draw propelling energy from the countries whose position and safety were under threat.[20] If Japan was to fight, the longer it waited the greater the risk that the battle might be lost for lack of oil or other essential raw materials. So the oil gauge influenced the time of decision.

Not only the time of decision, but the war plans. The wish to obtain economic reserves for a long war was an important factor in determining the spheres to be occupied. It was decided by Imperial Military Headquarters that to be sure of enough oil, rubber, rice, bauxite, iron ore, it was necessary to get swift control of Java, Sumatra, Borneo, and Malaya. In order to effect the occupation and protect the transport lines to Japan, it was necessary to expel the United States from the Philippines, Guam, and Wake, and Britain from Singapore. Thus it can be said that the points of attack and occupation were settled by placing these vital raw material needs alongside of the estimate of Japan's military means. And having settled these, the question of the weather entered in to hurry the final action.[21]

[19] These estimates of reserves (in the so-called Inner Zone of Japan) are derived from the figures contained in the reports of the United States Strategic Bombing Survey. However, in a memorandum submitted by the President of the Planning Board to the Liaison Conference of September 3, 1941, total reserve stocks were put at 52.8 million barrels.

The Survey in its report—*Oil in Japan's War*, p. 10—estimated that at the time of Pearl Harbor stocks had fallen to about 43 million barrels.

[20] The record of decline in American exports to Japan was (in millions of barrels):

| | | CRUDE PETROLEUM | GASOLINE | GAS AND FUEL OIL | RESIDUAL FUEL OIL | LUBRICATING OIL |
|---|---|---|---|---|---|---|
| Last five months | 1939 | 6.7 | 0.5 | 2.8 | 1.3 | 0.3 |
| | 1940 | 5.2 | 2.7 | 2.0 | 0.8 | 0.6 |
| | 1941 | 0.1 | 0.1 | 0.2 | .0 | .0 |

Unpublished statistics of Bureau of Foreign and Domestic Commerce.

[21] This brief comment on the way in which the wish to obtain economic reserves affected the plans with which Japan began the war is drawn from several studies made available to me by the Military Intelligence Division of the Supreme Headquarters of the Allied Command in Tokyo; especially the information furnished by Colonel Hattori (Takushiro), former Chief of the Operations Section of the General Staff of the Japanese Army. It corresponds also to the explanations of Admiral Toyoda (Soemu) former Commanding Officer, Kure Naval District.

The Army and Navy feared even to see two, three, or four *months* elapse. For on their strategic calendar October and November were the best months for landing operations. December was possible but difficult, January or later, impossible.[22] If the plan were to include an attack on Pearl Harbor by the Great Circle Route, navigational and weather conditions would, it was judged, become unfavorable after January.[23] Furthermore the sooner the southern operations were under way, the less the chance that the Soviet Union could attack from the north; if they could be completed before the end of winter, that danger need not be feared.[24]

Thus, leaving Konoye to go on with his talks with the United States, the Army and Navy threw themselves at once into the plans for action. The Operations Section of the Army began to get ready to capture Malaya, Java, Borneo, the Bismarck Archipelago, the Indies, and the Philippines; it was to be fully ready by the end of October. The Navy finished its war games. These included the surprise attack on Pearl Harbor and the American fleet there. At the end of the games the two general staffs conferred on the result and found it satisfactory.[25]

By the end of September these steps towards war—if diplomacy should fail—were well under way. Still Konoye and Toyoda found themselves reading the unchanging reports of American resistance. The President was still in the White House—planning to go no further than Warm Springs. Hull and his draftsmen were still dissecting every document which came from Tokyo with the scalpel of mistrust. In his apartment in the Wardman Park Hotel there seemed to be no sense of hurry. No calendar hung there with October ringed in red.

Time had become the meter of strategy for both governments. But one did not mind its passing, while the other was crazed by the tick of the clock.

---

[22] Tojo deposition, *Far East Mil. Trib.,* Exh. No. 3655. As stated by Admiral Shimada, Minister of the Navy, in his deposition, Exh. No. 3565: "With the advent of December, northeasterly monsoons would blow with force in the Formosan Straits, the Philippines, and Malayan areas rendering military operations difficult."

[23] This forecast of weather conditions was borne out by the event—in early December. "The start (for the attack on Pearl Harbor) was from Saeki, the training harbor, about November 17, 1941; then north and across the Pacific, just south of the Aleutians, then south to Pearl Harbor. We had studied this route for a long time. Upon returning we suffered from heavy seas and strong winds." Interrogation of Captain Watanabe, on Admiral Yamamoto's staff.

[24] As stated by General Tojo in his defense deposition, and by Colonel Hattori in his study for the Supreme Command of the Allied Powers.

[25] See evidence of records of Admiral Nagano and Admiral Yamamoto, Commander in Chief of the Combined Fleet. *ibid.,* Exh. Nos. 1126 and 1127. For interesting details, see Captain Ellis M. Zacharias, *Secret Missions* (New York [1946]), pp. 243, *et seq.*

## CHAPTER 35

# The Idea of a Roosevelt-Konoye Meeting Dies; the Deadlock Is Complete: October 1941

THOSE who were reading the "Magic" intercepts, could have been in no doubt that the Japanese government was in the throes of a most critical decision. Items such as the following in one of Toyoda's cables to Nomura must have spoken for themselves: "Now the international situation as well as our internal situation is strained in the extreme and we have reached the point where we will pin our last hopes on an interview between the Premier and President. . ."[1] The secret insight was confirmation—if any were needed—of the urgent pleas and warnings that Grew and Craigie were sending. Grew was advising a test of Japanese intentions and good faith. This could be had, he thought, by relaxing the economic and military measures which were exerting inexorable pressure on Japan, step by step, as Japan, step by step, altered its course. What the first steps were to be Grew did not say.[2]

Then on the evening of September 6 (Tokyo time), right after the fateful Imperial Conference, Grew dined with Konoye. The invitation was unusual. A Japanese Prime Minister does not consort with foreign diplomats. They met in the private house of a mutual friend, Prince Ito. Automobile tags were changed to escape recognition. All the servants were sent out and the dinner was served by the daughter of the house.

But when Hull and his staff read Grew's report of the three-hour talk, they could not see that privacy changed Japanese ideas or tactics.[3] The Prime Minister sought to allay doubt as to his ability to keep his word by repeating that all the military and naval leaders of Japan subscribed to his proposals. If he said "Yes" to Roosevelt, the generals and admirals at his side would say "Yes"; and the whole government would be committed. To prevent challenge to his decisions in Tokyo, they would be radioed to the Emperor, who would, Konoye asserted, see that they were accepted.

[1] Cable, No. 504, Toyoda to Nomura, Washington, August 26, 1941.
[2] Telegram, September 5, 1941, printed in *Foreign Relations: Japan*, II, 601–3.
[3] *ibid.*, II, 604–6.

But this stress on his accord with the military had ambiguous meaning to the State Department students of the latest Japanese written proposals that were in hand. These had been transmitted through both Grew and Nomura.[4] It can now be seen that they derived straight from the statement of Japan's minimum demands approved by the Imperial Conference on that day. Though vaguer in phrase, they were in root and essence the same; and need not, therefore, again be reviewed.[5]

## [2]

Of the long spell of talk, that which followed now was the most crammed and tense. Night after night the diplomats of the two countries probed for the real intent behind these opaque Japanese proposals. The same skeptical questions that had been asked before were asked again by the Americans. The same pleas for trust were made by the Japanese; and the same answer was given—that Japan should prove its intentions by plain words and plain acts. Even those parts of an accord that had been put in order before became disarranged, like the covers on the bed of a sleepless man as the weary night drags on.

The dispatches, memoranda, and statements which were exchanged during the weeks ahead (September–October) fill many, many pages.[6]

[4] To Grew by Toyoda on September 4 (Tokyo time), by Nomura to Hull, September 6.
[5] They are printed in *Foreign Relations: Japan*, II, 608–9. It is of interest to note the phraseology on one point about which little has been said in this narrative—the treatment of American business in China. The Japanese Government offered a promise not to restrict American economic activities in China "so long as pursued on an equitable basis." This subject engaged as much of the time of the negotiators as any other, and absorbed a great amount of drafting energy.
This Japanese formula (and the later and different one which Japan offered in early November), while ambiguous, represented some change in the Japanese position. They ran quite crisscross to basic Japanese plans and policies to make a highly planned and more or less exclusive bloc of Japan, Manchukuo, and China. Much capital and scarce materials had been spent in the effort to realize this program. Its essential features were most systematically stated in "The Outline for the Economic Construction of Japan, Manchukuo and China," approved by the cabinet on October 3, 1940. *Far East Mil. Trib.*, Exh. No. 861.
The first two paragraphs of the basic policy explain the purpose: (1) "The aim of the economic development of Japan, Manchukuo and China is to establish a state of self-sufficient economy among them as a unit by 1950 and at the same time to accelerate the establishment of the East Asia Co-Prosperity Sphere and thereby strengthen and secure their position in world economy. (2) The guiding spirit of the Japan-Manchukuo-China economy is to establish a national defense economy through the united co-operation of Japan, Manchukuo and China with Japan as the leader . . ."
[6] The curious can find most, but not all, of them in *Foreign Relations: Japan*, II, to which compilation reference has frequently been made.

No one but the specialist would want now to rummage in their details. Their import is clear. The two governments still remained separated by unyielding differences in purpose. The terms offered by the Japanese government would have permitted that country to emerge rewarded and strong from its ten-year venture in arms and stratagem. They would have allowed her to control China, keep American forces tied down in the Far East, and retain the chance of resuming the southern surge later. The terms offered by the American government would have meant that Japan accept defeat; give up the gains of past effort, and the prospect of future expansion. They would have meant, also, a triumphant China.

The course of diplomacy exposed these basic differences rather than healed them. Beyond them lay another trial which would, I think, have become plain if the talk had progressed. The American government in these months of talk was trustee for the Chinese, British, Dutch, French, and Russian governments.[7] Would any of these have been reconciled to leaving Japan in a position of dominance in the Far East, won during their time of struggle?

In sum, Hull and the Far Eastern wing of the State Department concluded that the Japanese proposals were vague in vital points and in conflict with the principles for which the United States stood.[8] Found suspect, also, was the timing of the acts of readjustment which the two governments were called upon to perform. Japanese forces were to be drawn out of China and Indo-China, economic opportunities in China were to be (more or less) equally shared, *when* a peace settlement had been reached with China. But the United States was to resume trade with Japan, it was to end help to China, it was to suspend military measures in the Pacific, *before* such a settlement was reached—as soon as Japan and the United States signed an accord.

[7] As the American government explained to the Japanese, e.g., Grew to Toyoda, September 10, 1941: "Any such premise as the foregoing passes over or ignores the intention of the United States Government, which has been repeatedly impressed upon the Japanese Ambassador, to confer with the Government of China, Great Britain, The Netherlands, etc., before it could agree to embark on any definitive negotiations with the Japanese government regarding a settlement involving the Pacific area." *ibid.,* II, 611.

On September 4 Hull had again assured the Chinese Ambassador in Washington that the American government was not considering, and would not consider, any arrangement with Japan that would permit the continuance of aggression in China. A report of this talk was cabled to the American Ambassador in Chungking for transmission to the Chinese government on the 12th.

From September 23 on, Hull gave Eden the substance of the main points of his current talks with Japan, on the understanding that no circulation be made to British diplomatic missions.

[8] Hull so informed Nomura, telling him on September 10 that in his opinion "the present proposals [those presented on the 6th] had narrowed down the spirit and the scope of the proposed understanding" as compared with previous ones. *ibid.,* II, 613.

On September 28 Hull reported his impressions of the state of the talks to the President, who replied: "I wholly agree with your penciled note—to recite the more liberal original attitude of the Japanese when they first sought the meeting, point out their much narrowed position now, earnestly ask if they cannot go back to their original attitude, start discussions again on agreement in principle, and re-emphasize my hope for a meeting." [9]

Grew, in a most solicitous telegram received the next day (the 29th), was pleading that we should seize what might be the last chance to avoid war.[10] On the one hand he predicted that if the American government waited for clear-cut and satisfactory promises, "the logical outcome . . . will be the downfall of the Konoye Cabinet and the formation of a military dictatorship which will lack either the disposition or the temperament to avoid colliding head-on with the United States." On the other hand, he thought that the gap might well be spanned if the President met with Konoye; that the Prime Minister was ready and able to lead Japan along our path, if given time and help. The chance had come, he thought, when Japanese policy could be genuinely changed if Roosevelt and Churchill patiently showed the way of "constructive conciliation." Konoye, Grew said he had been told, "is in a position in direct negotiations with President Roosevelt to offer him assurance which, because of their far reaching character, will not fail to satisfy the United States."

The world may long wonder what would have happened had the President agreed then to meet with Konoye. Grew and Dooman, at the time and later, had a sense that the refusal was a sad error. To them it seemed that the American government missed a real chance to lead Japan back to peaceful ways. Konoye, they thought, was sincere in his acceptance of those principles of international conduct for which the American government stood, and with the support of the Emperor would be able to carry through his promises. In words which Grew confided to his diary:

"It is my belief that the Emperor, the Government of Prince Konoye and the militant leaders of Japan (the leaders then in control) had come to accept the status of the conflict in China, in conjunction with our

[9] Hull, op. cit., II, 1033.
[10] This important telegram—No. 1529 from Tokyo, September 29—is printed in Foreign Relations: Japan, II, 645-50.

freezing measures and Japan's economic condition as evidence of failure or comparative incapacity to succeed."

Our attitude, he thought (and others since have thought the same), showed a lack both of insight and suppleness, if not of desire. The mistake sprang, in this view, from failure to appreciate why Konoye could not be as clear and conclusive as the American government wished; and to admit that Japan could correct its course only in a gradual and orderly way. Wise American statesmanship, thus, would have bartered adjustment for adjustment, agreeing to relax our economic restraints little by little as Japan, little by little, went our way. Instead, the judgment ends, it was dull and inflexible. By insisting that Japan promise in black and white, then and there, to conform to every American requirement, it made Konoye's task impossible.

It will be always possible to think that Grew was correct; that the authorities in Washington were too close to their texts and too soaked in their disbelief to perceive what he saw. That the American government was as stern as a righteous schoolmaster cannot be denied. Nor that it was unwilling either to ease Japanese failure, or to provide any quick or easy way to improve their hard lot. But the records since come to hand do not support the belief that a real chance of maintaining peace in the Pacific—on or close to the terms for which we had stood since 1931—was missed. They do not confirm the opinion that Konoye was prepared, without reserve or trickery, to observe the rules set down by Hull.[11] Nor that he would have been able to do so, even though a respite was granted and he was allowed to grade the retreat gently.

If Konoye was ready and able—as Grew thought—to give Roosevelt trustworthy and satisfactory promises of a new sort, he does not tell of them in his "Memoirs." Nor has any other record available to me disclosed them. He was a prisoner, willing or unwilling, of the terms precisely prescribed in conferences over which he presided. The latest of these were the minimum demands specified by the Imperial Conference of September 6, just reviewed. It is unlikely that he could have got around them or that he would have in some desperate act discarded them. The whole of his political career speaks to the contrary.

[11] For example, the decisions in regard to China. How reconcile two of Hull's principles (those stipulating non-intervention in domestic affairs and respect for the integrity and independence of China) with the terms specified on September 6 and reaffirmed by a Liaison Conference of September 13, as "Magic" revealed? China was to be required to assent to the stationing of Japanese Army units "for a necessary period" in prescribed areas in Inner Mongolia and North China, and for the stationing of Japanese warships and military units in Hainan, Amoy, and other localities. There was to be a Sino-Japanese economic coalition.

In proof of his ability to carry out his assurances, Konoye stressed first, that his ideas were approved by the Army and Navy; and second, that senior officials (Vice-Chiefs of Staff) of both branches would accompany him on his mission. If and when he said "Yes," they would say "Yes"; and thus the United States could count upon unified execution of any accord. But it seems to me far more likely that the Army and Navy had other thoughts in mind on assigning high officials to go along with him. They would be there to see that Konoye did not yield to the wish for peace or the will of the President. The truer version of the bond is expressed in the title of one of the sub-sections of Konoye's "Memoirs": "The Independence of the Supreme Command and State Affairs from Each Other: The Anguish of Cabinets from Generation to Generation."

Konoye could have honestly agreed that Japan would stop its southern advance and reduce its forces in China to the minimum needed to assure compliance with its wishes. That is really all. To the seekers of the New Order in East Asia this seemed much; to the American government it seemed too little. The error, the fault, in American policy—if there was one—was not in the refusal to trust what Konoye could honestly offer. It was in insisting that Japan entirely clear out of Indo-China and China (and perhaps out of Manchukuo) and give up all exclusive privileges in these countries.

In any case, the President and Hull were convinced that Konoye's purposes were murky and his freedom of decision small. Therefore they concluded that to meet with him before Japan proved its intentions would be a great mistake.[12] It could bring confusion into both American policies and our relations with the other opponents of the Axis. So Grew's earnest appeal for a daring try did not influence the responses to Japan that Hull's drafting squad was putting together. They took nothing that came from Tokyo for granted; wanted everything shown. The Army and Navy were both saying that they could use well all the time they could get. Both Stimson and Knox approved "stringing out

[12] Ott's judgment of the prospect was at the time the same as that reached by the American government. He thought that even though certain circles about Konoye genuinely sought a *détente* with the United States, the effort was certain to fail in the end. He reported that the purpose of Konoye's mission was being pictured to the Navy and activist circles as a last step to convince the Japanese people that a peaceful settlement was not possible. Acceptance of the American terms would, Ott predicted, swiftly result in grave inner convulsions. (See Most Urgent telegram, Ott to Ribbentrop, September 4, 1941. *Far East Mil. Trib.*, Exh. No. 801A.)

negotiations." But neither wanted Roosevelt to meet Konoye or to soften American terms just to gain time.[13]

[3]

Hull was guided by these thoughts in the prepared answer which he gave Nomura on October 2, the answer on which the plans of Japan hung. The Japanese proposals (of September 6), this said in effect, did not provide a basis for a settlement, and were on essential points ambiguous.[14] The meeting between the President and Konoye was put off till there was a real meeting of minds about the application of the four principles—which were the essential foundations of proper relations.

Upon reading this, the opinion nurtured by Konoye and Toyoda, that Japanese and American terms could be reconciled, dropped. This, the note of October 2, rather than the one of November 26 on which controversy has centered, ended the era of talk. For the crisis that followed in Japan brought into power a group determined to fight us rather than move further our way. Thereafter war came first, diplomacy second.

The Foreign Minister on October 7 observed to Grew that this note seemed to mean that the United States wanted Japan to revert "at once and unqualifiedly" to the position of 1937. The Japanese government was prepared to do so, he said, but it was essential that the American government understand that to undo the intervening events at a moment's notice was a matter of tremendous scope—entailing basic and gradual adjustments.[15] On the same day Ushiba, the private secretary of the Prime Minister, called on Dooman to say that this was the last chance both for Konoye and for us. "Prince Konoye," he said, "was at a loss to know what further he could do. . . . When Prince Konoye had taken that responsibility [for starting the talks], the Army gave him full and unqualified support, and if his high hopes are not fulfilled he will have to 'assume responsibility,' and there would be no one who would have the courage to take the risks which the Prince has taken or with sufficient prestige and political position to gain the support of the Army . . ."[16]

The heads of the American government probably accepted this as true. But Hull felt neither inclined nor compelled to state in new words

---

[13] Stimson diary, entry for October 6, 1941.
[14] The text is to be found in *Foreign Relations: Japan*, II, 656, *et seq.*
[15] Memorandum of Grew-Toyoda talk, October 7, *ibid.*, II, 663-65.
[16] *ibid.*, II, 662.

what was wanted of Japan.[17] Requests for fresh and exact definitions were—rightly or wrongly—feared as a device to get the American government to provide catchwords for blame. Hull sought rather, as he expressed it, to elicit from Tokyo some spontaneous proof that American principles were accepted.

On October 16 (Washington time) the news came that the Konoye Cabinet had fallen. Of their impression of the state of the talks at this time two main participants have borne witness. To Hull "the area of difference between us was wider than at the start of the discussions." [18] This in my summary view was too pessimistic an appraisal; the Japanese would have accepted in October less than they were bent on having in March. But it is of interest to note that the Japanese Foreign Minister, Togo, who took office after Konoye fell, on reviewing the record reached the same conclusion as Hull.[19] The impression is due in part, I think, to the fact that in October the American government was revealing more clearly than it did in March that it would not compromise with Japan. American defense production was gaining size and speed; the situation in the Atlantic was better; the British still had the Suez Canal; the Russians were holding before Moscow and winter was not far ahead. Japan could no longer determine whether the war in Europe was to be won or lost.

Konoye in his "Memoirs" sums up the position in which he now found himself. He had presided over an Imperial Conference (September 6) which had stipulated that if by the early part of October there was no reasonable hope of having its terms accepted, Japan should decide for war. The time had come, the effort had failed.

"In the end," as he later wrote in his "Memoirs," "the Japanese side insisted that 'It is now the United States' turn to say something,' and to this the Americans continued to say stubbornly 'It is Japan's turn.' The negotiations had now reached a complete deadlock." But now at the edge of this transit to war, he drew back. But before telling of what happened next, perspective demands that brief notice be taken of another integral element in the situation—how the Axis connection also stood at this time in the way of an accord.

[17] See memoranda of talks between Welles and Wakasugi, Minister-Counsellor of the Japanese Embassy, October 13, and between Hull and Wakasugi, October 16 and 17, *ibid.*, II, 680, *et seq.*

[18] Hull, *op. cit.*, II, 1035.

[19] Deposition of Togo, *Far East Mil. Trib.*, Exh. No. 3646.

## [4]

The American government, while talking with Japan, could not forget that it was allied with Germany and Italy. American planes and warships were now providing watch and ward over wide areas of the Middle and Western Atlantic and around Iceland.[20] Encounters were becoming frequent. On September 11 the President, having discussed his words with Hull, Stimson, and Knox, broadcast: "The aggression is not ours. Ours is solely defense. But let this warning be clear. From now on, if German or Italian vessels of war enter the waters, the protection of which is necessary for American defense, they do so at their own peril. The orders which I have given as Commander in Chief of the United States Army and Navy are to carry out that policy—at once." [21]

On September 26 the Navy issued orders to protect all ships engaged in commerce in our defensive waters—by patrolling, covering, escorting, reporting, or destroying German and Italian naval, land, and air forces encountered.[22] As the President wrote to Mackenzie King, Prime Minister of Canada, ". . . we have begun to have practically sole charge of the safety of things to twenty-six degrees longitude, and to a further extension in the waters well to the eastward of Iceland." [23]

Further, it was foreseen that before long American merchant ships, manned by American crews, would soon be making the whole voyage to Britain. By the end of September, agreement had been reached between the President and Congressional leaders that the Neutrality Act should be so amended as to permit American merchant ships to enter combat areas and the ports of belligerents. The President's message so recommending was sent to Congress October 8.

[20] On August 25 Atlantic fleet forces were ordered to destroy surface raiders which attacked shipping along sea lanes between North America and Iceland, or which approached these lanes sufficiently closely to threaten such shipping. On September 3 the Western Atlantic area of operations covered by the United States Atlantic fleet was extended eastward. These were changes, Nos. 2 and 4, to W.P.L. 51. *Pearl Harbor Attack,* Part 5, p. 2295.

[21] While this speech was in preparation, the President had the impulse to be more explicit in his statements but Hull warned against any reference to shooting.

[22] This was Western Hemisphere Defense Plan, No. 5 (W.P.L. 52), effective October 11, 1941.

[23] Letter, Roosevelt to King, September 27, 1941. Churchill understood these orders to mean that American ships would attack any Axis ships found in the prohibited zone and assume responsibility for all fast British convoys other than troop convoys between America and Iceland. See his message to General Smuts of September 14, 1941. Churchill, *The Grand Alliance,* p. 517.

Would this bring war with Germany? Hull did not think so; Hitler would not, he thought, declare a war as a result of any action of ours unless he thought it to his own advantage.[24] But should this turn out to be wrong, how would Japan construe its obligations under Article III of the Tripartite Pact? It was not possible to deduce a reliable answer from either the Japanese talk or texts. The American government sought to have Japan, in some form or other, cancel the obligation. The Konoye Cabinet lived in an agony of division over the issue. Unwilling to separate from Germany, but equally unwilling to lose a chance for a settlement with the United States, it fell into bigamous vows.

Formula after formula was served up to Washington. None was a conclusive repudiation of the tie. The American government was asked to feel safe with the assurance that Japan would construe its obligation independently. This was accompanied by covert hints that we need not fear the decision, if other matters were amiably adjusted. Thus on September 18, Ushiba, Konoye's secretary, said to Dooman that it was impossible for Japan to go farther than the formula already offered on the Tripartite Pact before the besought Konoye-Roosevelt meeting. "He added, however, that an understanding had been reached among the various influential elements in Japan which would enable Prince Konoye to give orally and directly to the President an assurance with regard to the attitude of Japan which, he felt sure, would be entirely satisfactory to the President." [25]

The German government was doing all it could to induce Japan to be faithful. It asked public reaffirmation of Matsuoka's version of the pact —that, in the event of war between Germany and the United States, Japan would join Germany. A deciphered cable sent by Oshima with a special request that it be shown to the Army and Navy related what Ribbentrop was saying: that the whole German government was displeased with the Japanese attitude and secrecy; and that if Japan took a "wishy-washy" attitude and proceeded with the talks without consulting Germany there was no telling what Germany might do.[26] Another deciphered cable made it clear that the Japanese government, while seeking to soothe Berlin, refused to do as asked. Oshima was

---

[24] The event proved Hull to be correct. On September 17 the German Navy asked Hitler to change its orders to permit, among other things, attacks on escorting forces in any operational area at any time. Hitler decided against such action for the time being, until the outcome of the fighting in Russia was decided, which he expected soon. *Fuehrer Conferences,* 1941, II, 33.

[25] *Foreign Relations: Japan,* II, 628.

[26] Telegram, No. 1198, Oshima to Toyoda, October 1, 1941.

told that just as German policy had been governed by German aims, so Japanese policy would be guided by Japanese aims; that the original purpose of the Tripartite Pact was to restrain the United States from entering the war, and this was still Japan's purpose.[27]

Thus the American government could gather that devotion to Germany probably would not stand in the way of an accord that Japan found desirable. But it did not want to buy off the threat. Nor to have to rely on secret demi-promises. It wanted the connection dissolved. As long as Japan refused to do so, its appeals to be believed were not in good standing. It was thought to be—it had to be—corrupted by evil association. Thus the Axis connection, courted in the first months of his Ministry, was one of the causes of the tragic dilemma in which Konoye now found himself.

[27] Telegram, No. 873, Toyoda to Oshima, October 8, 1941.

## CHAPTER 36

# The Army Insists on a Decision for War; Konoye Quits; Tojo Takes Over

IN THE statement of policy approved at the Imperial Conference of September 6, the men of peace and the men of war had each written a part. The time for the curtain call was set. The actors read over Clause 3: "If by the early part of October there is no reasonable hope of having our demands agreed to in the diplomatic negotiations mentioned above, we will immediately make up our minds to get ready for war against America (and England and Holland)."

Diplomacy was lost in the wings. The view gained force that there was nothing more that Japan could say or offer; that it suited the United States to drag on the talks as long as possible. In Konoye's words: "within Japan the urgency of the political situation increased with oppressive force." [1]

On September 18 an attempt had been made to kill the Prime Minister. As he was leaving his home for his office four men armed with daggers and short swords sprang at his car. Guards stopped and disarmed them. The Prime Minister was not hurt. The affair was kept most secret, but it left marks upon the nerves. Judgment of the situation was warped by the thought that unruly elements in and out of the Army might defy a conclusion they did not like and kill its sponsors. A premium was placed on the leadership of those who could manage these elements.

Konoye lacked commanding purpose and energy. Neither he nor the court dared try to impose any other will over that of the Army. The idea of resignation came to the top of his seesawing thoughts. As Prime Minister (in 1937) he was responsible before the Emperor for the war in China, even though the Army had run its own course; and as Prime

---

[1] The following account of this peace-war crisis is based on many pertinent documents and depositions presented to the International Military Tribunal for the Far East, interrogations of many of the participants in this crisis, the Konoye memorandum entitled "Facts Pertaining to the Resignation of the 3rd Konoye Cabinet," and "Kido's Diary," particularly the long note made in November, "Circumstances under which the Third Konoye Cabinet Tendered Resignation." *Far East Mil. Trib.*, Exh. No. 2250.

Minister (in 1941) he was responsible before the Emperor for the program adopted on September 6. The past had him by the heels.

Should Japan defer to us, or defer to the imperative contained in the resolution of September 6? Should it go on talking with the United States, perhaps bidding a little more for an accord? Or should it let no more time pass and declare for war? Over this choice a tense round of talk swiveled. The Foreign Minister, Toyoda, gave advice—under the guise of an estimate of the outlook—that conformed to Konoye's views: that all the resources of diplomacy were not exhausted and the talks should go on. But the Army refused consent, unless the Prime Minister could show some new chance that the United States would accept Japanese terms. Delay, it asserted, would be most costly, for the familiar reasons: enemy forces would be stronger; the weather would become less favorable for planned operations; the oil supply would be shorter and the risk of destruction in the oil fields in the Indies prolonged.

The Navy was divided and of two minds. Most of its chief figures were uneasy about the prospect. But, because of professional pride, all they would say was that the Navy would take orders. The Planning Board merely repeated its report that Japan had only enough oil for a short and decisive war; and that the outcome would depend on whether Japan could take and hold sources of supply in the southern regions—a matter about which the Navy was uncertain. The Emperor and his court were much troubled by the thought of fighting so hazardous a war. But as the crisis went on they became more worried over the danger of civil war than over the possible ruin of a foreign war. What the Court Circle came most to want was a decision that would not tear Japan apart —any decision.

It was agreed that the civilian and military heads of the government would meet on October 12 to make the fateful choice. The evening before, Admiral Oka, Chief of the Naval Affairs Bureau of the Ministry of the Navy, told Konoye that, with the exception of part of the General Staff, the "brains" of the Navy did not want war with the United States. But, he added, the Minister of the Navy, Oikawa, could not officially say so. Or, as later explained by that cabinet official, "It was my opinion that if the Navy made a public announcement that it 'lacked confidence in fighting the United States,' it would lead to the disruption of national opinions, cause the pitting of the Army against the Navy, and consequently develop into a grave internal problem." [2]

October 12 was Konoye's fiftieth birthday. The Minister of Foreign

[2] Deposition of Oikawa, *ibid.,* Exh. No. 3470.

Affairs, the Ministers of War and of the Navy, and the President of the Planning Board, went out to his villa at Ogikubo. The Foreign Minister said again he thought an accord might still be reached with the United States—if Japan agreed "in principle" to retire its troops from China; the United States agreeing then to allow troops to remain in some places for some time. On this matter Tojo asserted the Army could not yield; any accord must provide for limited occupation. For that, he argued, was essential to maintain stability in China, to preserve Japan's position in Manchuria and Korea, to prevent the spread of Communism, and to assure orderly economic progress. Further, he added, if the Army, after its vast exertions in China, were forced out entirely, its morale and its power to defend Japan would be destroyed. These things being so—and the United States refusing to recognize them —he concluded that Japan must go to war, and at once. Oikawa spoke as anticipated—saying the Navy did not want war since it was doubtful of the outcome; but it would leave the decision to the Prime Minister.

Konoye and Tojo talked over the disputed issues again on the morning of the 14th, before what was to be the last meeting of the cabinet. Konoye referred to the comparative weakness of Japan, because of which he found it hard to agree to enter a greater war. Tojo accused him and Toyoda of paying too much heed to the obstacles and risks. Aroused, Tojo left, saying: "All this must be due to the difference in our characters." When he appeared at the cabinet meeting his anger had not faded, and he gave an excited statement of the reasons for ending the talks with the United States.

Later that afternoon (the 14th) General Muto, the Chief of the Military Affairs Bureau in the Ministry of War, made a last attempt to avoid a crisis. He sent word to the Chief Secretary of the Cabinet, that the refusal of the Navy to take a position was making it impossible for the Prime Minister to reach a decision. If the Navy should say openly to the Army: "The Navy at this time does not want war," then the Army would be able to control its commands. Both the meaning and purpose of this message are obscure, despite later commentaries.[3] It was passed on to Admiral Oka. But his answer was the same—the Navy could not say that it did not want war. It was, he said, the duty of the Prime Minister to decide between peace and war, and the duty of the Navy to follow orders.[4] The Navy, in other words, would not pit itself against the Army.

---

[3] Among them, that of Muto in his deposition, *ibid.*, Exh. No. 3454.

[4] Depositions—Admiral Oka, *ibid.*, Exh. No. 3473; Tomita, Chief Secretary of the Cabinet, *ibid.*, Exh. 3467; and Oikawa, Minister for the Navy, *ibid.*, Exh. No. 3470.

Thus Konoye was left without effective means of reply to the message he received from Tojo late that night (the 14th). This stated that since the cabinet was not able to carry out the plan approved on September 6 it ought to resign; then a new and unobligated cabinet could decide whether or not to go forward with this plan. Konoye gave up. On the morning of the 15th he told the Emperor that the breach between himself and the Minister of War had grown so great that Tojo was now saying that he did not want to talk to him any longer as he was not sure he could control his feelings. The Emperor was distressed but reserved.

With animated haste, Konoye got the resignations of the members of his cabinet. On the evening of the next day he submitted them to the Emperor. His letter of explanation repeated his views of the situation and admitted failure.[5] The Emperor spoke a few sad words of regret. Konoye, on leaving the Imperial Presence, found Kido, Lord Keeper of the Privy Seal, waiting for him to discuss the question of the succession.

Both Konoye and Tojo had been showing favor to the idea of selecting Prince Higashi Kuni, a member of the Imperial House. But Kido detected a difference in the motives of various advocates of this choice. He scented peril for the Emperor, no matter which of them turned out to be the more shrewd. If, as Konoye seemed to think, this appointment led to a decision against the Army there was danger of revolt against the Emperor. If, as Tojo seemed to think, it led to a decision to go to war, and the war was lost, the Emperor would become the target of hatred. Thus Kido suppressed the suggestion.[6]

Instead he told Konoye that he thought the crisis could be managed only by someone fully acquainted with the making of the decision of September 6; that, in fact, it would be very hard for anyone except the Minister of War or Minister of the Navy to organize a cabinet. It is idle now to try to trace Kido's real train of thought when he turned the pointer to these two men.[7] The best surmise, I think, is that his primary wish was to avoid the danger of a protracted cabinet crisis. It may be surmised further that Kido foresaw the bargain that would be

[5] "Letter of Resignation by Prince Fumimaro Konoye to His Majesty the Emperor." Substantial differences of meaning are to be found between the translation of this letter included as Appendix VIII in the "Konoye Memoirs" (as printed in *Pearl Harbor Attack*, Part 20, pp. 4025–26) and the version presented to the war crimes tribunal (*Far East Mil. Trib.*, Exh. No. 1152).

[6] A detailed account of the back and forth soundings of Prince Higashi Kuni by Tojo, Konoye and others is given by Suzuki, who was an active intermediary, in his deposition, *ibid.*, Exh. No. 3605.

[7] His explanations are set forth at length in his "Diary" and deposition, *ibid.*, Exh. No. 3340.

struck; that Tojo would be selected; that if he were made Prime Minister, he would agree that the decision of September 6 might be reviewed; that the Navy, if thus granted more time, would accept Tojo; and that presently it would go where he led.

How much of this did Konoye foresee, when he fell in with Kido's suggestion? In any case he favored the transfer of power to Tojo, the adversary. As between the War Minister and Navy Minister, the first, he told Kido, would be better able to control the Army. Tojo, he seems to have thought, would not hastily plunge the nation into war in view of the wavering in the Navy; especially if the Emperor enjoined him to be prudent. Who is to know whether this was the full depth of his thought or a false bottom?

The formalities for making Tojo the next Prime Minister followed. The Council of Elder Statesmen met around noon on the 17th. Konoye, pleading a fever, did not attend. But he sent a letter. This went into his quarrel with the Army about the decision to go to war; and the terms of settlement with the United States.[8] After this was read, Kido explained the reasons for choosing Tojo. He answered doubts—and the Elders had many—by saying that this was the only way, first, to make it possible, peacefully, to review the program of September 6; and second, to bring about a unity of opinion between the Army and Navy.[9] The Council, after three hours of grave questioning, approved. Or rather, as later expressed by one of the group, no one objected "absolutely." [10]

The Emperor was advised. In the afternoon he summoned Tojo and conferred the Imperial mandate upon him. In doing so, he said: "You will see to it that the cooperation between the Army and Navy is closer than ever." As soon as Tojo left, the Minister of the Navy appeared, and to him the Emperor said: "As I told Tojo that the Army and Navy should cooperate more closely, you must also try to carry out my wish." In the anteroom outside of the Imperial Presence, the two Ministers were met by Kido. He gave them a further message—that the Emperor wished them both to study internal and external circumstances more broadly and deeply than before—and in doing so, not to feel bound by

---

[8] This long letter is given in Kido's deposition, *ibid.*, Exh. No. 3340. It is a clear exposition not only of his own opinions but those of the Army and Navy. It gives the impression that Konoye thought that the points of difference with the American Government were much smaller than Hull did. Even as regards the stationing of troops in China he still seemed to think the American Government would not be entirely obdurate.

[9] A resumé of the proceedings of this conference is given in Kido's deposition, *op. cit.*

[10] Deposition of General Abe, *Far East Mil. Trib.*, Exh. No. 3526.

the decision which had been taken in his presence on September 6.[11] Thus, the earlier resolution to go to war was rescinded.

Tojo described the policy of this cabinet as that of "the clean slate." But the chalk was placed in the hands of those who had made the earlier mark. They were the men who had carried the war deep into China and for whom retreat would mean failure. They were the men who made decisions by a military timetable. In fact Japan had turned back toward a Shogun administration, named by its opponents the *Bakufu* —literally "curtain government" in allusion to the fact that it was a government of generals whose camps were circled by curtains, as at Uraga when Commodore Perry arrived.[12]

---

[11] As given in Kido's deposition, he said to them: "I presume you have just received Imperial words in regard to cooperation between the Army and the Navy. As regards the fundamental line of national policy I am commanded to convey to you the Imperial desire that careful consideration be taken by studying both the internal and external situation more comprehensively and more profoundly than ever, regardless of the Resolution of the September 6th Imperial Conference."

[12] Arthur Walworth, *Black Ships Off Japan* (New York, 1946), p. 142. A most interesting account of Perry's visit to Japan and his negotiations.

# PART FOUR
## WAR

## CHAPTER 37

# The Last Offers to the United States
# Are Formulated: November 5, 1941

THE new cabinet took over on October 18. Tojo was promoted to be a full general and allowed to remain on active service. This enabled him to retain the post of Minister of War, as well as that of Prime Minister. He also kept for himself the office of Home Minister, in charge of the internal police. Oikawa, the Navy Minister, gave way to Admiral Shimada, a less resistant man. Admiral Toyoda was replaced as Foreign Minister by Togo, a senior member of the diplomatic service who had been cool to the alliance with Germany. He had qualms about serving in this cabinet. But they were overcome by Tojo's nebulous promise that he would make a sincere effort to adjust relations with the United States. General Suzuki stayed on as Head of the Planning Board and member of the cabinet. General Hoshino, another former Manchurian officer, was brought back into the inner group as Chief Secretary of the Cabinet.

Nomura, Tojo found, wanted very much to quit as Ambassador to the United States. In a series of cables to the Foreign Minister and Minister of the Navy he reported himself to be puzzled and at the end of his rope.[1] The Navy, he complained, was not supporting the Foreign Office as promised before he left for Washington. The American government had failed to be conciliatory as he had hoped. The cabinet had changed and he no longer knew what the government wanted him to do. "I cannot tell you how much in the dark I am." And in another place, "Now that I am a dead horse [i.e., without influence either in Japan or in the United States] I do not want to continue this hypocritical existence, deceiving myself and other people."[2] But the new cabinet would not let him go. He was urged to remain and to make

---

[1] Nomura to Togo, October 20 and 22 (CA), Army No. 23774 and Army No. 23859; both were deciphered by "Magic."

[2] Nomura in his manuscript (*op. cit.*) states that the main reasons he wanted to resign were: that he had been a failure; that because of cabinet changes he was out of touch; that Roosevelt and Hull thought him to be without influence in Tokyo. An alternative translation of this quoted sentence is: "I am now, so to speak, a skeleton of a dead horse. It is too much for me to be a sham existence, cheating others as well as myself."

a greater effort than before to save Japan. Nomura, the naval officer, felt he could not refuse.

But the first words of guidance received from the new cabinet (on October 21) must have confirmed his sense that he could accomplish nothing. It was a special message, sent with the concurrence of the Army and Navy, stating that the situation could not be solved unless the United States changed its views. Nomura's response seems to have taken the form of a report of a talk with his old friend, the retired Admiral Pratt. This transmitted Pratt's warning and advice: warning that if Japan moved either north or south, war would result; advice that Japan should keep its naval force unharmed—so that it could be taken along to the eventual peace conference.[3]

But the government was moving in the opposite direction. At its first Liaison Conference with the military leaders (October 23), General Sugiyama, Chief of the General Staff, firmly reiterated that the decision between peace and war must be made quickly. Diplomacy, he insisted, must keep pace with the military measures. These had been going forward without pause throughout the cabinet crisis.

The surveys and maps of the lands to be invaded were being put in final form. The Army and Navy were beginning to issue plans for joint operations. The organization of the Southern Army was being completed. Its command was chosen and installed at Saigon, the recently acquired base in Indo-China. The divisions which were to capture Singapore, Hong Kong, and Malaya were entering the last phases of intensive training. Materials and technicians were being recruited to operate the coveted oil fields in the Indies. The argument within the senior naval circles as to whether or not, as part of the first action, to attack the American fleet at Pearl Harbor was settled.[4]

Such was the situation when the cabinet and the Supreme Command met long into the night of November 1–2, and again during the day

[3] Telegram, Nomura to Togo, No. 1004, October 27, 1941. Wakasugi Minister-Counsellor of the Japanese Embassy, was giving the same advice.

[4] Of the many records of the contents and schedule of Japanese Army orders contained in the documents presented to the International Military Tribunal, Far East, the depositions of General Tanaka (Shinichi), Chief of the Operations Section of the Army General Staff, Exh. Nos. 2676, 3027, and 2244, are the most informative; for Navy orders and movements, the report made by Admiral James Richardson, Exh. No. 1249.

Instructive accounts of the development of plans for the attack upon Pearl Harbor and the arguments over them are to be found in the depositions of Commander Miyo (Tatsukichi) of the Operations Section of the Naval General Staff, *ibid.*, Exh. No. 3007 and of Captain Genda (Minoru), Staff Officer, First Air Fleet, *ibid.*, Exh. No. 3009.

The texts (whole or in part) of almost all the important naval orders and some of the Army orders are printed in various scattered parts and sections of *Pearl Harbor Attack*.

of the 2nd. These were the sessions when the whole dilemma of Japan was exposed. The past placed its hand on the shoulder of the present and thrust it into the dark future. There was a "tight, tense, and trapped feeling."[5] The Foreign Minister, Togo, brought into the meeting a proposal that any act of war should be deferred until the United States entered the European war. The Army and Navy participants said they could not consent to any such policy of delay.

Their position rested on a pyramid of deductions and fears. Diplomacy had failed to arrange a tolerable settlement with the United States. It would continue to fail, since the United States neither could nor would understand the reasons why Japan must maintain a strong protective position in China. It was demanding that Japan take all its forces out of that country, leaving it in disorder and hostile to Japan. This they could not contemplate. If the issue were faced at once a successful war could be fought. If it were postponed, Japan might be forced to submit to a ruinous peace or fight a losing war.

This being so, the high military command stated that if decision was deferred, it would no longer accept responsibility for the defense of the country. The fearful were routed with the cry (as later phrased by Tojo) that "rather than await extinction it were better to face death by breaking through the encircling ring to find a way for existence."[6]

The advice made a long backward arc through time, when the Japanese were in parley as to how to deal with Commodore Perry and the "black ships" at anchor in Tokyo Bay. Then the Prince of Mito advised Lord Abe, "If we don't drive them away now, we shall never have another opportunity. If now we resort to a willfully dilatory method of procedure, we shall gnaw our navels afterwards when it will be of no use."[7]

The cabinet, after the conference of September 6, had again looked into the question of whether the production of synthetic oil could be quickly and greatly increased. Konoye had argued that it was better to spend great sums for that purpose than to spend them in war. But the task proved beyond the powers of the Planning Board to conceive, much less accomplish. It might be done, the board reported, in two, three, or four years; if billions of yen were invested and other programs pared to provide the needful materials—steel, pipes, and machinery.[8]

[5] Words later used by Admiral Shimada, Minister of the Navy, to explain his consent to the decisions of the next few days. Deposition, *Far East Mil. Trib.*, Exh. No. 3565.

[6] Tojo deposition, *ibid.*, Exh. No. 3655.

[7] Walworth, *op. cit.*, p. 148.

[8] A summary of this report on Japan's supply of commodities if negotiations with the United States ended is given in Suzuki's deposition. *Far East Mil. Trib.* Exh. No. 3605.

Military prospects were also reviewed. Or rather the military leaders were asked to put themselves on record, for no one was bold enough to assert that they might be wrong. The Navy was obeying the Emperor's injunction to cooperate with the Army. Through Admiral Nagano it now said that the chances of winning the first battles were good; and, if they were won and strategic areas were quickly occupied, Japan would be able to sustain a long war.[9] The Japanese Navy, Nagano thought, would be able to cut American and British connections with the South and to destroy the American fleet if it came close. General Sugiyama assured the gathering that the prospects of victory were good; not only of first victory, but of final victory.[10]

Thus buoyed up, the Liaison Conference of November 2 made up its mind. After a night of uneasy doubt, the two hesitants, Togo, Foreign Minister, and Kaya, Finance Minister, went along with the rest. In essence it was decided that revised and final proposals should be made to the American government, and if these were not accepted very quickly, war should be begun.

The Emperor was told (on the evening of the 2nd) by Tojo and the Chiefs of Staff of this decision. Since he still spoke anxiously over the prospect of war, a conference of military counsellors was called in his presence (the 4th). Its outcome was the same: a unanimous report that the Supreme War Council deemed it proper and just that the Army and Navy High Command should take measures . . . to expedite operational preparations for war.

The stage was set for the formality of enactment. On the next day, November 5, an Imperial Conference after a short and muted session set its seal upon a program on which the participants were already agreed.

---

Konoye discusses his attitude towards the problem of oil in a supplemental memo to his "Memoirs," entitled "Supplying of Military Stores and Materials, Pro and Con of the Theory of Gradual Exhaustion." *Pearl Harbor Attack*, Part 20, pp. 4011–13.

[9] The war plans visualized the quick capture of the territories in a large, but limited, area of the Southwestern Pacific which it was believed could be held against the American fleet weakened by attacks upon Pearl Harbor and the Philippines, and engaged in the Atlantic.

Sir George Sansom has given a lucid account of this strategy and its later mistaken extension in an article in *International Affairs*, October 1948, entitled, "Japan's Fatal Blunder."

[10] Sato (Kenryo), Chief of the Military Affairs Bureau of the War Ministry, explained in an article published in *Nichi Nichi* (Tokyo), March 11, 1942, the basis for the confidence of the Army. He stated that since 1937 only 40 per cent of the Army budget had been used for the war in China, the rest for expansion; that the munitions industry had been increased seven-fold during that period; and that he reckoned the combat power of the Army was three times what it was before the outbreak of the war in China.

It was entitled "Essentials for Executing the National Purpose of the Empire." [11] They were few. Two last proposals, lettered A and B, were to be placed before the American government. The military forces were to be ready to fight by the beginning of December. If by November 25 no accord had been reached, the final decision to go to war should be placed before the Emperor. The German and Italian governments were then to be notified to this effect, and asked to make war at the same time. Japan was to remain at peace with Russia, even if Germany was thereby alienated.

Proposal A was a restatement of Japanese terms on the few most disputed points. [12] In substance the new formulas to be put before the American government were:

(1) Acceptance of the rule of economic equality in China and throughout the Pacific, provided it was adopted in all other parts of the world.

(2) Japanese army units of unspecified size were to remain in certain areas in North China, Mongolia and Hainan for a "necessary period." Nomura was instructed, if asked by the American government, to interpret this last phrase to mean "about twenty-five years." Japan was to commence the withdrawal of all other troops in China as soon as peace was restored between Japan and China, and complete the withdrawal "within two years with [sic] the firm establishment of peace and order."

(3) The Japanese forces in Indo-China would be withdrawn when the war in China was settled or a just peace established in East Asia.

(4) Japanese obligations under the Tripartite Pact were defined in new language without new meaning.

On these indistinct terms the American government was to persuade Chiang Kai-shek to make peace with Japan—under threat that the United States would cease to support him. The Foreign Minister, Togo, foresaw a refusal of this now stale scheme of adjustment. At his urging, the Imperial Conference also approved a second proposal, B, to be produced if and when A failed. This was to be the last call. It was regarded only as a temporary measure—a *modus vivendi*—under which Japan and the United States might carry on, at odds but without war. Of its features notice will be taken when this narrative again reverts to Washington.

[11] The text, poorly translated, is given in *Far East Mil. Trib.*, Exh. No. 779. The parts having to do with the offers to be made to the United States which were presented to Hull in official English translation are to be found in *Foreign Relations: Japan*, II, Proposal A, 709, 715–17; Proposal B, 755–56.

[12] When sending the text of Proposal A to Nomura he was told that "Every effort is to be made to avoid including the Four Principles [of Hull] in the formal agreements between Japan and the United States." *Far East Mil. Trib.*, Exh. No. 2925.

The heads of the Army and Navy hurried away from the Imperial Conference to dispatch their orders. On November 3, Admiral Yamamoto, Commander in Chief of the Combined Fleet, had approved Secret Operations Order No. 1. The opening parts ran:

"The Japanese Empire is expecting war to break out with the United States, Great Britain and the Netherlands.

"War will be declared on X day.

"This order will become effective on Y day." [13]

This was now sent off. So was the Army order which told those forces which were to join the Southern Army to leave Japan and Korea for their area of service.[14]

In a series of long messages over the same days (November 2–5) the Japanese government proceeded to make Nomura realize the vital nature of his next errands. Both before and after sending him the new texts, it told him in words, both earnest and forceful, that they were Japan's final orders and if they were rejected war would follow.[15] Thus, one passage in the message sent on the 4th read:

"Both in name and in spirit this offer of ours is indeed the last. . . . This time we are showing all our friendship; this time we are making our last possible bargain . . . the success or failure of the pending discussions will have an immense effect on the destiny of the Japanese Empire. In fact, we gambled the fate of our land on the throw of this die." [16]

Nomura was also told that all arrangements for the signing of the agreement had to be completed by November 25. Finally he was informed that in view of the gravity of the situation Ambassador Kurusu

[13] This is differently phrased in the version of Combined Fleet Secret Operations Order No. 1 (as drawn up on the Flagship *Nagato* on November 1). The first sentence of that translation begins "The Japanese Empire will declare war on the United States, Great Britain and the Netherlands."

[14] Deposition of General Tanaka, Chief of the Operations Section of the General Staff, *Far East Mil. Trib.*, Exh. Nos. 2244, 3027.

[15] This series of most interesting instructions and the explanations thereof are contained in telegrams from Togo to Nomura: Exh. Nos. 722 of November 2; 723 of November 3; 725, 726, 730 of November 4; 732, 735, and 736 of November 5; and 740 and 741 of November 6.

Another feature of the instruction was the concern shown to preserve secrecy regarding, not only the text of these proposals, but the very fact that they were being presented. Thus, in Telegram No. 741 of November 6, Nomura was told to do his utmost to avoid any public knowledge of the talk he was to have with the President, and to maintain the same secrecy in regard to all the other contacts with American officials.

[16] Telegram No. 725, Togo to Nomura, November 4, 1941.

was leaving Japan by clipper at once. The message from Togo telling him of this went on to state that "he [Kurusu] is carrying no additional instructions—so please tell him all." But there can be little doubt that Kurusu knew of the Japanese program and schedule of action.[17] But he probably was uninformed of the plan to dispose of the American fleet at Pearl Harbor.

Most of these messages from Tokyo were being read with sober attention by the President and the rest of those within the circle of "Magic." They knew what was about to be put before them; and knew that the Imperial government was calling it the "final step." Time was becoming exceedingly short and the situation very critical.

[17] So stated by Tojo in his deposition.

## CHAPTER 38

# November: The American Government Stands Fast and Hurries Its Preparations

THE character of the new cabinet caused concern rather than surprise. The name and image of Tojo were disliked, and unpleasant events were expected to follow.[1] He was the small, wiry and tough soldier who had pounded his way into the heart of China. The Far Eastern Division of the State Department was disposed to think that, as Prime Minister, he might think less of making war and more of making peace. But the President and all the War Council thought this unlikely. They added up the evidence in hand, wondering how much longer they could hold Japan in check.

The incoming reports from Grew were somber and his diary even more so. War, they said, was near unless the American government granted a reprieve by relaxing economic restraints. His message carrying the surest forecast was that of November 3. He warned, "Action by Japan which might render unavoidable an armed conflict with the United States may come with dangerous and dramatic suddenness."[2]

It was hard for Grew, a person of buoyant belief that any situation could be straightened out if the try was hard enough, to admit that this one could not be. There was regret, even reproach, between the lines of this cable of November 3, of which later he wrote in his diary, "I hope that history will not overlook this telegram."[3] His appeals for "constructive conciliation" had not been heeded. He repeated his view

[1] For a good appreciation of the situation see the report prepared by the Office of the Chief of Naval Operations, October 21, 1941, printed in *Pearl Harbor Attack*, Part 15, p. 1845, *et seq.*

[2] *Foreign Relations: Japan,* II, 701–704.

[3] His appeal to history reflected his sense that Washington, as so often before, would overlook it. Reviewing the critical period of negotiations (August–December 1941) after the outbreak of the war he wrote in his diary, "Our own telegrams brought no response whatsoever; they were never even referred to, and reporting to the Department was like throwing pebbles into a lake at night; we were not permitted to see even the ripples. For all we all knew our telegrams had not in any degree registered. Obviously I could only assume our recommendations were not welcome, yet we continued to express our carefully considered judgment as to the developing situation, a judgment which subsequent events prove to have been all too accurate." Diary, entry for December 1941.

that while principles must not be compromised, methods might be flexible. Japan, having been shown how hard was the road of the aggressor, might now turn back if given time and help, he thought. He was searching for an acceptable adjustment of the time balance between Japan's retreat and America's response. In doing so, he was carrying out the first duty of a good diplomat—never to let peace fail because men grow weary of the hunt for tolerable terms.

But there was one inlaid hindrance to any adjustment of this time balance, and of this Washington was more aware than Tokyo. By then, had the United States resumed shipments of war materials *before* Japan proved its intentions, the unwritten pact between the United States and the other opponents of the Axis might have come apart. For they would have remained exposed to Japanese threat and assault. This aspect in the situation now came to the fore. Urgent appeals were coming from Chungking as well as from Tokyo. So urgent, in fact, that the American government considered whether or not to threaten Japan with war.

Chiang Kai-shek between October 28 and November 5 sent a series of most worried messages to the President and Churchill. These said he expected Japan to commence an attack at once against the province of Yunnan for the purpose of closing the Burma Road and capturing Kunming. If this attack succeeded, he continued, China would be entirely cut off from the outside world, the Chinese armies might well be encircled, and his country forced out of the war. He urged that Japan be warned not to march upon Yunnan. And he asked that the American government turn over to China heavy bombers tagged for Singapore, and that the British government promise to use their forces stationed in Singapore to defend Yunnan. It may be surmised that the Generalissimo's anxieties were made more acute by the growing influence of the Communist forces among the farmers and workers of the north—as the Chungking troops suffered losses before the Japanese advance.

The State Department sought the opinion of the heads of the Army and Navy about these appeals. In a series of meetings (beginning on November 1), Hull said that he did not see any use of issuing any additional warnings to Japan if the American government could not back them up. He wished to know if the Army and Navy would be prepared to do so.[4] The Joint Army-Navy Board met to consider the answer to

---

[4] As recounted in the minutes of the meeting of the Joint Army-Navy Board of November 3, 1941, printed in *Pearl Harbor Attack*, Part 14, p. 1062, *et seq*.

this question, Stark and Marshall both attending. All present greatly wanted to avoid immediate involvement in the Far East.[5]

The Army was not ready to deal with an attack in the Philippines, though hopeful that within a short time it would become so. A substantial movement of mechanized equipment—tanks, self-propelled cannon, and other artillery—and of soldiers was under way.

The first squadron of nine Flying Fortresses (B-17s) had reached Manila weeks before. Other and larger squadrons were to follow soon. Even greater hope was attached to what Marshall termed, "the super Flying Fortresses, B-24 type planes," a reserve of which he planned to send to Manila. These planes were expected to have an operating radius of fifteen hundred miles, with a bombing load of seven tons. Once they arrived, it was thought the airfields and ports essential to Japanese southward advance would come within American striking range. They could reach Osaka with a full bomb load and Tokyo with a partial load.[6]

So eager was the wish to have these bombing groups in place to fend off or smash a Japanese attack, that a dangerous chance was taken. For it was realized that there was no adequate interception defense or warning system to guard these heavy planes. The creation of this force was, as Generals Marshall and Arnold told Brereton, the Commander, a "calculated risk."[7] Protection would come later with the arrival of a large number of the latest pursuit planes sent out by sea.

As explained by Stimson to the President in a letter of October 21: "A strategic opportunity of the utmost importance has suddenly arisen in the southwestern Pacific. . . . From being impotent to influence events in that area, we suddenly find ourselves vested with the possibility of great effective power . . . . even this imperfect threat, if not promptly called by the Japanese, bids fair to stop Japan's march to the south and secure the safety of Singapore . . ."[8]

At the same time the government hurried to establish a chain of airfields strung over the Southwest Pacific for these heavy bombers. These were to be located at many points along a looping southern route be-

---

[5] As expressed by General Marshall to the Navy Court of Inquiry: ". . . our state of mind at that period—I am referring now to both Stark and myself—was to do all in our power here at home, with the State Department or otherwise, to try to delay this break to the last moment, because of our state of unpreparedness and because of our involvements in other parts of the world." *ibid.*, Part 32, p. 560.

[6] For details see the letter from Marshall to Stark, September 12, 1941, *ibid.*, Part 16, pp. 2211-12. It is difficult to identify precisely what aircraft General Marshall had in mind. The B-24 was commonly known as the Liberator, the B-17 series, as the Flying Fortress.

[7] Lieutenant General Lewis H. Brereton, *The Brereton Diaries* (New York, 1946), p. 8.

[8] *Pearl Harbor Attack*, Part 20, pp. 4442-44.

tween Hawaii down to Australia, and from there back to the Philippines and Java. Later it was to be extended to Singapore and China. These stations would be points of transit, and bases of operation in the event of war. Maintenance crews, fuel, parts, and munitions were to be kept at each.

On October 15 (acting on Stimson's earlier resquest) the State Department had ordered its missions to ask the British, Australian, New Zealand, Dutch, and Free French (at New Caledonia) authorities to co-operate in the project. It was hoped that the local governments would do the job, but the War Department offered to provide technical and financial help, and, where necessary, to carry out the construction. By early November all had given their approval, and the work was begun on several of the fields.[9] A new command was established at Manila, the Far East Air Force, to supervise the operation and to conduct training flights.[10]

The British were bringing together the Fast Eastern fleet which had been contemplated in ABC-1, of about six battleships, two or three aircraft carriers, and some additional cruisers and destroyers. Some of these had already arrived in Singapore by early November. Others left for it shortly thereafter. The British were also moving some additional troops and aircraft to Malaya; the United States provided some aircraft to the British in Singapore on Lend-Lease and sent some experts and mechanics. These measures, Churchill had cabled the President on November 2, "ought to serve as a deterrent on Japan," and he added, "The firmer your attitude and ours, the less chance of their taking the plunge."

The American Navy was as desirous of delay as the Army. It wanted neither to spare nor risk warships and merchant ships in a fight in the Pacific. Besides, it was worried by the lack of tankers, the vulnerability of its lines of communication, the inadequacy of repair facilities in

---

[9] News items and reports emanating from Australia about this time upset the American government, which hoped to keep this whole operation secret. Thus Prime Minister Curtin announced publicly "we have taken several important decisions in cooperation with the other democratic powers in the Pacific reflecting an extraordinary advance on what might have been considered possible a year ago." *Sunday Sun,* Sydney, October 19, 1941. And on October 23, the day after the Australian government concurred in the bomber-base plan, the American press carried an Associated Press story from Sydney saying that negotiations were completed between the United States, Great Britain, China, the Netherlands East Indies, New Zealand, and Australia for a "united Pacific front." Hull, when questioned on October 22 about reports concerning new arrangements for defense in the Pacific, said there was nothing new on the subject. It is safe to conclude that the Japanese government knew what was going on.

[10] An account of these preparatory operations is to be found in *The Brereton Diaries,* pp. 25–37.

Manila and Singapore and of anti-aircraft protection at the Far Eastern bases.

On November 5, the same day that the Japanese government decided to go to war if its final proposals (A or B) were rejected, Stark and Marshall (with Chiang Kai-shek's appeal before them) summed up their judgment of the line to be held. Their memorandum to the President advised that:

(a) The basic military policies and strategy agreed to in the United States–British Staff conversations remain sound. The primary objective of the two nations is the defeat of Germany. If Japan be defeated and Germany remain undefeated, decision will still have not been reached. In any case, an unlimited offensive war should not be undertaken against Japan, since such a war would greatly weaken the combined effort in the Atlantic against Germany, the most dangerous enemy.

(b) War between the United States and Japan should be avoided while building up defensive forces in the Far East, until such time as Japan attacks or directly threatens territories whose security to the United States is of very great importance. Military action against Japan should be undertaken only in one or more of the following contingencies: (1) A direct act of war by Japanese armed forces against the territory or mandated territory of the United States, the British Commonwealth, or the Netherlands East Indies; (2) The movement of Japanese armed forces into Thailand to the West of 100° East, or South of 10° North; or into Portuguese Timor, New Caledonia, or the Loyalty Islands.[11]

(d) Considering world strategy, a Japanese advance against Kunming, into Thailand except as previously indicated, or an attack on Russia, would not justify intervention by the United States against Japan.

(e) All possible aid short of actual war against Japan should be extended to the Chinese Central Government.

. . .                                    . . .                                    . . .

Specifically, they recommend:

That the dispatch of United States armed forces for intervention against Japan in China be disapproved.

That material aid to China be accelerated consonant with the needs of Russia, Great Britain, and our own forces.

That aid to the American Volunteer Group be continued and accelerated to the maximum practicable extent.

That no ultimatum be delivered to Japan. [12]


The President followed this traced line. On the 6th he told Stimson that he might propose a truce in which there would be no movement

[11] The thought was that any movement of this kind would be a plan to go into the Gulf of Siam, on the way to attack the Malay-Kra Peninsula. ———

[12] *Pearl Harbor Attack,* Part 14, pp. 1061–62.

of armed forces for six months, during which China and Japan might come to terms. Stimson wanted time also but objected to this means of getting it. The movement of forces to the Philippines, he thought, should not be halted. And the Chinese, in his opinion, should not be left alone with the Japanese; they would, he correctly forecast, balk at any such arrangement.[13] The President placed the idea of a truce aside, but not far.

On this next day, November 7, the President asked the cabinet for advice. All agreed with a statement made by Hull that the situation was extremely serious and that Japan might attack at any time. The position being maintained in the talks with Japan was approved; the current program for the extension of military forces in the Southwest Pacific area was endorsed; the cohesion between our own activities in that area and those of Britain, Australia, and the Indies was noted with satisfaction. Thus it was decided to "carry on," and to leave Japan to decide whether to turn about or attack. The President took a poll, asking whether the people would back the government up if it struck at Japan in case it attacked English or Dutch territories in the Pacific. All the cabinet was of the opinion that it would. It was agreed that speeches should be made to acquaint the country with the situation.[14]

In the evening after this cabinet meeting Nomura paid his first call on Hull since the advent of the Tojo Cabinet. Earnestly he presented Proposal A and asked a quick answer. Hull, after a rapid glance at the contents (which he already knew) indicated his attitude by observing what a wonderful chance Japan had to launch forth on a real new order which would gain it moral leadership in the Far East.

Nomura asked to talk to the President, and was received on the 10th. He had an invisible naval escort not of his own choosing. Not many hours before he entered the White House, his former colleague, Vice-Admiral Nagumo, on board the aircraft carrier, *Akagi,* issued Striking Force Operations Order, No. 1. All ships in this force were directed to complete battle preparations by November 20, and to assemble in Hito-kappu Bay, Etorofu Island, Kuriles. This was the force that was to attack Pearl Harbor.

Nomura did not know either the schedule or geography written in this order, one of many placing the Japanese Navy in location for war. But he knew that he was in a race with such orders, and that only some miracle of conversion could stop them. The smoke was over the funnels. Thus he pleaded for acceptance of what he came to offer on the

[13] Stimson diary, entry for November 6, 1941.
[14] *ibid.,* entry for November 7, and the written statement by Hull, *Pearl Harbor Attack,* Part 2, p. 429.

ground that Japan was doing all it could in the light of reason and of history. But his two American listeners were unmoved. Their books, open and secret, contained the record of Japan's desertion of the ways of peace and order.

The President met the plea by saying, in substance, that Japan should prove its intentions by actions, prove them by beginning to move its troops out of China and Indo-China.[15] This answer could hardly have surprised Nomura. For on the evening before the Postmaster General, Walker, had said to him, "I tell this only to you, swearing to God. Both our 'boss' and the Secretary of State have received an authentic report that Japan has decided a policy of taking action." [16] Nomura had not contradicted.

Proposal A thus died; it was, in truth, dead before it was delivered.

The speeches meant to awaken the American people to the crisis were delivered (on November 11) by Secretary of the Navy Knox and Welles. But at the same time a last, harried effort was begun to find some way to keep war from coming. Kurusu was on his way; and with his arrival, it was known, the last act would begin, the act that would end with peace or war.

The buzzer brought alongside Hull's desk officers of the Department rarely consulted about the Far Eastern crisis. Ideas, forms, and formulas were solicited from technicians, drafters of trade treaties. The Secretary was seeking some feasible offer of economic reward which might offset the Japanese sense of being driven into war in order to live decently. A statement by Togo to Grew had made an impression: that if Japan were forced to give up suddenly all the fruits of the long war in China, collapse would follow.[17]

A belated try was begun to prove that Japan could gain more by peaceful world-wide trading and financial arrangements than by force. But the search produced little new. What promises of special aid or opportunity could the United States, speaking for itself alone, make without infringing on principle? Not enough to wean Japan away from its dreams of great empire.

[15] Hull's memorandum of this important talk is printed in *Foreign Relations: Japan*, II, 715-19.
[16] Nomura manuscript (*op. cit.*), entry for November 9, 1941. The Ambassador transmitted a report of this talk with Walker to Tokyo on the 10th.
[17] Grew's report of this talk is printed in *Foreign Relations: Japan*, II, 710-14. Togo also repeated that economic pressure of the sort to which Japan was subject might menace its national existence more than force, and might cause Japan to resort to force. Nomura, reading from a manuscript, made the same statements to the President and Hull the same day. *ibid.*, II, 717.

The formal answer which Hull gave Nomura to Proposal A asked the same questions and posed the same tests as before. Would Japan agree to regard the Tripartite Pact as a dead letter? Would it prove its peaceful intentions in regard to China? Hull followed this answer by a suggestion meant to illuminate the other route by which Japan could prosper. The two governments, he proposed, might make a joint declaration on economic policy. Of such he submitted a text. But it smelled of the study lamp, and was hitched to the future rather than the crisis. Japan was to retain no vestige of privileged economic place in China.[18]

On the day before (November 14) the State Department had sent the delayed answer to Chiang Kai-shek's call for help. This sought to be calming. Despite Churchill's support, Chiang's request that the American government serve Japan with urgent warning (implying that the United States would go to war if the warning went unheeded) was passed by.[19]

The intercepted messages, now more numerous than ever, gave an almost daylight picture of the mind of the Japanese government. The cabinet was chafing at the passage of time. Nomura was trying to dissuade it from a swift plunge into war. He warned that the war would be long, and small victories would not count. Then he added: "In spite of the fact that it is my understanding that the people and officials, too, are tightening their belts, I am going to pass on to you my opinion, even though I know I will be harshly criticized for it. I feel that should the situation in Japan permit, I would like to caution patience for one or two months in order to get a clear view of the world situation. This, I believe, would be the best plan."[20]

The answer was read in Washington a few days later, as Nomura and Kurusu were presenting Proposal B (for a *modus vivendi*—a way of getting along for a while longer): "I am awfully sorry to say that the situation renders this out of the question. The deadline for the solution

[18] The reader will find Hull's memo of this talk of November 15 and the text of the joint declaration, *ibid.*, II, 731-37.
[19] Churchill had cabled the President that "what we need now is a deterrent of the most general and formidable character." The joint embargo, he observed, was steadily forcing Japan to decide between peace and war, and he urged the President to warn Japan not to attack Yunnan. On the 9th, the President had answered that he doubted whether the attack on Yunnan was imminent. After citing the current support being given to China and current efforts to strengthen the Philippines, he said he thought a new formalized verbal warning or remonstrance might have at least an even chance of producing the opposite effect.
[20] Telegram, No. 1090, Nomura to Togo, November 14, 1941.

of these negotiations is set . . . and there will be no change. Please try to understand that. You see how short the time is; therefore do not allow the United States to sidetrack us and delay the negotiations any further." [21]

Kurusu had arrived.[22] The British, Dutch, and Chinese governments asked more bluntly for news. The President went on with plans to visit Warm Springs, but there was a gleam of excitement in his manner. Now in this time of last answers, he left the management of the situation to Hull, relying on the guidance and protection of that subtle adviser. The Secretary of State wanted peace not war, but a firm peace based on law and justice as he saw them, not a scraggly, bought peace. Over and over he reviewed the situation with men who were beginning to feel that they had passed their whole lives in his office. No matter how often the wheel of thought went around, it always made the same circle. For by then it was welded to ideas and relationships that could not be changed without great trouble.

[21] Army 24878, CA Urgent, November 16, 1941, Togo to Nomura.
[22] Nomura had asked for professional diplomatic assistance as early as August 4 when he cabled the Japanese Foreign Office: "I deeply fear that I should make a miscalculation at this point and besides there is a limit to my ability. I therefore earnestly ask you to send at earliest convenience some senior in the diplomatic service who is well versed in affairs in and out of Japan (for example Ambassador Kurusu) to co-operate with me. I am unable to perceive the delicate shades of the policy of the government and am quite at a loss what to do." *Far East Mil. Trib.*, Exh. No. 2921.

## CHAPTER 39

# Japan's Final Proposal for a Truce
# Is Weighed and Found Wanting

KURUSU arrived in Washington. A clipper brought him, and his flight across the Pacific was watched as though he were a bird whose coming could bring fair weather or foul. But the government knew that he was only a trained expositor of matters already decided.

Hull on the 17th introduced him to the President. The ensuing talk was only a snarled survey of the area of dissension. The President did not sprinkle his words with geniality, as he usually had with Nomura. There was no liking either for the man or for his mission. As for the man, Hull spoke for both when he wrote: "Kurusu seemed to me the antithesis of Nomura. Neither his appearance nor his attitude commanded confidence or respect. I felt from the start that he was deceitful." [1] As for the mission, that was unpromising, even if not false. His purpose, looked at in the best light, was to persuade the American government to accept the latest Japanese terms in preference to war. Looked at in the worst light, it was to engage American interest while the assault plans were being secretly completed. Just before the meeting, another cable of warning had been received from Grew. Be on guard, he said, against sudden naval and military actions, for Japan would probably exploit every possible tactical advantage, such as surprise and initiative.

On the next day, the 18th, the talk took an unmapped turn. Nomura, speaking as though the idea were his own, asked whether it might not be possible to arrange a type of accord other than that over which the two governments were now so completely at odds. Perhaps, he suggested, a partial agreement which would at least avert immediate trouble. His thought, he said, was that the two governments might restore the situation as it was before July, when Japan moved into Southern Indo-China, and the United States and Britain imposed their embargo. [2]

Hull, up to that point had been ungiving. But here was a chance, at

---

[1] Hull, *op. cit.*, II, 1062.
[2] It is possible that the idea which had been in both Roosevelt's and Hull's mind was passed on to the Japanese by Postmaster General Walker.

least, to gain time. Time that would fit us (and our associates) better for war. Time that might enable the Japanese government to persuade the Army to yield more, and the people to accept the thought of retreat. As broached, it was only an idea, incomplete and without authority. Hull said just enough to show he was attracted, no more. He asked Nomura whether, if such an arrangement were made, the talks would continue. Nomura said they would. Hull then observed that he could see how this step might enable the Japanese leaders to hold their position and to organize public opinion in favor of a peaceful course. Therefore he would acquaint the British and Dutch governments with the suggestion and see what they thought.

Nomura and Kurusu stood on tiptoe in the effort to put this idea across. That night (November 18) they hurried off message after message to Tokyo.[3] Togo, the Foreign Minister, had sent them some days before the text of Proposal B—terms for a truce to be offered as a last resort. But its rejection was foreseen by them.[4] The two Japanese diplomats were trying to prevent the final crash by proffering easier and simpler truce terms.

As soon as the Japanese had left, Hull asked Sir Ronald Campbell, British Chargé d'Affaires, to call. He told Campbell of the status of the talks and of the idea of a partial arrangement to allow the Japanese government to direct public opinion. On the next morning he spoke to the Chinese Ambassador and the Australian and Dutch Ministers in the same sense and with a certain show of eagerness.

But "Magic" brought the news that the notions of the two Ambassadors had been rejected in Tokyo. The Foreign Minister frowned on their flow of advice that Japan should accept a loose "give and take" truce rather than a long drawn-out war.[5] They were told that the Japanese government could not agree to withdraw from Indo-China, merely in return for relaxation of trade controls; that it was afraid that the American government would soon bring up other and further conditions. They were ordered to present at once the whole of Proposal B, as stencilled by the Imperial Conference on November 5.[6]

Another snatched message sent on the same date conveyed the fact

---

[3] The texts of these telegrams, Nos. 1131, 1133, and 1134, from Washington to Tokyo, are printed in *Pearl Harbor Attack*, Part 12, pp. 146–52. Nomura sought to make sure that these messages would reach the Prime Minister. Nomura manuscript (*op. cit.*).

[4] Nomura said as much in Telegram No. 1134.

[5] Telegram No. 1136 of November 19, 1941, Nomura to Togo, *Pearl Harbor Attack*, Part 12, p. 158.

[6] Telegrams Nos. 798 and 799 of November 19, 1941, Togo to Nomura and Kurusu, *ibid.*, Part 12, p. 155.

that a new code was being sent to Nomura. Signals would be given in the daily Japanese language short-wave newscasts. Comments upon the direction of the wind would inform whether diplomatic relations were about to be broken with the United States, Great Britain, or Russia, or all of them. Thereafter, American listeners were posted to catch the signals.

Nomura placed Proposal B before Hull on November 20. The English text, as cabled some days before, had been intercepted and read. Hull knew that it was regarded in Tokyo as the last bargain; the hinge on the breech of the cannon.

There were five numbered points on the white piece of paper which Nomura gave to Hull. They have been printed in many other places, but I think the reader will want them before him as he follows the narrative:

"1. Both the Government of Japan and the United States undertake not to make any armed advancement into any of the regions in the South-eastern Asia and the Southern Pacific area excepting the part of French Indo-China where the Japanese troops are stationed at present.

"2. The Japanese Government undertakes to withdraw its troops now stationed in French Indo-China upon either the restoration of peace between Japan and China or the establishment of an equitable peace in the Pacific area.

"In the meantime the Government of Japan declares that it is prepared to remove its troops now stationed in the southern part of French Indo-China to the northern part of the said terirtory upon the conclusion of the present arrangement which shall later be embodied in the final agreement.

"3. The Government of Japan and the United States shall cooperate with a view to securing the acquisition of those goods and commodities which the two countries need in Netherlands East Indies.

"4. The Government of Japan and the United States mutually undertake to restore their commercial relations to those prevailing prior to the freezing of the assets.

"The Government of the United States shall supply Japan a required quantity of oil.

"5. The Government of the United States undertakes to refrain from such measures and actions as will be prejudicial to the endeavors for the restoration of general peace between Japan and China." [7]

Whoever insisted on the last paragraph—Tojo and the Army certainly did—insisted on war.

Hull glanced over the text to make sure it was the same as that which

[7] *Foreign Relations: Japan*, II, 755-56.

was known. It was. Then, on two points in particular he spoke out. Linking Japan's treatment of China to Hitler's actions, he defended our aid to China. Kurusu remarked that perhaps this point (No. 5) in the Japanese terms might be construed to mean that the United States would end its help only at the time when talks between Japan and China would have started. Hull also dwelt on the fact that this truce would leave Japan a full member of the Axis pact, and hence still a potential enemy of the United States and Great Britain. To this Kurusu had no answer.[8]

Hull found no dissent, either within the State Department or at the White House, to his opinion that the proposal was "clearly unacceptable." His reasons for finding it so are summed up again in his "Memoirs":

"The commitments we should have to make were virtually a surrender. We on our part should have to supply Japan as much oil as she might require, suspend our freezing measures, and resume full commercial relations with Tokyo. We should have to discontinue aid to China and withdraw our moral and material support from the recognized Chinese Government of Chiang Kai-shek. We should have to help Japan obtain products of the Netherlands East Indies. We should have to cease augmenting our military forces in the western Pacific.

"Japan, on her part, would still be free to continue her military operations in China, to attack the Soviet Union, and to keep her troops in northern Indo-China until peace was effected with China. . . . Japan thus clung to her vantage point in Indo-China which threatened countries to the south and vital trade routes.

"The President and I could only conclude that agreeing to these proposals would mean condonement by the United States of Japan's past aggressions, assent to future courses of conquest by Japan, abandonment of the most essential principles of our foreign policy, betrayal of China and Russia, and acceptance of the role of silent partner aiding and abetting Japan in her effort to create a Japanese hegemony over the western Pacific and eastern Asia."[9]

Inspection of such Japanese records as I have seen leaves room for doubt about some features of this judgment. It is not certain that the meaning which Hull attached to some of the points in Proposal B is the necessary meaning; or that his total estimate of the Japanese offer to begin to retreat was just. Perhaps so, probably so, but not surely so.

---

[8] *ibid.*, II, 753–55.
[9] Hull, *op. cit.*, II, 1069–70.

It would be a barren exercise, I think, now to re-examine, feature by feature, the face and soul of this last Japanese formula for peace. The result would be inconclusive; for even its authors were divided and mixed up in their intentions. And even a less suspicious reading would have, I think, led to the same rejection. For the situation had grown too immense and entangled for haggling. Japan had forced the creation of a defensive coalition more vast than the empire of the Pacific for which it plotted. This was not now to be quieted by a temporary halt along the fringe of the Japanese advance.

Acceptance of this Japanese proposal would have imperilled the trustful unity of the coalition. As the next few days were to show, China would have felt itself deserted, if not betrayed. Elsewhere the will to carry on the fight against Germany without pause or compromise might have been corrupted. The Japanese Army and Navy would have been left in place to take advantage of any future weakness.

Even—to carry conjecture further—if the American government had taken these risks and entered into this accord, there would have been war in the Pacific. For it seems to me almost certain that the truce would have broken down as soon as signed. Quarrels would have started over the military movements in which both sides were engaged. Japan would not have ceased its preparations for attack. Nor can it be thought that we or the British would have ended the movement of planes and ships and anti-aircraft and radar to the Philippines and Malaya. Each side would have thought the other to be taking crooked advantage of the truce.

If these disputes did not bring the truce to a quick end, arguments over oil would have done so. Very different notions existed in Tokyo and Washington as to what was expected under the phrase "a required quantity of oil." The Japanese government had told Nomura to let us know before signing how much it had in mind. It wanted four million tons a year from the United States, and one million tons a year from the Indies.[10] The American government would not have agreed to supply anything like such quantities, which were enough to keep Japanese reserves intact.

In sum, the paper given by Nomura to Hull on November 20 would have marked only the start of new disputes, not the end of old ones.

[10] One million according to the intercepted telegram from Togo to Nomura, No. 833, sent from Tokyo on November 26. These figures were, the Foreign Minister said, to be taken as the basis of negotiation and were not the absolute minimum. *Pearl Harbor Attack*, Part 12, p. 177. Other Japanese documents put the amount to be asked of the Indies at two million tons. *Far East Mil. Trib.*, Exh. No. 2944.

## [2]

War might be in the secret messages; it might be in the nerves; but the wish to avoid it was still alive. Hull began to compound a counter-offer to Proposal B which might defer the climax without giving Japan an advantage, or destroying the faith of our allies. The drafting squad ransacked the files for old memoranda, and drew upon a refreshingly new one from the Treasury.

The President sent across to the State Department his ideas of the terms on which a simple stay might be arranged. These were: some oil and rice for Japan at once, and more later; an introduction of the Japanese and Chinese governments, so that the two could talk the situation over in a friendly fashion without American participation. Japan, in return, was to promise not to send any more troops south or north and to agree not to invoke the Tripartite Pact, even if the United States got into the European war.[11]

Hull was afraid both of being tricked and of being misunderstood. Therefore he resorted to a form of response that might have provided useful protection if a truce had been effected, but which surely would have prevented one. Along with the counterproposal for a *modus vivendi* Japan was to be asked to subscribe to a statement of principles to be observed by both countries thereafter.

Tentative drafts of these two papers were, by the 22nd, ready for submission to other governments. Hull called to his office the emissaries of Great Britain, Australia, the Netherlands, and China. He explained to them that the heads of the Army and Navy were beseeching him to postpone the crisis, if he could, to gain some more time. He showed the visitors copies of the drafts, from which they took notes. Casey spoke out incisively, saying that he felt that the wish of the military was enough to command. The others said little. But Hull had the sense that all except the Chinese Ambassador fell in with his thought. He asked whether under the accord Japan would be obligated not to extend its invasion into China. Hull answered that it would not. The diplomats left to report to their governments.

Later that day Hull talked with Nomura and Kurusu in an attempt to find out whether they held any further concessions in reserve. They

[11] These suggestions were contained in a personal, undated memorandum given by the President to the Secretary of State. According to a note appended in the State Department, this was written "shortly after November 20, 1941." But it may have been written earlier.

had none. The news drawn from the caught cables and elsewhere did not encourage the opinion that it was any use to stretch our principles. Large Japanese forces were moving into their bases in Southern Indo-China, and Japanese transports were gathering at the point in the Japanese mandated islands nearest the Indies. A "Magic" cable sent from Tokyo on the 22nd (Tokyo time) informed Nomura that it was awfully hard for the Japanese government to consider a change in the deadline for the American reply, "for reasons beyond your ability to guess." But, the message continued, "if you can bring about the sign-ing of the pertinent notes we will wait until November 29." "After that," the "Magic" cable read, "things are automatically going to happen." [12]

Another message sent out on the same day by Admiral Yamamoto, the Commander in Chief of the Combined Fleet, to the Task Force in the Kuriles, was not intercepted. It began:

"The Task Force will move out from Hitokappu Wan on 26 Novem-ber and proceed without being detected to Rendezvous set for December 3.

"X-day will be December 8."

Over the weekend the drafts of the two texts were retouched, and agreement with the Army and Navy confirmed. The military men strongly favored the effort to buy time. But since they esteemed it as a chance to make the Pacific outposts stronger, they wanted a truce which would not immobilize them.[13] On this point they were satisfied.

Then on Monday, the 24th, the diplomats of the ABCD powers were consulted again. Hull made a vigorous exposition of the benefits to all of committing Japan to a peaceful course for three months. He sensed apathy in their comment. "They seemed to be very much gratified," he noted after the meeting was over, "[but] they seemed to be think-

---

[12] Telegram No. 812, Togo to Nomura, November 22, 1941.

[13] Memorandum of General Gerow, Acting Assistant Chief of Staff, November 21, 1941. *Pearl Harbor Attack,* Part 14, p. 1103. Admiral Stark was willing, if necessary, to agree not to increase American combatant naval and military forces in the Philippines. Memo-randum of the same date to Secretary Hull, *ibid.,* Part 14, p. 1104.

The program for the air reinforcement of the Philippines (as summarized in a memo prepared by the Assistant Chief of Staff on November 28 for Stimson and Marshall) was:

B-17s in the Philippines, 35; scheduled to arrive by Jan. 1, 1942, 48 more
P-40s in the Philippines, 81; scheduled to arrive by Jan. 1, 1942, 101 more
A-24s (dive bombers), 52 en route, due to arrive by Dec. 25.

The program was delayed because deliveries from factories were behind schedule and because of adverse winds to Hawaii, which postponed flight of the squadrons.

ing of the advantages to be derived without any particular thought of what we should pay for them, if anything." The Dutch Ambassador reported that his government would support the truce. None of the others had as yet heard from home. Aggrieved at having to worry through this miserable decision with so little aid, Hull said to them: ". . . each of their Governments was more interested in the defense of that area of the world than this country, and at the same time they expected this country, in case of a Japanese outbreak, to be ready to move in a military way and take the lead in defending the entire area." [14] In mind were the urgent current pleas of the British and Dutch military representatives in Singapore and Batavia for full agreement on combined military action if Japan moved south.

The intercepts, which Hull could not mention, made clear that time left for talk was all but gone. He merely said, on parting from the diplomats, that he did not know whether or not he would present the text discussed without knowing the views of their governments.

That evening the President, at Hull's initiative, sent a message to Churchill, outlining the terms of the offer in mind. In return primarily for a Japanese promise not to advance north or south, the American and other governments were to permit Japan to obtain a monthly quota of oil for civilian needs, and limited amounts of foodstuffs, drugs, cotton, ship bunkers and supplies. "I am not very hopeful," the message ended, "and we must be prepared for real trouble, possibly soon." This last sentence was added by the President himself to the draft which Hull had submitted.

At noon the next day (the 25th) Hull, Stimson, and Knox went to the White House where they were joined by Stark and Marshall. The talk seems to have been more concerned with what to do when and as Japan attacked than with the patchwork truce. The President, according to Stimson's notes, "brought up the event that we were likely to be attacked perhaps (as soon as) next Monday [December 1], for the Japanese are notorious for making an attack without warning, and the question was what we should do. The question was how we should maneuver them into the position of firing the first shot without allowing too much danger to ourselves." [15] The Secretary's language was, I think, hurried and elliptic. The Japanese force was the attacking force. If left to choose the place and time for the first encounter, the defense might suffer. But if any of the defenders fired the first shot, they might

---

[14] Hull's memorandum of this meeting is printed, *ibid.*, Part 14, pp. 1143-46.
[15] Stimson diary, entry for November 25, 1941.

be regarded as attackers. The problem of keeping the roles straight—without paying heavily for it—was far from easy.

After this meeting the members of the War Council returned to their offices. Stark and Marshall were disturbed by the rate at which the situation seemed to be heading to a showdown.[16] They resumed work upon a joint memorandum to the President which was already well started.

Stimson found further news waiting for him. The Japanese were embarking a large force—from thirty to fifty ships—at Shanghai and the first elements of this expedition had been sighted proceeding south of Formosa along the Chinese coast. This news he telephoned to the President and Hull. Then he met again with Marshall and Stark. He was concerned lest the paper which Stark and Marshall were finishing should be construed by the President as a recommendation to reopen the talks with Japan on a basis of compromise. They assured him it was not to be so understood. Warnings to be sent to our commanders in the Pacific were also drafted.

Hull returned from the White House to a schedule of appointments. Halifax brought an unhelpful message from Eden. This stated that the British government, having complete confidence in Mr. Hull's handling of the negotiations, would support him if he felt it best to put forward a counterproposal. But he added that in his, Eden's, view, ". . . our demands should be pitched high and our price low." The Japanese government, the message went on, should be asked to withdraw all its armed force from Indo-China, and to promise to suspend further military advances in China. It also expressed doubt about the resumption of any oil shipments.[17] Hull briefly reviewed with Halifax the advantages of a truce, but did not say what he would do.

Loudon, the Dutch Minister, came next. He again reported his government to be in favor of the truce proposal, but was of the opinion that the quantities of oil to be delivered should be limited, so that Japan's war potential would not be increased.[18]

The Chinese Ambassador, Hu Shih, was waiting. He had anxious complaints from Chiang Kai-shek.[19] In essence, the Generalissimo said that he had the impression that the American government had put China to one side and was inclined to appease Japan at its expense. He was afraid that if the economic blockade was relaxed, the morale of the

[16] *Pearl Harbor Attack*, Part 5, p. 2316.
[17] The texts of this message and of this talk between Hull and Halifax are printed, *ibid.*, Part 14, pp. 1162, *et seq.*
[18] *ibid.*, Part 4, p. 1692.
[19] *ibid.*, Part 14, pp. 1167, *et seq.*

Chinese troops would be sorely shaken, and the spirit of resistance of both people and Army might collapse. Chiang Kai-shek took pains to see that this message got to the President and friends in the cabinet quickly and undiluted. He sent an even stronger version to T. V. Soong, his brother-in-law (who was in Washington), for transmission to Knox and Stimson.[20] Owen Lattimore, an American appointed by Chiang Kai-shek to be his political adviser, cabled Lauchlin Currie, one of the President's secretaries, asking him urgently to inform the President of the Generalissimo's very strong reaction.[21]

A few months before, the Chinese government had shown itself similarly adverse and frightened. Alarmed by reports of a deal whereby, in return for Japanese promises in regard to the rest of the Pacific area, the United States would resume shipments of oil and scrap iron, it had protested. Hull on September 4 had sent assurances that the American government would not enter any arrangement that would allow aggression in China to continue. Further, he said that it would not alter or end the measures taken to impede Japan unless Japan altered the situations which had caused the United States to resort to them. The Chinese Foreign Minister had then half apologized for his anxieties. His way of doing so had been to tell a Confucian anecdote, of the mother at the spinning wheel, who, because of faith in her son, ignored the first two reports that he had committed a murder, but rose to investigate when a third neighbor brought the same story. The episode showed, whether realized or not, that the policy of the United States was almost as closely linked to the fate of China as to that of Britain. Both had been encouraged to spend themselves. How, then, could the United States, unless they freely concurred, treat with their enemy?

Now, in this crisis, Chinese trust faltered again. Chiang's messages seemed to both the President and Hull foolishly excited and unjust. Was not American fidelity amply proved? Hull explained to the Chinese Ambassador, Hu Shih, how all the opponents of Japan would gain by a truce; how China would be relieved by the retirement of Japanese troops from Indo-China, which he intended to ask; how even, perhaps, the war from which China was suffering so much could be brought to a good end. His exasperation found words before the call ended. The American government, he remarked, could, of course, cancel the proposal; but if it did so it was "not to be charged with failure to send our

[20] *ibid.*, Part 2, p. 774.
[21] *ibid.*

fleet into the area near Indochina and into Japanese waters, if by any chance Japan makes a military drive southward." [22]

It was dark outside by the time Hu Shih left. Still Hull called together again the members of his staff who had shared with him the long and failing effort to convince or outwit Japan. Those present at this late afternoon session recall several interrupting telephone calls from outside. The identity of the talkers on the other end of the wire is no longer remembered; perhaps the President called, perhaps some reporter of further news of Japanese military movements. But they caused a further ebb in the belief that it was worth-while to proceed with the idea of a truce.

The group separated for a hurried half-eaten dinner, then met again at Hull's apartment in the Wardman Park. All agreed that the meager American offer would only be for the record; that Japan would not accept it or any tolerable variant of it. Time and again, as Hull knew, the Japanese envoys had been told that the proposal made to the United States was Japan's last word. [23] The gesture, therefore, would not prevent or delay the Japanese southward invasion.

The very making of the offer seemed likely to have troublesome, if not ruinous, effects. It would be self-defeating to give a true and full explanation to the American people. A confused domestic debate was apt to follow and be in full flow when the war crisis came. More worrisome still was the prospect that, despite whatever was said, the other nations fighting the Axis would feel let down. There was no time to convince Chiang Kai-shek that China would not suffer and would not be deserted. [24] The other members of the coalition were showing themselves lukewarm—not opposing the truce, but not welcoming it. Was it, as Hull averred, only a maneuver, or was it a wavering in the ranks?

Sometime during the night of the 25th, Churchill's answer to the President arrived. [25] It left the American government free to do what it

[22] The texts of the telegram which the Chinese Ambassador showed Hull, and of Hull's memorandum of this conversation are printed *ibid.*, Part 14, pp. 1167, *et seq.*

[23] An intercepted cable sent only the day before by the Japanese Foreign Minister to Nomura and Kurusu had reiterated that Japan could make no further concessions from Proposal B *in toto*. Telegram, Togo to Nomura, No. 821, of November 24, *Pearl Harbor Attack*, Part 12, p. 172.

[24] The intercepted message, No. 821, from Togo to Nomura on the 24th read in part: ". . . our demand for a cessation of aid to Chiang . . . is a most essential condition." *loc. cit.*

[25] There is a conflict of report as to when this cable or its substance was known to the

thought best, but seemed to fall in with the view that a truce with Japan was unfair to China. Doubt seemed to overrule enthusiasm.[25a] The text is given so that the reader may judge for himself:

MOST SECRET FOR THE PRESIDENT FROM THE FORMER NAVAL PERSON. "Your message about Japan received tonight. Also full accounts from Lord Halifax of discussions and your counter project to Japan on which Foreign Secretary has sent some comments. Of course, it is for you to handle this business and we certainly do not want an additional war. There is only one point that disquiets us. What about Chiang Kai Shek? Is he not having a very thin diet? Our anxiety is about China. If they collapse our joint dangers would enormously encrease. We are sure that the regard of the United States for the Chinese cause will govern your action. We feel that the Japanese are most unsure of themselves." [26]

Hull, in the course of the night, added up the sum of pros and cons. The reason for going ahead with the counterproposal had come to seem unreal. What we had to offer, it was all but certain, would not buy even time. The objections seemed many and hard to meet. He decided to discard it and let events take their course. The verdict was reached after tormenting uncertainty. But once reached, a calm sense followed that he had done all that a man could do.

One other happening of this day, November 25, might have been pertinent had our decision taken the other turn. Hull and Knox concurred in a recommendation of Admiral Land, Chairman of the Maritime Commission, that merchant vessels, under the American flag, be

---

President and Hull. According to the time stamps on the face of the original, it was sent from London at 6 a.m. on November 26, received by the code room of the State Department at 12:55 a.m., November 26, which is before the time of dispatch, allowance being made for five hours time difference. It also carries the notation that it was sent over to the White House at 9:05 a.m., on the 26th.

But two of the participants in the afternoon and evening meetings with Hull on the 25th have the remembered impression that either the cable or the substance of it was known to them then; they recall even Hull's comments that Churchill's message did not seem to agree entirely with Eden's. Despite the absence of any record, it is possible that the substance of this message was transmitted earlier in the day through the British Embassy in Washington or some other channel. Hull's reference to this point in his book (*op. cit.*, II, 1081) can be read either way, but suggests that Hull knew its contents on the night of the 25th.

[25a] In the minute that Churchill sent to Eden on November 23 he indicated favor towards the counterproposal being prepared by the State Department, provided the United States and Britain remained free to continue their aid to China. But on this point he found the draft which Hull submitted inadequate. Churchill, *The Grand Alliance*, pp. 595–96.

[26] *Pearl Harbor Attack*, Part 14, p. 1300.

sent to Archangel and Britain, hitherto forbidden zones.[27] They agreed that ships should be put on these routes gradually and when properly equipped.[28] There was to be, at all events, no letup in the program of resistance to Germany. The mind is left to wonder what would have happened had the truce been signed, and this extension of our aid to Britain and Russia been made.

[27] Congress had passed (November 7–14) amendments to the Neutrality Act which lifted the ban upon the entry of American vessels into these waters. The President had signed the amendments on November 17. This bill was passed in the face of German attacks on American merchant and naval vessels in the Western Atlantic (the U.S.S. *Kearny,* October 17; the U.S.S. *Reuben James,* October 31).

[28] Admiral Land made the suggestion to the White House on November 19. The President asked Hull and Knox on the 22nd to confer with Land about the matter and let him have a joint recommendation. On the 25th the three sent a memorandum to the President recommending that (1) ships under the American flag be sent to Archangel as soon as they are available; (2) ships under the American flag go to Great Britain as they become available, but that this be done gradually, beginning with only a small number.

The President also consulted Hopkins who wrote him on the 24th that he agreed with Admiral Land. Hopkins' memorandum was sent to Land on the 25th with the notation, "OK, F.D.R."

## CHAPTER 40

# As Stubborn as Ever; the American Answer, November 26, 1941

HULL wrote out what he proposed to say to the President: "In view of the opposition of the Chinese Government and either the half-hearted support or the actual opposition of the British, the Netherlands and the Australian Governments, and in view of the wide publicity of the opposition and of the additional opposition that will naturally follow through utter lack of an understanding of the vast importance and value otherwise of the *modus vivendi,* without in any way departing from my views about the wisdom and the benefit of this step to all the countries opposed to the aggressor nations who are interested in the Pacific area, I desire very earnestly to recommend that at this time I call in the Japanese Ambassadors and hand to them a copy of the comprehensive basic proposal for a general peaceful settlement, and at the same time withhold the *modus vivendi* proposal." [1]

Early on the 26th he read this to the President, who quickly agreed. Both knew, it may be surmised, that the Japanese would have ignored the discarded sketch of a truce. For what was offered, they would not have recalled the expeditions then heading south and west.[2]

That afternoon at 5 o'clock Hull gave the Japanese Ambassadors his "comprehensive basic proposal." In this statement the American government had its full say. Described as "Strictly Confidential, Tentative and Without Commitment," it plotted out both present and future in the Far East. Only a student of dead detail, an ironist besides, would now read it through. Both memory and judgment will now, I think, be

[1] *Pearl Harbor Attack,* Part 14, p. 1176. Longer explanations of his thought were given in oral and written testimony before the Congressional Joint Committee on the Investigation of the Pearl Harbor Attack, *ibid.,* Part 2, p. 453; Part 11, pp. 5369–73, as well as in his *Memoirs.*

[2] A few details will suffice to establish that conclusion. Japan was called upon not to advance in any regions in which it had military forces; and not only to withdraw all forces from southern Indo-China but to reduce the total of the forces in all of Indo-China to the small numbers that were there on July 6. There was no promise to stop aid to China, or the flow of American and British weapons and troops into the Southwest Pacific. As for oil, it provided only a monthly allowance for "civilian needs" of low-grade products.

sufficiently served by a summary of the three main features.[3] Japan and the United States were mutually to promise to abide by the principles for which we had been standing right along. They were to sponsor a non-aggression pact among all countries concerned in the Far East which, in effect, would have been re-validation of the Nine-Power Treaty. Japan was to withdraw all military, naval, air, and police forces from China and Indo-China.

The system of political and social order proposed was in direct contrast to the dream that had driven Japan on. It conceived of a community of orderly and equal states, who would respect each other's independence and security, and treat and trade with one another on identical terms. The Japanese program conceived that Japan would be the stabilizing center of life throughout East Asia. All other countries of the region would be clustered about Japan. It would be the roof of the temple; they the pillars. It would be the organizer; they the followers. It would be the lawgiver; they the grateful recipients. Here in this document there was a denial of all that Japan had set out to do by stratagem or by force.

But there seems to me no warrant for making it an ultimatum—either in the political or the military sense.[4] Japan was left with four choices: to assent to the American proposal and reverse its policy; to abstain from any further armed advance north or south, but to continue the war in China as best it could; to begin its retreat and see what return for doing so might be had from China, the United States, and Great Britain; or to carry through its bid for victory to the end. It chose the last.

The American officials who knew of our answer had little doubt that it would. Their thoughts switched further from the tactics of negotiations to the tactics of war. On the next day (the 27th) Hull told Stimson, "I have washed my hands of it, and it [the situation] is now in the hands of you and Knox, the Army and Navy."

[3] It is printed in *Foreign Relations: Japan*, II, 768–70.

[4] The Japanese Government called it that. The Foreign Minister, Togo, in his defense deposition, *Far East Mil. Trib.*, Exh. No. 3646, tells of the views expressed at the Liaison Conference of November 27: "The reaction of all of us to it [Hull's note] was, I think, the same. Ignoring all past progress and areas of agreement in the negotiations, the United States had served upon us what we viewed as an ultimatum containing demands far in excess of the strongest positions theretofore taken."

Charles A. Beard, *President Roosevelt and the Coming of the War*, pp. 235–36, avoids the name but not the substance, describing the note as a proposal for "a sweeping withdrawal from China under a veiled threat of war and under the pressure of economic sanctions likely to lead to war." More justly he describes it a few pages later (p. 238) as "the maximum terms of an American policy for the whole Orient."

Stimson had no regrets or misgivings.[5] Knox and Stark came that morning to his office. General Marshall was out of town and General Gerow was again acting in his stead. There were two crucial matters to be decided. What action should the American government take in the face of threatened Japanese assault? What further warnings should be sent to the commanders of our forces in the Far East?

The Army and Navy had for weeks past been trying to extract a conclusive answer to the first question from the President, the Commander in Chief.[6] There was a war plan, "Rainbow No. 5," which had been prepared for the contingency that now was in sight. But there was no enacting decision or agreement to put it into force. It had been shaped in conference with the British and Dutch authorities, and was based on the conception that if war came all would be in it together. The British and Dutch governments had made a score of attempts to obtain assurances that in the event of attack upon their territories (or Japanese entry into Thailand) the United States would join in the defense. But the American government had just as persistently refused to give any explicit promise to that effect.

Admiral Hart, Commander of the United States Asiatic Fleet, to which it was expected the first call for action would come, had been authorized to talk the situation out.[7] The British military commanders in the Far East (under Admiral Phillips) were echoing Churchill's plea for firm assurances, and again urging that the United States join in a warning to Japan that a new transgression would mean war. The American naval men had said that they could not agree to this, but that they would take the matter up with the President and make a recommendation.[8]

Stark and Marshall had been trying to frame an answer to Hart. This was the prompting reason for the paper on which they had been at work,

[5] Stimson diary, entry for November 27, 1941.
[6] Admiral Stark, when asked by Senator Ferguson in the course of the Pearl Harbor Investigation if he had tried to find out what we would do in case of an attack on the British possessions, replied that he had put the question more than once but the President had said he could not answer it. "Just that he did not know; at least he said that he could not answer it. At one time I believe he said to me, 'Don't ask me these questions,' because . . . I felt that he could not answer them." *Pearl Harbor Attack,* Part 5, p. 2332.
[7] All previous attempts, going as far back as October 1940, had failed to arrive at any agreement. A proposal brought to Argentia by the British had been turned down by Marshall and Stark. On November 21 the whole subject had been reviewed by Admiral Ghormley in London with the British Admiralty, as a result of which new instructions had been sent by Stark to Hart.
[8] Testimony of Admiral Richmond Kelly Turner, War Plans Officer for the Chief of Naval Operations, *ibid.,* Part 4, pp. 2048-49.

and which they had held back pending the outcome of the last diplomatic turn. Now the decision could no longer be put off. It was November 27; and the Japanese warships and troop transports were just around the bend, headed for no one knew where. Were the American ships and planes in the neighborhood to wait till they landed? Were they to wait even longer if territories under the American flag were left alone?

Stark and Marshall tendered their advice to the President in a memorandum sent to him that day (the 27th).[9] The phrasing of one paragraph was a leftover from earlier drafts. "The most essential thing now, from the United States viewpoint," it read, "is to gain time." Therefore, "precipitance of military action on our part should be avoided so long as consistent with national policy." Stimson received assurance that the authors did not mean by this statement to urge a reopening of the talks.[10]

The line laid down was definite and conformed essentially to that which had been drawn in the conferences held in Singapore in the spring of the year.

"It is recommended that:

prior to the completion of the Philippine reinforcement, military counteraction be considered only if Japan attacks or directly threatens United States, British, or Dutch territory as above outlined:

in case of a Japanese advance into Thailand, Japan be warned by the United States, the British, and the Dutch governments that advance beyond the lines indicated may lead to war;

prior to such warning no joint military opposition be undertaken; steps be taken at once to consummate agreements with the British and Dutch for the issuance of such warning." [11]

[9] It was, in fact, except for some small changes, completed the day before. Marshall signed it on the 26th, before he left Washington, or on the 28th after his return. The text is printed, *ibid.*, Part 14, p. 1083.

[10] Stimson talked this question over with Knox, Stark, and General Gerow (in Marshall's absence) on the morning of the 27th—in all probability before the memo was sent to the President.

[11] Admiral Hart (on October 27) had recommended to Stark that the Asiatic fleet be retained in the Philippine Islands area. But Stark thought it unwise to do so because of inadequate air forces and antiaircraft defenses for such a base and the danger that superior Japanese forces could cut off the American naval forces from the British and Dutch forces in the south. Thereupon Hart proceeded with plans to establish a task force of cruisers and destroyers under Admiral Glassford to be deployed southward on the receipt of war warnings, or in the event of a Japanese attack. But it was decided (November 20-26) in agreement with the British to include Luzon (along with Malaya, Singapore, and Java) among the positions to be defended against Japanese attack.

Stimson and Knox agreed with these conclusions, and Stimson tried at once to get the President to rule upon them. But he would not, still keeping clear of any open promise to go to war, or joint warning which would be the equivalent. The problem of arranging for coordinated action was again passed back to the local commanders in the Asiatic region. The idea was that they should arrive at an "executory supplement" to "Rainbow No. 5." They were so engaged when the war started.

Whether or not the American forces would have gone into action right away if American territories had not been attacked remains a matter of conjecture. But it seems most probable that, at the point and hour where the danger flared high and clearly, the President would have followed the advice that his two senior military advisers gave on November 27. It may be guessed with confidence that he thought (1) that if the Philippines (or Guam, or Hawaii) were attacked the question would settle itself; (2) that if they were left alone the best tactic to be pursued was similar to that being followed in the Atlantic—a gradual movement of the American naval and air forces into combined action with the British, Dutch, and Australians. The Asiatic fleet would almost certainly have become engaged at once in the defense of the Malay Barrier.

On that same day (November 27), also, the war warnings that failed to protect were dispatched. Stimson proposed and the President approved the transmission to MacArthur and other field commanders of the "final alert," informing them of the situation and telling them to be on the "qui vive for any attack." [12] These were sent off—the message to Admiral Kimmel at Pearl Harbor beginning, "This dispatch is to be considered a war warning." [13]

The American people were vaguely aware that talks with Japan had come to a lingering end. But they were not clearly told that we might very soon be at war with Japan. Whatever else Japan might do, they did not expect it to attack territory under the American flag; and, short of that, they thought only of supporting operations, as in the Atlantic. Even those men who walked the corridors of the State, War, and Navy Buildings did not truly feel the great change that lay ahead.

Up to then we had been managers of the war, riders of the storm. Now we were soon to become part of it, of its flame and fire. We were

[12] Stimson diary, entry for November 27, 1941.
[13] *Pearl Harbor Attack*, Part 5, pp. 2124-25.

going soon to land men on the bare coral ledges in the vast Pacific, on the African beaches, on the shores of Italy, and where the Atlantic rolled over the Normandy sands. The faces of the Japanese soldiers were going to be closer to many Americans than the image of home. That was, within a few days, to be decided in Tokyo.

## CHAPTER 41

# The Last Arrangements and Formalities for War

THERE, the resolution approved at the Imperial Conference on November 5 dictated the future. It had followed a pattern set by earlier use; a pattern cut to suit divided authority. Time and again since 1931 the more aggressive elements in Japan, especially the Army, had set a mark. Having done so, they allowed diplomacy a short time to reach this mark by persuasion, guile, or threat. Meanwhile the armed forces got ready to act if diplomacy failed. The advances into China and Indo-China had been arranged that way. Once again the Army had agreed to give diplomacy a last chance. A brief and bound chance.

The talkers had been allowed the days that were left in the month of November. They had ticked away like a hidden bomb. Scores of messages were exchanged between the Japanese government and its Embassy in Washington. But they were all one in meaning. The first said the same thing as the last: the American government will not choose peace on fair terms; it will not agree to end aid to China and to provide oil, unless we give up everything for which we have been waging war.

On November 13 both the plans and the time schedule of action in the event that no accord was reached with the United States had been confirmed at another Liaison Conference in the presence of the Emperor.[1] Within the Foreign Office and court circles there had been some scant expectation that we would agree to Proposal B. Hearing from Nomura that Hull had said that he must have more time to consult other governments, the Japanese cabinet had agreed to wait for the American answer a few days longer—till the 29th. "After that," the answer to Nomura said, "things are automatically going to happen." Indeed they were; the task force assembling in the Kuriles was being

---

[1] *Far East Mil. Trib.,* Exh. No. 878. "Measures to be taken towards Foreign Countries relative to the Outline for the Execution of National Policies," which was decided at the council in the presence of the Emperor held on November 5. The strategy was in several ways shaped by the wish to conceal or disguise the intention of going to war.

told that on the morning of the 26th it was to proceed to the Hawaii area.

The long Ten-Point Memorandum on principles, which was our response to Proposal B, was received in Tokyo on the morning of the 27th. Along with it Nomura and Kurusu sent a convoy of troubled comment. They thought the answer hard and dumbfounding. But they found nothing in it compelling Japan to resort to war. They were afraid, as "Magic" let Washington know, that the United States and Britain might try to forestall Japan by occupying the Indies, thus bringing on war. Even this late, Nomura advised his government to keep on with the effort to reach a peaceful accord. He recalled a remark the President had made in an earlier talk—that there would be "no last words." [2] But, he added, if his counsel was not taken, it would be best not to keep up a false front of friendliness, and to strike from behind it. Kurusu, also, tried to be calming. He attributed our statement in part to knowledge of the Japanese military movements and concentrations in the south.[3]

Another Liaison Conference was called as soon as the American paper was read (November 27). This summarily dismissed our statement of principles as a humiliating ultimatum. It was resolved to proceed with the program adopted on November 5; that is, to go to war as soon as the striking forces were in position. Stratagem had failed. Force would be used. Japan would do or die.

As was natural, the men who made this decision pleaded later that it was compelled by the terms placed upon peace by the United States. Thus, the former Foreign Minister, Togo, one of the more conciliatory members of the government, argued that "Japan was now asked not only to abandon all the gains of her years of sacrifice, but to surrender her international position as a power in the Far East. That surrender, as he saw it, would have amounted to national suicide. The only way to face this challenge and defend ourselves was war." [4]

This was not a valid attitude. The idea that compliance with the American terms would have meant "extinction" for Japan, or so deeply hurt it that it could not guard its just interests, is an absurdity. Japan was not asked to give up any land or resources except those which it

[2] Intercepted Telegrams, Nos. 1180, 1189, and 1190, Nomura to Togo, November 26, 1941, set forth the Ambassador's views at length.

[3] Telegram, No. 1206, Nomura to Togo, November 27, and memorandum of telephone conversation between Kurusu and Yamamoto on November 27th.

[4] Togo deposition, *Far East Mil. Trib.*, Exh. No. 3646.

held by force of arms. Its independence was not in peril. Its Army, Navy, and Air Force would have remained in being. Its chances to trade with the rest of the world would have been restored. Its struggle against the extension of Communism could have combined with that of China and the West. Extinction threatened the plan for expansion in Asia, but not Japan or the Japanese.

On the 28th, Tojo turned down Nomura's appeals. So did the Lord Privy Seal, Kido. They were not, as Nomura probably hoped, reported to the Emperor. Nomura and Kurusu were duly told: "With the report of the views of the Imperial Government that will be sent to you in two or three days, talks will be de facto ruptured. This is inevitable. However, I do not wish you to give the impression that the negotiations are broken off. . . . From now on do the best you can." [5] This was read in Washington.

The coming day (the 29th, Tokyo time) was the day of the deadline —the day after which things were automatically going to happen. It was spent in continuous consultation. The Senior Statesmen met with the cabinet in the morning, with the Emperor at lunch, and with the cabinet again later in the afternoon. Several of them plainly spoke their doubts as to whether Japan should attempt to fight a great war.

Thus Konoye said: "To my great regret I am forced to conclude . . . that the continuance of diplomatic negotiations would be hopeless. Still is it necessary, however, to resort to war·at once even though diplomatic negotiations have been broken off? Would it not be possible, I wonder, while carrying on things as they are to later find a way out of the deadlock by persevering to the utmost under difficulties?"

Another former Prime Minister, Yonai, uttered a prayer that "We may take care not to lose everything by trying to avoid becoming poor gradually." [6]

To all such words of prudence, to wait or watch longer, Tojo had the same flat answer: To go on with broken economic relations would mean gradual weakening of Japan. The Senior Statesmen, thus having served their Emperor, went home to dinner and to bed. They were only a

[5] Telegram, Togo to Nomura and Kurusu, No. 844, November 28, 1941.

[6] A resumé of many of the statements made by the Senior Statesmen before the Emperor is given in Kido's defense deposition. It corresponds with Konoye's account of the meeting as given in the important supplementary note to his "Memoirs," already cited, "Pro and Con of the Theory of Gradual Exhaustion."

group of respected callers, whose time seemed past. Four years later some would be sought out again to manage the surrender.

That same day the government received a repetition of assurances that if Japan got into war with the United States and Great Britain, Germany would enter at once.[7] Ribbentrop quoted Hitler as saying that there were fundamental differences in the very right to exist between Germany and Japan and the United States. To wipe out any doubt about the military prospect, he also informed the Japanese government that Hitler said he was now determined to crush Russia to an even greater extent than he had planned at first; that next spring German troops would cross the Urals and chase Stalin deep into Siberia.[8] This was also intercepted and read in Washington.

A mite of worry still bothered the Emperor. His brother, Prince Takamatsu, had told him that as the Navy's hands were full it wished to avoid war. But the Navy Minister and Chief of the Naval General Staff, when called to the Palace, answered the Emperor's questions with confidence.[9] Thereupon the Emperor acceded to Tojo's request that an Imperial Conference be held the next day to review for the last time the plan of war.

Without waiting for morning to come around the Japanese government began to complete its war pact with Germany and Italy. Oshima was instructed (on November 30) to inform Hitler and Ribbentrop that the talks with the United States were at an end. He was to tell them "that there is an extreme danger that war may suddenly break out between the Anglo-Saxon nations and Japan through some clash of arms and that the time of the start of this war may be quicker than anyone dreams." He was to explain further that Japan wanted to move south

[7] On November 21 Ott had been asked by the Japanese Foreign Office if Germany would agree that there should be no separate peace if Germany and Japan became involved in war, for no matter what reason. Ott, on Ribbentrop's instruction, said that was only natural and that Germany would be willing so to agree in writing. When thus informed, the War Ministry and Tojo expressed gratitude. *Far East Mil. Trib.*, Exh. Nos. 601, 602.

The more direct assurance that Germany would join the war at once was given by Ribbentrop to Oshima on the 29th. Exh. No. 603.

[8] Telegram, No. 1393, Berlin to Tokyo, November 29th.

[9] As related by Admiral Shimada, Minister of the Navy, in his deposition, *Far East Mil. Trib.*, Exh. No. 3565. "The Navy was never confident of achieving victory over the United States but we were confident that we were better prepared at that time to fight than we would have been at any later date . . . Admiral Nagano and I on November 30th told the Emperor that the Navy had made adequate preparations."

"By 1941 the Japanese Navy was more powerful than the combined Allied Fleets in the Pacific. And, having received the best of upkeep and lavish modernization, it was in a better state of readiness for combat." Morison, *op. cit.*, III, 20.

and to refrain for the time being from any direct move against Russia. The authors of this cable gave Oshima the answer to any possible reproach that Hitler might make. He was to say, if need be, that during the whole period of the talk with the United States "the Japanese Government stuck adamantly to the Tripartite Alliance as the cornerstone of its national policy." It had hoped to find the solution within the scope of the alliance in order to restrain the United States from entering the war. But when in the later meetings it became clear that the United States demanded a divorce from the alliance, Japan could no longer continue the talks.[10]

The Imperial Conference met at 2 o'clock in the afternoon of December 1. Tojo presided. It was now clear, he declared, that Japan's claims could not be obtained through diplomatic measures; and it was wholly out of the question, both from the viewpoint of national power and of military strategy, to allow the present situation to continue longer.[11] The heads of the Army and Navy said they were ready and burning to serve the nation. The Emperor spoke not a single word. The decision for war was transmuted into "the way of the Emperor."

The drafting of the final statement to be given to the American government was begun. Tojo and Kido conferred about the text of the Imperial Rescript which was to be issued. On the next day (December 2) the Chief of Staff of the Army informed commanders in all South Sea areas that the war would start on December 8 (Tokyo time). An Imperial naval order sent the same notice to naval commanders. If, they were also told, an accord was reached before then, all the forces of the combined fleet would be ordered to reassemble and return to their bases. They were on their way, to be turned about only by a signal from Heaven.

The few remaining days of peace were spent in trying to keep the Americans and Britishers lulled, and in sealing the war pact with Ger-

[10] Telegrams, Nos. 985 and 986, November 30, Togo to Oshima, *Far East Mil. Trib.*, Exh. No. 802. These messages were read in Washington before they could be got to Hitler, who was at military headquarters on the Eastern Front because the Russians were counter-attacking near Moscow. Some of the men who read them in Washington were the same men who had heard Nomura explain that the American government should not make a serious issue of Japan's participation in the Tripartite Pact.

[11] The explanations given by the Prime Minister, Tojo, and Foreign Minister, Togo, at this conference are to be found, *ibid.*, Exh. Nos. 2954 and 2955.

many and Italy. Nomura and Kurusu kept contact with Hull. Togo was suavely patient with Grew.

On the 3rd, the Japanese Ambassador in Rome informed Mussolini that war with the United States and Britain in the immediate future was possible. Mussolini said he would declare war on the United States and Great Britain at once if Japan did. The Duce, according to Ciano, was pleased by the news and said: "Thus we arrive at the war between continents, which I have foreseen since September 1939." [12] The British intercepted the report of the promise which was sent to Tokyo.[13]

The Japanese government had trouble in getting from Hitler a final confirmation of the similar German promise. Ribbentrop gave as the reasons the storm around Berlin, and Hitler's faraway absence and absorption in the Russian battlefront. Perhaps these were the only reasons, perhaps not. There might well have been a tardy tremor of doubt as to whether Japan in the role of ally would count for as much as a belligerent United States. Ciano noted in his diary on December 4: ". . . the Berlin reaction to the Japanese step is extremely cautious. Maybe they will go ahead, because they can't do otherwise, but the idea of provoking American intervention is less and less liked by the Germans. Mussolini, on the other hand, is happy about it." [14] On the 5th, Ribbentrop submitted to Mussolini a plan for triple action on Japan's entry into the war. The first article of the proposed treaty began: "Should a state of war arise between Japan and the United States, Germany and Italy for their part shall also consider themselves to be at war with the United States, and shall conduct this war with all the armed forces at their disposal." [15]

Ciano complained that after delaying two days, Germany was now insisting on an answer at once. But it was given, at once. The British interceptors learned of all this also.

[12] Ciano, *op. cit.*, entry for December 3, 1941.

[13] Telegram, No. 985, Rome to Tokyo, December 3, 1941.

[14] Ciano, *op. cit.*, entry for December 4, 1941. Reporting to Ribbentrop on a talk with the officials of the Japanese Foreign Office as late as December 5, Ott said that he had "advised them to avoid a direct attack [on the Philippines] in order to place the responsibility for the war on the United States in accordance with instructions received." Telegram, December 5, Ott to the German Foreign Office, *Weizsaecker Brief*, Document No. NG 4367. For this Ott was on the 7th reprimanded by Ribbentrop. Erich Kordt, *Wahn und Wirklichkeit* (Stuttgart [1948]).

But, on December 14, after the successful attack on Pearl Harbor, Hitler told Oshima that Japan's entry into the war was a great relief to Germany; and that he thought that Japan had given the right kind of declaration of war. Further, he confided that he did not think American fighting capacity was high. "How could troops whose God is the dollar hold firm to the last!" *Far East Mil. Trib.*, Exh. No. 609.

[15] *Pearl Harbor Attack*, Part 35, p. 685.

One thing remained to be settled, whether to strike without warning. The Army and Navy, particularly Admiral Nagano, the Chief of the Naval General Staff, wanted to avoid any risk of spoiling the surprise attack. The Foreign Minister, Togo, objected. He said it was improper not to give some advance formal notice and that Japan's good repute and honor would suffer. He had been the First Secretary of the Japanese Embassy in Washington when the Briand-Kellogg Pact for the renunciation of war was signed. This was his last gesture towards a foregone ideal.

The Liaison Conference of November 30 had agreed to permit the Army and Navy to set the time of notice. The Navy suggested 12:30 p.m. on December 7 (Washington time). This, it said, would allow sufficient time before the attack to preserve Japan's good name. The Foreign Office was not told of the exact hour of the attack. Later, the Navy asked that the hour be put off till 1 p.m., and again the Foreign Office agreed.[16] Had the notice been presented precisely at the arranged time, there would have been some twenty minutes before the planes arrived over Pearl Harbor. That long, at least, would have been needed to read to the revealing final sentence. This was the last and foolish stratagem.

But the Pearl Harbor attack was only a disabling action. The real invasions about to begin were in the south—in the Philippines, Malaya, the Indies, Borneo. The Japanese soldiers were sent there to conquer colonial lands, which for several centuries had been under the hands of the West. Their mission, their rulers avowed, was to bring peace and stability throughout Greater East Asia. They were, rather, time has since shown, the destroyers of peace and order there, as they had been in China. Before the Japanese invasion the peoples of the countries in the Pacific south of Japan had a secure and improving way of existence, though not as free or just a way as could be wished. The Japanese armies ruined this without bringing justice or freedom. In the Southwest Pacific—as in China—they widened the already open path for suffering and for revolution.

[16] The full story of the discussion of the timing of the notice to the United States is told in the deposition made by Togo, *Far East Mil. Trib.*, Exh. No. 3646.

## CHAPTER 42

# The Clasp of War Is Closed

DURING the last few days of somber waiting the President faced three entwined questions. First: should he promise the British and Dutch that the United States would join them if Japanese forces attacked their territories or crossed certain bounds? Second: should he so warn Japan —openly or secretly? Third: should he inform Congress about the fast-coming crisis and the action he proposed to take?

The President, at one time or another, was on the point of doing each or all of these things. After listening, to Hull most especially, he did none of them. His mind could not settle on any program that seemed to fit the many uncalipered angles of the situation. Until the objects of the Japanese military movement that was under way became clear, it was hard to know what action was essential, and what Congress and the people would approve. And in the event that Japan struck at the Philippines, Guam, or Hawaii, he would not have to argue with those who still believed that the United States should take no part in foreign wars. It was best, he concluded, to wait until the event itself dramatized the danger and marked the response.

Japan, in other words, was left not only to strike the first blow, but to decide, as well, whether and in what way the issue of war or peace was brought before the United States. This course lessened the risk of blunder and costly confusion at the instant hour. But it caused the growth, as the American people learned more of what had taken place before the Japanese attack, of a sense that they had been led in ignorance.

Behind the scenes there was hurried suspense—intent reading of the news of Japanese ship movements, grim talk as to whether and how American forces should be engaged, anxious uncertainty over when and what to tell the country and Congress.

The Japanese envoys continued to drive down each day from the Embassy on Massachusetts Avenue to the State Department. They still bowed as they entered Hull's office. But no chance of change any longer attached to their visits. They had been told, it was known, to keep on talking in order to make military surprise the more complete. Hull listened only for clues to the Japanese program of action, and to keep the record straight.

On the 28th the War Council, meeting with the President, agreed (in accord with the Stark-Marshall memo) that if the Japanese attacked British or Dutch territories, or if they rounded the southern point of Indo-China and landed in the Gulf of Siam, and the British fought, the United States would have to fight. It favored the issuance of a warning to that effect. When the group dispersed it was understood that the President would send a private message to the Emperor. This was to be at once a friendly expression of the wish for peace and a warning. He was also to "deliver a special message to Congress reporting on the danger and reporting what we would have to do if the danger happened." [1]

The State Department was put to work at once on these two messages, using material and ideas sent by Stimson and Knox. There was no time to be lost, for Congress was going to meet on Monday (December 1) and unless held together would adjourn almost at once. The President left for Warm Springs, remarking to reporters that the Japanese situation might bring him back any time. Stimson rushed such drafts as he had written down to him by plane on the 29th. Then he and Knox again worked over with Hornbeck the message for the Emperor. "This was in the shape of a virtual ultimatum to Japan that we cannot permit her to take any further steps of aggression against any of the countries of the Southwest Pacific, including China." [2]

During these same days (November 27–December 1) the British government again tried its utmost to get a definition of our intentions. On the 30th Halifax asked Hull what the American government would do if the British resisted a Japanese attempt to establish a base on the Kra Isthmus. Hull answered that he would submit the question to the President, who would be back in Washington the next morning. Later that day a message came from Churchill, urging a declarative warning.

"It seems to me," this read, "that one important method remains unused in averting war between Japan and our two countries, namely a plain declaration, secret or public as may be thought best, that any further act of aggression by Japan will lead immediately to the gravest consequences." [3]

[1] Stimson's written statement for the *Pearl Harbor Attack*, Part 11, p. 5427, and entries in Stimson diary for November 28 and 29, 1941.
[2] *ibid.*, November 30, 1941.
[3] *Pearl Harbor Attack*, Part 2, p. 476.

About this and other messages to the same effect the sceptical mind can still play. Ever since learning of Hull's decision to discard the truce counter-offer, the British, Australian, and Dutch Ambassadors in every visit to the State Department expressed regret and stressed a desire for more time to prepare.[4] It is hard to believe that Churchill thought a warning could now halt Japan; that the Japanese government had not already taken American entry in the war into full account.

Churchill commented later about this message, "I did not know that the die had already been cast by Japan or how far the President's resolves had gone."[4a] Besides, at a hazard, his pen may have been touched by a wish to bring the President to the point of final decision; to have him say, through the warning, whether or not the United States would fight at once even if its lands were not attacked. This was an answer to which the British felt themselves entitled.

In any case, the President, on Hull's advice, postponed the warning message to the Emperor until the attack had all but begun. Of the reasons which caused him to do so, I have found no convincing record or account.[5]

Hull had also been poring over drafts of the message to Congress. This, too, he concluded, had better be reserved "until the last stage of our relations, relating to actual hostility, has been reached." He so advised the President. For this counsel, Hull, then and later, gave two reasons. A full account of the situation, he thought, would give material to Jap-

---

[4] For example, in Halifax's talk with Welles on the 27th, with Hull on the 30th, *ibid.*, Part 14, pp. 1179–81, and 1249–52, Casey's talks with Hull on the 29th and 30th, *ibid.*, Part 14, pp. 1194, *et seq.*, and Part 19, pp. 3689–90.

The earlier comments of the British and Dutch Governments on the truce counter-proposal have been recounted in Chapter 39. The position of the Australian Government towards the truce counterproposal could hardly have seemed helpful to Hull, for its approval seemed to be coupled with wishes that could not then have been satisfied. The Minister for External Affairs, Evatt, explained his attitude to the House of Representatives on November 27th (Canberra time, and almost certainly before he had been informed of Hull's decision not to make a counterproposal) as follows: "We are content to allow the leadership and initiative in this matter to be retained by the United States of America. . . . At the same time, I must express the hope that the talks will result in an agreement . . . I do not see why it should be impossible for Japan to retrace its steps and make possible the easing of the present economic restrictions, while Japan restores the *status quo* by withdrawing its fighting forces and equipment from French Indo-China. But all this would be of no avail if aggression in one particular quarter were to be abandoned only to be succeeded by aggression elsewhere. Obviously Britain could not look on with equanimity if Japanese forces attacked Russia in the north-west Pacific or if the pressure in China were to be redoubled in intensity." *Parliamentary Debates* (Canberra, Australia), CLXIX, 976.

[4a] Churchill, *The Grand Alliance*, p. 599.

[5] The reasons given by Hull for this advice seem unconvincing and mixed up. They are: (a) that the Emperor was only a figurehead; (b) that it would anger Tojo's Cabinet; (c) that it would be construed as a sign of weakness. Hull, *op. cit.*, II, 1092.

anese advocates of war with which to rouse their people against us. Further it would cause excitement in Congress where isolationist feeling was still strong, stir division within the United States. This might be taken as a sign of weakness and bring on the war crisis sooner than otherwise.[6]

Who is to know whether that is how, and how far, his mind and the President's along with his, travelled? There is reality, sad reality, in the fact that a revelation of the whole situation probably would have produced a serious, even though brief, division in the country. Old fights would have been fought again. Old and bitter charges would have been heard again. Even old slurs against the foreign countries with which now, more closely than ever, the United States would have to stand. But there is little reality in the thought that this quarrel might have hastened the war crisis or made a difference in Japanese morale. The attack was known to be actually in motion—though the points of attack were not spotted.

Whatever the inner core of thought and purpose, the message to Congress was also deferred. The President went down the road a little longer by himself.[7] He told Hull (December 1) to query Nomura again about the meaning of the reported large troop movements into Indo-China. He asked for a copy for his own private files on the intercept of the cable sent on November 30 by the Japanese Foreign Minister, Togo, to the Japanese Ambassador in Berlin, Oshima. One passage, at least, of this message for Hitler and Ribbentrop, will return to the reader's mind: "that there is an extreme danger that war may suddenly break out between the Anglo-Saxon nations and Japan through some clash of arms and that the time of the start of this war may be quicker than anyone dreams."

The next three days (December 1–4) thus passed without any new American initiative. On the 4th Congress adjourned for a long weekend.

The signs that the end was close became as plain as though they were written on a blackboard for children. "Magic" produced more telltale cables. One from Tokyo (the 5th, Tokyo time) ordered most of the

[6] This is a short and disputable summary of the several longish and turgid explanations which the Secretary of State has given. These vary from each other in distribution of emphasis, except on one point—the wisdom of avoiding at that time of crisis a turbulent and divisive argument over the whole field of American foreign policy. An oral explanation is to be found in *Pearl Harbor Attack*, Part 2, pp. 553, *et seq.*; written explanations, *ibid.*, Part 11, pp. 5375 and 5409, and Part 2, pp. 553, *et seq.*; and in Hull, *op. cit.*, II, 1091–92.

[7] But Harry Hopkins, who had lunched with the President on December 1, assured Stimson that the President had not weakened in his policy. Stimson diary, entry for December 1, 1941.

members of the Japanese Embassy staff to leave Washington by plane within the next couple of days. Another from Nomura (the 5th, Washington time) informed Tokyo, "We have completed destruction of codes . . ." [8]

The President now decided (on the 6th) that the time had come for the last-minute note to the Emperor.[9] It said nothing that had not been said before. Washington knew that it was being addressed to a throne that rested on weak silence.

Whether or not it was truly expected that an answer, a significant answer, would be received before some first clash, somewhere in the Pacific, is not to be known from the records in hand. Probably a wan hope, nothing more. How could there have been more?

From the Far East and London reports came that two large fleets of Japanese cruisers, destroyers, and transports were moving around the southern point of Indo-China.[10] Cambodia Point is about 250 miles from Kota Bharu (where the Japanese landed first in Malaya) and about 500 miles from Singapore.

The Dutch and British were still asking to be told what we would do if the expeditions at sea landed in the Indies, Malaya, or Thailand. To the Dutch, Admiral Stark, after consulting the President, had given advice (on the 4th) that Japan might be warned that if its ships entered

---

[8] Telegrams: No. 896, December 5th, Tokyo to Washington; No. 1268, December 5, Washington to Tokyo.

[9] The decision to send it off was probably made (on the 6th) before the President and Hull saw the intercept which informed them that the final Japanese answer to the American statement of November 26 was about to be sent to Nomura. But it did not actually leave the State Department till after the intercept was available. Final reading and revision in the State Department delayed the dispatch to Grew, which left the Code Room at 9 o'clock the night of the 6th (11 a.m. of the 7th in Tokyo).

One is also left to surmise what the President would have done next if war had not come. But he seems to have decided if no answer was received to his message to the Emperor by the evening of December 8, that he would have made a full recital to Congress on the 9th, and followed it up by the issuance of a declarative warning such as Churchill had besought him to issue some days before. This is the schedule he mentioned in his talk with the Australian Minister, Casey, on the late afteroon of December 6 (*Pearl Harbor Attack, Report*, p. 429), and in his talk with the Chinese Ambassador, Hu Shih, on the morning of the 7th.

[10] Two separate messages were received from Winant—the first at 10:40 a.m., and the second at 3:05 p.m. (Washington time). These transmitted Admiralty reports that at 3 a.m. that morning (Greenwich time) two Japanese expeditions were seen off Cambodia Point, sailing westward—destination uncertain, perhaps Bangkok, perhaps Kra (fourteen hours sailing time).

Admiral Hart also cabled the Navy Department on the 6th that the British Commander in Chief at the China Station reported two large convoys, escorted by cruisers and destroyers, in the same neighborhood and proceeding on a western course; and that his own scouting force had sighted thirty ships and one large cruiser in Camranh Bay. *Pearl Harbor Attack*, Part 2, pp. 493–94, and Part 15, p. 1681.

certain waters close to the Indies, it would be considered an act of war. But he had given no promise that the American government would, for its part, so regard it.[11]

The British government was similarly holding back from any warning or anticipatory measures. Thus on December 6 the President was informed, via Harriman and Hopkins, that it was Churchill's belief that "it would be the policy of the British to postpone any action—even though this delay might involve some military sacrifice—until the President has taken such action as, under the circumstances, he considers best." [12]

On that same evening (the 6th, Washington time) the Navy and Army Departments received the report of the arrangements worked out among Admiral Hart, Commander of the Asiatic Fleet, General MacArthur and Admiral Phillips.[13] MacArthur cabled Marshall: "Complete coordination and cooperation most satisfactorily accomplished." Hart cabled Stark: "Am sending Glassford to command TF [Task Force] 5. Recommend you empower me to put all or part of the command under British strategic direction or even direct command . . ." Hart was so sure of approval, and so sure the battle was about to start that he began to carry the arrangement into effect without waiting for the answer. On

[11] Stark's testimony, *ibid.*, Part 11, pp. 5215-19. The Dutch had sought a joint Dutch-American-British declaration of a defense zone south and west of the Davao-Waigeu-equator line. But Eden had turned down the suggestion saying that a unilateral declaration by the Indies would be less provocative. Stark was afraid, however, that if the Dutch closed this area to shipping it would delay important American shipments to the Philippines, and give Japan a reason for closing many other sea areas. Therefore he suggested that if the Dutch considered some warning to Japan essential it had best take the form of a statement to Japan that if Japanese naval vessels or expeditionary forces crossed this line, they would be considered hostile and attacked. Correspondence on this subject is printed, *ibid.*, Part 15, pp. 1770-73.

[12] Sherwood, *op. cit.*, p. 424. The previously cited cable from Winant to Hull stated that the British were delaying the answer to Thailand because of a desire "to carry out President's wishes in message transmitted by Welles to Halifax." But no record of any message bearing specifically on this point has been found.

Sometime on this day (the 6th) the President seems to have approved the issuance of a warning to be given by the American, Dutch, and British Commonwealth Governments —in case the Japanese forces invaded Thailand. *Pearl Harbor Attack, Report*, pp. 429-431.

[13] The text of the Hart-Phillips accord is printed in *Pearl Harbor Attack*, Part 4, pp. 1933-34. It was a fairly definite plan of initial distribution of naval forces throughout the whole region.

By December 7, 1941, arrangements for combined military action between the British, Australians, and Dutch were so complete that they were in fact obligatory. The Australians, in agreement with the Dutch assumed responsibility for Timor, Ambon, and the islands south of the Dutch New Guinea coast. The defense of the Indies was divided into three parts, with the British Malayan command taking over the northern portion of Sumatra—to enable the Dutch to concentrate the bulk of their strength in defense of Java. These arrangements looked well on the map but were most vulnerable. See article by Major Basil Hall, "Pacific Front Line," *The Army Quarterly* (London), October, 1946.

the evening of the 6th (Manila time), as recorded by Morison, he told Admiral Phillips: "I have just ordered my destroyers at Balikpapan [Borneo] to proceed to Batavia on the pretext of rest and leave. Actually they will join your force." [14]

In the War Department, too, some lights burned late on this night of the 6th. Ships with important military supplies for the Philippines were on the ocean; and a flight of big bombers had just left the West Coast for Hawaii, en route to the Philippines.[15]

After dinner the awaited message to Nomura was taken out of the air. The assistant to the Naval Aide hurried to put before the President the first thirteen (of fourteen) sections of this final answer from Japan. The President read them, and to Hopkins, pacing back and forth, said, in effect, "This means war." [16] War from the east. He would still wait, and not because of secret knowledge begin it. The roles of disturber and of resister must not be confused in the last minute.

In private houses and on the streets of Washington, the morning of the 7th seemed like any other quiet Sunday morning. Even the readers of "Magic" did not greatly change their routine or manner.

The last of the fourteenth part of the note which Japan was about to present had been caught and deciphered.[17] It was in the President's hands soon after breakfast. Japan was saying that all talk was at an end, and bitterly placing the blame upon us. The Japanese intent seemed clear; even before seeing this last section of its answer the President had concluded Japan was about to take some action that would mean war. But would it make some further declaration? And when?

In one way or another we would soon learn, the President must have thought. For a little later the carrier of the "Magic" messages brought another. This informed that the Japanese government had ordered its envoys to present its answer to Hull at one o'clock that day—little more than two hours off. The President waited to let events instruct. He may well, though it is not of record, have spent part of that time in study of the text of a joint warning to Japan—submitted by Churchill.[18]

[14] Morison, *op. cit.*, III, 157.
[15] Stimson diary, entry for December 6, 1941.
[16] As reported by Commander L. R. Schulz who delivered the message to the President.
[17] The last paragraph read "The Japanese Government regrets to have to notify hereby the American government that in view of the attitude of the American government it cannot but consider that it is impossible to reach an agreement through further negotiations." The whole note is printed in *Foreign Relations: Japan*, II, 787–92.
[18] According to Sherwood, *op. cit.*, p. 425, this text was not delivered to Roosevelt until

In the Pentagon building Marshall and his staff fumbled with and over a last minute alert to the commanders at the outposts—the Philippines and Hawaii. In the Navy building Stark and his staff discussed Hart's reports of the arrangements he had made with Phillips.

At half-past ten Stimson and Knox went to Hull's office. Soon after, his secretary entered to say that the Japanese Embassy was on the telephone asking for an engagement for Nomura and Kurusu at one o'clock. With the flimsies of the last two "Magic" messages in mind, but out of sight, Hull agreed to the hour. It would be early dawn over the Pacific islands. The three cabinet officers stayed together till past noon, wondering where the action would start and going over plans for what should be said or done. "We three," Stimson recorded in his diary, "all thought we must fight if the British fought." They were ready so to argue before Congress and the nation with all the authority of their office.[19]

At twelve-thirty the President received the Chinese Ambassador, Hu Shih, who had shuttled back from New York on learning that he was sought. With an air of leisure and gusto Roosevelt read aloud the text of his note to the Mikado. Now and again he paused to explain why he used such and such a phrase. When Mrs. Roosevelt came in to remind that time was getting on (and a big family luncheon assembling), he motioned to the Ambassador to resume his seat, and went on to the last word.

The President then told his thoughts of the moment. In Hu Shih's present memory these remain very much alive in words believed to be close to the original.[20] "This is," Hu Shih recalls his saying at the end of the reading, "my last effort for peace." And then, "I am afraid it may fail." The President went on to say that if he got no reply to his message by the evening of the 8th, the American government would publish its text. But he added that he had just learned that "those fellows" (his term for Nomura and Kurusu) had asked for an urgent appointment with Hull. The Japanese government, he thought, was probably hurrying its answer to our last note (of November 26). In this hurry, the President went on to state he expected "foul play"; he had a feeling that within forty-eight hours something "nasty" might happen in Thailand, Malaya, the Dutch Indies, and "possibly" the Philippines.

Hu Shih took his leave at 1:10.

---

the 7th, and it is not known whether or not Roosevelt had a chance to read it before the arrival of the news of the Pearl Harbor attack.

[19] Stimson, entry for December 7, 1941.

[20] As told by Hu Shih to the author.

Undetected, a Japanese task force was coming upon Hawaii. Over the flagship *Akagi* flew the flag which had been displayed on the battleship *Mikasa* when, in 1905, the Japanese fleet moved into battle against the Russians in Tsushima Straits.[21] The planes were leaving the decks of the carriers. Their errand, each crew had been told, was to destroy the power of the United States to cheat Japan out of its deserved place on the earth.

In the Japanese Embassy a great scurry was going on. The code clerks had selected trivial messages to decipher before the fourteenth part. A diplomatic secretary was doing over pages his awkward fingers had wrongly typed. There were a few last-minute revisions from Tokyo to be made. Nomura and Kurusu could have snatched what was ready and kept their one o'clock engagement with Hull. But they put it off till the typed message was in fair shape. The Ambassadors arrived at the State Department at two. They were shown into Hull's room at twenty minutes past two.[22] This was about two and a half hours after the landing at Kota Bharu (British Malaya) had begun; an hour after the first bomb fell on Pearl Harbor. American battleships were settling in the sand.

The envoys sat awkwardly in the deep black leather chairs. Nomura gave over the accusing paper. Hull made a show of looking at it. Both refrain and phrases were familiar; Japan had sought only to bring stability to East Asia and peace to the world; the United States had failed to grasp its true intentions. With quickened voice, Hull called it false and distorted in every line. The envoys made no answer. Now enemies, they opened the door for themselves. The elevator was waiting, empty, to take them to the street. As they walked across the sidewalk to their car, the light but gleaming structure of the White House stood before them. The President was talking on the telephone to Hull. The clasp of war was closed.

---

[21] Zacharias, *op. cit.*, p. 250.

[22] These details are taken mainly from the deposition of Yuki (Shiroji), assistant to Kurusu. *Far East Mil. Trib.*, Exh. No. 2967.

62, 139n.; report Sept. 1941 on Far East strategy, 263n.

Joint Staff planning (American-British), arrangements for, 125-128; approved, 138-139; conferences, Washington, Jan.–March 1941, 165, 165n., 166, 168-169; conference, Singapore, Apr. 1941, 170, 190; for southwest Pacific, 322, 322n.

Jonasson, Hermann, Prime Minister of Iceland, 221

jute, export to Japan ended, 157

Kahn, Dr. Herman, viii
Kan-in, Prince, 78
Kase, Shun-ichi, 210n.
Kato, Sotomatsu, Japanese Ambassador at Vichy, 224, 224n., 232
Kaya, Okinobu, Finance Minister, 294
Keenan, Joseph B., vii
Keitel, Field Marshal Wilhelm, 253n.
Keyserling, Mrs. Mary D., viii
Kido, Marquis Koichi, vi, 29n., 32n., 36n., 66n., 78n., 79n., 80, 80n., 86, 87n., 105, 105n., 116, 116n., 147n., 148n., 152n., 175n., 181, 209n., 211n., 212, 212n., 224n., 225, 252, 252n., 253n., 267, 267n., 328n., 330; comment on Emperor's position, 95; made Lord Keeper of Privy Seal, 80; opposes choice Higashi Kuni as Prime Minister, 285, 285n.; part in selection of Tojo as Prime Minister, 285-286, 286n.
Kimmel, Admiral H. E., Commander in Chief of Pacific Fleet, 156, 168n.; war warning of Nov. 27, 1941 sent to, 324
King, Mackenzie, Prime Minister of Canada, 279, 279n.
Kittredge, Captain T. B., vii
Kleffens, Eelco N., van, viii
Knox, Frank, Secretary of the Navy, and oil restrictions July–Aug. 1940, 89-91, 97, Oct. 1940, 123, Nov. 1940, 136; on measures toward Japan, 126, 127n.; on aid to Britain, 141; 155, 197, 198n., 220, 220n., 232, 279, 304, 314, 319n., 321, 322, 323n., 324, 334; on Joint Staff Conferences, 166n.; approves ABC–1 report, 168; and freezing order, July 1941, 239; opposes compromise with Japan to gain time, 276-277; meeting with Stimson and Hull, Dec. 7, 1941, 340
Kobayashi, Ichizo, Minister of Commerce and Industry, 96n., 104, 104n., 130
Koiso, General, 96n.
Kokuhonsha, reactionary society, 18
Komei, Emperor, 31
Konoye, Prince Fumimaro, and start of war with China, 9, 10, 18; 1st cabinet, 27-28, 88; and Axis pact, 27-28; forma-

tion of 2nd cabinet, July 1940, 80-82; character of, 81-82; policy decisions, 84-86, 85n.; concepts of self-defense, 86-87; cabinet plans for New Order in East Asia, summer 1940, 95, 96n.; cabinet demands right to enter Tonkin, 96; 96n., 146, 148, 175n., 200, 203n., 217, 220, 223, 224, 225, 251, 253, 253n., 256, 257, 264, 276, 276n., 283-284, 293, 294n.; sponsors Tripartite pact, 112-116, 119, 121, 123, 146n.; approves Neutrality Pact with USSR, 186n., 187-189n.; cabinet, crucial dilemma, spring 1941, 188, 188n., 189, 189n., 191, 192, 192n., 193, 193n., 194-195; cabinet, critical decision of, 209-218, 215n.; reaction to German attack on USSR, 210, 210n., 211, 211n.; 2nd Konoye cabinet resigns, 225; 3rd Konoye cabinet and Tripartite pact, 230-231, 280-281; seeks meeting with Roosevelt, 249-250, 252-254; explains purpose in seeking Roosevelt meeting, 252-253, 253n.; secrecy about meeting, 259n.; message to Roosevelt, 259-260; struggle against army for time to negotiate, 264-267, 265n., 267n., 268n.; final plea to U.S., Sept. 6, 1941, 271; desperate position after American note, Oct. 2, 1941, 277, 278, 282, 282n.; last efforts to carry on, 280-281; attempted assassination of, 282; 3rd cabinet, resignation of, 282, 282n., 285, 285n., 286, 286n.; opposes start of war, 328, 328n.

Kordt, Erich, 331
Korea, 4
Kota Bharu, 337, 341
Krock, Arthur, 222
Kurusu, Ambassador Saburo, 15, 67, 310, 312, 327, 327n., 331; replaced by Oshima, 148; signatory of Tripartite pact, 119; mission to U.S., 296-297, 304, 305, 306, 306n., 307; plea to Tokyo to defer war action, 308, 308n.; last talk with Hull, Dec. 7, 1941, 340-341
Kwantung Army, 81, 81n., 211, 212, 217, 218n., 251-252

LaGuardia, Mayor Fiorello H., 236
Land, Admiral Emory S., Chairman of the Maritime Commission, 318, 319n.
Langer, William L., viii
Lansing-Ishii Agreement, 193
Laos, province of Indo-China, 104
Lattimore, Owen, political adviser to Chiang Kai-shek, 316
lead, 124, export to Japan ended, 157
League of Nations, 13
Leahy, Admiral William D., 127n.

Lend-Lease Act, 153, 153n., 197, 245n., 301; caution before passage of, 153-154; passage of, imperilled, 155

Liaison Conferences, Imperial: of July 27, 1940, 84, 84n., 85n., 86, 95, 95n., 110, 112, 149; Sept. 19, 1940, 105, 110n., 114n., 117,; Sept. 26-27, 1940, 146; Jan. 30, 1941, 181; Feb. 1, 1941, 152; Feb. 3, 1941, 181, 181n.; Feb. 13, 1941, 184n.; April 18, 1941, 192, 193; June 13, 1941, 210; June 25 and July 2, 1941, 212, 212n., 213, 215, 215n.; resolution quoted, 215-216; July 10 and 12, 1941, 223; Aug., 1941, 254; Sept. 4-6, 1941, 264, 267, 271, 272, 275, 278, 282, 283, 293; Sept. 13, 1941, 275n.; Oct. 23, 1941, 292; Nov. 2 and 5, 1941, 294, 308, 326, 326n.; Nov. 27, 1941, 321n., 327; Nov. 30, 1941, 329, 332; Dec. 1, 1941, 330

Lindbergh, Charles A., 124

Lindley, Ernest K., 122n., 153

Lindsay, Sir Ronald, British Ambassador in Washington, 15, 21

Lothian, Lord, British Ambassador in Washington, 43-44, 56, 69-71, 73; and oil restrictions, July 1940, 89-90, 94; 99, 103n., 105, 140n.; talks with Hull on joint staff planning, 125-126, 126n., 127, 127n., 135, 137, 138n.

Loudon, Alexander, Dutch Ambassador in Washington, 138n., 247, 308, 312, 314, 315

lubricants, statistics Japanese purchases of, 88, 88n.; control of, 91, 93, 199


MacArthur, General Douglas, vii; on defense of Philippines, 263; war warning to, Nov. 27, 1941, 324; and arrangements for use of Asiatic Fleet in event of war, 338

machinery, metal-working, embargo on, 74

Mackensen, Hans-George von, German Ambassador to Italy, 28n.

"Magic", described, 173; revelations of, 219, 220, 226, 227, 228, 228n., 229, 231n., 232, 233, 234n., 239, 249, 250, 259, 260, 271, 275n., 280, 291n.; 297, 305, 308, 313, 314, 317n., 327, 330n., 336, 337n., 339, 340

magnesium, embargo on, 74

Malaya, reinforcement of, 301; invasion of, 332

Manchukuo, 4-7, 17, 37, 81, 81n., 200n.; Japanese plans for economic bloc with, 272n.

Manchuria, see Manchukuo

manganese, 104n.; in Netherlands East Indies, 59n.; Philippine export to Japan ended, 206

manila fiber, 40

Marris, A. D., Counsellor of British Embassy, 135

Marshall, General George C., 62, 140n., 155, 166n., 170, 197, 229n., 256n., 322, 322n., 323n.; and American policy, 128, 128n.; and staff conversations with the British, 138, 165n.; aid to Britain, 141; and the ADB report, 170; advice to Roosevelt on lines of defense, 170; and freezing order, July, 1941, 239, 241; and schedule for defense of Philippines, 263, 263n.; on wish to gain time, 300, 300n.; on air force, 300, 300n.; –Stark joint memos on strategic line of defense, preparation of, 302, 315, 322, presented to President, 323, 323n., substance of, 302, 323, decision based on, 334; and war warnings, 340

Masland, John W., 165n.

Matsudaira, Chief Secretary of the Privy Council, 29n.; Household Minister, 78

Matsui, General Iwane, 17, 17n.

Matsumoto, Shunichi, 113n.

Matsuoka, Yosuke, made Foreign Minister, 80; character of, 81, 81n., 84, 115, 115n., 120, 161, 172; note to Roosevelt, July 1940, 87; 85n., 96, 96n., 98n., 101, 104n., 112-113, 116, 123, 129, 129n., 131, 150, 151, 152, 152n., 153, 174, 175, 182, 188, 188n., 189n., 194n., 209, 215, 217, 220, 221n., 223; explanations of Tripartite pact, 111-113, 116, 117, 119-121; seeks entry of USSR into Tripartite pact, 145-146; plans trip to Germany and USSR, 148, 160-161; talks in Berlin and Moscow, March–April 1941, 180-187 and ns.; talks with Hitler and Ribbentrop 184-186; concludes Neutrality Pact with USSR, 186-187, 186n.; opposition to negotiations with U.S., April–May, 1941, 193-195, 194n.; final efforts to aid Germany, May–July 1941, 200, 200n., 202-205, 208, 211, 214, 223, 224n.; minimizes break in Nomura-Hull talks, 207n., 208; dropped from cabinet, 222, 224-225

Maxwell, Colonel Russell L., made administrator export control, 74

Mayeda, Admiral, 222

Meiji, Emperor, 116, 267

*Mikasa*, battleship, 341

Military measures, American, in the Pacific, plans and progress, 262-263

Millis, Walter, 220n.

Mito, Prince of, 293

Miyo, Commander Tatsukichi, 292n.

mander in Chief of Pacific Fleet, 57n., 106n., 124, 127, 127n., 292n.

Roling, Mr. Justice, 85n.

Roosevelt, Franklin D., decision not to apply Neutrality Act to war in China, 10; Brussels Conference, 13-14; quarantine speech, 11, 12; avoids British proposals, May 1939, 21; attitude on renewal treaty with Japan, 41-42; action regarding Netherlands East Indies, May 1940, 56-57; and foreign policy, May–June 1940, 59-60, 70-71; and National Defense Act, 72, 73, 73n., 74, 74n.; order July 1940 on oil and scrap iron, 88, 90, 92, 94; orders scrap embargo, Sept. 1940, 105-106; campaign statements, Sept. 1940, 102, 102n., 128, 133, 133n., 134; interpretation of Tripartite pact, 122n.; and oil restrictions, 124, 124n., 206, 206n., 207; approves staff talks with Britain, 125-127, 126n., 127n., 138-139; policy after 1940 elections, 133, 134, 140, 141, 142; administration National Defense Act, 142-143; on meaning of Lend Lease Act, 153-154; denies British requests, Jan.–Feb. 1941, 155, 155n.; talks with Nomura, 160, 175, 257, 258, and Kurusu, 307; and Staff Conferences, 166n., 190; and ABC—1 report, 168, 169, 169n.; Pan-American Day Speech, 195; naval movements in the Atlantic, 196, 196n., 197, 197n.; declares "unlimited emergency", 204; decision to occupy Iceland, 221; and retaliation against Japanese moves south, 227; and aid to USSR, 228; statement about oil for Japan, July 1941, 236-237, 261n.; and freezing of Japanese funds, 235, 237, 238; issues orders to freeze Japanese funds, 237, 238; proposes Indo-China be neutralized, 238, 251, and that Thailand be neutralized, 249n.; 250, 297, 299, 305n., 307, 307n., 316, 318n., 324; meeting with Churchill, 255-257; warning to Japan, Aug. 1941, 257; secrecy about meeting with Konoye, 259n.; evades meeting with Konoye, 260, 276; rejection of Japanese offer, Sept. 1941, 274; orders to Navy in Atlantic, Aug.–Sept. 1941, 279, 279n.; proposes amendment Neutrality Act, Oct. 1941, 279; defines line of defense in southwest Pacific, Nov. 1941, 302; considers Japanese truce proposal, 302-303, 309; ideas on truce counter-offer, 312, 312n.; message to Churchill about truce, 314; and expectation of Japanese attack, Dec. 1, 1941, 314; approves decision to discard truce idea, 320; and action in event of attack on

British or Dutch territories, 322n., 324, 333, 334; dilemmas and decisions in the week before Pearl Harbor, 333-341; message to Emperor, 334, 335, 337, 337n.; talk with Hu Shih just before news of Pearl Harbor, 340

Roosevelt-Konoye meeting, proposed, 249-250; Konoye's purposes, 252-253; Japanese pleas for, 258-259; secrecy about, 259n.; Hull decides against, 259; personal message to President about, 259-260; failure of project for, 271-278; comments on, 274-278, 280

Roosevelt, Mrs. Eleanor, 340

Roosevelt, Theodore, 124

Royal Dutch Shell Company, 97, 98, 99, 105

rubber, 40, 104n., 177, 236, 243, 246n., 269; in Netherlands East Indies, 59n., 131, 131n., 207, 207n.; of Indo-China, 233, 234n.

Saionji, Prince, vi; comments on pact with Axis, 1939, 30-31, 32, 34n., 36n.; 78, 80, 81, 96n., 116n., 120

Saito, Toshiye, 187n.

Sakamoto, Ryuki, 187

Sakhalin, North, 147, 184n.

salt, industrial, 104n.

sanctions, see Embargoes

Sansom, Sir George, 294n.

Sato, Kenrye, General, 294n.

Sato, Naotake, talks with Ribbentrop, 77, 77n., 79

Savord, Ruth, viii

Sawada, General Shigero, 78n.

Sayre, Francis B., Assistant Secretary of State, 11, 53, 72

Schmidt, Max, 173, 174

Schmidt, Dr. Paul Otto, German interpreter, 146, 184n.

Schulenburg, F. W., German Ambassador in Moscow, part in German-Soviet accord, 32n., 33, 33n.; 147, 186n., 187, 187n.

Schulz, Commander L. R., 339

Schwellenbach, Senator Lewis B., Resolution of, 11n., 22n., 50

Scobey, Colonel W. P., 169n.

scrap iron and steel, 11, 49, 54; in Netherlands East Indies, 59n., 131n.; discussion of embargo on, June 1940, 72; restricting order, July 1940, 88, 92, 93, 94; embargoed, Sept. 1940, 101-103, 105-109, consequences of, 106-109; Japanese stock pile, 109n.; Japanese protests against embargo on, 129

self-defense, concept of, 86

Lightning Source UK Ltd.
Milton Keynes UK
UKHW021808091118
332085UK00003B/405/P